THE GULF COOPERATION COUNCIL
Record and Analysis

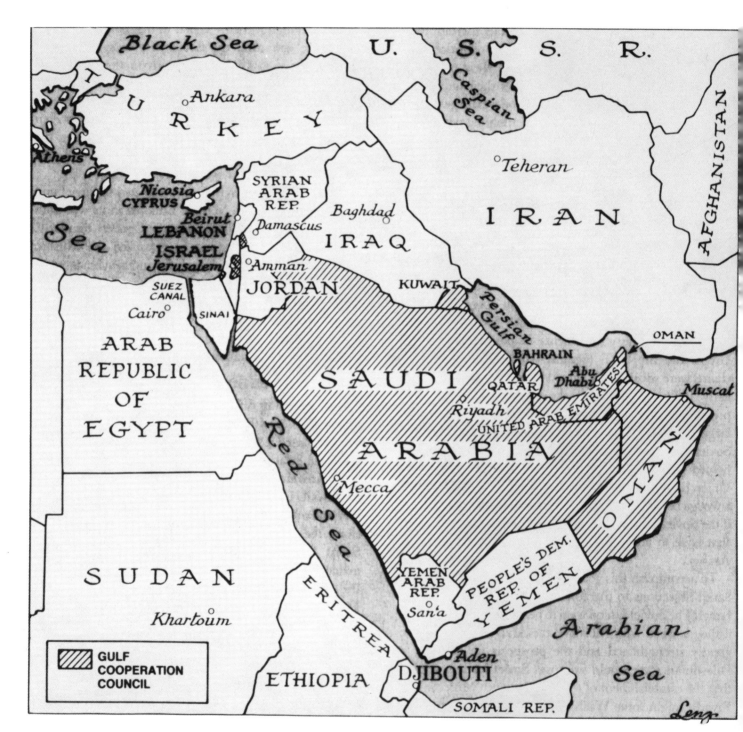

GULF
COOPERATION
COUNCIL

THE GULF COOPERATION COUNCIL
Record and Analysis

R. K. Ramazani
with the assistance of
Joseph A. Kechichian

With a Foreword by Sultan Bin Mohamed Al-Qasimi

UNIVERSITY PRESS OF VIRGINIA
CHARLOTTESVILLE

THE UNIVERSITY PRESS OF VIRGINIA
Copyright © 1988 by the Rector and Visitors
of the University of Virginia

First published 1988

LIBRARY OF CONGRESS
Library of Congress Cataloging-in-Publication Data
Ramazani, Rouhollah K., 1928–
    The Gulf Cooperation Council : record and analysis / R.K. Ramazani
with the assistance of Joseph A. Kechichian ; with a foreword by Bin Mohamed al
-Qasimi
        p.   cm.
    Bibliography: p.
    Includes index.
    ISBN 0-8139-1148-6
    1.Majlis al-Taʻāwun li-Duwal al-Khalīj al-ʻArabīyah—History.
2. Majlis al-Taʻāwun li-Duwal al-Khalīj al-ʻArabīyah—History—
Sources. 3. Arabian Peninsula—Relations. I. Kechichian, Joseph
A. II. Title.
DS201.M353R36   1988
341.24'77—dc19   87-37170
                                                                CIP
        Printed in the United States of America

To the Secretariat General
of the
Gulf Cooperation Council
in Recognition of
Its Vision of the GCC as an Arab Confederation

Contents

Appendixes

Foreword

Although the West considers Arab unity an impossible dream, the Arabs themselves believe in it as their only way to salvation and progress, if not for their mere survival. The Americans seem to have forgotten that it took them a revolution and a civil war to bring together desperately heterogeneous people who had nothing in common except their will to survive. Once they decided to unite, the British threat could only cement and strengthen their Union and even a bitterly fought debilitating civil war could not bring down that Union. Now, no one would have the slightest doubt about the eternal nature of the American Union.

More recently, and after many centuries of almost continual wars amongst themselves, the peoples of Europe with their decidedly different backgrounds, cultures, customs, and, most certainly, languages entered the first stages of a union that would hopefully lead them into the United States of Europe. The European Economic Community is now, after sixteen years, an established fact. And it is expanding every year.

The Gulf Cooperation Council is now also an established fact although it is only six years old. At first it was greeted with skeptical pessimism, and predictions of failure abounded. The critics overlooked some essential facts about the Arabs of the Gulf States. They did not seem to realize that these Arabs have a great deal in common among themselves. Certainly they are by far more homogeneous than the nations of Europe, members of the EEC. Like all other Arabs, the Arabs of the Gulf believe in Arab unity and they know that they live in a dangerous world. There are powers in the neighborhood that have coveted a piece of territory here or there. There are the two great powers who wish to dominate the area from the east or the west, the north or the south. For the last seven years the Iraq-Iran war has brought those dangers ever closer to the area. The GCC, which was born in the midst of these dangers, struck the right chord and was accepted by the Gulf Arabs as a step in the right direction. The governments proposed it but the people accepted it, and very quickly it became part of all facets of life in the member states.

An example has been set for the rest of the Arab world. If total unity is not attainable immediately, then cooperation is a second best. The path has been opened in a most unexpected way; it remains for the others to follow. The GCC will grow stronger and more studies of its activities are certain to follow.

Sultan Bin Mohamed Al-Qasimi
Member of the Federal Supreme Council
and Ruler of Sharjah

Preface

Although it was established in 1981, the Gulf Cooperation Council (GCC) has not been adequately understood. Except for a ritualistic acknowledgment of its existence on the occasion of the GCC's annual summit meetings, the Western press has practically ignored its development. A survey of leading American and British newspapers over the first five years of the GCC's life has turned up not a single editorial on this nascent organization. Coverage of its activities between summit meetings has been rare, inadequate, and often relegated to back pages.

This lack of adequate understanding of the GCC is not merely a function of poor coverage in the Western press. It reflects, to a large extent, the persistence of misconceptions about the GCC, which are perpetuated by its avowed supporters and detractors. Some have depicted it as an anti-Israeli alliance or an anti-Iranian coalition. Some have charged that it is "a tool of the United States," while others have characterized it as "a stalking horse of Saudi Arabia." Some have called it "a rulers' club" of the Gulf monarchies, while others have labeled it "an extended royal family."

This book is published to set the record straight. There is no better way of doing so than by providing the record. This volume partially documents the GCC's various activities during its first five years, from its founding in 1981 through its fifth anniversary in 1986. It makes no claim to completeness, despite the fact that a total of 122 documents have been identified and reproduced here for the first time. The concept of "document" used here has been rather inclusive. In addition to the text of the Charter of the GCC and other basic statutes, agreements, communiqués, and official statements, the texts of a select number of interviews given by GCC leaders and officials have been included in the hope that they will shed light on the meaning of official documents. The documents are numbered sequentially throughout the volume, divided into five chapters in terms of their overall relevance to the analytical sections. When referred to in these chapters, the documents are identified by the letter D and the number.

No record, however, simply speaks for itself. This volume, therefore, includes analysis as well. It is an empirical analysis rather than an ideological one. It explores the overriding question of what is the nature of the GCC. In doing so, it considers two prior questions: Why was the GCC created in the first place, and what did it actually do during the first five years after its establishment? In search of answers to these questions, this book analyzes the factors behind the formation of the GCC and also four major strategies that the GCC states used in practice in order to attain their objectives. Chapter One explores why the GCC was established by Bahrain, Kuwait, Oman, Qatar, Saudi Arabia, and the United Arab Emirates (UAE). Chapters Two through Five examine the GCC activities meant to cope with the perceived threat of subversion and terrorism, to deter the spread of the Iraq-Iran war, to integrate the economies of the GCC countries, and to coordinate their diplomatic courses of action. The concluding Chapter Six attempts to answer the central question about the nature of the GCC and to speculate about its future on the basis of the empirical findings of the previous five chapters. Each chapter contains an analytical section and a collection of documents.

In addition to trying to set the record straight, it is hoped that this volume will assist further research on the GCC. Three sets of materials have been appended to the main text of analytical chapters and documentary record. They consist of statistical tables, a chronology of GCC events, and an annotated bibliography of select books and articles in Western and Arabic languages. Without any claim of completeness, these materials have been prepared for the first time as further aids to research on the GCC.

With this volume, the University of Virginia has demonstrated its increasing interest in becoming the principal center for research in North America on the GCC. Founded by Thomas Jefferson, the author of the American Declaration on Independence, the university favors efforts to promote harmony and cooperation among nations. Ever since the establishment of the GCC, the university has supported studies bearing significantly on GCC affairs. It supported my *Security of Access to Persian Gulf Oil Supplies in the 1980's* (The Energy Policy Studies Center, University of Virginia, 1982) and my *Revolutionary Iran: Challenge and Response in the Middle East* (Baltimore and London: Johns Hopkins University Press, 1986). It also sponsored the pioneering doctoral dissertation of Joseph A. Kechichian on "The Gulf Cooperation Council: Search for Security in the Persian Gulf" (1985).

For the support of this volume by the University of Virginia, I would like to thank Edwin E. Floyd, former Vice President and Provost, for his sustained confidence in, and support of, my scholarly research and writing over the years. I am grateful for the enthusiastic endorsement by David C. Benjamin, former Associate Provost for Research, of the research project that led to the production of this book. I feel indebted to Emmett B. Ford, Jr., Research Administrator, for his understanding of the difficulties I encountered in conducting research on this book. Paul R. Gross, Vice President and Provost, supported the completion of the first and the start of the second phase of the GCC Project, for which I am thankful. I have been fortunate to have had the help of Joseph A. Kechichian in completing this study. I am happy to associate his name with this book in recognition of his superb research assistance to me. Jean Perkins and Karen Miller painstakingly keyboarded the documents, and Andrew T. Parasiliti proofread them for publication. I thank them all, but as the sole author of this book I alone am responsible for any errors of fact or interpretation that I might have made. Neill H. Alford, Jr., Clifton McCleskey, and Merrill D. Peterson helped with the decision to publish this book upon the untimely death of my friend W. Walker Cowen, the Director of the University Press of Virginia.

I am deeply indebted to Sultan Bin Mohamed Al-Qasimi for graciously agreeing to write the foreword to this book. As an Arab scholar as well as a leader, he considers the establishment of the GCC as an expression of the basic desire for Arab unity. He also sees the survival of the GCC in the course of perilous events in the Gulf region as concrete evidence of the capacity of the governments and people of the Arab world to cooperate toward their goal of unity.

I would also like to thank the officials of the GCC Secretariat, especially His Excellency Abdel Karim al-Hamadi, for the courtesy shown to me during my visits to Riyadh. I have found my conversations with GCC officials and particularly with government, business, and academic leaders in the GCC states most helpful to my analysis of GCC affairs. I hope the staff of the Secretariat General as well as these leaders in the GCC countries will find useful this volume by an American scholar on the first five years of GCC activities. Without the invaluable support of the University of Virginia this book would never have been published, and I hope that it will be the first step in the direction of building cooperative research and publication bridges between the University of Virginia and the Secretariat General of the GCC.

To my wife, Nesta, I offer heartfelt thanks for stylistic criticism of the first draft of the book manuscript.

THE GULF COOPERATION COUNCIL
Record and Analysis

1

Founding the Gulf Cooperation Council

ANALYSIS

Five years after the founding of the Gulf Cooperation Council (GCC) in 1981 by Bahrain, Kuwait, Oman, Qatar, Saudi Arabia, and the United Arab Emirates (UAE), the debate over the reasons for its creation continued. A number of observers, particularly from the Gulf Arab countries, have seen the GCC as an organic growth rooted in the pre-GCC interaction of the six member states, particularly in the economic field. Others have emphasized various kinds of threats, ranging from that of Israel to those of the Soviet Union, the United States, and Iran. Still others, in fact most observers, have attributed the birth of the organization to the threat of the Iraq-Iran war.

The detractors of the GCC have compounded the problem of analyzing its origins. Anti-Western regimes, especially those led by the Soviet Union, have characterized the GCC as a military "arm of NATO." Anti-American observers have dubbed it a "tool of the United States" in the pursuit of its alleged imperialist game in the Middle East. Some have labeled it as a "latter-day Central Treaty Organization" (CENTO), that moribund brainchild of Secretary of State John Foster Dulles. And finally, the antimonarchical radical left and extremist right have depicted it as a "stalking horse of Saudi Arabia."

The admirers of the GCC, on the other hand, have viewed it favorably for various reasons. Some see it as a budding confederation among the Gulf Arab states. Others consider it an example of the capacity of Arabs to work toward the goal of complete unity, while still others see it as an economic community similar to the European example.

Official Perceptions of the GCC

The founding of the Gulf Cooperation Council officially took place between 4 February and 26 May 1981. On 4 February the foreign ministers of Saudi Arabia, Kuwait, Bahrain, Oman, and the United Arab Emirates (UAE) met in Riyadh, Saudi Arabia, and decided to set up a cooperation council among their states, to form a secretariat general for this purpose, and to hold periodic meetings at the summit level and the level of foreign ministers. In a statement issued on that date and read to journalists that night by Saudi foreign minister Prince Saud al-Faysal, the founding of the organization was attributed to such considerations as the "special relations," "joint characteristics," "joint creed," "similarity of regimes," and "unity of heritage" of the member states and their "desire to deepen and develop cooperation and coordination among them in all fields in a manner that brings good, development and stability to their peoples." The formation of the organization was said to be "within the framework of the Arab League Charter, which urges regional cooperation" (D1 and D2).

A special committee of experts began a two-day meeting in Riyadh on 24 February for the purpose of "formulation of the fundamental system" for the GCC before submitting the results to the foreign ministers of the member states on 8 March. The committee was chaired by the head of the Saudi delegation, Ambassador Shaykh Ismail ash-Shura, and included experts from all the other five GCC states. The experts also held another meeting in Muscat, Oman, where the session was inaugurated on 7 March by Salim Ismail Suwayd of the Omani Foreign Ministry. As a result of the meetings of the experts, four basic draft documents on the structures and functions of the GCC were presented to the foreign ministers for their initials in Muscat. These basic documents included the Charter of the GCC (D4), Rules of Procedures of the Supreme Council (D5), Rules of Procedures of the Ministerial Council (D6), and Internal Statute for the General Secretariat, all of which were initialed by the foreign ministers except for the last document, which was reviewed but its approval postponed until the appointment of a secretary general who would be able to express his view on it. At the end of their meeting on 10 March, the foreign ministers recommended that the first summit meeting of the GCC should be held on 26–27 May in the city of Abu Dhabi, UAE.

The first GCC summit actually began on 25 May, and hence the basic documents of the organization carry the dates when they were approved by the leaders of the six countries on 25–26 May. The following day, Abdallah Yaqub Bisharah, secretary general of the GCC, held his first press conference in Abu Dhabi (D11). Among many points made, the secretary general reportedly said that the organization had attracted worldwide interest; that its members refused to be viewed as mere oil states and waterways; and that they had a greater role to play in the world. He also said that the members remained, as before, independent sovereign states; they were equal despite the establishment of the GCC headquarters in Saudi Arabia and the appointment of the secretary general from Kuwait; and the council was "not exactly political . . .[because] priority is given to economic issues."

How did the officials and leaders of the GCC perceive the organization during this founding period? A sampling of views should include those of Saudi Arabia, Kuwait, and Oman for the important reason that before the establishment of the GCC, each had developed its own proposal for regional cooperation. In response to a correspondent, Saudi interior minister Prince Nayif flatly stated that Saudi Arabia "did not have contacts with the Gulf states on the subject of Gulf security cooperation prior to the declaration of the Gulf cooperation project in which we have participated." Although no date for the interview was given, the Saudi newspaper *Al-Jazirah* published it on 14 February, which falls within the official founding period of the GCC.[1] The prince further stated that "our intention is to establish complete cooperation in all fields—political, economic, security, unity of jurisdictions—on the basis that the Islamic Shariah is the fundamental source of our legislation and system." In regard to the security of the oilfields, the prince said: "I see no reason why a joint security action should not exist within the framework of a Gulf cooperation plan that includes the economy, a united political stand, military defense cooperation and other issues. . . . There can be joint security to prevent threats to oil wells such as sabotage and to organize the security of wells and their sites. All this is possible, and we have been cooperating satisfactorily on information." The Saudi minister of defense and aviation, Prince Sultan, believed that the GCC arose in the "shadow of cooperation and coordination, which had already been growing at the highest and best levels." Furthermore, he thought that "the Gulf states and their peoples were aware of all that is being hatched against them and that this is what makes them confident that the Gulf Cooperation Council will serve all these states and peoples."[2]

The Kuwaiti officials seemed to emphasize the nonaligned character of the GCC. For example, the crown prince and prime minister, Shaykh Saad al-Abdallah, was reported on 17 February 1981 to have said that the GCC "was not a new grouping or an alliance but a framework for organizing constructive cooperation among the member states." He added that "many peoples in the world had covered a long distance on the path of regional cooperation, hence the Islamic countries are in bad need for such cooperation," and the GCC "was the outcome of a sincere effort aimed at coordinating and developing cooperation already existing between countries having common destiny and history."[3]

In contrast with the official Saudi and Kuwaiti perspectives, the Omani view of the GCC unequivocally stressed the problem of security, particularly as it concerned the freedom of navigation in the Strait of Hormuz. With respect to the question of regional cooperation in general, in an interview given to *Al-Mustaqbal* magazine in May 1981 Sultan Qabus stated: "There have been many previous attempts in this direction, the first in 1974, but none have been successful. When the idea of Gulf cooperation was revived during the Amman summit, we immediately supported and agreed to it. When we received a working paper in At-Taif, we responded to the idea and paid much attention to it." "The region," he continued, "is facing threats from all directions. The USSR is in Afghanistan, while South Yemen is a Soviet military base in the full meaning of the word. There are thousands of Cuban soldiers in Ethiopia. We are the gateway to Arabia and the oil route. Any aircraft in the Horn of Africa, Kabul or Tashkent is capable of covering a distance of 450 miles to drop mines in the Strait of Hormuz, closing the strait and severing the West's economic artery."[4]

Although these and other official perspectives of the GCC members held immediately after the establishment of the organization hint at previous attempts at regional cooperation and at the kind of general concerns that motivated the leaders of the six states to band together, both the background of the GCC and the incentives for its formation require a brief analysis. (Those readers who are interested in the formal structures and functions of the GCC may find the documents appended at the end of this chapter useful.)

The Quest for Regional Cooperation

How can one date the birth of the idea of regional cooperation in the Gulf? The answer is complicated by the fact that the founders of the GCC made frequent references to "Islam" and "Arabism," ideas which are as old as Muslim and Arab histories. Both the notions of Islamic community (*umma*) and Arab community (*qawmiyyah*) long preceded the birth of the new congeries of sovereign states and are regarded by some observers to be related to the movement toward regional cooperation. The founders of the GCC have claimed that it was established within the framework of the Arab League insofar as the idea of Arabism is concerned. They also have claimed that it is within the context of Islam as evidenced by the fact that in January 1981 the Organization of the Islamic Conference (OIC) issued the landmark Mecca Declaration stating that "security and stability of the Gulf as well as the safety of its waterways are absolute responsibility of the Gulf states without any foreign interference." Alternatively, one may trace the idea back to May 1976, as an official GCC publication seems to do, when Shaykh Jabir al-Ahmad al-Sabah, the prime minister and crown prince of Kuwait, called for "the establishment of a Gulf Union with the object of realizing cooperation in all economic, political, educational and informational fields . . . to serve the interests and stability of the peoples of the region."[5]

From the perspective of power politics, however, it may be said that the idea of regional cooperation in the Gulf region paralleled the regional conflict that arose after the demise of *Pax Britannica*. Although the shah of Iran was one of the earliest advocates of the idea of regional cooperation, he was suspected by the Arabs of using it as a cloak for *Pax Iranica*. Because of their greater weakness, the smaller states were attracted to the ideal of collaboration partly as a means of thwarting the bid for hegemony by the larger states. It is little wonder that the Dubai Agreement of February 1967—the month after the British government announced its decision to withdraw its forces from the Gulf in 1971—marked the beginning of intensified efforts to unite the seven Trucial Coast Emirates with Bahrain and Qatar. These efforts had the support of the British, who were urged by some of the shaykhly leaders to reverse their decision to withdraw. Although Bahrain and Qatar stayed out of the proposed union, a new federated state of the United Arab Emirates was formed in 1971.

In the intervening decade between the formation of the UAE and the establishment of the GCC, although both Arab-Iranian and intra-Arab conflicts marked the affairs of the region, many disputes were peacefully settled. Iran resolved its conflict with Saudi Arabia (1968), Abu Dhabi (1971), Qatar (1970), and Iraq (1975), while Saudi Arabia settled its disputes with Iraq (1975) and Abu Dhabi (1974). The two large conservative states set the example for the smaller Gulf states such as Abu Dhabi and Qatar, which also settled their disputes.

The idea of regional cooperation got its greatest boost, however, when Iran and Iraq settled their ancient and bitter controversy over the Shatt al-Arab boundary river in 1975. The two countries had nearly gone to war the previous year after years of border skirmishes. The passing of the threat of war as a result of a peaceful settlement was hailed by numerous states from within and outside the Gulf region, and the critical mediatory role of Algeria was acknowledged by all concerned. Only a few months after the Algiers Agreement (March 1975), during the Islamic Conference in Jiddah (July 1975), the Gulf foreign ministers agreed, for the first time, to hold a summit meeting to discuss mutual defense cooperation and other issues such as the territorial integrity of all littoral states, limits on foreign fleets, freedom of navigation, a ban on foreign military bases in the Gulf, mutual aid against internal coups, and the division of Gulf waters. In November 1976 various plans were discussed by all eight states of the Gulf in Muscat without any agreement being reached. Saudi Arabia and the smaller Gulf states were wary of both Iranian and Iraqi ambitions to dominate the region.

Such fears seemed to be aroused especially whenever security issues came up. With respect to non-security issues, progress toward cooperation seemed more feasible. For example, seven Gulf states, including non-Arab Iran, reached an agreement for the protection of the marine environment in 1978.[6] Furthermore, despite the suspicion of Saudi Arabia and the smaller Gulf states of fellow-Arab Iraq, they did reach agreement with Iraq in regard to a number of nonsecurity issues. One of these was the establishment by the seven Gulf Arab states of the Gulf Organization for Industrial Consulting (GOIC) in February 1976 "to achieve industrial cooperation and coordination among the member states." By the time of the establishment of the GCC, the GOIC had expanded its personnel from three to some eighty people and had conducted various studies on the basic Gulf industries and downstream operations. It had also drawn up long-term regional strategies for the aluminum, petrochemical, cement, and iron and steel industries.[7] The examples of regional cooperation among the Arab states of the Gulf before the establishment of the GCC could be easily multiplied to indicate three points: one, to show that during the pre-GCC decade there had been more cooperation, both bilateral and multilateral, among the Arab states of the Gulf than between them and non-Arab Iran; two, to reveal that there had been far more cooperation among the six Arab states which subsequently formed the GCC than between them and Arab Iraq; and three, to emphasize that most attempts at cooperation foundered on the rock of security issues, even when Iran was excluded and whether or not Iraq was included. In other words, each major Arab state of the Gulf had its own security scheme.

To take up each one briefly, the Iraqi security plan was the most ambitious of all Arab plans. It reflected the Iraqi bid for Arab leadership in the face of Egypt's isolation by the Arab world as a result of President Sadat's signing of the Camp David accords and the peace treaty with Israel. In 1978 and 1979 Iraq led the Arab hard-line platform against Egypt in two conferences held in Baghdad. In 1980 Saddam Hussein unfurled the banner of the Arab Charter after the revolutionary destruction of the shah's regime and a momentary decline of Iran's preponderant power in the Gulf region. The Iraqi security scheme called for creating a collective Arab Gulf Security Force, as a supplement to the Arab League Joint Defense Pact, and a Joint Military Command which would control the force as an independent unit financed by the participating member states.

As a matter of fact, the Iraqi security proposal was largely designed to counter the plan of Oman. *Al-Thawra*, the mouthpiece of the Baath party of Iraq, dubbed the Omani security proposal as a "new imperialist alliance," and the Iraqi government did everything to discredit it among the Arab states. The Omani Gulf security concept was centered on the concern of the sultanate with the safety of navigation through the Strait of Hormuz. The Omani Musandam Peninsula juts out into this vital international waterway. As early as 1974, the shah and Sultan Qabus had agreed to the "joint patrol" of the strategic waterway, but the Iranian Revolution overturned that arrangement. The Omanis tried to sell their scheme to the revolutionary regime in September 1979 but failed. The charge that the Omani plan was an imperialist plot stemmed from the fact that it envisaged financial and technical aid from major oil-consuming industrial nations. Rejected by both Iran and Iraq, the plan was subsequently confined to the establishment of a Joint Arab Gulf Force to which participating Arab states would contribute money for arms purchases, but not to the exclusion of assistance from Western industrialized nations. Although as early as 1975 Henry Kissinger and Sultan Qabus had "initiated" an agreement for the American use of the British-controlled Masirah Island airstrip off the coast of Oman, Oman did not agree to accord such "facilities" to the United States until 4 June 1980, well after the Iranian Revolution.

The Omani plan not only was opposed by Iran and Iraq but also was rivaled by regional security ideas of two other prospective GCC states. At the time, Kuwait represented the opposite pole of Oman in its foreign policy orientation. It was then the only future GCC state that had diplomatic relations with the Soviet Union and was the most ardent advocate of nonalignment in world politics. In Kuwait's view, if there was to be a regional security plan, it would have to be premised, above all else, on the principle of self-reliance. Such a plan presumably would end foreign dependency and aim at military defense by creating a joint command and standardizing military equipment and training.

The Saudi plan seemed to strike a middle course between the Omani and Kuwaiti extremes. It neither rejected the idea of foreign aid, the way the Kuwaiti scheme seemed to do, nor accepted such assistance as wholeheartedly as the Omani proposal did. It significantly differed from rival security plans in two major respects. First, it was clearly confined to "collective cooperation" between Saudi Arabia and the other prospective GCC states. Second, it emphasized collaboration among the participant states with respect to internal stability of the incumbent regimes. It would be tempting to attribute this Saudi preoccupation with domestic stability to the traumatic siege of the Grand Mosque in Mecca in 1979,[8] but as will be seen, other factors also contributed to the Saudi fear of acts of subversion and sabotage.

Emergence of a Common Security Concern

The overriding pre-GCC concern of Saudi Arabia with the security and stability of the House of Saud and other royal families no doubt contributed to the creation of the GCC. But several subsequent commentaries about the founding of the organization have muddied the waters. To begin with, neither the Charter of the GCC nor the statements of its founding fathers clarified its political philosophy. To be sure, the leaders of the six members talked about cooperation in all fields "in order to serve their interests and strengthen their ability to hold on to their beliefs and values." But nowhere did they spell out what these words meant. The resulting ambiguity was compounded by the comments of outsiders, attributing the birth of the GCC variously to the fight against Israel, the machinations of NATO, the prodding of the United States, the dictation of Saudi Arabia, and so on.

On a more serious note, however, the creation of the GCC has been almost universally attributed to the fear of its founders of the spread of the Iraq-Iran war. In the light of the analysis that will follow, it should become amply clear that this has been an unwarranted assumption. At best, the war was a catalyst, not the cause, of the GCC's creation. It helped to crystallize and unify the various prewar concepts of security as well as to point out the need for tidying up the already existing bilateral and multilateral cooperation in many nonmilitary fields. Finally, the war provided a perfect excuse for excluding Iraq from membership in the GCC. On the unlikely assumption that Iraq would join a regional organization which was not closely tied to the Arab League, Iraqi membership would have compromised the GCC's official neutrality in the war.

More than any other single factor, the Iranian Revolution helped to coalesce the security concerns of Saudi Arabia and the other monarchies in the Gulf region. As the largest Arab monarchy, Saudi Arabia was in a position to lead the others toward cooperative efforts. The impact of the Iranian Revolution on Saudi Arabia was manifold. The revolution destroyed the most powerful monarchy in the Gulf area. It was the second revolution to send shock waves throughout the Gulf region, the first being the revolution in Iraq that destroyed the monarchy in 1958. The Iraqi revolution had been followed by deteriorating relations between Riyadh and Baghdad, when the Baathist regime tried to subvert the Gulf monarchies. The Iranian example, however, appeared more menacing. The balance of forces seemed to have changed further against the monarchical regimes in the region because Iran, like Iraq, replaced the monarchy with a republic. Whatever course the new Iranian republic took, its very existence would threaten Saudi Arabia and other Gulf monarchies. As the revolution began to unfold in Iran, the Saudis feared that the communist forces might win out, substantially increasing the communist threat to conservative regimes. The Marxist regime in South Yemen would find an ally in Iran, which would no longer act as an anticommunist and anti-Soviet bulwark in the Gulf region. But the Saudis, like everybody else, misread the Iranian revolutionary dynamics. They were as surprised as anybody else when the militant religious forces on the right in effect toppled the moderate Bazargan government on 6 November 1979, two days after the seizure of the United States Embassy in Tehran.

This event, which the Khomeini forces labeled the "second revolution," brings us to yet another reason for the Saudi security concern about the Iranian Revolution. The unfolding of the revolution coincided with the most traumatic domestic threat to the House of Saud in history. The seizure of the Grand Mosque by ultrafundamentalist Muslims threatened the stability of the House of Saud. There was no sign of Iranian or pro-Khomeini Saudi Shia involvement in this incident. But the general Iranian propaganda agitation for exporting the "Islamic Revolution" compounded the threat of subversion by indigenous forces in all Gulf Arab monarchies, especially in Saudi Arabia, where a radical Sunni fundamentalist group was in rebellion. More critically, the indigenous Saudi Shias also rebelled in November 1979 and February 1980, no doubt inspired by the Iranian paradigm and propaganda.[9]

Although Iran's revolutionary example seemed menacing in all these respects, the other effects of the revolution paradoxically seemed propitious for the House of Saud. Because the Saudi concern with the threat of the revolution was shared by the other Gulf monarchies, the emerging perception of a common threat aided the Saudi bid for leadership. Furthermore, the momentary decline of Iranian preponderance in the Gulf region, as a result of domestic revolutionary chaos, preoccupation with the hostage crisis, and defense against the Iraqi invasion, seemed to have created a power vacuum in the area, for Iraq was also preoccupied with the war. In these circumstances the Saudis could finally realize their historical goal of extending their protective power and influence throughout the Arabian Peninsula and its periphery. The creation of a regional cooperation organization would aid them in attaining that goal. Such a limited peninsular, rather than Gulf-wide, conception of cooperation would be aided by the great amount of commonality already in existence. The six nations shared a common religion, an Arab heritage, a similarity of regimes, and a tradition of cooperation in social and economic fields. Yet, the real catalyst for action was their perception of the common threat of the Iranian Revolution to their regimes. A regional organization led by Saudi Arabia and backed by the world's largest pool of energy would also aid the Saudi role in world affairs, particularly in the Arab world, where Sadat's Egypt was universally ostracized for having signed the Camp David accords and the peace treaty with Israel.

Of the Arab monarchies alarmed by the eruption of the Iranian Revolution, ranking second only to Saudi Arabia was Bahrain. The shah in 1970 had dramatically relinquished the ancient Iranian claim to sovereignty over Bahrain and had been the first leader to recognize the island's independence. But soon after the revolutionary forces took power, and before the fall of the government of Bazargan, when revolutionary chaos reigned, a firebrand cleric, Ayatollah Sadeq Ruhani, threatened that Iran would "annex" Bahrain unless it adopted an Islamic government after the Iranian model. The threat created an uproar throughout the Arab world from the Gulf to Egypt where President Sadat offered aid to Bahrain and other Gulf states to counter the Iranian threat, which embarrassed the Bazargan government. It denounced the "unauthorized" statement of Ruhani and sent envoys to Bahrain and Saudi Arabia to put out the fire. Like the Saudis, the Bahrainis also experienced two Shia upheavals in 1979 and 1980. These added to the mounting sense of vulnerability within the Khalifah Sunni ruling family. Unlike Saudi Arabia, where the Shias are a small minority, the Shias in Bahrain constitute the majority of the citizen population.[10]

Even Kuwait could not escape the onslaught of the Iranian revolutionary crusade. As an independent-minded and fairly liberal ruling elite, the Sabah royal family officially welcomed the Iranian Revolution, and Kuwait was the first Gulf Arab state to send its foreign minister on a goodwill mission to Iran. Ayatollah Khomeini personally received Sabah al-Ahmad al-Sabah, who expressed confidence in improving Kuwait's relations with Iran, partly because of Iran's pro-Palestinian stance. Yet, the Kuwaiti ruling family soon would face the threat of Iranian political incitement within the borders of Kuwait itself. According to the Kuwaiti interior minister, "a nephew of Ayatollah Khomeini" by the name of Ahmad al-Mahri used religious sermons in a mosque for "political purposes." The cleric and his father, Abbas al-Mahri, who had been appointed by Khomeini as a Friday prayer leader in Kuwait, and the rest of their family were expelled from Kuwait.[11]

The threat posed by the Iranian Revolution convinced these three major royal families that the time for a united front had come if they were to ensure their survival. It is no wonder, therefore, that the Saudi security scheme emphasized, more than any other proposal, the need for cooperation in assuring internal security among the six conservative monarchies. Yet, to leave the matter here would convey the false impression that the GCC was created simply as a counterrevolutionary alliance against revolutionary Iran. There were other major factors at work as well.

One such factor was the perceived threat of the Soviet Union, which was seen to be twofold. First, the invasion and occupation of Afghanistan intensified the long-standing fear of both the Soviet Union and communism felt by the conservative monarchies. The presence of over 100,000 Soviet troops in Afghanistan brought the threat of the Soviet Union that much closer to the Gulf and the Strait of Hormuz. It also tightened the perceived noose around the neck of the conservative regimes by adding the Soviet presence there to the existence of Soviet proxies in South Yemen and Ethiopia. The Saudis had always considered communism and Zionism the two faces of the evil of imperialism. Even the Kuwaitis, who had diplomatic relations with Moscow, rejected the Soviet justification of their invasion in terms of the Moscow-Kabul treaty of 1978 and vowed to continue to help Afghan refugees with food and medicine.[12]

The other dimension of the Soviet threat was the so-called Brezhnev proposals for neutralizing and demilitarizing the Gulf region. In the Gulf, everyone knew that these proposals were advanced by the Soviets as a means of countering the Carter Doctrine. To the Gulf leaders, the Soviet stance was essentially self-serving because it would, if implemented, make it difficult for them to seek foreign military aid, especially from the United States, as a means of strengthening their armed forces. The Saudi information minister, Dr. Muhammad Abduh Yamani, for example, reacted to the Soviet proposals by saying that "the Gulf area is in no need of custodianship and that its people are capable of defending it."[13] If accepted, he believed, the Soviet proposal would amount to actual interference in the name of noninterference. The Omani undersecretary of foreign affairs, Yusuf al-Alawi, sounded the same note straightforwardly. He rejected the Brezhnev proposals, reportedly saying that "these proposals will provide the Soviet Union with the opportunity to interfere in the area's domestic affairs."[14]

It was, however, the perceived threat of the Soviet military presence in Afghanistan, rather than the Brezhnev proposals, that helped crystallize the need for the creation of an indigenous and eventually self-reliant regional organization. The Saudi foreign minister, Prince Saud al-Faysal, for example, told the newspaper *Al-Jazirah* in an interview that the events in Afghanistan "confirmed the need for Gulf states to depend on themselves for the protection of their independence and resources" and urged "friendly nations" to offer arms supplies to the Gulf states to help them achieve "self-reliance for self-defense."[15] Having preceded the formation of the GCC, this statement by a Saudi leader shows the impact of the Soviet invasion of Afghanistan on Saudi thinking in favor of collective self-help. Newspaper accounts later expressed the Saudi thought on the matter more frankly than the official policy statements. An article in the Saudi newspaper *Ukaz*, for example, said on 11 February 1981 that "the objective of creating the Gulf Cooperation Council is to protect the Arab entity against all challenges, against the Soviet challenge in Afghanistan which seeks domination and hegemony, and in many parts of Asia and Africa. Can we forget what is happening in Africa at the hands of Soviet mercenaries?"[16]

We would be remiss, however, to limit this analysis to the two factors discussed above. The fear of the Iranian Revolution and the potential Soviet intervention in the Gulf region was paralleled by the concern over the potential threat of American intervention in the area. In a region of the world which has been bedeviled by imperial rivalries ever since Alexander's soldiers roamed its lands—that is, long before the world's largest oil pool was discovered in the Middle East—the memories of foreign intervention are always fresh. The United States was viewed in many respects as the legatee of British imperialism, despite its lack of direct control over the area. Its aid to the creation of the state of Israel in 1948 was regarded by many Arabs as the most blatant example of American political interference in favor of a local client. They knew of other examples as well. In 1975 Henry Kissinger threatened that the United States would intervene in Arab oil fields in the event of "some actual strangulation of the industrialized world." Five years later the United States finally committed itself to direct military intervention in the Gulf if necessary to protect the uninterrupted flow of Gulf oil supplies to world markets.

The Carter Doctrine was to the Gulf people as a red flag to a bull. Without consulting the regional states, in 1980 President Jimmy Carter told the Congress in his State of the Union Address: "Let our position be absolutely clear: An attempt by any outside force to gain control of the Persian Gulf region will be regarded as an assault on the vital interests of the United States. It will be repelled by use of any means necessary, including military force." The fact that the Gulf Arab leaders knew that President Carter's statement was precipitated by the Soviet invasion of Afghanistan made no real difference in their reactions. They still opposed the Carter Doctrine because it reflected the underlying superpower competition in the region. As the president himself had admitted, his doctrine could not be effectively implemented without the support of the local states. But the regional states would extend none of that kind of support if it meant having American military bases on their soil. Saud al-Faysal, the foreign minister of Saudi Arabia, categorically opposed the establishment of such bases by any foreign country on Saudi territory, despite decades of security relations between Riyadh and Washington. Crown Prince and Prime Minister Shaykh Saad al-Sabah of Kuwait opposed "all foreign intervention in the Gulf no matter what its origin."

The same theme was sounded by other Arab leaders. They also insisted that the Gulf area had no need for any foreign intervention and the regional states themselves could look after the security of their oil supplies. None of this, of course, meant that they were really capable of stopping the Soviet interdiction of oil supplies if Moscow was to disrupt their flow. The Gulf Arab leaders believed that the United States could deter Soviet mischief by establishing a military presence "over the horizon," outside the Gulf waters in the Arabian Sea near the Strait of Hormuz. Although all leaders seemed to oppose American military bases in the region, military "facilities" could be provided. Despite the objection of would-be fellow-GCC Arabs, Oman provided facilities for the United States about four months after President Carter delivered his message to Congress. The Gulf Arab leaders were keenly aware of the need for foreign military aid if they were to be able to create their own collective deterrent force. In fact, their request for such aid, particularly from the United States, skyrocketed after the formation of the GCC.

Preserving the Monarchical Regimes

All said, the founding of the GCC reflected the developments of 1979–81, which the six Arab monarchs felt threatened the very survival of their regimes. The birth of the GCC was not inevitable. In the decade between the departure of the British forces from the Gulf region and the founding of the organization, bilateral cooperation in a great variety of fields had taken place among the six founding members. No matter how important the previous efforts for cooperation, however, they still did not provide sufficient conditions for creating such an organization. To be sure, the pre-GCC tradition of cooperation greatly facilitated the post-GCC activities, especially in nonmilitary fields, but they did not in themselves provide the necessary stimulus for creating the GCC.

The perceived threat of the Soviet Union to the Gulf region did not impel the Gulf monarchies to band together either. They generally feared the perceived Soviet intention of using Afghanistan as a launching board for imperialist expansion in the Gulf and the Indian Ocean, but the threat did not appear that imminent. In fact, there were differences between, for example, the Omani and the Kuwaiti perceptions of the Soviet threat to the region. But even the Omanis, or for that matter the Saudis, who were more alarmed by the Soviet invasion of Afghanistan, did not seem to believe that the Soviet Union posed an immediate threat to the security and stability of the incumbent regimes.

Nor did the potential American military intervention in the Gulf region seem to pose such a threat. After all, Saudi Arabia had enjoyed decades of a security relationship with the United States, and Oman had already pledged to provide the United States with facilities necessary for military contingencies, especially for protecting the freedom of navigation through the Strait of Hormuz. Kuwait had always pursued a more independent policy toward the United States, but when the chips were down even that small city-state would probably opt for American, rather than Soviet, aid to maintain its security. Of course, if the Soviets themselves happened to pose a threat to Kuwaiti security, American protection could become all the more desirable.

Finally, the threat of the spread of the Iraq-Iran war—although an increasing threat after the formation of the GCC—did not at the inception of the GCC pose enough of a threat to be regarded as the cause of the GCC's creation. In fact, during the months between the outbreak of the Iraq-Iran war and the founding of the GCC, Iran was in no position whatever to expand the war to the six monarchies. It was first invaded by Iraqi forces, which escalated the longtime border skirmishes to the level of total war (*harb al-shamilih*) on 22 September 1980. And then for nearly a year Iran was unable to launch an offensive against the Iraqi forces occupying some 800 square miles of the Iranian oil-rich province of Khuzistan. When Iran was finally able to launch its first successful offensive in September 1981, the GCC had already been in existence for about half a year.

The common security concern, therefore, that impelled the leaders of the six states to create the GCC was the perceived threat of the contagion of the Iranian Revolution. Of all the perceived dangers, this was considered to be the most real and imminent threat to the ruling regimes in the six countries. During the crucial 1979–81 period before the founding of the GCC, three of the six states—Bahrain, Kuwait, and Saudi Arabia—had in one way or another faced the threat of Iranian-inspired rebellion within their own societies and a virulent antiroyalist campaign from Iran. Although the other three countries did not share such an experience at the time, Oman, Qatar, and the UAE as similar monarchies fully empathized with the experience of the other three. Their leaders believed that the overthrow of the royal families, particularly in Kuwait and Saudi Arabia, could seriously jeopardize the survival of the others as well.

This perceived threat of revolution to the six ruling families before the founding of the GCC carried over into the first five years of the GCC's existence. For half a decade, the six faced increasingly the threat of perceived Iranian-inspired acts of subversion and terrorism, a perception that Iranian revolutionary leaders vehemently denied. Nevertheless, from the perspective of the six, the post-GCC experience with acts of political violence confirmed their belief that if they did not hang together, they would hang separately.

Notes

1. *Foreign Broadcast Information Service, Daily Report: Middle East and Africa*, V, no. 032, 18 Feb. 1981 (Hereafter *FBIS-V-MEA-*).

2. *FBIS-MEA-V-81-076*, 21 April 1981.

3. *FBIS-MEA-V-81-032*, 18 Feb. 1981.

4. *FBIS-MEA-V-81-085*, 4 May 1981.

5. Gulf Cooperation Council, *Gulf Information and Research Center* (n.p., 1983).

6. Oman did not sign this agreement. For the text of this convention and the related protocol, see R. K. Ramazani, *The Persian Gulf and the Strait of Hormuz* (Alphen aan den Rijn, The Netherlands: Sijthoff and Noordhoff, 1979), pp. 163–75.

7. For details, see *Middle East Magazine*, April 1981, pp. 70–72.

8. *Middle East Magazine*, January 1981, p. 16.

9. See R. K. Ramazani, "Iran's Islamic Revolution and the Persian Gulf," *Current History*, January 1985, pp. 5–8, 40–41.

10. For details, see R. K. Ramazani, "Shiism in the Persian Gulf," in Juan R. I. Cole and Nikki R. Keddie, eds., *Shiism and Social Protest* (New Haven and London: Yale University Press, 1986), pp. 48–54. See also R. K. Ramazani, *Revolutionary Iran: Challenge and Response in the Middle East* (Baltimore and London: Johns Hopkins University Press, 1986), pp. 48–53.

11. For details, see Ramazani, *Revolutionary Iran*, pp. 42–48.

12. See ibid., pp. 119–23.

13. *FBIS-MEA-V-81-045*, 9 March 1981.

14. Ibid.

15. Reported in *Arab News*, 3 March 1980.

16. *FBIS-MEA-V-81-028*, 11 Feb. 1981.

Documents

Document 1

Foreign Minister's Statement on the Founding of the Gulf Cooperation Council (Riyadh Communiqué)

4 February 1981

The United Arab Emirates, the State of Bahrain, the Kingdom of Saudi Arabia, the Sultanate of Oman, the State of Qatar and the State of Kuwait, out of consideration of their special relations and joint characteristics stemming from their joint creed, similarity of regimes, unity of heritage, similarity of their political, social and demographic structure, and their cultural and historical affiliation; and out of these states' desire to deepen and develop cooperation and coordination among them in all fields in a manner that brings good, development and stability to their peoples, these states' foreign ministers met in Riyadh in the Kingdom of Saudi Arabia on 4 February 1981 and resumed their consultations with a view to setting up the operational sys-

tem [*at-tanzim al-amali*] and the organizational structure to crystallize and develop the desired cooperation and co-ordination among their states. They agreed to set up a co-operation council among the said Arab Gulf states, to form a secretariat general for this purpose and to hold periodic meetings on the summit level and the level of foreign ministers with a view to attaining the desired objectives of these states and their peoples in all fields.

This step comes in conformity with the Arab nation's national objectives and within the framework of the Arab League Charter, which urges regional cooperation that is aimed at strengthening the Arab nation and emphasizing these states' affiliation to the Arab League and their enhancement of its role in attaining the aims and principles of its charter in a manner that serves the Arab and Islamic issues.

The foreign ministers decided to hold another meeting in Muscat on 8 March 1981. It is to be preceded by the two meetings of experts, on 24 February 1981 and 4 March 1981, in Riyadh and Muscat with a view to completely systematizing what has been agreed upon with regard to establishing a cooperation council for the Arab Gulf states.

Source: *Al-Hadaf* (Kuwait), 5 Feb. 1981, p. 5, as translated in *FBIS-MEA-V–81–026*, 9 Feb. 1981, p. C1.

Document 2

The Decision to Establish the Gulf Cooperation Council

14 February 1981

In the name of God, the compassionate and the merciful:

Out of their realization of special relations, common characteristics and similar regimes that govern them; out of their feeling of the importance of establishing close coordination in all spheres, especially the economic and social domains; out of their belief in a common destiny and unity of objectives; and out of their desire to realize coordination, integration and closer relations in all spheres, the UAE, the State of Bahrain, the Kingdom of Saudi Arabia, the Sultanate of Oman, the State of Qatar, and the State of Kuwait have decided to establish an organization that aims at deepening and bringing closer relations, ties and cooperation among its members in various spheres. The organization shall be named the Cooperation Council for the Arab States of the Gulf [*luduwa al-khalij al-arabiyah*]. Its headquarters shall be in Riyadh, Saudi Arabia. The council will be the vehicle by means of which the maximum coordination, integration and closer relations will be realized. It will also draw up regulations in the spheres of economy, finance, education, culture, social affairs, health, communications, information, passports and nationality, travel, transport, trade customs, freight and legal and legislative affairs.

The Cooperation Council for the Arab States of the Gulf Organizational structure:

The council shall consist of:

A. The Supreme Council, to which will be attached a body for resolving disputes.

B. The Ministerial Council.

C. The Secretariat General.

The Supreme Council:

1. Shall consist of the heads of state of the member states.

2. The presidency of the council shall be rotated in alphabetical order.

3. The council shall meet in normal sessions twice a year. Emergency session may be held.

4. Each member has the right to call for an emergency meeting. The meeting shall take place if seconded by another member.

Competency of the Supreme Council:

It will draw up the high policy of the Cooperation Council and the basic lines it will follow. It will discuss the recommendations, laws and bylaws presented to it by the Ministerial Council and the Secretariat General in preparation for their endorsement. It shall form the body for resolving disputes.

Body for resolving disputes:

It shall be attached to the Supreme Council. It shall resolve existing disputes or any that may occur between member states. It also shall be the reference for interpretation of the basic bylaws of the Cooperation Council.

The Ministerial Council:

1. It shall be composed of the foreign ministers of the member states, or any ministers deputizing for them.

2. It shall draw up the basic regulations for the Secretariat General.

3. The Ministerial Council shall prepare for meetings of the Supreme Council and studies, topics, recommendations, bylaws and laws presented to the Supreme Council. It will also make preparations for meetings of the council.

4. The council shall meet six times every year, that is, once every 2 months. Emergency sessions may be held at the proposal of two member states.

5. It shall draw up policies, recommendations, studies and projects which aim at developing cooperation and coordination among member states in various spheres.

6. It shall encourage aspects of cooperation and coordination between the various activities of the private sector.

7. It shall endorse routine reports as well as regulations and bylaws concerning administrative affairs, and those proposed by the Secretariat General of the Cooperation Council.

8. It shall work to encourage, develop and coordinate existing activities between states in various spheres. Such activities shall be binding should the Ministerial Council endorse them. The council shall recommend competent ministers to draw up policies as well as studies apt to bring to fruition the objectives of the Cooperation Council.

Secretariat General:

The Cooperation Council shall have a secretary general appointed by the Supreme Council. The Supreme Council shall define the conditions and period of office of the secretary general. He shall be chosen from subjects of the Cooperation Council states.

The secretary general shall be responsible directly for all actions of the assistant secretary generals, the Secretariat General and the good course of work in its various sectors. The Secretariat General shall have a data information apparatus.

Competency of the Secretariat General:

1. Preparation of studies concerning cooperation and coordination.

2. Follow up the implementation of resolutions and recommendations of the Supreme Council and the Ministerial Council by the member states.

3. Preparation of reports and studies required by the Ministerial Council.

4. Preparation of routine reports on the work of the Co-operation Council.

5. Preparation of budgets and final accounts.

6. Preparation of the draft of financial and administrative bylaws which shall make the body elaborate and commensurate with the growth of the Cooperation Council and its increasing responsibilities.

Secretariat General budget:

The Secretariat General shall have a budget toward which all member states shall contribute in equal proportions.

[Signed] Kingdom of Saudi Arabia, the State of Bahrain, the State of the UAE, the State of Kuwait, the State of Qatar and the Sultanate of Oman.

Minutes of Meeting

LD142210 Riyadh SPA in Arabic 1750 GMT 14 Feb 81

[Minutes of the meeting of the foreign ministers of Kuwait, Bahrain, Qatar, the UAE, the Sultanate of Oman and Saudi Arabia on 4 February 1981 in Riyadh]

[Text] [No dateline given] The foreign ministers of Kuwait, Bahrain, Qatar, the UAE, the Sultanate of Oman and the Kingdom of Saudi Arabia have met. They endorsed the plan for a cooperation council for the Arab states of the Gulf, the bylaws of which were attached. The foreign ministers have also decided to hold another meeting in Muscat on 8 March 1981, provided that it is preceded by another two meetings of experts on 24 February 1981 and 4 March 1981 in Riyadh and Muscat in order to formulate integral bylaws on what has been approved concerning the establishment of the Cooperation Council of the Arab states of the Gulf. It has been agreed to recommend to the states concerned appointing a minister for cooperation affairs among the Gulf states in the future.

Source: *FBIS-MEA-V–81–031*, 17 Feb. 1981, pp. C1-C3.

Document 3
The Structure of the GCC
10 March 1981

His Excellency Abd al-Aziz ar-Rawwas, minister of information and youth affairs, opened the sixth Arab Gulf information ministers conference in the Muscat Intercontinental Hotel conference hall at 1030 today.

The conference began with a recitation of verses from the holy Koran. His Excellency Abd al-Aziz ar-Rawwas, who is the conference chairman, then delivered the sultan's speech. He welcomed their excellencies the ministers and the participating delegations, and said that it is auspicious that the meeting is taking place in the light of continuous contacts among our states to construct the greater edifice to Gulf fraternity and effective cooperation among the region's states and peoples in harmony with the inevitability of history and common destiny.

He said that none of them had spared their efforts to unite our voice and ranks. We could not make our voice heard and respected in the world unless we reverted to a united voice in a manner that would yield prosperity for our region and people.

His Excellency Abd al-Aziz ar-Rawwas said it was because of this that there is an urgent and pressing need for a new information policy that would lift us to a cultural level from which our nation would derive vitality and transform the role of our Gulf information policy into an active one in the various international fields.

The new information policy we propose is above all political, but it cannot be a substitute for other institutions that have defined duties and tasks. If we make objectivity our guide in information work and exert the required efforts to raise the level of proficiency of our cadres and improve their performance we will be able to attain our goals with the same level of scientific proficiency and technical capacity as that which at present we seek from abroad. For this reason, if we infuse the existing information institutions with experienced information expertise and train the workers in the field of information then we should be able to develop the capacity to attain our goals.

His excellency went on to say that there is a positive phenomenon that had emerged during the last few years, namely, the Arabic newspaper published by Arabs living abroad. Permit me in your name to hail our colleagues who had made of their [*word indistinct*] a reality accompanied by the development of Arab corporations in the field of journalism and information. In this manner they carried the Arab voice to our sons and brothers living abroad. He said that it is time the Gulf information institutions which we established by joint efforts during previous conferences were developed.

The right approach which we believe will crystallize these institutions in a manner that will make them more effective and beneficial will not be possible without organizational, coordination and consultation among us through a permanent secretariat of a level commensurate with the tasks of the Gulf information policy. One of its principal concerns should be the evaluation of the work of the existing institutions and a follow-up of the implementation of the required information policy.

His excellency said that the depth of the relations that link us in this region, headed by relations of faith, blood, and neighborliness, were bound—with God's support—to lead us to full coordination in all fields in a manner that will serve the interests, hopes and aspirations of the peoples in our region and the stability of our states.

Decisions Reported

The foreign ministers of the Cooperation Council of the six Gulf Arab states concluded their meeting this afternoon at the guest palaces at Al-Ghubrah. After the final session

His Excellency Qais Abd al-Munim Zawawi, minister of state for foreign affairs, made the following statement to newsmen:

This morning the foreign ministers of the state of the United Arab Emirates, the State of Kuwait, the State of Bahrain, the Kingdom of Saudi Arabia, the State of Qatar and the Sultanate of Oman met in Muscat for their second preparatory meeting to finalize the statutes relating to the Cooperation Council of the Gulf Arab states.

The ministers discussed the following draft bills and statutes presented to them by the committee of experts following its meetings in the cities of Riyadh and Muscat:

The basic statute [*an-nizam al-asasi*] for the Cooperation Council;

The internal statute [*an-nizam ad-dakhili*] for the Supreme Council;

The internal statute for the Ministerial Council;

The internal statute for the General Secretariat.

The ministers approved the first three statutes. With regard to the internal statute for the General Secretariat, the ministers reviewed it but resolved not to make any final decision until the appointment of a secretary general who will express his view about the statute.

The ministers recommended that the Supreme Council should hold its session at the beginning of May and November every year. The council recommended a meeting of leaders to be held 26–27 May 1981, in the city of Abu Dhabi. This meeting is to be preceded by the foreign ministers meeting on 24 May.

His Excellency Qais Zawawi said the initialling of the statutes will take place later today.

Their excellencies the foreign ministers of the six Gulf states have now gone to Salalah where they will be received by His Majesty Sultan Qabus.

Source: *FBIS-MEA-V–81–047*, 11 March 1981, pp. A1-A3.

Document 4
Charter of the GCC
25 May 1981

Cooperation Council for the Arab States of the Gulf: The States of the United Arab Emirates, the State of Bahrain, the Kingdom of Saudi Arabia, the Sultanate of Oman, the State of Qatar, and the State of Kuwait,

Being fully aware of their mutual bonds of special relations, common characteristics and similar systems founded on the Creed of Islam; and based on their faith in the common destiny and destination that link their peoples; and in view of their desire to effect coordination, integration and interconnection between them in all fields; and based on

their conviction that coordination, cooperation and integration between them serve the higher goals of the Arab Nation; and, in order to strengthen their cooperation and reinforce their common links; and in an endeavor to complement efforts already begun in all vital scopes that concern their peoples and realize their hopes for a better future on the path to unity of their States; and in conformity with the Charter of the League of Arab States which calls for the realization of closer relations and stronger bonds; and in order to channel their efforts to reinforce and serve Arab and Islamic causes, have agreed as follows:

Article One, Establishment of Council

A council shall be established hereby to be named The Cooperation Council for the Arab States of the Gulf, hereinafter referred to as Cooperation Council.

Article Two, Headquarters

The Cooperation Council shall have its headquarters in Riyadh, Saudi Arabia.

Article Three, Cooperation Council Meetings

The Council shall hold its meetings in the state where it has its headquarters, and may convene in any member state.

Article Four, Objectives

The basic objectives of the Cooperation Council are:

1. To effect coordination, integration and interconnection between member states in all fields in order to achieve unity between them.

2. Deepen and strengthen relations, links and scopes of cooperation now prevailing between their peoples in various fields.

3. Formulate similar regulations in various fields including the following:

   a. Economic and financial affairs
   b. Commerce, customs and communications
   c. Education and culture
   d. Social and health affairs
   e. Information and tourism
   f. Legislation and administrative affairs.

4. Stimulate scientific and technological progress in the fields of industry, mineralogy, agriculture, water and animal resources; the establishment of scientific research centers, implementation of common projects, and encourage cooperation by the private sector for the good of their peoples.

Article Five, Council Membership

The Cooperation Council shall be formed of the six states that participated in the Foreign Ministers' meeting held at Riyadh on 4 February 1981.

Article Six, Organizations of the Cooperation Council

The Cooperation Council shall have the following main organizations:

1. Supreme Council to which shall be attached the Commission for Settlement of Disputes.

2. Ministerial Council.

3. Secretariat-General.

Each of these organizations may establish branch organizations as necessary.

Article Seven, Supreme Council

1. The Supreme Council is the highest authority of the Cooperation Council and shall be formed of heads of member states. Its presidency shall be rotatory based on the alphabetical order of the names of the member states.

2. The Supreme Council shall hold one regular session every year. Extraordinary sessions may be convened at the request of any member seconded by another member.

3. The Supreme Council shall hold its sessions in the territories of member states.

4. A Supreme Council shall be considered valid if attended by two thirds of the member states.

Article Eight, Supreme Council's Functions

The Supreme Council shall endeavor to achieve the objectives of the Cooperation Council, particularly as concerns the following:

1. Review matters of interest to the member states.

2. Lay down the higher policy for the Cooperation Council and the basic line it should follow.

3. Review the recommendations, reports, studies and common projects submitted by the Ministerial Council for approval.

4. Review reports and studies which the Secretary-General is charged to prepare.

5. Approve the bases for dealing with other states and international organizations.

6. Approve the rules of procedures of the Commission for Settlement of Disputes and nominate its members.

7. Appoint the Secretary-General.

8. Amend the Charter of the Cooperation Council.

9. Approve the Council's Internal Rules.

10. Approve the budget of the Secretariat-General.

Article Nine, Voting in Supreme Council

1. Each member of the Supreme Council shall have one vote.

2. Resolutions of the Supreme Council in substantive matters shall be carried by unanimous approval of the member states participating in the voting, while resolutions on procedural matters shall be carried by majority vote.

Article Ten, Commission for Settlement of Disputes

1. The Cooperation Council shall have a commission called "Commission for Settlement of Disputes" and shall be attached to the Supreme Council.

2. The Supreme Council shall form the Commission for every case separately based on the nature of the dispute.

3. If a dispute arises over interpretation or implementation of the Charter and such dispute is not resolved within the Ministerial Council or the Supreme Council, the Supreme Council may refer such dispute to the Commission for Settlement of Disputes.

4. The Commission shall submit its recommendations or opinion, as applicable, to the Supreme Council for appropriate action.

Article Eleven, Ministerial Council

1. The Ministerial Council shall be formed of the Foreign Ministers of the member states or other delegated Ministers. The Council's presidency shall rotate among members every three months by alphabetical order of the states.

2. The Ministerial Council shall convene every three months and may hold extraordinary sessions at the invitation of any member seconded by another member.

3. The Ministerial Council shall decide the venue of its next session.

4. A Council's meeting shall be deemed valid if attended by two thirds of the member states.

Article Twelve, Functions of the Ministerial Council

The Ministerial Council's functions shall include the following:

1. Propose policies, prepare recommendations, studies and projects aimed at developing cooperation and coordination between member states in the various fields and adopt required resolutions or recommendations concerning thereof.

2. Endeavor to encourage, develop and coordinate activities existing between member states in all fields. Resolutions adopted in such matters shall be referred to the Ministerial Council for further submission, with recommendations, to the Supreme Council for appropriate action.

3. Submit recommendations to the Ministers concerned to formulate policies whereby the Cooperation Council's resolutions may be put into action.

4. Encourage means of cooperation and coordination between the various private sector activities, develop existing cooperation between the member states' chambers of commerce and industry, and encourage the flow of working citizens of the member states among them.

5. Refer any of the various facets of cooperation to one or more technical or specialized committee for study and presentation of relevant proposals.

6. Review proposals related to amendments to this Charter and submit appropriate recommendations to the Supreme Council.

7. Approve the Ministerial Council's Rules of Procedures as well as the Rules of Procedures of the Secretariat-General.

8. Appoint the Assistant Secretaries-General, as nominated by the Secretary-General, for a renewable period of three years.

9. Approve periodic reports as well as internal rules and regulations related to administrative and financial affairs proposed by the Secretary-General, and submit recommendations to the Supreme Council for approval of the budget of the Secretariat-General.

10. Make arrangements for the Supreme Council's meetings and prepare its agenda.

11. Review matters referred to it by the Supreme Council.

Article Thirteen, Voting at Ministerial Council

1. Every member of the Ministerial Council shall have one vote.

2. Resolutions of the Ministerial Council in substantive matters shall be carried by unanimous vote of the member states present and participating in the vote, and in procedural matters by majority vote.

Article Fourteen, Secretariat-General

1. The Secretariat-General shall be composed of a Secretary-General who shall be assisted by assistants and a number of staff as required.

2. The Supreme Council shall appoint the Secretary-General, who shall be a citizen of one of the Cooperation Council states, for a period of three years which may be renewed for one time only.

3. The Secretary-General shall nominate the Assistant Secretaries-General.

4. The Secretary-General shall appoint the Secretariat General's staff from among the citizens of member states, and may not make exceptions without the approval of the Ministerial Council.

5. The Secretary-General shall be directly responsible for the work of the Secretariat-General and the smooth flow of work in its various organizations. He shall represent the Cooperation Council with other parties within the powers vested in him.

Article Fifteen, Functions of the Secretariat-General

The Secretariat-General shall undertake the following functions:

1. Prepare studies related to cooperation and coordination, and to integrated plans and programmes for member states' common action.

2. Prepare periodic reports on the Cooperation Council's work.

3. Follow up the execution by the member states of the resolutions and recommendations of the Supreme Council and Ministerial Council.

4. Prepare reports and studies ordered by the Supreme Council for Ministerial Council.

5. Prepare the draft of administrative and financial regulations commensurate with the growth of the Cooperation Council and its expanding responsibilities.

6. Prepare the Cooperation Council's budget and closing accounts.

7. Make preparations for meetings and prepare agenda and draft resolutions for the Ministerial Council.

8. Recommend to the Chairman of the Ministerial Council the convocation of an extraordinary session of the Council whenever necessary.

9. Any other tasks entrusted to it by the Supreme Council or Ministerial Council.

Article Sixteen, The Secretary-General and the Assistant Secretaries-General and all the Secretariat General's staff shall carry out their duties in complete independence and for the common interest of the member states. They shall refrain from any action or behavior that is incompatible with their duties and from divulging the secrets of their jobs either during or after their tenure of office.

Article Seventeen, Privileges and Immunities

1. The Cooperation Council and its organizations shall enjoy on the territories of all member states such legal competence, privileges and immunities as required to realize their objectives and carry out their functions.

2. Representatives of the member states of the Council, and the Council's employees, shall enjoy such privileges and immunities as are specified in agreements to be concluded for this purpose between the member states. A special agreement shall organize the relation between the Council and the state in which it has its headquarters.

3. Until such time as the two agreements mentioned in item 2 above are prepared and put into effect, the representatives of the member states in the Cooperation Council and its staff shall enjoy the diplomatic privileges and immunities established for similar organizations.

Article Eighteen, Budget of the Secretariat-General.

The Secretariat-General shall have a budget to which the member states shall contribute equal amounts.

Article Nineteen, Charter Implementation

1. This Charter shall go into effect as of the date it is signed by the heads of states of the six member states named in this Charter's preamble.

2. The original copy of this Charter shall be deposited with Saudi Arabia's Ministry of Foreign Affairs which shall act as custodian and shall deliver a true copy thereof to every member state, pending the establishment of the Secretariat-General at which time the latter shall become depository.

Article Twenty, Amendments to Charter

1. Any member state may request an amendment of this Charter.

2. Requests for Charter amendments shall be submitted to the Secretary-General who shall refer them to the member states at least four months prior to submission to the Ministerial Council.

Article Twenty-One, Closing Provisions

No reservations may be voiced in respect of the provisions of this Charter.

Article Twenty-Two

The Secretariat-General shall arrange to deposit and register copies of this Charter with the League of Arab States and the United Nations, by resolution of the Ministerial Council.

This Charter is signed on one copy in Arabic language at Abu Dhabi City, United Arab Emirates, on 21 Rajab 1401 corresponding to 25 May 1981.

United Arab Emirates
State of Bahrain
Kingdom of Saudi Arabia
Sultanate of Oman
State of Qatar
State of Kuwait

Source: *American-Arab Affairs*, no. 7 (Winter 1983–84): 157–62.

Document 5

Rules of Procedures of the Supreme Council

25 May 1981

Article One, Definitions

These regulations shall be called Rules of Procedures of the Supreme Council of the Gulf Arab States Cooperation Council and shall encompass the rules that govern procedures for convening the Council and the exercise of its functions.

Article Two, Membership

1. The Supreme Council shall be composed of the heads of state of the Cooperation Council member states. The Presidency shall be rotatory based on the alphabetical order of the states' names.

2. Each member state shall notify the Secretary-General of the names of the members of its delegations to the Council meeting, at least seven days prior to the date set for opening the meeting.

Article Three

With due regard to the objectives of the Cooperation Council and the jurisdiction of the Supreme Council as specified in Articles 4 and 8 of the Charter, the Supreme Council may perform the following:

1. Form technical committees and select their members from member states' nominees who specialize in the committees' respective fields.

2. Call one or more of its members to a specific subject and submit a report thereon to be distributed to the members sufficiently in advance of the meeting set for discussing that subject.

Article Four, Convening the Supreme Council

1. a. The Supreme Council shall hold one regular session every year, and may hold extraordinary sessions at the request of any one member seconded by another member.

b. The Supreme Council shall hold its sessions at the heads of state level.

c. The Supreme Council shall hold its sessions in the member states' territories.

d. Prior to convening the Supreme Council, the Secretary-General shall hold a meeting to be attended by delegates of the member states for consultation on matters related to the session's agenda.

2. a. The Secretary-General shall set the opening date of the Council's session and suggest a closing date.

b. The Secretary-General shall issue the invitations for convening a regular session no less than thirty days in advance, and for convening an extraordinary session, within no more than five days.

Article Five

1. The Supreme Council shall at the start of every session decide whether the meetings shall be secret or public.

2. A meeting shall be considered valid if attended by heads of state of two thirds of the member states. Its resolutions in substantive matters shall be carried by unanimous agreement of the member states present and participating in the vote, while resolutions in procedural matters shall be carried by majority vote. Any member abstaining shall document his being not bound by the resolution.

Article Six

1. The Council shall hold an extraordinary session based on:

a. Resolution issued in a previous session.

b. Request of a member state seconded by another state. In this case, the Council shall convene within no more than five days from the date of issue of the invitation for holding the extraordinary session.

2. No matters may be placed on the extraordinary session's agenda other than those for which the session was convened to discuss.

Article Seven

1. Presidency of the Supreme Council shall, at the opening of each regular session, go to a head of state by rotation based on the alphabetical order of the member states' names. The President shall continue to exercise the functions of the Presidency until such functions are entrusted to his successor at the beginning of the next regular session.

2. The head of a state that is party to an outstanding dispute may not preside over a session or meeting called to discuss the subject of the dispute. In such case, the Council shall designate a temporary president.

3. The President shall declare the opening and closing of sessions and meetings, the suspension of meetings, and clotures, and shall see that the Cooperation Council Charter and these Rules of Procedures are duly complied with. He shall give the floor to speakers based on the order of their requests, submit suggestions for acceptance by the membership, direct voting procedures, give final decisions on points of order, announce resolutions, follow up on works of committees, and inform the Council of all incoming correspondence.

4. The President may take part in deliberations and submit suggestions in the name of the state which he represents and may, for this purpose, assign a member of his state's delegation to act on his behalf in such instances.

Article Eight, Supreme Council Agenda

1. The Ministerial Council shall prepare a draft agenda for the Supreme Council, and such draft agenda shall be conveyed by the Secretary-General, together with explanatory notes and documentation, to the member states under cover of the letter of convocation at least thirty days before the date set for the meeting.

2. The draft agenda shall include the following:

a. A report by the Secretary-General on the Supreme Council's activities between the two sessions, and actions taken to carry out its resolutions.

b. Reports and matters received from the Ministerial Council and the Secretariat-General.

c. Matters which the Supreme Council had previously decided to include on the agenda.

d. Matters suggested by a member state for necessary review by the Supreme Council.

3. Every member state may request inclusion of additional items on the draft agenda provided such request is tabled at least fifteen days prior to the date set for opening the session. Such matters shall be listed in an additional agenda which shall be sent, along with relevant documentation, to the member state, at least five days before the date set for the session.

4. Any member state may request inclusion of extra items on the draft agenda as late as the date set for opening a session, if such matters are considered both important and urgent.

5. The Council shall approve its agenda at the start of every session.

6. The Council may, during the session, add new items that are considered urgent.

7. The ordinary session shall be adjourned after completion of discussions of the items placed on the agenda. The Supreme Council may decide to suspend the session's meeting before completion of discussions on agenda items, and resume such meetings at a later date.

Article Nine, Office and Committees of Supreme Council

1. The Supreme Council Office shall be formed, in every session, of the Council President, the Chairman of the Ministerial Council and the Secretary-General. The Office shall be headed by the Supreme Council President.

2. The Office shall carry out the following functions:

a. Review the text of resolutions passed by the Supreme Council without affecting their contents.

b. Assist the President of the Supreme Council in directing the activities of the session in a general way.

c. Other tasks indicated in these Rules of Procedures or other matters entrusted to it by the Supreme Council.

Article Ten

1. The Council may, at the start of every session, create any committees that it deems necessary to allow adequate study of matters listed on the agenda. Delegates of member states shall take part in the activities of such committees.

2. Meetings of committees shall continue until they complete their task, with due regard for the date set for closing the session. The resolutions shall be carried by majority vote.

3. Every committee shall start its work by selecting a chairman from among its members. The rapporteur of the committee shall act for the chairman in directing the meeting in the absence of the chairman. The chairman, or other rapporteur in the chairman's absence, shall submit to the Council all the explanations that it requests on the committee's reports. The chairman may, with the approval of the session's President, take part in the discussions, without voting if he is not a member of the Supreme Council.

4. The Council may refer any of the matters included in the agenda to the committees, based on their specialization for study and reporting. Any one item may be referred to more than one committee.

5. Committees may neither discuss any matter not referred to them by the Council, nor adopt any recommendation which, if approved by the Council, may produce a financial obligation, before the committee receives a report from the Secretary-General regarding the financial and administrative results that may ensue from adopting the resolution.

Article Eleven, Progress of Deliberations and Suggestions

1. Every member state may participate in the deliberations and committees of the Supreme Council as stipulated in these Rules of Procedures.

2. The President shall direct discussion of the items as presented in order on the meeting's agenda and may, when necessary, call the Secretary-General or his representative to the meeting to explain any point as necessary.

3. The President shall give the floor to speakers in the order of their requests. He may give priority to the Chairman or rapporteur of a committee to submit a report or explain specific points.

4. Every member may, during deliberations, raise points of order which the President shall resolve immediately and his decisions shall be valid unless contradicted by a majority of the Supreme Council member states.

Article Twelve

1. Every member may, during the discussion of any subject, request suspension or adjournment of the meeting or discussion of the subject, or cloture. Such requests may not be discussed, but the President shall put them to the vote, if duly seconded, and decision shall be by majority of the member states.

2. With due regard to provisions of item 4 of the preceding Article, suggestions indicated in item 1 of the Article, shall be given priority over all others based on the following order:

a. Suspend the meeting.

b. Adjourn the meeting.

c. Postpone discussion of the matter on hand.

d. Cloture of discussion of the matter on hand.

3. Apart from suggestions concerning language or procedural matters, draft resolutions and substantive amendments shall be submitted in writing to the Secretary-General or his representative who shall distribute them as soon as possible to the delegations. No draft resolution may be submitted for discussion or voting before the text thereof is distributed to all the delegations.

4. A proposal that has already been decided upon in the same session may not be reconsidered unless the Council decides otherwise.

Article Thirteen

The President shall follow the activities of the committees, inform the Supreme Council of correspondence received, and formally announce before members all the resolutions and recommendations arrived at.

Article Fourteen, Voting

Every member state shall have one vote and no state may represent another state or vote for it.

Article Fifteen

1. Voting shall be by calling the names in the alphabetical order of the states' names, or by raising hands. Voting shall be secret if so requested by a member by decision of the President. The Supreme Council may decide otherwise. The vote of every member shall be documented in the minutes of the meeting if voting is effected by calling the names. The minutes shall indicate the result of voting, if the vote is secret or by show of hands.

2. A member may abstain from a vote or express reservations over a procedural matter or part thereof, in which case the reservation shall be read at the time the resolution is announced and shall be duly documented in writing. Members may present explanations about their stand in the voting after voting is completed.

3. Once the President announces that voting has started, no interruption may be made unless the matter relates to a point of order relevant to the vote.

Article Sixteen

1. If a member requests amendment of a proposal, voting on the amendment shall be carried out first. If there are more than one amendment, voting shall first be made on the amendment which in the President's opinion is farthest from the original proposal, then on the next farthest, and so on until voting is completed on all proposed amendments. If one or more such amendments is passed, then voting shall be made on the original proposal as amended.

2. Any new proposal shall be deemed as an amendment to the original proposal if it merely entails an addition to, omission from or change to a part of the original proposal.

Article Seventeen

1. The Supreme Council may create technical committees charged with giving advice on the design and execution of Supreme Council programmes in specific fields.

2. The Supreme Council shall appoint the members of the technical committees from specialists who are citizens of the member states.

3. The technical committees shall meet at the invitation of the Secretary-General and shall lay down their work plans in consultation with him.

4. The Secretary-General shall prepare the committees' agendas after consultation with the chairman of the committee concerned.

Article Eighteen, Amendment of Rules of Procedures

1. Any member state may propose amendments to the Rules of Procedures.

2. No proposed amendments may be considered unless the relevant proposal is circulated to the member states by the Secretariat-General prior to tabling with the Ministerial Council by at least thirty days.

3. No basic changes may be introduced to the proposed amendment mentioned in the preceding item unless the text of such proposed changes have been circulated to the member states by the Secretariat-General before tabling with the Ministerial Council by at least fifteen days.

4. Except for items based on the provisions of the Charter, and with due regard to preceding items, these Rules of Procedures shall be amended by a resolution of the Supreme Council approved by majority of the members.

Article Nineteen, Effective Date

These Rules of Procedures shall go into effect as of the date of approval by the Supreme Council and may not be amended except in accordance with procedures set forth in the preceding Article.

These Rules of Procedures are signed at Abu Dhabi City, United Arab Emirates on 21 Rajab 1401 AH corresponding to 25 May 1981 AD.

United Arab Emirates
State of Bahrain
Kingdom of Saudi Arabia
Sultanate of Oman
State of Qatar
State of Kuwait

Source: *American-Arab Affairs*, no. 7 (Winter 1983–84): 162–67.

Document 6

Rules of Procedures of the Ministerial Council
25 May 1981

Article One

1. These regulations shall be called Rules of Procedures of the Ministerial Council of the Gulf Arab States Cooperation Council and shall encompass rules governing Council meetings and exercise of its functions.

2. The following terms as used in these shall have the meanings indicated:

Cooperation Council—The Gulf Arab States Cooperation Council

Charter—Statute establishing the Gulf Arab States Cooperation Council

Supreme Council—The highest body of the Gulf Arab States Cooperation Council

Council—Ministerial Council of the Gulf Arab States Cooperation Council

Secretary-General—The Secretary-General of the Gulf Arab States Cooperation Council

Chairman—The Chairman of the Ministerial Council of the Gulf Arab States Cooperation Council

Article Two, State Representation

1. The Ministerial Council shall be composed of the member states' Foreign Ministers or other delegated Ministers.

2. Every member state shall, at least one week prior to the convening of every Ministerial Council's ordinary session, convey to the Secretary-General a list of the names of the members of its delegation. For extraordinary sessions,

the list shall be submitted three days before the date set for the session.

Article Three, Convening the Sessions

1. The Ministerial Council shall decide in every meeting the venue of its next regular session.

2. The Secretary-General shall decide, in consultation with the member states, the venues of extraordinary sessions.

3. If circumstances should arise that preclude the convening of an ordinary or extraordinary session at the place set for it, the Secretary-General shall so inform the member states and shall set another place for the meeting after consultation with them.

Article Four, Ordinary Sessions

1. The Council shall convene in ordinary session once every three months.

2. The Secretary-General shall set the date for opening the session and suggest the date of its closing.

3. The Secretary-General shall address the invitation to attend a Council ordinary session at least fifteen days in advance, and shall indicate therein the date and place set for the meeting, as well as attach thereto the session's agenda, explanatory notes and other documentation.

Article Five, Extraordinary Sessions

1. The Council shall hold an extraordinary session at the request of any member state seconded by another member.

2. The Secretary-General shall address the invitation to the council's extraordinary session and attach a memorandum containing the request of the member which asked for the meeting.

3. The Secretary-General shall specify in the invitation the place, date and agenda of the session.

Article Six

1. The Council may itself decide to hold extraordinary sessions, in which case it shall specify the agenda, time and place of the session.

2. The Secretary-General shall send out to the member states the invitation to attend the Council's extraordinary meeting, along with a memorandum containing the Council's decision to this effect, and specifying the date and agenda of the session.

3. The extraordinary session shall be convened within a maximum of five days from the date of issue of the invitation.

Article Seven

No matters, other than those for which the extraordinary session was called, may be included on its agenda.

Article Eight, Agenda

The Secretary-General shall prepare a draft agenda for a Council's ordinary session and such draft shall include the following:

1. The Secretary-General's Report on the Cooperation Council's work.

2. Matters referred to him by the Supreme Council.

3. Matters which the Council had previously decided to include on the agenda.

4. Matters which the Secretary-General believes should be reviewed by the Council.

5. Matters suggested by a member state.

Article Nine

Member states shall convey to the Secretary-General their suggestions on matters they wish to include on the Council's agenda at least thirty days prior to the date of the Council's ordinary session.

Article Ten

Member states or the Secretary-General may request the inclusion of additional items on the Council's draft agenda at least ten days prior to the date set for opening an ordinary session. Such items shall be listed on an additional schedule which shall be conveyed along with relevant documentation to the member states at least five days prior to the date of the session.

Article Eleven

Member states or the Secretary-General may request inclusion of additional items on the Council ordinary session's agenda up to [the] date set for opening the session if such matters are both important and urgent.

Article Twelve

The Council shall approve its agenda at the beginning of every session.

Article Thirteen

A Council's ordinary session shall end upon completion of discussion of matters listed on the agenda. The Council may, when necessary, decide to suspend its meetings temporarily before discussion of agenda items is completed and resume its meetings at a later date.

Article Fourteen

The Council may defer discussion of certain items on its agenda and decide to include them with the others, when necessary, on the agenda of a subsequent session.

Article Fifteen, Council's Chairmanship

1. Chairmanship of the Council shall be entrusted every six months to a head of delegation on rotation based on the alphabetical order of the member states' names, and if necessary, to the next in order.

2. The Chairman shall exercise his functions until he passes his post on to his successor.

3. The Chairman shall, as well, preside over the extraordinary sessions.

4. The representative of a state that is party to an outstanding dispute may not chair the session or meeting assigned for discussing such dispute, in which case the Council shall name a temporary Chairman.

Article Sixteen

1. The Chairman shall announce the opening and closing of sessions and meetings, the suspension of meetings and cloture of discussions, and shall see that the provisions of the Charter and these Rules of Procedures are duly respected.

2. The Chairman may participate in the Council's deliberations and vote in the name of the state he represents. He may, for such purpose, delegate another member of his delegation to act on his behalf.

Article Seventeen, Council's Office

1. The Council Office shall include the Chairman, Secretary-General, and heads of working subcommittees which the Council decides to form.

2. The Council Chairman shall preside over the Office.

Article Eighteen

The Office shall carry out the following tasks:

1. Help the Chairman direct the sessions' proceedings;

2. Coordinate the work of the Council and the subcommittees;

3. Supervise the drafting of the resolutions passed by the Council;

4. Other tasks indicated in these Rules of Procedures or entrusted to it by the Council.

Article Nineteen, Subcommittees

1. The Council shall utilize preparatory and working committees to accomplish its tasks.

2. The Secretariat-General shall participate in the work of the committees.

Article Twenty

1. The Secretary-General may, in consultation with the Chairman of the session, form preparatory committees charged with the study of matters listed on the agenda.

2. Preparatory committees shall be composed of delegates of member states and may, when necessary, seek the help of such experts as they may deem fit.

3. Each preparatory committee shall meet at least three days prior to the opening of the session by invitation of the Secretary-General. The work of the committee shall end at the close of the session.

Article Twenty-One

1. The Council may, at the start of each session, form working committees and charge them with specific tasks.

2. The work of the working committees shall continue until the date set for closing the session.

Article Twenty-Two

1. Each subcommittee shall start its work by electing a chairman and a rapporteur from among its members. When the chairman is absent, the rapporteur shall act for him in directing the meetings.

2. The chairman or rapporteur of each subcommittee shall submit a report on its work to the Council.

3. The chairman or rapporteur of a subcommittee shall present to the Council all explanations required about the contents of the subcommittee's report.

Article Twenty-Three

1. The Secretariat-General shall organize the technical secretariat and subcommittees of the Council.

2. The Secretariat-General shall prepare minutes of meetings documenting discussions, resolutions and recommendations. Such minutes shall be prepared for all meetings of the Council and its subcommittees.

3. The Secretary-General shall supervise the organization of the Council's relations with the information media.

4. The Secretary-General shall convey the Council's resolutions and recommendations and relevant documen-

tation to the member states within fifteen days after the end of the session.

Article Twenty-Four

The Council's Secretariat and subcommittees shall receive and distribute documents, reports, resolutions and recommendations of the Council and its subcommittees and shall draw up and distribute minutes and daily bulletins, as well as safeguard the documents and carry out any other tasks required by the Council's work.

Article Twenty-Five

Texts of resolutions or recommendations made by the Council may not be announced or published except by decision of the Council.

Article Twenty-Six, Deliberations

Every member state may take part in the deliberations of the Council and its subcommittees in the manner prescribed in these Rules of Procedures.

Article Twenty-Seven

1. The Chairman shall direct deliberations on matters in hand in the order they are listed on the Council's agenda.

2. The chairman shall give the floor to speakers in the order of their requests. Priority may be given to the chairman or rapporteur of a certain committee to present its report or explain certain points therein. The floor shall be given to the Secretary-General or his representative whenever it is necessary.

3. The Council Chairman may, during deliberations, read the list of the names of members who requested the floor, and with the approval of the Council, close the list. The only exception is exercise of the right of reply.

Article Twenty-Eight

The Council shall decide whether the meetings shall be open or secret.

Article Twenty-Nine

1. Every member may raise a point of order which the chairman shall resolve immediately and his decision shall be final unless opposed by majority of the member states.

2. A member who raises a point of order may not go beyond the point he raised.

Article Thirty

1. Every member may, during discussion of any matter, suggest the suspension or adjournment of the meeting, or discussion of the matter on hand or cloture. The Chairman shall in such cases submit the suggestion to the vote directly, if the suggestion is seconded by another member, and it requires the approval of the majority of the member states to pass.

2. With due regard to the provisions of the preceding item, suggestions indicated therein shall be submitted to the vote in the following order:

    a. Suspension of meeting

    b. Adjournment of meeting

    c. Postponement of discussion of the matter in hand

    d. Cloture of discussion of the matter in hand.

Article Thirty-One

1. Member states may suggest draft resolutions or recommendations, or amendments thereto, and may withdraw such suggestions unless they are voted upon.

2. Drafts indicated in the preceding item shall be submitted in writing to the Secretariat-General for distribution to delegations as soon as possible.

3. Except for suggestions concerning language or procedures, drafts indicated in this Article may not be discussed or voted upon before their texts are distributed to all delegations.

4. A suggestion already decided upon in the same session may not be reconsidered unless the Council decides otherwise.

Article Thirty-Two

The Chairman shall follow the work of the committees, inform the Council of incoming correspondence, and formally announce before members the resolutions and recommendations that have been arrived at.

Article Thirty-Three, Voting

1. The Council shall pass its resolutions with the unanimous approval of the member states present and participating in the vote, while decisions in procedural matters shall be passed by a majority vote. The member abstaining from the vote shall document his nonsubscription to the decision.

2. If members of the Council should disagree on the definition of the matter being put to the vote, the matter shall be settled by majority vote of the member states present.

Article Thirty-Four

1. Every member state shall have one vote.

2. No member state may represent another state or vote for it.

Article Thirty-Five

1. Voting shall be by calling the names in the alphabetical order of the states' names, or by raising hands.

2. Voting shall be by secret ballot if so requested by a member or by decision of the Chairman. The Council, however, may decide otherwise.

3. The vote of every member shall be documented in the minutes of the meeting if voting is effected by calling the names. The minutes shall indicate the result of voting if the vote is secret or by show of hands.

4. Member states may explain their positions after the vote and such explanations shall be written down in the minutes of the meeting.

5. Once the Chairman announces that voting has started, no interruption may be made except for a point of order relating to the vote or its postponement in accordance with the provisions of this Article and the next Article.

Article Thirty-Six

1. The Council Chairman with the help of the Secretary-General shall endeavor to reconcile the stands of member states on disputed matters and obtain their agreement to a draft resolution before submitting it to the vote.

2. The Council Chairman, the Secretary-General or any member state may request postponement of a vote for a specific period during which further negotiations may be made concerning the item submitted to the vote.

Article Thirty-Seven

1. If a member requests amendment of a proposal, voting on the amendment shall be carried out first. If there is more than one amendment, voting shall first be made on the amendment which the Chairman considers to be farthest from the original proposal, then on the next farthest, and so on until all proposed amendments have been voted upon. If one or more amendments are passed, then voting shall be made on the original proposal as amended.

2. A new proposal shall be deemed as an amendment to the original proposal if it merely entails an addition to, omission from, or change to a part of the original proposal.

Article Thirty-Eight

1. Any member state or the Secretary-General may propose amending these Rules of Procedures.

2. No proposed amendment to these Rules of Procedures may be considered unless the relevant proposal is circulated to the member states by the Secretariat-General at least thirty days before submission to the Council.

3. No basic changes may be introduced to the proposed amendment mentioned in the preceding item unless the texts of such proposed change have been circulated to the member states at least fifteen days prior to submission to the Council.

4. Except for items based on provisions of the Charter, and with due regard to preceding items, these Rules of Procedures shall be amended by a resolution of the Council approved by majority of its members.

Article Thirty-Nine, Effective Date

These Rules of Procedures shall go into effect as of the date of approval by the Council and may not be amended except in accordance with procedures set forth in the preceding article.

Thus, these Rules of Procedures are signed at Abu Dhabi City, United Arab Emirates, on 21 Rajab 1401 AH corresponding to 25 May 1981 AD.

United Arab Emirates
State of Bahrain
Kingdom of Saudi Arabia
Sultanate of Oman
State of Qatar
State of Kuwait

Source: *American-Arab Affairs*, no. 7 (Winter 1983–84): 167–74.

Document 7

Rules of Procedures of the Commission for the Settlement of Disputes

25 May 1981

Preamble

In accordance with the provisions of Article Six of the Charter of the Gulf Arab States Cooperation Council; and in execution of the provision of Article Ten of the Cooperation Council Charter, a Commission for Settlement of Disputes, hereinafter referred to as The Commission, shall be set up and its jurisdiction and rules for its proceedings shall be as follows:

Article One, Terminology

Terms used in these Rules of Procedures shall have the same meanings established in the Charter of the Gulf Arab States Cooperation Council.

Article Two, Commission's Seat and Meetings

The Commission shall have its headquarters at Riyadh, Saudi Arabia, and shall hold its meetings on the territory of the state where its headquarters is located, but may hold its meetings elsewhere, when necessary.

Article Three, Jurisdiction

The Commission shall, once installed, have jurisdiction to consider the following matters referred to it by the Supreme Council:

1. Disputes between member states.

2. Differences of opinion as to the interpretation or execution of the Cooperation Council Charter.

Article Four, Commission's Membership

1. The Commission shall be formed of an appropriate number of citizens of member states not involved in the dispute as the Council selects in every case separately depending on the nature of the dispute, provided that the number shall not be less than three members.

2. The Commission may seek the advice of any such experts as it may deem necessary.

3. Unless the Supreme Council decides otherwise, the Commission's task shall end with the submission of its recommendations or opinion to the Supreme Council which, after the conclusion of the Commission's task, may summon it at any time to explain or elaborate on its recommendations or opinions.

Article Five, Meetings and Internal Procedures

1. The Commission's meeting shall be valid if attended by all members.

2. The Secretariat-General of the Cooperation Council shall prepare procedures required to conduct the Commission's affairs, and such procedures shall go into effect as of the date of approval by the Ministerial Council.

3. Each party to the dispute shall send representatives to the Commission who shall be entitled to follow proceedings and present their defense.

Article Six, Chairmanship

The Commission shall select a chairman from among its members.

Article Seven, Voting

Every member of the Commission shall have one vote, and shall issue its recommendations or opinions on matters referred to it by majority of the members. In case of a tie, the party with the Chairman's vote shall prevail.

Article Eight, Commission's Secretariat

1. The Secretary-General shall appoint a recorder for the Commission, and a sufficient number of employees to carry out secretarial work.

2. The Supreme Council may create an independent organization to carry out the Commission's secretarial work when the need arises.

Article Nine, Recommendations and Opinions

1. The Commission shall issue its recommendations or opinions in accordance with the Cooperation Council's Charter, international laws and practices, and the principles of Islamic Shariah. The Commission shall submit its findings on the case in hand to the Supreme Council for appropriate action.

2. The Commission may, while considering any dispute referred to it and pending the issue of its final recommendations thereon, ask the Supreme Council to take interim action called for by necessity or circumstances.

3. The Commission's recommendations or opinions shall spell out the reasons on which they were based and shall be signed by the chairman and recorder.

4. If an opinion is passed wholly or partially by unanimous vote of the members, the dissenting members shall be entitled to document their dissenting opinion.

Article Ten, Immunities and Privileges

The Commission and its members shall enjoy such immunities and privileges in the territories of the member states as are required to realize its objectives and in accordance with Article Seventeen of the Cooperation Council Charter.

Article Eleven, Commission's Budget

The Commission's budget shall be considered part of the Secretariat-General's budget. Remunerations of the Commission's members shall be established by the Supreme Council.

Article Twelve, Amendments

1. Any member state may request for amendments of these Rules of Procedures.

2. Requests for amendments shall be submitted to the Secretary-General who shall relay them to the member states by at least four months before submission to the Ministerial Council.

3. An amendment shall be effective if approved unanimously by the Supreme Council.

Article Thirteen, Effective Date

These Rules of Procedures shall go into effect as of the date of approval by the Supreme Council.

These Rules of Procedures were signed at Abu Dhabi

City, United Arab Emirates on 21 Rajab 1401 AH corresponding to 25 May 1981 AD.

United Arab Emirates
State of Bahrain
Kingdom of Saudi Arabia
Sultanate of Oman
State of Qatar
State of Kuwait

Source: *American-Arab Affairs*, no. 7 (Winter 1983–84): 174–76.

Document 8
Bylaws of the GCC
26 May 1981

During their closed meeting today, the heads of the six Gulf states participating in the Arab Gulf Cooperation Council approved the bylaws of the Supreme Council, which is the supreme authority of the Cooperation Council and one of its three main organs, in addition to the Ministerial Council and the General Secretariat. The following is the text of the Supreme Council's bylaws:

Article One:

The following shall be called the Bylaws of the Supreme Council of the Arab Gulf Cooperation Council. They contain the rules regulating the convocation of the council and the exercise of its tasks.

Article Two: The Supreme Council's Membership and Tasks

1. The Supreme Council shall consist of the heads of the Cooperation Councils' member states. Its presidency shall be periodic in accordance with the alphabetical order of the names of these states.

2. Every member state shall notify the secretary general of the names of its delegates to the council's meeting at least 7 days before its opening date.

Article Three:

Taking into consideration the Cooperation Council's aims and the Supreme Council's jurisdictions as stipulated in articles four and eight of the statutes, the council shall perform the following:

1. To form technical committees and choose its members from member states' nominees, who are specialized in these committees' fields of work.

2. To entrust one or more of its members with the task of studying a certain subject and submit a report about it to be distributed among the members sometime before the session is held to discuss it.

Article Four: The Convocation of the Supreme Council

1. A. The Supreme Council shall hold two ordinary sessions a year. Extraordinary sessions can be held upon the request of any member with the second of another member.

B. The Supreme Council shall hold its sessions on the level of the heads of state.

C. The Supreme Council shall hold its sessions in the countries of the member states.

D. Before the convocation of the Supreme Council, the secretary general shall call for a meeting to be attended by the representatives of the member states in order to hold consultations about the affairs concerning the session's work.

2. A. The secretary general shall fix the dates the sessions shall begin. He shall also propose the dates they shall end.

B. The secretary general shall address invitations to attend the ordinary session at least 30 days before the convocation date and 5 days at most before the convocation of an extraordinary session.

Article Five:

1. The Supreme Council shall decide whether the sessions will be secret or public at the beginning of every session.

2. The Supreme Council's convocation shall be sound if it is attended by the heads of two-thirds of the member states. It shall adopt its decisions on objective issues by the unanimous vote of the states present and on procedural affairs by the majority. The member who abstains from voting must record that he will not abide by the decision.

Article Six:

1. The Supreme Council shall hold an extraordinary session:

A. Upon a decision adopted at a previous session.

B. Upon the request of a member state and the approval of another. In this case, the council shall convene within 5 days after the invitation for the extraordinary session.

2. The agenda of the extraordinary sessions shall not include topics other than those for which they were held.

Article Seven: Supreme Council Presidency

1. At the beginning of every ordinary session, the presidency of the Supreme Council shall be alternately assumed by the heads of member states in accordance with the alphabetical order of the names of the countries. The president shall continue exercising the functions of the presidency until his successor assumes this responsibility at the beginning of the next ordinary session.

2. The head of a state which is party to an existing conflict cannot preside over the session or the meeting devoted to the discussion of this conflict. In this case, the council shall appoint a temporary president.

3. The president shall open and close the sessions or meetings, suspend sessions, decide when to end the discussions, guarantee respect for the Gulf Cooperation Council's statutes, give the floor to those who ask for it first, submit proposals on which opinions are to be given, direct the operation of voting, decide on various points of the statutes, announce resolutions, follow up the work of the committees and inform the council about the letters it receives.

4. The president shall have the right to participate in

deliberations and discussions on behalf of the country he represents. He shall also have the right to delegate a member of his delegation for this purpose.

Article Eight: The Supreme Council's Agenda

1. The Ministerial Council shall prepare the Supreme Council's draft agenda and the secretary general shall communicate it to the member states with explanatory memorandums, documents and the letter inviting the council to convene, at least 30 days before the date of convening the council.

2. The draft agenda shall contain:

A. The secretary general's report on the Supreme Council's work during the period that falls between the two sessions and the measures taken to implement its decisions.

B. Reports and topics coming from the Ministerial Council and the Secretariat General.

C. Topics that the Supreme Council had previously decided to list on its agenda.

D. Topics proposed by a member state which it considers as necessary to be discussed by the Supreme Council.

3. Each member state shall have the right to list additional topics on the Supreme Council's draft agenda at least 15 days before the set date of the council's session. These topics will be listed in an additional agenda that will be sent to the member states along with their documents at least 5 days before the date of the session.

4. Any member state shall have the right to list additional topics to the session's agenda until the date that has been set for its opening if these topics are [at] the same time important and urgent.

5. The council approves its agenda at the beginning of every session.

6. The council shall have the right to list additional topics to the agenda during the session if they are urgent.

7. The ordinary session shall end after the completion of the discussion of the items listed on the agenda. The Supreme Council shall have the right to suspend the meetings of the session temporarily before having completed the discussion of the agenda and to resume the meetings at a later date.

Article Nine: The Supreme Council's Bureau and Committees

1. The Supreme Council's Bureau shall consist, at every ordinary session, of the council's chairman, the chairman of the Ministerial Council and the secretary general. The chairman of the Supreme Council shall preside over the bureau.

2. The bureau shall assume the following tasks:

A. A review of the formulation of the resolutions that are adopted by the Supreme Council without changing their content.

B. The task of assisting the Supreme Council chairman in the management of the session in a general manner.

C. Other tasks that are contained in the statutes or those which are entrusted to the bureau by the Supreme Council.

Article Ten:

1. At the outset of every ordinary session, the council shall form the committees it deems necessary and in such a way that the opportunity is given for making a detailed study of the issues on the agenda. Representatives from the member states shall participate in the work of these committees.

2. The committees' meetings shall continue in order to complete their work, taking into consideration the specific date for ending the session. The committees shall issue their resolutions with majority votes.

3. Every committee shall begin its work with the election of a chairman and rapporteur from among its members. If the chairman is absent he shall be represented by the committee's rapporteur who shall manage its sessions. If the chairman is absent, his representative or the rapporteur shall give the council all the required clarifications on the contents of the committee's report. The rapporteur or chairman's representative can, with the approval of the chairman of the session, participate in the deliberations without voting, unless he is a member of the council.

4. The council shall refer issues listed on the agenda to committee in accordance with their specialization in order to have them study these issues and prepare reports on them. An issue can be referred to more than one committee.

5. The committees cannot discuss any issue unless it is referred to them by the council. The committees also cannot adopt any recommendations on any issue that is listed on their agenda and whose adoption entails a financial commitment by the council before they receive a report from the secretary general on the financial and administrative effects pertaining to the adoption of these recommendations.

Article Eleven: The Progress of Deliberations and Proposals

1. Each member state shall have the right to participate in the deliberations of the Supreme Council and its committees in accordance with the statutes.

2. The chairman directs the deliberations on the issues to be discussed according to their order in the session's agenda. When necessary the chairman can invite the secretary general or the person who represents him at the meeting to clarify what he considers necessary.

3. The chairman yields the floor in accordance with requests made. The floor may be given to the chairman or rapporteur of a committee to submit the committee's report or explain points contained in it.

4. Any member can raise a point of the statutes during the deliberations on which the chairman shall immediately decide. The chairman's decision will be executed unless it is reversed by a majority vote of the Supreme Council.

Article Twelve:

1. During the discussion of any issue, any member can propose the suspension or postponement of the session, the postponement of the discussion of the issue in question or the ending of discussion. The proposal shall not be the sub-

ject for discussion but shall be submitted to a vote by the chairman if it is seconded by another member. The adoption of this proposal shall be made with a majority vote of member states.

2. Taking into consideration the contents of paragraph four, article eleven, proposals made in accordance with paragraph one this article shall be given preference to all other points preceding them according to the following order:

A. the suspension of the session
B. the postponement of the session
C. ending discussion of the issue under discussion.

3. Excluding proposals on formulation and on procedural matters, draft resolutions and fundamental amendments shall be submitted in writing to the secretary general or to the person who represents him for distribution to the delegations as soon as possible. The discussion of a draft resolution or its submission to a vote cannot take place before the distribution of their test to all the delegations.

4. Any proposal on which a decision has been taken during the same session cannot be reconsidered unless the council decides otherwise.

Article Thirteen:

The chairman shall follow up the committees' work, inform the Supreme Council of the messages received by it and officially announce before the members the recommendations reached.

Article Fourteen: Voting

Each member state shall have one vote and no state shall represent another state or vote for it.

Article Fifteen:

1. Voting shall be made by calling the name in accordance with the alphabetical order of the states' names or by raising the hand. Voting shall be in the form of a secret ballot if asked to be so by a member or upon a decision by the chairman. The Supreme Council shall have the right to decide otherwise and to write down in the session's minutes the vote of every member if the ballot is made by calling the roll. The result of the ballot shall be included in the minutes if the ballot is secret or made by raising hand.

2. Every member shall have the right to abstain from voting or to express a reservation about a procedural decision or part of it. The reservation shall be read out when the decision is announced and shall be written down. The members shall have the right to explain their stands toward the voting when said voting ends.

3. Once the chairman announces the beginning of voting, no one shall interrupt him unless this interruption pertains to a legal point concerning the voting.

Article Sixteen:

1. If a member asks for the amendment of a proposal, a vote shall be held first on this amendment. Should there be more than one amendment, voting will begin on the amendment whose subject is seen by the chairman as furthest detached from that of the original amendment. Voting shall then be on the amendment next furthest detached and so forth until all proposed amendments are voted upon. If

one or more amendment is approved, the amended original proposal shall then be voted upon.

2. Any new proposal shall be considered an amendment of the original proposal if it includes the mere addition, omission or change of any part of the original proposal.

Article Seventeen:

1. The Supreme Council shall form technical committees entrusted with the task of offering consultation in the preparation and implementation of the Supreme Council's programs in certain fields.

2. The Supreme Council shall appoint the technical committees' members from among the specialist citizens of the member states.

3. The technical committees shall meet upon the invitation of the secretary general and shall prepare their working plan through consultations with him.

4. The secretary general shall draw up the technical committees' agenda after consultations with the competent committee's chairman.

Article Eighteen: Amendment of the Bylaws

1. Every state has the right to suggest the amendment of these bylaws.

2. It is impermissible to examine the request to amend the bylaws unless the proposal regarding this amendment is sent to the member states by the General Secretariat at least 30 days before submitting it to the Ministerial Council.

3. It is impermissible to introduce any basic changes on the amendment proposal as cited in the previous paragraph unless the text of these proposed changes has been sent to the member states by the General Secretariat at least 15 days before it is submitted to the Ministerial Council.

4. With the exception of the articles based on the provisions of the statutes, taking into consideration the above-mentioned paragraphs, these bylaws are amended by a decision adopted by the Supreme Council upon the approval of the majority of its members.

Article Nineteen: The Validity of the Bylaws

These bylaws shall be valid as of the date they are approved by the Supreme Council. They shall not be amended except in accordance with the measures cited in the previous article.

These bylaws have been signed in the city of Abu Dhabi in the UAE on 22 Rajab 1401 Hegira, corresponding to 26 May 1981.

The United Arab Emirates
The State of Bahrain
The Kingdom of Saudi Arabia
The Sultanate of Oman
The State of Qatar
The State of Kuwait

Source: *FBIS-MEA-V–81–107*, 4 June 1981, pp. A6-A10.

Document 9

Abu Dhabi Supreme Council Summit: Final Communiqué

26 May 1981

In the name of God, the merciful, the compassionate.

Final statement of the first meeting of the Supreme Council of the Cooperation Council of the Arab Gulf countries:

In response to the invitation of his highness the president of the UAE and with the help of God, a meeting was held in Abu Dhabi 21–22 Rajab 1401 Hegira, corresponding to 25–26 May 1981, of their majesties and their highnesses Shaykh Zayid ibn Sultan Al Nuhayyan, president of the UAE; Shaykh Isa ibn Salman Al Khalifah, amir of the State of Bahrain; King Khalid ibn Abd al-Aziz Al Saud of the Kingdom of Saudi Arabia; Sultan Qabus ibn Said of Oman; Shaykh Khalifah ibn Hamad Al Thani, amir of the State of Qatar; and Shaykh Jabir al-Ahmad al-Jabir as-Sabah, the amir of Kuwait.

Out of the fraternal spirit that exists among these countries and their peoples; in completion of the efforts begun by their leaders to lay down a model formula that includes their countries and enables these countries to cooperate and coordinate among themselves; out of their belief in the importance of cooperation among these countries; in response to their peoples' expectations and aspirations for increased cooperation and efforts to achieve a better future; and in accordance with the results of the meetings of their foreign ministers in Riyadh on 4 February 1981 and in Muscat on 9 March 1981:

Their majesties and highnesses agreed to establish a council of their countries to be called the Cooperation Council of the Arab Gulf States (*Majlis at-Taawun li Duwal al-Khalij al-Arabiyah*). They signed the statutes of the council, which are aimed at developing cooperation among these states enhancing their relations; achieving coordination; integration and closer links; deepening and strengthening the ties and relations that exist among their peoples in various fields; implementing joint projects and drawing up similar systems in economic, cultural, information, social and legislative fields in order to serve their interests and strengthen their ability to hold on to their beliefs and values.

Their majesties and highnesses also decided to appoint Abdallah Bisharah secretary general of the Cooperation Council. Riyadh, in the Kingdom of Saudi Arabia, shall be the council's permanent headquarters.

Out of their realization of the inevitability of economic integration among their countries and a social merger among their peoples, they believe that the current circumstances of their states and the similar issues and problems they face, in addition to their similar economic and social systems, make it necessary to lay down the bases for and establish the institutions and apparatus that will make this economic integration and social merger a living reality.

In order to achieve these goals, in accordance with Article 4 of the council's statutes, they decided to set up specialized committees as outlined in detail in the enclosed working paper approved by the supreme council.

Their majesties and highnesses reviewed the current situation in the area. They reaffirm that the region's security and stability are the responsibility of its peoples and countries and that this council expresses the will of these countries and their right to defend their security and independence. They also affirm their absolute rejection of foreign interference in the region from any source. They call for keeping the entire region free of international conflicts, particularly the presence of military fleets and foreign bases, in order to safeguard their interests and the interests of the world.

They declare that guaranteeing stability in the Gulf is linked to the achievement of peace in the Middle East, and this underlines the need to achieve a just solution for the Palestinian question—a solution that safeguards the Palestinian people's legitimate rights, including their rights to repatriation and the establishment of an independent state, and ensures Israeli withdrawal from all the occupied Arab territories, the foremost of which is Jerusalem.

Their majesties and highnesses discussed the serious situation arising from the escalation of Zionist aggression against the Arab nation. They discussed in a spirit of national responsibility Israel's persistence in violating fraternal Lebanon's sovereignty and independence and the savage bombardment of Lebanese cities and towns and Palestinian refugee camps, its war of extermination launched against the Palestinians, its aggression against the Arab Deterrent Forces and its threats to fraternal Syria. They affirm their full support and backing for Syria. They appeal to all parties in Lebanon to discard their differences, put an end to the bloodshed in Lebanon and embark on reconciliation talks within the framework of Lebanese legitimacy.

Their majesties and highnesses support the efforts being made to end the Iraqi-Iranian war, since it is one of the problems that threaten the region's security and increases the possibility of foreign intervention in the region. They stress the need to redouble efforts to find a final settlement to the dispute.

Their majesties and highnesses also reaffirm their commitment to the Arab League Charter and the resolutions of Arab summit conferences. They reiterate their support for the Islamic Conference Organization and their commitment to its resolutions. They express their adherence to the principles of nonalignment and to the UN Charter.

In response to the invitation of His Majesty King Khalid ibn Abd al-Aziz of the Kingdom of Saudi Arabia, it was decided to hold the second meeting in Riyadh in Muharram, 1402 Hegira, corresponding to the first half of November 1981.

Issued in Abu Dhabi 22 Rajab, 1401 Hegira, 26 May 1981.

Source: *FBIS-MEA-V–81–101*, 27 May 1981, pp. A1-A2.

Document 10
GCC Working Paper
26 May 1981

The emergence of the council for cooperation among the Gulf states is in response to the historical, social, cultural, political and strategic reality through which the Gulf region passed and is passing. The need for such a council is more urgent at present than ever before for the good of the peoples of the region.

The natural solidarity which links the Arab states in the Gulf merits appearance in a joint framework after all the positive and effective bilateral and collective measures adopted to date. It also merits better, clearer channeling in the interest of the peoples of the region.

The contemporary trend is toward big political and economic unities for the preservation of stability and security and to bridge the gaps into which many countries in other parts of the world have fallen, learning a lesson after paying dearly in blood, men and money. These gaps are the presence of inconclusive, long-standing territorial disputes in which energies and efforts are wasted and peoples lose a great deal.

If challenges are enough to create effective cooperation in any part of the world, the circumstances of the Gulf region are even more opportune for such cooperation. We constitute part of an ethnicity which has one religion, a joint civilization and joint values and customs. Moreover, our geographical location and oil resources make us vulnerable to international and political designs which almost amount to blackmail. This urges us all toward joint cooperation.

Today's world emphasizes the importance of links between nations. Hence, the regional merger, particularly in the Gulf region, will be an aid and support to the objectives of the Arab and Islamic nation, and becomes more urgent and a local demand in this historical phase.

Effective mobilization of resources and expertise in building a Gulf organization will enhance the situation and will render the organization worthy of transporting this Arab region to balanced developmental horizons, benefiting all the sons of the region in general and the Arabs in particular.

The challenges confronting this region are increasing as the industrialized world's need for oil increases. Gulf merger has become [*words indistinct*] toward a new, broad tendency to formulate an economic and political [*word indistinct*] which will keep the region away from international competition and bargaining. International designs will not be able to find a foothold in a merged region which has one voice, opinion and strength. However, they will be able to find a thousand footholds if this region, which is rich in oil and men, remains made up of small entities that can be easily victimized.

Talk of "the power vacuum" in the region and the resource which has no owners can end forever if the rightful owners firmly and resolutely perform their collective role.

The Cooperation Council countries can jointly have a say in the international and regional fields, which will express its respected and feared place in the world economy in the relations of these countries with east, north and south. These countries can also provide active support for the causes of the Arab nation.

Arab union, since the dawn of Arab liberation after World War II, has been the center of the attention of the Arab peoples. Positive steps in that direction have sprung up in an area which embraced Islam, sheltered Arabism and has been safeguarding pan-Arab interests since the beginning of history.

The real and hard tasks which await us should be faced collectively. The oil on which we are relying at present is an exhaustible wealth. It generated huge wealth in the past decade but it also generated high tension and changes in human behavior. The peoples of the Gulf look to their governments to solve the difficult equation of achieving real development on the one hand, and safeguard social peace, security and progress on the other.

This equation cannot be solved unless we study our priorities with farsightedness: this establishment of a comprehensive development that stands upon a firm foundation and a solid base of production on the one hand, and the training of manpower, which is the more important capital, on the other. We should answer the important question of how to transform oil into comprehensive and stable development in the interest of our peoples. The historic opportunity to make our choice is available to us now, but it may not be available in the future. The embryo of the industrial revolution was the naval compass, gunpowder and printing. Now, however, humanity is pushing into space and the development of modern nuclear physics, using fast and direct communications. Whoever lags behind remains among the backward states and nations. Briefly, it is an age of scientific breakthroughs which dictate the use of scientific tools in political, economic, industrial and educational affairs. The first priority of this organized scientific thinking is for us to reach a genuine and comprehensive merger in the economic, social and political fields.

These are the challenges facing us. Through sound merger plans among our countries and peoples, we can face these challenges, nurture our material and human investments and achieve comprehensive development for our peoples in a fair and wise manner. Furthermore, as a group, we can contribute to the efforts for peace in the world, which is turbulent.

In order to achieve and implement these aims, the council decided to form the following committees made up of the competent ministers. These committees will have temporary tasks and will cooperate and coordinate with the General Secretariat. They will begin their work in accordance with the dates proposed by the secretary general:

I. The Committee for Economic and Social Planning

This committee will devise and coordinate joint action in economic and social planning to achieve homogeneity among the national economic plans and draw up bases for future integrated planning in order to bring about economic integration among the member states.

II. The Committee for Financial, Economic and Trade Cooperation

This committee will study ways to coordinate financial and economic cooperation in light of the general aims of joint economic action. Among its functions are:

A. Financial and monetary cooperation:

1. Seeking to standardize laws and regulations governing investment in order to draw up a common investment policy that will gear external and internal Gulf investment of these states and the aspirations of their peoples for development and progress.

2. Coordinating banking and monetary policies and enhancing coordination among the monetary establishments and central banks in these states in order to come out with a standard Gulf currency that will complete the aspired for economic integration.

3. Coordinating financial and monetary policies of the member states on the external level in the field of extending international and regional aid for development.

B. Transfer of funds and individuals and the exercise of economic activity:

1. Drawing up bases for the treatment of subjects of the Cooperation Council member states without any discrimination in any of these states, in accordance with what is agreed upon in the following domains:

a. freedom of movement, work and residence;
b. freedom of ownership, inheritance and bequests;
c. freedom of exercise of economic activity.

2. Seeking to remove the obstacles which impede the movement of revenues and capital and coordinating and unifying trade, financial and customs regulations in a manner that gives similar treatment to the subjects of the member states in all the states.

3. Encouraging the private sector in the member states to establish joint projects and companies in order to tie together the economic interests of the citizens in all fields.

C. Trade exchange:

1. Seeking to lift the customs barriers among the member states of this council regarding their products and seeking to standardize a customs tariff between these states and the outside world.

2. Applying the principle of total exemption from customs duties levied on the local products of the member states and treating these products as national commodities.

3. Coordinating the policies of import, export and food reserves.

4. Creating a collective negotiating force in the field of export and import.

D. Transport and communications:

1. Cooperating in the field of sea and land transport and communications and coordinating on the establishment of construction projects, such as buildings, airports, water stations, power stations and roads, and developing existing establishments in these spheres.

2. Seeking to coordinate aviation and air transport policies among the council's member states.

III. The Committee for Industrial Cooperation

This body will be entrusted with the following:

A. Coordinating industrial activity among the member states by formulating policies and proposing ways to bring about industrial transformation in the member states on the basis of an integration that insures the highest benefit to each state and provides reassurance and prosperity to all their peoples.

B. Studying the standardization of the industrial laws and regulations of the member states.

C. Seeking to channel local production toward meeting the needs of the member states.

D. Preparing laws and regulations for the importation of technology and expertise and choosing the most suitable in light of the objectives and requisites of development in the member states.

E. Distributing industry in the member states by encouraging the establishment of industries. Accordance with economic feasibility, that complement the essential projects distributed in the member states.

F. Formulating policies and implementing integrated programs for training and technical, vocational and artisan rehabilitation on all levels and at all stages among the member states.

IV. The Oil Committee

This committee will be formed of the foreign, oil and finance ministers and will undertake the following:

A. Coordinate the policies of the council's members in the field of oil industry in all its stages of drilling, refining, marketing and pricing; transporting and exploiting natural gas; and developing sources of energy.

B. Draw up a unified oil policy and joint stands toward the outside world and international organizations.

V. The Committee for Social and Cultural Services

This committee will devise scopes for joint action in the fields of education, health, labor, social affairs and culture and will draw up bases for their integration and homogeneity.

The secretary general calls on the finance and economy ministers to draw up a unified economic agreement to replace the current bilateral agreements, in accordance with the principles agreed upon during their meetings in Dhahran, Saudi Arabia on 16 Rajab 1401 Hegira, corresponding to 20 May 1981. This should be accomplished within the next 2 months and will be referred to the Ministerial Council, which will submit it to the Supreme Council at its next session.

Source: *FBIS-MEA-V–81–107*, 4 June 1981, pp. A10-A13.

Document 11

GCC Secretary General Bisharah's Press Conference

27 May 1981

Abdallah Bisharah, secretary general of the Arab Gulf Co-operation Council, has said that the council is a historic accomplishment to rally the forces of the region's states in the interest of their peoples as well as the interest of the Arab and Third Worlds.

In a press conference held today at the end of the meetings of the cooperation council's supreme council in Abu Dhabi yesterday, the secretary general added that the council enjoys an economic power, in addition to the Gulf states' important strategic position, which draws the attention of the big powers. These facts, he said, give the council's states a strong voice and a great influence on relations among states on the world level. Moreover, the strength of the council's states stem from these states' similar political and economic systems and their similar cultural and social values.

The secretary general stressed that the council's member-states aim at keeping the region away from the big powers' rivalry and struggle.

He added: The unprecedented factor I sensed during the closed meeting at King Khalid's suite yesterday morning was that the leaders were determined to achieve their aims and to carry on work for the establishment of the council.

He said that the council is neither a confederal nor a federal one, but a cooperation council. We say this, he added, believing that the strength of this cooperation stems from the harmony we seek to achieve and which we believe is existing in all fields. He added that this council is not inspired by the big powers, but stems from the awareness of the region's peoples of the need to establish it.

He announced that during the past 2 days future economic activity was discussed and the conferees agreed to establish five committees on economic cooperation. He added that the secretary general was asked to call for a meeting of the finance ministers in order to reach a comprehensive and unified economic agreement to replace the present bilateral agreements.

Bisharah said that the heads of state discussed the political situation in the Gulf and its complications. They showed complete agreement regarding all the topics and reaffirmed their commitment to the Islamic Conference summit resolutions. These topics, he said, were related to Afghanistan, Palestine, bases in the Indian Ocean and foreign threats. However, he added, the heads of state did not go into the details of these topics because the council's aim was to concentrate on issues related to the Gulf and to assert its commitment to the Islamic Conference summit resolutions.

Bisharah went on to say: There can be no economic progress without stability. Therefore, the heads of state decided to continue to exchange viewpoints, to call the ministerial council into session to thoroughly discuss other topics and to submit a report about them to the second summit conference of the cooperation council to be held in Riyadh in November.

He stressed that the council would enjoy the interest of the world due to its economic power and its ability to affect the world economic situation. He said: Since there can be no economic stability without the industrial states' participation, there can be no economic stability without our council's participation; and if technology is important to the issue of dialogue between the north and south, raw materials and energy are considered basic and vital in this dialogue.

The secretary general strongly reiterated that the member-states object to foreign intervention, the establishment of bases and the presence of fleets and foreign influence, adding that the purpose of this is to keep the region free of and removed from any foreign intervention. He cited the contents of the final statement, which stressed that the region's security is the responsibility of its states.

He stated that the council cannot be separated from the Arab states, since it is not an independent group. Rather, we constitute an important tributary that flows into the main Arab river. We constitute an important power in the major course of Arab policy and believe that our council both strengthens and bolsters the Arab League.

He added that the council includes states which are members of the Islamic Conference Organization and are the cradle of Islam. The Prophet's cradle is also in the land of Mecca, which is considered the Kiblah of all Muslims. The council's importance does not only lie in its economic importance but also in its spiritual, strategic and political importance.

Addressing the reporters, he said: You cannot find leaders who can sit together at ease and agree on important issues within two hours. He praised the supreme council's meeting, saying that this was a wonderful beginning for this council, reflecting its determination and persistence to achieve all its goals.

In the course of his reply to a question on his contacting international and regional organizations, Abdallah Yaqub Bisharah affirmed that he will conduct such contacts, saying: We do not live in isolation, nor do we live on an island in the middle of an unknown ocean.

He pointed out that the council's states have drawn the world's interest and refuse to be viewed as mere oil states and waterways. Rather, he added, these states insist on contributing to making humanity happy. He added that the role of the council's states goes beyond their being a group of states which constitutes a source for the production of energy. Rather, he pointed out, these states have a greater role to play and have sharp teeth.

Bisharah pointed out that the cooperation council's charter does not include anything to the effect that all member-states should give up their sovereignty. Rather, this council comprises independence and sovereign states. He further pointed out that the kings and leaders have left a Gulf region that is much stronger than it was.

He stated that the council's member-states are equal whatever their position, resources, foreign policy or affiliations might be. The presence of the general secretariat's headquarters in Saudi Arabia does not mean that Saudi Arabia has a stronger voice, nor does the appointment of a Kuwaiti as secretary general mean that Kuwait has a stronger voice than the others. We are all equal and the council's budget is equally divided among the states, thus affirming our equality.

The secretary general said that the council is not exactly political. He added that the council's charter does not specifically refer to politics. Rather, he pointed out, priority is given to economic issues.

The secretary general affirmed that the member-states will not change their firm policy on the Palestinian people's right and on bolstering and supporting the Syrian struggle and Lebanon. At the end of his press conference he affirmed that the council will not separate itself from the Arab world since the Gulf would then suffer and its security would be jeopardized. He added that the Gulf states want to participate in and bolster the Arab nation's issues, particularly the Palestinian people's issue and this people's restoration of their legitimate rights. Indeed, he said, these are among the priorities of our pan-Arab work.

Source: *FBIS-MEA-V–81–102*, 28 May 1981, pp. A1-A2.

2
Coping with Subversion and Terrorism

ANALYSIS

The overriding common objective of preserving the six monarchies against the tremors of the Iranian Revolution was challenged repeatedly by acts of political violence during the first five years of the GCC's existence. The founding of the GCC did not automatically secure the royal families in the six states against an attempted coup d'état in Bahrain or from a whole range of terrorist acts in Kuwait, including an attempt against the life of the amir. For all practical purposes, Kuwait was transformed into a hotbed of terrorism.

The GCC states, individually and severally, tightened internal security to an unprecedented extent. In trying to cope with the ever-present threat of acts of political violence, they imposed ever-growing restrictions on visas, travel, information, and publication. They deported thousands of suspects. They sought to prevent infiltration across their borders. Even the more liberal-minded Kuwaitis tried to impose the death penalty for any act of terrorism that resulted in the loss of life. Despite all these and other similar security measures, they failed to conclude an internal security agreement that would include as signatories all the six governments. Except for Kuwait, they did, however, conclude four bilateral security agreements with Saudi Arabia in the wake of the discovery of the coup plot in Bahrain.

Yet, the broader and deeper problem of political fragility continued to plague the GCC societies in varying degrees. This problem will be explored after first discussing the incidents of political violence.

Acts of Political Violence

On 13 December 1981 the government of Bahrain announced that it had arrested a group of "saboteurs," allegedly trained by Iran. Subsequently, the Bahraini interior minister charged that the group had planned to assassinate Bahraini officials. He said that it belonged to the "Islamic Front" (*al-Jabhah al-Islamiyah*) headquartered in Tehran and that its "sixty" members were Shia Muslims. The actual number turned out to be seventy-three: sixty Bahrainis, eleven Saudi dissidents, one Omani, and one Kuwaiti national. No Iranians were among the group. At the time, five unidentified armed men reportedly presented a written memorandum to the Bahraini Embassy in Tehran in which they claimed responsibility for the group arrested in Bahrain. Bahrain asked Iran to recall its chargé d'affaires. After a long-drawn-out investigation and trial, the plotters were finally sentenced in May 1982, receiving jail sentences ranging from seven years to life imprisonment.

Despite the years that have passed since the discovery of the plot, the facts of the case are still unclear. Shortly after the discovery, it was reported that the sabotage network included twelve members headed by Hadi Modarresi, "who escaped from the Shah's regime and took refuge in Bahrain. He left Bahrain in August 1979 when his passport expired."[1] On the other hand, some have learned from on-site conversations that Hojatollislam Modaressi actually was deported from Bahrain because of his connections and communication with Iran. Most observers seem to believe that this was a poorly planned and quixotic coup attempt. A few, however, seem to exaggerate it to the point of alleging that "five Iranian hovercrafts loaded with troops and equipment were standing by the port of Bushehr" to help the plotters in the execution of the plan.[2] Perhaps the less doubtful fact is that the Islamic Front for the Liberation of Bahrain was one of many such fronts set up in Iran in 1981. The Iranian government adopted a "plan for an Islamic front," which, according to Prime Minister Mir-Hussein Musavi, who was then the foreign minister, was to be "followed up" by Iran's Ministry of Foreign Affairs. "The fight against imperialism," according to Musavi, "should take place all over the world." While the Iranians publicly admitted their support of these fronts, they vehemently denied any part in planning the plot or arming the plotters. The Bahraini and other GCC members, however, seemed to be certain there was Iranian involvement.

The reactions of the GCC members to the Bahraini incident may be viewed from several perspectives. Bahraini officials were at first quite panicky, and their rhetoric was accusatory. The harshest statement came from the Bahraini prime minister, Shaykh Khalifah ibn Salman al-Khalifah, who reportedly asserted on 23 January 1982 that "the Iranian regime constitutes a primary threat to the Gulf states just as the Zionist entity is threatening the Arab east." He also reportedly said that "the Iranian regime's threat is embodied in its expansionist policy of sabotage against the Arab Gulf states and in its attempt to incite and sow sedition," adding that the "relations between Israel and the Iranian regime are well-known." The prime minister also stressed the need for economic sanctions against Iran by all other Gulf states, claiming that his own country had "ceased its dealings with Iran, including those in shipping and air flights," and had "banned the entry of Iranian nationals into Bahrain."[3] Moreover, the prime minister categorically stated in an interview that there was "no internal danger [in Bahrain]." Asked what "external danger" there was, he replied: "The external danger is Iran and the present regime in Tehran. This Iranian regime is instigating the Shiites in Bahrain and in the Gulf under slogans of the Islamic revolution and with a sectarian motive against the Arab Gulf states and their regimes. The regime in Iran is exploiting the Shiites in Bahrain and the Gulf, encouraging their political ties with the ruling ayatollahs in Tehran, training them in the use of weapons and acts of sabotage and sending them to their countries to foment chaos and shake security."[4]

In some ways the Saudi denunciation of the plot surpassed even Bahrain's accusations. The most condemnatory statement came from the Saudi interior minister, Prince Nayif, charging that by its "conspiracy" against Bahrain, Iran actually "violated Islam." A few other remarks of the prince are worth quoting directly: "We had hoped that Iran, our neighbour and friend, would not have such [conspiratorial] intentions. But after what has happened in Bahrain, our hopes have unfortunately been dashed and it has become clear to us that Iran has become a source of danger and harm to Gulf nations and their security. At the very beginning of their revolution, the men in power in Iran said that they would not be the policemen of the Gulf. Today they have unfortunately become the terrorists of the Gulf."[5]

Not only did Saudi Arabia outdo its GCC partners in denouncing the Khomeini regime, it also took leadership in swiftly signing several bilateral security agreements with them. After signing the first security agreement with Bahrain, Saudi Arabia signed three others with the United Arab Emirates, Qatar, and Oman. Following the signing of the security agreement with the UAE on 21 February 1982, Prince Nayif said its terms were similar to those of the agreement with Bahrain. It provided for the exchange of equipment, expertise, and training and for extradition of criminals and border cooperation. The security agreement with Qatar, signed the same day, contained similar provisions, including efforts for combating infiltration across the borders, exchange of information, and extradition of criminals. Two days later Prince Nayif signed a fourth agreement, this one with Oman. According to him, while this agreement was similar in many respects to those signed with the other GCC partners, it was "more comprehensive." Despite the hope of Prince Nayif, Kuwait refused then, and has ever since refused, to sign a similar agreement with Saudi Arabia.

Two other direct consequences of the Bahrain incident should be considered. First, the GCC Ministerial Council held its first extraordinary session in Bahrain on 6–7 February 1982 primarily because of the Bahraini crisis, although it did take up other issues as well. The council's final statement declared the GCC's support for Bahrain in safeguarding its safety and stability and protecting its sovereignty. It also applauded Bahrain's determination to resist "the acts of sabogate that are carried out by Iran." More important, the GCC members took this opportunity to state unequivocally their consensus on the principle of collective security: the GCC viewed "any aggression against any GCC member as an aggression against all GCC members." This principle also stressed that "the region's security and stability is a collective responsibility that falls on all GCC countries" (D14). In addition, for the first time, Saudi Arabia took the initiative in considering the idea of a collective security force. On 23 February 1982 Prince Nayif reportedly said that Saudi Arabia supported the formation of a "Gulf internal security force to defend Gulf security and to be called the Gulf Rapid Deployment Force (*Quwwat al-Tadakhkhul as-Sari al-Khalijiyah*)."[6]

There is no point in belaboring here the tortured fate of a GCC draft agreement on collective defense which was a major by-product of the Bahraini incident. A swift review will suffice. The GCC interior ministers agreed on a formula for a unified internal security agreement at their first meeting in Riyadh on 23–24 February 1982 when the Saudi-Omani bilateral agreement was signed. Again in a meeting in Riyadh on 17 October 1982, the interior ministers failed to agree on a joint security pact. Reportedly Kuwait feared that such a pact "would threaten the country's democratic traditions."[7] Apparently Kuwait finally decided to draft its own amendments to the proposed security pact. Interior Minister Shaykh Nawwaf al-Ahmad al-Jabir al-Sabah declared that such amendments were "necessary and suitable,"[8] and on 21 May 1985 he assured the Kuwaiti National Assembly that the government would not sign the security treaty unless it was amended to remove points that conflicted with the constitution of the nation.[9]

What was the real objection of Kuwait to signing a bilateral security agreement with Saudi Arabia and to joining other GCC partners in a multilateral internal security agreement? Two major speculations persist. First, Kuwait feared that a bilateral security agreement with Saudi Arabia might hurt its image of a nonaligned state because of Saudi Arabia's dependence on the United States for security. Second, given the relatively hard-line stance of Saudi Arabia toward Iran, the signing of either a bilateral or a multilateral agreement, or both, might identify Kuwait too closely with Saudi Arabia and cause even greater Iranian annoyance with it. Although this second suggestion might have been the case right after the Iranian Revolution, it no longer seems to be true. Kuwait-Iran relations soured considerably, particularly after the 1983 multiple bombings in Kuwait, while Saudi-Iranian relations seemed to improve somewhat after the exchange of visits between the two countries' foreign ministers in 1985.

The main objection of Kuwait to such security agreements probably reflected the concern of its leaders with their domestic political implications. Compared to any other GCC state, Kuwait is a relatively open society. Its nascent parliament has shown increasing influence in the Kuwaiti political process since its reopening in 1981, particularly since the latest parliamentary elections of 1985. The policies of the al-Sabah royal family were subjected to growing parliamentary scrutiny until the suspension of the assembly in the summer of 1986. The intrusion of security forces from other GCC states into Kuwaiti territory in hot pursuit of suspected criminals may, it is feared, be used by the more conservative Saudis to impinge on political liberties within Kuwaiti society.

The Kuwaiti concern with the adverse implications of the proposed internal security agreement for political freedom at home apparently centers on Article 12 of the draft agreement. It provides:

> Pursuit patrols belonging to any of the member countries have no right to cross the border of a neighboring country, except for a distance not to exceed 20Km in order to arrest those being pursued. Those pursued and all they have with them, including their vehicles, are to be handed over to the nearest post belonging to the country in whose territory the chase began, if they were arrested within the said distance. The principle of the immediate handing over of [those pursued] will be applicable if said persons were arrested at a farther distance by patrols belonging to the sovereign country, in the event they took part in the pursuit operation. [D20]

No other GCC country experienced the kind of threat to its internal security that Kuwait did during the first five years of the GCC's existence. In spite of sundry insignificant terrorist attempts in Qatar, the UAE, and Saudi Arabia, terrorism in the Gulf was largely the curse of Kuwaiti society. In less than two years the tiny city-state suffered four major assaults on its internal security. The GCC viewed all of them as attacks on the security and stability of its member states.

The first major attack on Kuwait's stability took place on 12 December 1983. The targets of terrorist attacks included the United States Embassy building, the skeleton of which still haunted the embassy premises three years later, and the French Embassy. Other targets included the headquarters of American Raytheon, the airport control tower, the Ministry of Electricity and Water, a major petrochemical refining complex, and other facilities. As in the truck bombings of the American Marines and the French paratroopers in Lebanon (23 October 1983), the "Islamic Jihad" claimed responsibility. Quietly, the GCC regimes blamed Iran, while Western sources did so loudly. A Kuwaiti court tried twenty-five defendants on 27 March 1984. Five were acquitted of involvement in the bombings; six were sentenced to death, three of whom were tried in absentia; seven to life imprisonment, four of whom were tried in absentia; four to fifteen years in prison, one to ten years, and two to five years. The day after the bombings, the GCC strongly denounced the "criminal terroristic acts" and affirmed its member countries' firm and total stand on the side of Kuwait and their support for Kuwait in facing up to such "criminal acts" and all acts that detract from Kuwait's independence and sovereignty (D21).

As in the case of the Bahrain plot, in this incident none of the accused was Iranian. Out of a group of twenty-five, seventeen were Iraqis, three were Lebanese, three were Kuwaitis, and two were stateless. In the Bahrain case, some sources claimed that the perpetrators belonged to the Islamic Front for the Liberation of Bahrain, while others believed they belonged to the Iraqi Shia underground movement called *al-Dawa*. In this Kuwaiti case, however, there was no doubt that they all belonged to the *Dawa* party.

The second assault on Kuwaiti security involved the hijacking of a Kuwaiti Airline plane. For six days, beginning on 4 December 1984, a group of Shia terrorists hijacked the plane to Tehran and held it there. It had been on its way from Dubai to Karachi with 155 passengers and 11 crew members on board. Apparently an Iranian fighter plane attempted to prevent it from landing in Iran when it entered Iranian airspace. It was allowed to land, however, because the pilot of the Kuwaiti plane claimed that he was running out of fuel. The Iranian officials condemned the hijacking and the killing of two Americans on board. Eventually Iranian troops stormed the plane, captured the hijackers, and freed the remaining passengers. The Iranian judicial authorities promised to put the hijackers on trial and punish them for their crimes. Despite all this, many observers in the GCC states and elsewhere in the world seemed to take the view that Iran had been in some kind of collusion with the hijackers. In this case, as in the case of the Bahrain plot and Kuwaiti multiple bombings, the finger of blame was once again pointed at Iran, despite its vehement denials.

A third assault on Kuwaiti stability was launched in a direct attack on the head of state on 25 May 1985. An explosive-laden car rammed into the motorcade of the amir, Shaykh Jabir al-Ahmad, killing two members of the Amiri Guard and a passerby and wounding eleven others. The so-called Islamic Jihad Organization's spokesman congratulated the amir on his escape and expressed the hope that the message had been clearly understood. Contacting a foreign news agency in Beirut, the spokesman also warned that a new blow would be soon directed against the "reactionary Arab regimes."[10] Kuwaiti security authorities said on 26 May that they had identified the perpetrator of the attack after "assembling pieces of his fingers and examining his fingerprints."[11] The culprit was an Iraqi who carried a Pakistani passport. Contrary to all evidence, the Iraqi ambassador denied that the man had been an Iraqi and flatly said that the *Dawa* "party to which the criminal belongs is an Iranian party 100 percent."[12] The GCC Secretariat condemned the act. It said that while it "strongly condemns this criminal attempt and all terrorist attempts and acts designed to threaten the security and stability of this vital region in the world, it affirms that this attempt will make Kuwait and its sister countries more determined to continue the march of welfare and construction to serve the issues of the Arab nation and Islamic solidarity." (D27).

A fourth act of political violence that shocked citizens and governments of Kuwait and other GCC members took place on 11 July 1985. Bombs were exploded at two popular cafés in the Sharq and Salmiyah areas where families and friends often gather for recreation. At first it was reported that the explosions led to nine deaths and fifty-six wounded, but later the numbers were raised to eleven dead and eighty-nine wounded. It was also believed that the victims of the incident were of a variety of nationalities, including eighteen Kuwaitis, one citizen from the UAE, one Iranian, two Egyptians, two Iraqis, and others of undetermined citizenship. Among the Kuwaiti casualties was a senior Interior Ministry official. The responsibility for the bomb blasts was claimed by the "Arab Revolutionary Brigades Organization," which had in the past claimed responsibility for attacks on diplomats from Jordan and the UAE in Europe, India, and the rest of the Gulf region. Once again the finger of blame was pointed at Iran, but not by Kuwaiti or GCC officials. Even the Kuwaiti newspaper *Al-Ray al-Amm*, which always seemed willing to blame every incident on Iran, was hard put to do so this time. It simply based its accusation on what the political forces opposed to the Khomeini regime had said. The GCC Secretariat as usual condemned the act as "criminal," asserted that it was "directed against innocent citizens," and claimed that "such vile actions will only make Kuwait and its sister GCC states stronger and more solid" (D34).

Despite all this bitter experience with acts of political violence, the GCC states failed to sign an internal security agreement. Paradoxically, Kuwait, the sole object of acts of terrorism among the GCC states, was the most reluctant of all to sign such an agreement. In reaction to the attempt against the life of the amir, Crown Prince and Prime Minister Shaykh Saad warned that the attack on the ruler "may force us to sacrifice liberal ways we have become used to in secure times." Furthermore, the Kuwaiti cabinet approved a stern antiterrorism bill on 9 June 1985, providing for the death penalty for terrorist acts that result in loss of life. But that was as far as Kuwait would go. As it stood, the draft internal security agreement was still unacceptable.

The effect of the failure of the GCC states to conclude such an agreement, however, should not be exaggerated. In practice, they have cooperated bilaterally and multilaterally in combating acts of political violence. For example, they have exchanged riot control equipment, expertise, and intelligence information. Individually, they have also taken parallel measures in fighting terrorism by such means as deporting suspects and restricting visas, travel, and publication. Apparently, the sharing of information was what helped to abort the Bahrain plot. Reportedly, the UAE immigration authorities tipped their Bahraini counterparts off about the suspects. Furthermore, in the relatively closed societies of the GCC where the balance between the requirements of security and liberty is not a paramount concern of the governments, they can repress any expression of dissent that is judged to threaten a regime's stability. This practice could be collectivized if the draft internal security agreement is approved without change. For all practical purposes, Article 1 bunches together "opponents of regimes" and "criminals" (D20).

The Challenge of Political Fragility

The GCC liberals as well as their Western counterparts tend to reduce the underlying causes of the problem of political violence to the lack of political participation in the GCC states. This is the single greatest concern of the modernized intelligentsia in the GCC societies as well as many other Third World societies. Indeed, the absence of opportunities and institutions for expressing legitimate political opposition may contribute to the problem of political radicalization and violence. But to believe that if the GCC regimes offered political participation to their citizens, the problem of political violence would vanish is as simplistic as to believe that political repression will do the trick. Both the conservative and liberal approaches are monistic, reductionist, and simplistic.

Empirically, the causes of political violence in the GCC societies are multifaceted, complicated, and dynamic. They are social, economic, political, cultural, and psychological in nature. They are interconnected, and therefore, none is isolable from the others. And they vary from place to place and from time to time. The GCC Secretariat did well in condemning all acts of political violence during the first five years of the life of the organization. The GCC states also did well in tightening internal security both individually and severally, even though they failed to conclude an internal security agreement. Such an agreement would give binding expression to the norm that was articulated for the first time during the first extraordinary meeting of the Ministerial Council on 6–7 February 1982. The council posited then that the political stability of the GCC member states ought to be a collective responsibility. During the second five years of its existence, the GCC Secretariat and the GCC members will do even better if they seriously explore the underlying causes of political fragility and violence in the GCC community.

Since every act of political violence was attributed to the machinations of Iran, it is necessary to explore first the contribution of the revolutionary regime to the factors behind these acts. How did the ideology and the practice of the Khomeini regime fuel social and political ferment? In other words, what were the effects of Iran's revolutionary paradigm in the GCC societies at large?

Iran's revolutionary example tended to destabilize the GCC regimes in four major ways. First, there were those individuals and groups of people within the six countries to whom the Khomeini ideology had a special appeal. Khomeini claimed that his ideology was "all-Islamic" and nonsectarian. For such people, the fact that Shia particularism cannot be separated from Khomeini's overall ideology did not seem to matter; they took him at his word. Nor did the fact that Khomeinism is the official creed of the Iranian state seem to disturb them. Second, many politically aware GCC citizens and expatriates welcomed the absolutist and uncompromising Khomeinist crusade against the superpowers, against the "pro-American" Gulf regimes, and against the perceived ostentatious living, corruption, and waste of the middle and upper classes. Third, to the lower classes in the GCC communities, the populist emphasis of the Iranian model had a particular appeal. Somehow, many Gulf Arabs were inclined to believe that only in revolutionary Iran had the oil wealth been equitably distributed. Fourth, a combination of Iran's antagonism toward the United States and its call for the destruction of Israel as well as its demand for a full-fledged Palestinian state had a heady effect on many Gulf Arabs, regardless of their wealth, status, or profession.

Iran's revolutionary paradigm, however, did not enjoy a universal appeal throughout the GCC communities. Many GCC citizens simply did not believe the "all-Islamic" claim of the Khomeini ideology; they perceived it as a particularistic Shia belief system. Many Gulf Arabs also disliked the Iranian type of governance, the "guardianship of the jurisprudent" (*vilayat-i faqih*). After the Iranian Revolution, the role of the religious leaders (*ulama*) in the political processes of most GCC states increased; nevertheless, they did not have the political power that the Iranian clerics had enjoyed even before the revolution. One aspect of Iran's revolutionary example in particular repelled many members of the modernized middle classes in the GCC countries. The purges, summary executions, and suppression of middle-class-based political opposition groups disillusioned those who had at first hailed the Iranian Revolution for its overthrow of the shah's dictatorial regime and for its elimination of the perceived American domination in Iran.

In fine, during the GCC's first five years, Iran's revolutionary paradigm did not pose the kind of formidable threat to the stability of the GCC regimes that has been often portrayed. The single most lasting effect of the Iranian revolutionary example has been the intensification of political consciousness throughout the Gulf region. In the future, the challenge to the stability of the GCC regimes, therefore, will be in part the widespread political awakening among the GCC citizens, which Iran's revolutionary example intensified to an unprecedented degree. However, it would be a mistake to view the whole problem of stability in the GCC societies merely in terms of the challenges presented by heightened political awareness among the GCC citizens. Doing so could lead to the facile prescription that the solution to the problem of fragility in the GCC societies should be sought in the magic formula of political participation. Moreover, it could lead to a perilous disregard of other complicating factors that underlie the problem of political fragility.

One such factor is the possibility of an increase in social and political ferment in the GCC countries in the future as a result of the growing number of young people. In the United States, the effects of the "baby boom" of the earlier decades were felt in the 1960s when many young men and women rebelled against established norms and practices, especially on university campuses. This problem of political "rejuvenation" challenges regimes in most Third World countries. About 60 percent of their populations are under twenty years of age as compared with about 40 percent in the more developed regions. The GCC societies are no exception. Taking the most politically active age group in these countries, that is, those between ten and thirty-four years of age, about 46 percent of the population was in that age group in 1980. Projecting this figure into the year 2000, it will increase to about 48 percent. In the United States, by comparison, Americans of the same age group in 1980 accounted for 43 percent of the population and will decrease to about 35 percent in the year 2000 (see Appendix A, table 1).

One of the most striking aspects of the problem of political violence of the Gulf region is the involvement of young people. Many of the individuals who participated in the Bahrain coup plot were teenagers, and others were only in their twenties. In the more serious example of the multiple bombings in Kuwait, of the twenty-one terrorists whose ages are known, all but three were under thirty years of age, and of the twenty-one convicted, sixteen were in their twenties. If indeed political violence goes hand in hand with the problem of political rejuvenation, then the GCC states cannot disregard this correlation in trying to cope with the problem of political fragility.

Nor can the GCC authorities overlook the relationship between political fragility and the high percentages of foreigners in the GCC countries. Since the problem of large numbers of expatriates in these societies is well known, we need not belabor the point (see App. A, table 2).[13] Suffice it to say that just because this problem is not as acute in, for example, Oman, where about 18 percent of the population are foreigners, as it is in Qatar, where over 70 percent of the population are aliens, it does not necessarily mean that the problem can be overlooked. Also, simply because a great many expatriates are leaving the GCC states because of the declining oil revenues, that does not necessarily mean that all are leaving for that reason. Ever since the multiple bombings in December 1983, Kuwait has expelled many thousands of expatriates, some 20,000 since the assassination attempt against the life of the amir in May 1985. Finally, most of those involved in acts of terrorism have been GCC nationals.

Another important factor that lies behind the problem of political fragility is the psychological predisposition of the GCC citizens. Although it has been argued elsewhere that revolution of the sort that Iran experienced is not in the cards for the GCC countries,[14] and that Iran's revolutionary paradigm is not all that appealing to the GCC populations, there is no room for complacency. Societal alienation is a major destabilizing factor. In Iran, it led to the "revolution of rising alienation," which stemmed from no single economic, political, moral, or ideological source.[15] Rather, it reflected cumulative popular dissatisfaction with the effects of complex domestic and foreign policies pursued by the shah's regime over many years. Various individuals and groups were disaffected for various reasons. For example, to many modernized intellectuals it was political repression that mattered most, while to the uprooted masses of peasantry it was the wretched conditions of their lives that fostered their growing estrangement from the shah's regime.

Although no one seems to know how far the process of societal alienation has gone in the GCC member states, there is little doubt that it is taking place. There is a highly politicized younger generation in the GCC societies. This generation provides the main social and political base for recruitment by various political groups, be they the underground cells of the *Dawa* party or the open gatherings of such groups as the Kuwaiti *Jamaat Islah* or the pro-Iranian *Jamaat Saqafah*. These examples do not imply that only such Islamic groups recruit alienated individuals. All kinds of secular groups and individuals are also politically active whether they consider themselves nationalist, or communist, or Marxist. From an ideological perspective, secularism challenges Islam in the GCC societies despite the proverbial "resurgence of Islam." For example, the Muslim fundamentalists in Kuwait, both Shia and Sunni, did not do so well in the 1985 parliamentary elections as in the 1981 elections, but the nationalists did surprisingly well.

The alienation of one particular group in the GCC societies is a potential source of destabilization. The Gulf region is the Shia heartland of the world.[16] Most of those who have participated in acts of political violence have been Shia Muslims. In Bahrain they constitute the majority of the citizen population, and there are large numbers of Shias in other GCC states (see App. A, table 3). It is not, however, simply their sect or their number that makes the Shias, especially those of the lower classes, a potential source of destabilization in the GCC countries. Rather, it is their sense of victimization, regardless of the country in which they live. Shia dissidents rebelled in Bahrain and Saudi Arabia in 1979 and 1980. The more objective Sunni Muslims of the GCC states admit that the Shias have historically been mistreated. The Saudi, the Bahraini, and other GCC governments in recent years have tried to improve the living conditions of the Shias as a means of redressing their grievances. Yet, the perception of being socially, economically, and politically "deprived" (*mahroomin*) persists among many Shias, except for those who happen to be affluent. The latter actually have more in common with their Sunni counterparts than with their fellow Shias.

If in the past it was feared that rapid modernization, fueled by a massive rise in oil revenues, could trigger societal dislocation, income maldistribution, and life-style disruption, it is now feared that economic recession, as a result of a drastic fall in oil prices, will produce many new sources of societal alienation. The alarmists may exaggerate the odds, but new problems caused by an unprecedented recession are already here. Today's oil bust can be as disruptive as yesterday's oil boom. Given their varying levels of development and their different needs and life-styles, the GCC citizens are hurting unevenly. Nevertheless, all are suffering, including the Saudis, who now have the world's second largest deficit after the United States and who in March 1986 were forced for the first time to announce their decision to defer their 1986–87 budget.

There is a danger that in trying to head off an economic crisis, the GCC governments may inadvertently trigger a social crisis. They are cutting back on spending, abandoning dispensable projects, and withdrawing subsidies, especially of water and electricity. They are also causing increasing complaints. Some Saudi academics said in 1986 that they lost about 30 percent of their income because many of their fringe benefits were cut off. They are not the only disgruntled people: businessmen, bankers, and other professionals are also hurting, and complaining. Optimistically, one could say that after all, this era of austerity may be a blessing in disguise, for it will force the people to cut down waste and abandon ostentatious living. But the problem is that the burden of belt-tightening may well fall on those who have no belt to tighten. The Shia poorer classes are particularly vulnerable. Many members of the middle class who have been unhappy with the lack of political freedom may well become restless now that their material comfort has been somewhat threatened. The politically disaffected Saudis, for example, may now become more vocal in their complaints about the ever-suspended promise of a consultative assembly, while their Bahraini counterparts may take to the streets to press their longtime demand for the reopening of their suspended parliament.

GCC's Complicated Agenda

Given these multiple causes of political fragility in the GCC states, the task of realizing the overriding goal of preserving similar monarchical regimes in the six countries involves more than coping merely with the acts of political violence. It requires coping with all the causes that constitute the environment of political violence. In their draft internal security agreement the GCC leaders equate "assault on heirs apparent, royal family members, ministers and those ruling in the member countries" with such ordinary—not "political"—crimes as cold-blooded murder. This is in keeping with the United Nations resolution that unequivocally condemns as criminal "all acts, methods and practices of terrorism." But in the "anarchical society" of states in which each nation sits as the judge of its own cause, this norm is not yet an enforceable world law. Until it becomes so, prevention of crime will be at least as important as the punishment of the criminal, a precept that is widely accepted even in national societies in which the legal norm is enforceable. In fine, the GCC governments will have to go beyond coping with the threat of subversion and terrorism by punishment and will have to improve the overall societal environment as a means of combating political violence at its roots.

As if this were not formidable enough a challenge to the embryonic new organization, the fear of the spread of the Iraq-Iran war complicated the GCC's agenda of cooperation among the six member states. When they established the GCC only about six months after the outbreak of the Iraq-Iran war, the Arab leaders did not have the slightest idea that the war could continue even after the sixth anniversary of the nascent organization, becoming the most protracted and disastrous war in the contemporary history of the Middle East. Nor could they foresee that the GCC's efforts for defense cooperation, economic integration, and diplomatic coordination would all be affected, in varying degrees, by the developments in the war.

Notes

1. *FBIS-MEA-V-82-001*, 4 Jan. 1982.

2. Safa Haeri, "Drôle de Putsch à Bahrein," *L'Express*, no. 1591 (8 Jan. 1982): 42–43; see also "Prime Minister Interviewed on Iranian Threat," *FBIS-MEA-V-82-019*, 28 Jan. 1982, pp. C1–C3.

3. *FBIS-MEA-V-82-019*, 28 Jan. 1982, pp. C2–C3.

4. *Al-Mustaqbal*, 23 Jan. 1982, pp. 10–12.

5. Adnan Sadiq, "*Al-Majallah* Publishes the Whole Story concerning Iran's Conspiracy against the Gulf," *Al-Majallah*, 16 Dec. 1981, [translated in *Joint Publication Research Service–Near East/ North Africa Report*, no. 2527 (19 April 1982): 8–11], p. 11.

6. *FBIS-MEA-V-82-037*, 24 Feb. 1982.

7. *Middle East Economic Digest*, 22 Oct. 1982, p. 2 (Hereafter MEED).

8. Ibid., 22 July 1983, p. 4.

9. Ibid., 24 May 1985, p. 20.

10. *FBIS-MEA-V-85-102*, 28 May 1985.

11. *FBIS-MEA-V-85-103*, 29 May 1985.

12. Ibid.

13. J. S. Birks and C. A. Sinclair, *Arab Manpower: The Crisis of Development* (New York: St. Martin's, 1980); see also Ismail Serageldin et al., *Manpower and International Labor in the Middle East and North Africa* (Washington, D.C.: The World Bank, June 30, 1981), and Joseph A. Kechichian, "Demographic Problems Facing the Gulf Cooperation Council," *International Demographics* 2, no. 4 (April 1983): 3, 12.

14. See R. K. Ramazani, "America and the Gulf: Beyond Peace and Security," *Middle East Insight*, Jan./ Feb. 1982, pp. 2–9.

15. See, for example, R. K. Ramazani, "Iran's Revolution: Patterns, Problems, and Prospects," *International Affairs* 56, no. 3 (Summer 1980): 443–57.

16. See R. K. Ramazani, "Shiism in the Persian Gulf," pp. 30–54.

Documents

Document 12

Saudi Interior Minister Prince Nayif ibn Abd al-Aziz Denounces "Iranian Plot"

14 December 1981

The Kingdom of Saudi Arabia considers the security of Bahrain and of the Gulf countries the security of the Kingdom; it stands by the brothers in Bahrain and all brothers in the Gulf against such acts, and it stresses its stand with all its capabilities by the side of brothers. According to the evidence we have, the Kingdom of Saudi Arabia is undoubtedly one of the targeted countries for such acts by the Iranian Government. In stressing this stance of ours, we denounce the occurrence of such acts by a neighboring country which should have been cooperating with all in maintaining security in the area and not be misleading some of its delusioned sons and forcing them to disturb the security of their homelands. The Iranian Government also ought to put an end to such irresponsible acts which are undoubtedly contrary to the security of the Arab and Islamic peoples. God is the guide to the right path.

Source: *FBIS-MEA-V–81–240*, 15 Dec. 1981, p. C4.

Document 13

GCC Ministerial Council: First Extraordinary Meeting—Opening Address by Shaykh Muhammad ibn Mubarak Al-Khalifah, Foreign Minister of Bahrain

6 February 1982

In the name of God, the merciful, the compassionate. Your highnesses, excellencies, delegation members, ladies and gentlemen of the press and the information media.

Welcome to your country, Bahrain, which takes pride in receiving you today among your kinsmen and harbor[s] love, friendship and fraternity toward you and those you represent.

I have the honor to convey to you the greetings of His Highness Shaykh Isa ibn Salman Al Khalifah who wishes you success in your present efforts through which you are writing a page of the history of this important epoch and charting the edifice of cooperation in this dear part of our great Arab homeland.

Today we are witnessing the dawn of an important event in the history of contemporary Arab awakening, an event that is based on serious and constructive work that is free of the negative aspects of the past, that aims to unite the views and rally the ranks and constitutes a significant tributary of the broader Arab action following the emergence of signs of corrosion in the nation's body—as the result of the intensification of conflict in the parts of the nation, whose rights have become a free-for-all for usurpers and covetous enemies.

Today we are turning a bright new page that will illuminate to us the correct path for building the future of the region and ensuring its protection so as to safeguard its present and future.

The establishment of the GCC through the awareness and determination of their majesties and highnesses was in response to the needs of the present period and in response to the challenges of the Arab nation and also to confront the international changes that have begun to impose themselves. This event in which we are participating is in itself a great achievement equal to the challenge of civilization that we have begun to experience and react to.

Brothers, we are brought together today by a fraternal gathering that is free of complicated official formalities in order to exchange and clarify our views, deepen our common understanding of the pressing issues that have a direct effect on the GCC countries, and strive to turn our hopes into action. The steps that were approved at the first [GCC] summit in Abu Dhabi, the second summit in Riyadh and the ministerial meetings that followed are proof of our sincere determination to carry out what we have resolved to do. At the same time these steps constitute an important progress along the long path that lies before us in our march to achieve our peoples' aspirations and serve our future generations.

History does not wait. Our noble religion calls on us to unite and fraternize and urges us to work together, for God supports a community that is united. Our Arab nationalism is also based on cooperation and unity. In view of all this, we have resolved to proceed, believing that joint action pays dividends, that cooperation has a positive effect and that strength is effective in serving the greater homeland, and achieving its progress and aspirations.

I ask God to grant us success.

Peace and God's mercy and blessings be upon you.

Source: *FBIS-MEA-V–82–026*, 8 Feb. 1982, p. C3.

Document 14
GCC Ministerial Council: First Extraordinary Meeting Statement
7 February 1982

The GCC Ministerial Council held its first extraordinary session in the State of Bahrain from 6 to 7 February 1982.

During its meeting the council reviewed the recent events in the State of Bahrain and declared its full support for the State of Bahrain in safeguarding its safety and stability and protecting its sovereignty and its determination to resist the acts of sabotage that are carried out by Iran with the aim of undermining security and stability, spreading chaos and confusion and threatening the interests of citizens—on the basis of the GCC's fundamental principles which view any aggression against any GCC member as an aggression against all GCC members, and which stress that the region's security and stability is a collective responsibility that falls on all GCC countries.

The council also reviewed the Iraqi-Iranian war and noted Iraq's constant readiness to find a just solution to the war. The council declared its support for all the efforts to end this war by peaceful means and calls on Iran to respond to the efforts of the Islamic Conference [Organization], the nonaligned countries and the United Nations to find a peaceful solution that safeguards the legitimate rights of the disputing parties. The council supports Iraq's request to discuss this matter at the forthcoming Arab summit so as to adopt a unified Arab stand.

The council reviewed in detail the current Arab situation and the Middle East question in particular. The council affirmed its support for Syria and for the Arab nation's efforts to resist the Zionist expansion represented by the annexation of the Golan Heights and the occupied Arab territories. The council reaffirmed its support for the Palestinians and for a just and comprehensive solution to this problem to safeguard the Palestinian people's legitimate rights in establishing an independent state on their land under the PLO's leadership and their right to self-determination and the return of Jerusalem to Arab sovereignty.

The council also calls for discarding Arab differences and unifying Arab ranks to confront all the challenges facing the Arab nation—challenges that are represented by the Zionist threat.

The council expressed its sincere thanks and appreciation to Shaykh Isa ibn Salman Al Khalifah, the amir of the State of Bahrain, for Bahrain's generous hospitality and for the facilities it provided and arrangements it made, which had a good effect on the success of the session's work. The council wishes the Bahraini Government and people security, stability, progress and prosperity under his wise leadership.

Source: *FBIS-MEA-V–81–026*, 8 Feb. 1982, pp. C5-C6.

Document 15
Press Conference Held by Shaykh Muhammad ibn Mubarak Al-Khalifah, Foreign Minister of Bahrain, and Abdallah Bisharah, GCC Secretary General
7 February 1982

[Excerpts] [Question] Are there undeclared resolutions approved by the GCC emergency ministerial conference meeting regarding Iranian-Gulf relations?

[Shaykh Muhammad] We, in the GCC, are working collectively in a clear and frank way. As I have said, this meeting was held to exchange views, explain things and adopt stands which we believe will be convenient to treat these issues. In my view, such issues were discussed during this meeting. We were all convinced of the need to confront any aggression or any intervention in our internal affairs. I believe the meeting has achieved the goals we sought.

[Question] Your Excellency, you (?stated) that there is no possibility of confrontation between Iran and the Gulf but that if any aggression should take place it would be confronted. You stated, though, that there is a move to achieve a kind of neighborliness and to stop the bloodshed in the Iraqi-Iranian war. What steps can be taken in this direction?

[Shaykh Muhammad] I request that the questions not be stated in a way to escalate the situation. We, here, want to arrive at solutions that serve the region's welfare, stability and development. I believe all of us are working to resolve any existing difference. As I have said, we want stability and coexistence to prevail in this region. In view of what I have said, this is the method we will adopt. We want to fortify the Gulf homes. Our goal is to strengthen and bolster collective action.

[Abdallah Bisharah] I beg your pardon. I want to add one point regarding the policy of the GCC countries. This policy did not stem from the emergency conference but from the summit resolutions—the first summit in Abu Dhabi and the second in Riyadh. This policy is: The security, stability and territorial integrity of the Gulf countries is a responsibility that should be borne by the sons of the GCC countries and the sons of the Gulf. Consequently, our responsibility—when we want to discuss a temporary issue or a permanent one—is that discussion must continue to ensure the unity of the GCC members and to stave off threats and ensure their territorial independence and sovereignty. This means that our policy is to look for internal solidity. We believe that when this is achieved—which we are trying to do and which we have begun working on— threats and dangers will automatically diminish and shrink.

[Question in English] Could you summarize in English the decisions taken by the council on the threats posed by Iran to the security of the Gulf states and the responsibility, if any, of Iran for the events here in Bahrain in December?

[Shaykh Muhammad, in English] Well, actually we will be ready to give you a full translation of this communiqué later on and it applies actually to the question you (?asked on) where we stand on this issue. We made it very clear in this communiqué.

[Question in English] Can you elaborate at all (?on what) we have, in your own words?

[Shaykh Muhammad, in English] You see, our policy here is based on cooperation of the Gulf states against any threat or aggression from outside. And the collective security of the GCC conference is the responsibility of those states. So this is really the main point mentioned in that paragraph concerning the situation in the Gulf area.

[Abdallah Bisharah, in English] The genesis, in fact the thought, of the charter of the GCC is based on a collective endeavor and a collective endeavor generates collective responsibility. When we talk about the territorial integrity of the member states and the political independence, we bear in our mind and stress the point that it is a collective responsibility that should be shouldered by all member states. And this is the approach we have taken. It is an approach which we did not invent but emanates from the charter of the GCC.

[Question] No doubt the problem now has two faces: the first is internal stability and security. Also, the foreign aspect is keeping the region away from areas of domination. After the conference, will we allow the Rapid Deployment Force to carry out training in any of the Gulf states?

[Shaykh Muhammad] Thank you. I want to say the responsibility for defending this region is that of the Gulf states alone. We are now at the beginning of the road. We are now coordinating among our countries in the security field, both internally and defensively. We have great hopes

and we are now at the beginning of the road. We hope this goal will be achieved: that our defense forces will complement each other to confront any foreign ambitions. As for internal security, it is the responsibility of each country. Nevertheless, there is coordination. As for foreign troops, we are against carrying out any kind of training in this region. Thank you.

[Question in English] I don't know what you were saying in Arabic, but you were speaking about collective responsibility and collective security. How does this go? If Iran should bomb Kuwait again as they have in the past, would this be considered an attack on Bahrain and an attack on Saudi Arabia?

[Shaykh Muhammad, in English] Well, you see, yes, our meaning of collective security is any threat to any of the states is a threat to the others. And when those states are being attacked, the others collectively will act together against any aggression. But to make this effective it needs lots of coordination, and that is what we just have started. You know, we speak about the first meeting of the defense ministers and the first meeting of the interior ministers. [words indistinct] Quite a time before we make our force in this area an effective one. But that doesn't mean that if there is any threat against one of those states, all other five will collectively try their best to defend that part. So I think this is one of the main principles of the creation of the Gulf Cooperation Council. But, as I said from the beginning, to make this effective needs lots of work among the people who are specialized in the field of defense. And I think they just started, and I hope they are going to continue. And we will see in the future, the near future, the real arrangement between the Gulf states to defend themselves.

[Question] Weinberger said he is coming to the Gulf to discuss how the United States will help in preserving Gulf security. Do you not think this contradicts your slogan that Gulf security is the responsibility of its sons?

[Shaykh Muhammad] I again talk about reply to statements. We in the GCC—since the first moment of the GCC—said the responsibility for Gulf security and defense is that of its states. As for other statements, we have repeatedly answered them. I cannot prevent any official of any country from making statements, but I want to clarify our stand. This is the stand of the Gulf countries. Defending it is the responsibility of its sons alone and therefore we have started work on military and security coordination.

[Question in English] Minister, do you believe that the Gulf countries will support an application by Egypt for readmission to the Arab League? And was this question of relations with Egypt discussed either in the closed session of the council or in bilateral discussion between members?

[Shaykh Muhammad, in English] No, this matter has not been discussed because we think the situation in Egypt has not yet reached a stage where you can be considered [as heard] because I think the Camp David process is going on one wheel even when the other wheel is not working on the Palestinian issue. And we think that what we said about Camp David is happening etc. these arrangements. [as *heard*] and therefore there is no new element to rank this kind of discussion valid. But certainly the door is open for Egypt in the future, and I cannot predict what kind of stand Egypt will take. And if Egypt coordinates with the other Arab states, certainly it's a major country in the Arab world and the Arab League. But certainly, at this moment, I don't think there is a new element to make that to be discussed.

Source: *FBIS-MEA-V–82–028,* 10 Feb. 1982, pp. C1-C3.

Document 16

GCC Information Ministers: Seventh Conference Statement on the Iraqi-Iranian War

23 February 1982

The seventh conference of the Arab Gulf states' information ministers, while expressing deep concern over the continuation of the Iraqi-Iranian war in view of the bloodshed and the exhaustion of energies this war is causing, hopes that this war will end as soon as possible in a manner that ensures the legitimate rights of both sides.

Having studied the situation and its developments and also its probable effect on the security and independence of the region in particular and to world peace, the council calls upon the Iranian officials to respond to the repeated efforts by Iraq regarding to end the fighting between the two neighboring countries, out of the principles and teachings of our true faith. The conference would also like to ask Iran to respond to the efforts of the Islamic Conference Organization, the committee of the nonaligned countries, the United Nations and other parties in this respect, now that Iraq has declared its readiness to cooperate with all these parties.

The conference, which feels pain due to the continuation of fighting between the two Muslim countries, believes that the continuation of this war is bound to affect the security and stability of the region. The war is drawing the attention of the superpowers, who are trying to find a foothold in this region because of the natural resources and the important strategic location which God has bestowed on us.

Furthermore, the continuation of the war between the two countries will benefit only the enemies of the Arab and Muslim nations.

Source: *FBIS-MEA-V–82–038,* 25 Feb. 1982, p. C1.

Document 17

GCC Information Ministers: Seventh Conference Final Statement

23 February 1982

At the conclusion of its meeting in the sister state of Kuwait, the seventh conference of the Arab gulf states' information ministers wishes to praise the tangible results achieved by the numerous information institutions set up in this region.

The conference asserts that the information action of the Arab Gulf states complements and backs up Arab information action. The conference also asserts that the positive experiment in implementing the decisions of these conferences is considered a valuable contribution in developing and guiding Arab information action on both the Arab and international levels.

In harmony with the resolutions of the Arab Summits and the meetings of the Arab information ministers, the conference of the Arab Gulf states' information ministers asserts the need for action within the common pan-Arab aims and for Arab information to avoid everything that harms the Arab nation or distorts its image.

The conference calls on all Arab media to work for unity, the closing of ranks and to bear in mind the dimensions of the responsibility shouldered by all for further solidarity among the sons of our Arab nation.

The conference decided to convey its sincere thanks and appreciation to his excellency the deputy prime minister, foreign minister, minister of information in the State of Kuwait and chairman of the conference for his wise management of the conference and the great efforts made for its success. The conference thanked the committee of experts, the drafting committee and the secretariat committee for their efforts to accomplish their work speedily and accurately, which has facilitated the task of the conference.

The conference also decided to send cables of thanks to his highness the amir of the State of Kuwait and to his highness the heir apparent and prime minister of Kuwait for hosting the conference and for the warm hospitality and reception.

The eighth conference of the Arab Gulf states' information ministers will be held in the United Arab Emirates in February 1983. The conference will be preceded by a meeting of the experts' committee.

Source: *FBIS-MEA-V–82–038,* 25 Feb. 1982, pp. C1-C2.

Document 18

Statement by Saudi Interior Minister Prince Nayif ibn Abd al-Aziz at the End of the Second GCC Interior Ministers Conference, Riyadh

18 October 1982

May the brothers allow me to make a short speech before we conclude our conference. I thank His Excellency Brother Muhammad ibn Khalifa [Bahraini interior minister] for his nice speech and I thank all the brother ministers for their effective participation in our meeting. I also thank the secretary general and General Secretariat of the GCC for their successful efforts in preparing all things to make our conference run orderly and in a manner that made it discuss and deliberate things on clear, studied and coordinated grounds.

Undoubtedly, the GCC has made great progress in all fields in a short period of time. Undoubtedly, the security field which all of you represent here is of paramount importance in the cooperation of the GCC member states. Undoubtedly, also, we have made worthwhile progress in achieving many things. Furthermore, our deliberations of issues were positive, and I believe everyone hoped to finish all the issues listed on the agenda. Nonetheless, our aim is not to finish what we have but to finish it in a way that serves the common goals and interests. Therefore, the participants found that regarding the comprehensive and unified security agreement, which is one of the most important issues, some issues that arose during the discussion of this agreement needed to be settled, although we highly appreciate the efforts exerted by the experts or the committee of experts that met and gave us a perfect agreement which we all hope to sign as soon as possible, God willing.

I hope that everyone will understand that we, here and in a conference of this nature, are not concerned about appearances or some formalities, but we are concerned about depth, positive matters and constructive, useful and positive cooperation. On this basis and out of this concept our affairs are being managed, and we will achieve further cooperation and further positive action in that field shortly, God willing.

Source: *FBIS-MEA-V–82–203*, 20 Oct. 1982, C1.

Document 19

Statement Issued by the GCC Interior Ministers, Riyadh

18 October 1982

Their highnesses and excellencies, the GCC Interior Ministers, held their second conference at the Headquarters of the GCC General Secretariat in Riyadh on Sunday and Monday, 30 Dhulhijjah 1402 and 1 Muharram 1403 Hegira [17 and 18 October 1982]. Out of their interest to bolster security cooperation among the GCC states, to complement the resolutions of their first conference and to accomplish integration in security affairs, the ministers studied and approved the recommendations submitted to them by the Committee of Heads of Passports, Immigration and Labor. They commissioned the General Secretariat to complete the studies of some recommendations.

The ministers also studied thoroughly the plan of the comprehensive security agreement that was prepared by the experts committee. After exchanging viewpoints, and with the spirit of collective responsibility which necessitates focusing on collecting the points that are related to the security agreement plan, and out of their desire to provide the necessary elements that require additional research, the ministers decided to continue contacts until they complete the final details in light of the observations that were made during the discussions.

The ministers also studied the recommendations of the experts committee on the establishment of a center for security information that will be used in the preparation of qualified national cadres in accordance with the prerequisites of collective action. They decided to approve these recommendations and to commission the General Secretariat to take the steps to prepare the necessary studies.

Their Highnesses and excellencies, the ministers, decided to hold their third conference after the General Secretariat completes the studies that have been delegated to it on the resolutions that were adopted during this conference.

Source: *FBIS-MEA-V–82–203*, 20 Oct. 1982, pp. C1-C2.

Document 20

Draft GCC Security Agreement Reviewed at the Bahrain GCC Summit

17 November 1982

Out of a spirit of sincere brotherhood, stressing the bases and principles set by the GCC countries, adhering to the principle that preservation of the security and stability of the GCC countries is the joint responsibility of the GCC countries, counting on one's own capabilities and the available powers to protect security and stability and moreover to defend the Islamic faith and idealistic views from destructive atheistic views and party activities, and in order to make the current security cooperation among the GCC countries reach a desirable and comprehensive standard, the GCC member countries have agreed on the following:

Chapter 1: General Views

Article 1: Abstaining from giving refuge to criminals and opponents of regimes whether they be citizens of the GCC countries or other countries, in addition to combating their activities harming the security of any of the GCC countries.

Article 2: Abstaining from allowing the circulation or transfer of pamphlets, printed material or posters that are antagonistic to the Islamic faith or that harm morality, or those directed against the ruling regimes of the GCC member countries.

Article 3: Every country which signs [this agreement] undertakes to adopt the necessary measures to prevent its citizens from interfering in the internal affairs of the other member countries.

Article 4: Exchange of information and expertise that helps in developing the means to fight crime in its various forms, in addition to exchange of laws and regulations dealing with activities of the Interior Ministries besides exchange of books, magazines and printed material issued by these ministries, in addition to explanatory methods and training films that are available.

Article 5: Providing the necessary facilities in the field of education and training for those who work in the GCC Interior Ministries and in the specialized institutes and colleges.

Article 6: All the countries will inform the member countries of scheduled conferences, educational sessions and cultural seminars and those dealing with the fields of specialization of the Interior Ministries, particularly those dealing with crime fighting, traffic, education and training, so that the information can be passed on in enough time to those who would be most likely to attend.

Article 7: The Interior Ministries of the member countries should hold consultations. Moreover, their representatives should cooperate in order to coordinate and unify their stands on issues on the agenda of Arab and international conferences.

Article 8: Work in the direction of unifying the laws and regulations dealing with emigration, passports, residency, nationality and other matters included within the responsibilities of the Interior Ministries of the member countries.

Article 9: The member countries should cooperate and provide the necessary facilities for the concerned authorities in these countries in order to put this agreement into effect.

Chapter 2: Combating of Infiltration and Smuggling

Article 10: The member countries should exert the necessary efforts to combat infiltration through the common borders and undertake legal or suitable disciplinary measures against those who carry out such acts or play a role in these activities.

Article 11: The infiltrators will be arrested by the concerned authorities of the member countries and legal or disciplinary measures will be taken against them. They will be arrested in accordance with the following:

A. Those who infiltrate the territories of one of the member countries illegally will be returned to the border post of the country from which they entered illegally.

B. Those with unknown identities and the infiltrators who cross the border of a country after infiltrating another country's border or even making several infiltrations will be subject to the country that arrests them in regard to dealing with their cases.

Article 12: Pursuit patrols belonging to any of the member countries have no right to cross the border of a neighboring country, except for a distance not to exceed 20 km in order to arrest those being pursued. Those pursued and all they have with them, including their vehicles, are to be handed over to the nearest post belonging to the country in whose territory the chase began, if they were arrested within the said distance. The principle of the immediate handing over of [those pursued] will be applicable if said persons were arrested at a farther distance by patrols belonging to the sovereign country, in the event they took part in the pursuit operation.

Article 13: The following should be observed during pursuit:

A. Pursuit vehicles should bear official marks and should be distinctive.

B. The number of pursuit vehicles must not exceed three.

C. The squad of pursuit patrols must not exceed 13 persons.

D. Vehicles and individuals are to be armed lightly in accordance with what the interior ministers will later agree upon.

E. Pursuit operations should stop as soon as the patrols reach the nearest city, village or a group of bedouin camps.

The rules of this article apply to sea pursuit provided the means listed in the above points are made applicable.

Article 14: Security authorities at the borders are to be informed of the pursuit whenever possible and pursuit patrols should inform the nearest official body at the site where an arrest is made as soon as the pursuit operation is concluded in the territory of the neighboring country, whether the result is positive or negative. This should be in accordance with an official report signed by both sides.

Article 15: Patrol meetings and joint patrols can be organized at the adjacent border regions of the member countries when there is a need to do so. Regular meetings are to be held between the officials of border posts of the member countries for this purpose.

Chapter 3: Crime Prevention

Article 16: The names of dangerous ex-convicts and suspects are to be exchanged and the movements of such persons are to be reported. They are to be prevented from traveling whenever possible. Names of personae non grata are also to be exchanged.

Article 17: Contacts among specialized bodies are to be consolidated through criminal detection and search in the member countries in order to report any information available to these bodies on criminal operations that took place or that are being planned in the territories of these countries or abroad.

Article 18: The special body in each member country shall inform counterparts in the other countries of what they have in regard to new crimes, the methods by which they were committed and the measures that were adopted to pursue them and eliminate them.

Article 19: The specialized bodies in each of the member countries shall search for suspects, criminals and escapees, place them under observation or even under detention pending investigation when necessary, prior to their extradition in accordance with the rules of this agreement. In order to achieve cooperation in this field, official contacts through post, cable, telephone or other means will be approved.

Article 20: The specialized authorities in each member country shall offer—in accordance with the laws and systems enacted therein—the required help with regard to crimes that are to be pursued by one of the member countries particularly as pertains to delivering extradition or present memoranda, implementing authorizations to question suspects or witnesses and carrying out other services such as examining, searching and arresting.

Article 21: The member countries shall adopt the necessary measures to preserve the secrecy of the information and materials exchanged between them whenever such things are characterized as secret by the country that delivers them. It is not allowed to hand the information and materials delivered in accordance with this agreement over to any other country that is not a GCC member except upon the approval of the country that delivers them.

Chapter 4: Extraditing Criminals

Article 22: Extraditing criminals among the member countries becomes mandatory if the following two conditions exist in the request:

A. If, according to its classification by the specialized body of the requesting country and in accordance with the rules enacted therein, the crime represents an offense whose penalty is not less than a 6-month imprisonment.

B. If the crime is committed in the territory of the requesting country or outside the territories of both countries provided that both countries' laws allow punishment for an offense perpetrated outside their territories.

Article 23: The country that is requested to extradite criminals has the right to refuse to do so in the following situations:

A. If the person to be extradited held its nationality at the time of perpetrating the crime, provided that it will in this case prosecute him according to its laws and systems and in accordance with a report to be prepared by the authorities concerned in the requesting country. It also has to inform the requesting country of the result of its judgment.

B. If the crime took place in the territory of the requesting country by the person to be extradited is not one of its nationals provided that the offense he is charged with is an indictable offense according to the law or system of the country requested to extradite him.

C. If the crime took place outside the territories of both countries, provided that the laws or systems of the country requested to extradite the offender do not consider his offense indictable if committed outside its territory if the indicted person is not a citizen of the requesting country.

D. If the crime or penalty had already been dropped when the extradition request was received, in case the crime was committed in the territories of the requested country, provided the wanted person is not a citizen of the requesting country and provided the crime is not murder.

Article 24: Extradition is not allowed in the following cases:

1. If it is a political crime. The following are not regarded as political crimes:

A. Sabotage, terrorism, murder, robbery and theft accompanied by acts of force whether committed by one person or a number of persons.

B. Any financial assault against the leaders of the member countries, their assets, branches or wives.

C. Assaulting the heirs apparent, royal family members, ministers and those ruling in the member countries.

D. Military crimes.

E. Punishment for the above-mentioned crimes in Articles A, B, C, D, if the laws or rules of the two countries cover such acts.

2. If the crime was committed in the territories of a country which is requested to extradite.

3. If the individual in question is a member of the diplomatic corps and has diplomatic immunity or any other individual with immunity according to international law or any other treaties and characters.

4. If the person to be extradited has been tried or was under investigation or on trial for the crime for which his extradition is requested, whether it was in the country which is requested to extradite or in the other in which the crime was committed, the latter is duty-bound to the country requesting extradition.

Article 25:

A. If the country which receives the extradition request has a number of requests from other countries regarding the same person for the same crime, the deciding factor will be which country's interests were harmed by the crime rather than where the crime was committed.

B. If the requests for extradition are for various crimes, the deciding factor will be the dates the extradition requests were made.

Article 26: If the wanted person is being prosecuted legally or has been sentenced for another crime in the country which received the extradition request, the decision on this request will be postponed until his prosecution ends, or it has been decided not to try him, or he is declared innocent or not responsible, or he is sentenced for punishment or exempted, or his detention has ended due to the dropping of the charges. It is possible to send the wanted person temporarily to the country requesting him so that he may appear before the authorities concerned on the condition that these authorities guarantee to send him back after his questioning or trial for which his extradition was demanded, and keep him detained according to the sentence or decision issued by the authorities of the country which extradited him.

Article 27:

A. The extradition request from the concerned side in the requesting country must be presented to the concerned side in the country which is requested to extradite.

B. The file of the request must include:

1. A detailed statement on the identity of the wanted person and his description, with an accompanying photograph if possible.

2. Memorandum of arrest or request for appearance from the concerned authority if the person has not been sentenced.

3. Certified copy of the texts that demand punishment for the deed and a detailed statement from the concerned side which includes relevant correspondence and evidences proving the responsibility of the wanted person.

4. A certified copy of the sentence whether the wanted person has been sentenced or not.

5. A statement from the authorities concerned with the case not to drop the charges in accordance to the laws or rules of their country.

6. Confirmation that the request corresponds to the rules of this agreement.

Article 28: An exception to the above-mentioned articles is that the country which is requested to extradite can extradite the wanted person, if he admits that he committed the crime he is charged with, the crime is one of those which requires extradition according to the articles of this agreement, and the wanted person agrees to be extradited without a file requesting his extradition, then the concerned authorities can order his extradition.

Article 29:

A. The authorities concerned in the country requesting extradition and the country being asked to extradite will decide according to the laws or the pertinent rules of each during the presentation of the request.

B. The concerned side in the country which is requested to extradite will inform the concerned side in the country requesting extradition about the decision issued on the extradition request whether negative or positive, and explanations will be provided when an extradition request is denied.

Article 30: The detention of an individual who has been requested for extradition should not exceed 30 days in the country which has received the extradition request. The individual should be released if during the above-mentioned period a request file does not arrive or the concerned country does not ask for the renewal of his detention for a maximum of 30 more days, on condition that the period of temporary imprisonment will be deducted from the sentence imposed by the country which requested the extradition.

The authorities concerned, which are requested to extra-

dite by post, cable or telephone, can ascertain the validity of this request by asking for further information from the authorities concerned in the country which made the request.

Article 31: The country which is requested to extradite turns over everything related to the crime in the possession of the wanted person when arrested in accordance with the rules or laws of the country which has received the extradition request.

Article 32: The wanted person is to be tried in the country requesting his extradition for the crimes he was extradited for and any deeds related to it, as well as any crimes he committed after his extradition. It is also possible to try him for crimes which were not listed in the extradition request as long as the statute of limitations has not run out in accordance to the laws or rules of the two countries.

Article 33: The country requesting extradition pays all the expenses required for the execution of the extradition request. It also pays all the expenses of the individual involved, including those incurred in returning to the place he was extradited from if his nonresponsibility or innocence is proved.

Article 34: The country requesting extradition must come forward to receive the wanted person within 30 days after the date the notification cable was sent regarding the issuance of the extradition decision, or else the country which is requested to extradite can release the wanted person. He cannot be detained for extradition again for the same crime.

Article 35: This agreement does not impair the bilateral agreements made between countries. In the event that the rules of this agreement contradict the rules of any of these bilateral agreements, the two countries should apply the more applicable rules in extraditing criminals.

Article 36: This agreement will be ratified by the signing countries in accordance to their legal systems within 4 months after its signing. The ratification documents will be kept at the GCC General Secretariat, which will prepare a file on the ratification documents of each country and will notify all other member countries upon receipt of said documents.

Article 37: This agreement becomes valid after 1 month from the date that all ratification documents are received from the signatory countries.

Article 38: Agreement among one-third of the signatory countries is required to revise or cancel the terms of this agreement.

Article 39: Any member country party to this agreement can withdraw from it by announcing its intention to do so to the GCC General Secretariat. The withdrawal becomes effective 6 months after notification of intention. This agreement remains valid regarding extradition requests until the end of the 6-month period.

Source: *Al-Anba* (Kuwait), 17 Nov. 1982, p. 6, as translated in *FBIS-MEA-V–82–225*, 22 Nov. 1982, pp. C1-C6.

Document 21

GCC Secretariat Statement on the Explosions in Kuwait

13 December 1983

With most profound sorrow, the GCC has followed reports received about the criminal explosions that have occurred in sister Kuwait. These incidents have come as an extremely strong shock to the GCC member countries, which most vehemently denounce all forms of violence and reject all kinds of sabotage.

While strongly denouncing these criminal terroristic acts which took lives of innocent people, the GCC member countries wish to affirm their total and firm stand by sister Kuwait and their absolute support for it in the face of such criminal acts and all acts that harm its sovereignty and independence. These acts, which aim at spreading anarchy and chaos, will only further consolidate GCC cohesion in the face of all acts of violence and terrorism. They will act as a continuous and strong incentive for them to back each other and intensify their efforts to cooperate and coordinate among themselves in order to safeguard their stability, security, and safety while working hard and continuing with their efforts to bolster the Arab and Islamic causes.

The GCC member countries pray to God Almighty to protect the Arab and Islamic nation's security and continue to endow it with stability and save it from all harm.

Source: *FBIS-MEA-V–83–240*, 13 Dec. 1983, p. C1.

Document 22

Statement by the Minister of State for Cabinet Affairs, Shaykh Abd al-Aziz Husayn, on Casualty Figures following the Explosions in Kuwait

12 December 1983

The security machinery is continuing its investigations into the explosions which took place this morning. It has found cooperation from all citizens and the various spheres of state machinery.

The number of victims of the incidents are: four dead—one a Syrian citizen working in the American Embassy, the second an Egyptian working at the airport. The nationalities of the other two are not yet known. They were killed at the American Embassy. The number of injured still in hospitals reached 62, among them 6 Kuwaitis, 13 Indians, 11 Egyptians, 10 Jordanians, 4 Bangladeshis, 3 Syrians, 7 Pakistanis, 2 Iranians, and 1 each from Sri Lanka, Britain, Switzerland, France, and Lebanon.

There is no truth in news agencies reports on an unexploded bomb being discovered in a police station.

Source: *FBIS-MEA-V–83–240*, 13 Dec. 1983, p. C5.

Document 23

Kuwait's State Security Court Statement on Bombings Suspects

23 January 1984

In an exclusive statement, the spokesman said that 19 of the accused were charged with 4 counts of murder, 87 counts of attempted murder and a variety of other offenses, while the remaining six are charged with aiding and abetting the perpetrators and foreknowledge of the incidents. Four of the 25 are still at large and will be tried in absentia for their role in the seven explosions which shook the capital and its environs on December 12. The accused include 17 Iraqis, 3 Lebanese, 3 Kuwaitis and two stateless persons, the statement said.

The 19 main defendants, according to the spokesman, along with one perpetrator who died while carrying out the bombing raid at the U.S. Embassy, would stand trial for responsibility for the blasts at all seven locations: the U.S. and French Embassies, the airport control tower, the Electricity and Water Ministry's control center, the Shuaybah industrial area, and offices and residences of American firms in the country.

The statement said that investigations revealed that the accused planned and prepared for the bombings with the intention of killing those inside and nearby the targeted buildings. The plan included allotting individual roles to be played in the actions among the group, and procuring explosives, detonators and large quantities of highly inflammable gas cylinders, as well as gasoline and petroleum containers.

Various vehicles were used to plant the explosives in the targeted locations, with timing devices set to cause the blasts, the statement asserted.

The 25 defendants named were:

1—Badir Ibrahim Abd ar-Rida, 30—Iraqi
2—Elias Fuad Saib, 23—Lebanese
3—Ahmad Ali Husayn (Abu Haydar),—Iraqi (at large)
4—Mustafa Ibrahim Ahmad (abu Zahra)—Iraqi (at large)
5—Abdil Husayn Aziz Abbas, 28—Iraqi
6—Jamal Jaafar Muhammad—Iraqi (at large)
7—Amir Abd az-Zahra Sulayman al-Awad, 22—Iraqi
8—Husayn Qasim Hassan, 27—Iraqi
9—Adil Abd ar-Razzaq Shaykh Hadi, 30—Iraqi
10—Nasrallah Matuk Saywan, 30—Iraqi
11—Jabbar Abbas Jabbar, 22—Iraqi
12—Husayn al-Sayyid Yusif al Musawi, 28—Lebanese

13—Azzam Khalil Ibrahim, 28—Lebanese
14—Ibrahim Sabah Frayhaj (Ahmad), 29—Iraqi
15—Yaarib Faiq Mahdi, 24—Iraqi
16—Hassan Flayj al-Hamad, 26—Iraqi
17—Saad Yasin Abdallah al-Dhayabi, 21—Kuwaiti
18—Yusef Majid Wahib, 21—Iraqi
19—Abdil Muhsin Rashash Abbas, 20—Iraqi
20—Haytham Mahfuz Abd al-Karim—Iraqi (at large)
21—Nasir Matar Dahsh, 25—no nationality
22—Ahmad Abd al-Karim Niimah (Kazim), 29—Iraqi
23—Sharif Mutlaq Nasir, 44—no nationality
24—Abd ar-Rida Dawud Madwah, 53—Kuwaiti
25—Abd as-Samad Jawad Abdallah as-Saffar, 32—Kuwaiti

Also named as being involved in the blasts was Raad Muftin Ajayl, an Iraqi who drove an explosive-laden lorry into the U.S. Embassy compound and died as a result of the blast.

The attorney general's office said that the premeditated murder charges were being brought for the death of three blast victims at the U.S. Embassy and one at the airport control tower. In addition, charges of attempted premeditated murder are being leveled on 87 counts, in the cases of those victims of the blasts who were injured: 59 at the U.S. Embassy, 8 at the French Embassy, 11 at Shuaybah, 6 at the airport, 2 at the offices of the American firm, and one at the American residential bloc.

Specific charges are leveled at certain of the defendants according to the role they played in the incidents as revealed by security investigations.

Defendant 2 is specifically charged, along with others, of setting timers and detonators for the blasts.

Defendant 7 is charged with driving a car to Kuwait airport to a place prepared by defendant 7 in order to cause the blast.

Defendants 8 and 9 are charged with carrying out the Shuaybah explosion, while defendants 10 and 11 are accused of responsibility for the French Embassy incident.

Defendants 12–15 are accused of planting the bombs at the American offices and residential building, with two vehicles being used at each location to set off the blasts.

Defendants 16 and 17 were specifically accused of responsibility for the explosion outside the Electricity and Water Ministry control center, although the statement noted that in this case the coincidental absence of passersby meant that no one was killed or injured.

Defendant 10 is, in addition, accused of training a number of people in the use of firearms and ammunition for illegal purposes, while defendants 11, 16 and 17 are charged with receiving such training with prior knowledge of the intended purpose.

Other charges leveled against the first 19 accused include arson, intent to damage public utilities, illegal importation of explosives and materials used in their manufacture and detonation, as well as illegal possession of unlicensed weapons and ammunition.

Defendants 20–22, while not accused of direct partici-

pation in the blasts, are charged with aiding and abetting the crimes prior to the date of the explosions.

The last three defendants, on the other hand, are being charged with prior knowledge of intention to commit the aforementioned crimes without giving prior warning to public authorities in time to prevent them from being carried out.

The law stipulates that premeditated murder and attempted murder carry maximum penalties of death and life imprisonment, while the other charges leveled by the prosecutors warrant lighter sentences.

Source: *FBIS-MEA-V–84–016,* 24 Jan. 1984, pp. C1-C2.

Document 24
Report on the Trial of Embassy Bombings in Kuwait
11 February 1984

The State Security Court trying twenty-five persons on charges of subversive activities, decided Saturday to hold its sittings in camera.

The court convened under stringent security precautions to hear twenty-one defendants. Four of the accused are being tried in absentia. The court is presided over by Ghazi as-Sammar, and the session was entirely devoted to reading the indictment sheet of the 21 persons involved in the chain of blasts which rocked the country last December 12. The court includes as members Counsellor Ismael Zazou and Judge Faysal al-Murshid.

Of the defendants, 19 face death sentences for premeditated murder. Other charges include attempted murder; subversive action against a number of foreign embassies and public installations and utilities with the intention of causing damage; importing and possessing arms, explosives and ammunition without permits; and training for the use and manning of explosives.

After the court started proceedings, the president called on the defendants by name and took note of the four defendants still at large. Three of the defendants requested a defence council while the court has already appointed 10 Kuwaiti lawyers for the rest of them.

The defendants' names were read as follows:
1. Badir Ibrahim Abd ar-Rida, 30—Iraqi, currently imprisoned at the central prison
2. Elias Fuad Saib, 23—Lebanese, currently imprisoned at the central prison
3. Ahmad Ali Husayn (Abu Haydar) wanted—still at large
4. Mustafa Ibrahim Ahmad (Abu Zahra) wanted—still at large
5. Abdil Husayn Aziz Abbas, 28—Iraqi, currently imprisoned at the central prison
6. Jamal Jaafar Muhammad, wanted—still at large

7. Amir Abd az-Zahra Sulayman al-Awad, 22—Iraqi, currently imprisoned at the central prison
8. Husayn Qasim Hassan, 27—Iraqi, currently imprisoned at the central prison
9. Adil Abd ar-Razzaq Shaykh Hadi, 27—Iraqi, currently imprisoned at the central prison
10. Nasralla Matuk Saywan, 30—Iraqi, currently imprisoned at the central prison
11. Jabbar Abbas Jabbar, 22—Iraqi, currently imprisoned at the central prison
12. Husayn al-Sayyid Yusif al-Musawi, 28—Lebanese, currently imprisoned at the central prison
13. Azzam Khalil Ibrahim, 22—Lebanese, currently imprisoned at the central prison
14. Ibrahim Sabah Frayhaj (Ahmad), 29—Iraqi, currently imprisoned at the central prison
15. Yaarib Faiq Mahdi, 24-Iraqi, currently imprisoned at the central prison
16. Hassan Flayj al-Hamad, 26—Iraqi, currently imprisoned at the central prison
17. Saad Yasin Abdallah ad-Dhayabi, 21—Kuwaiti, currently imprisoned at the central prison
18. Yusef Majid Wahib, 21—Iraqi, currently imprisoned at the central prison
19. Abdil Muhsin Rashash Abbas, 20—Iraqi, currently imprisoned at the central prison
20. Haytham Mahfuz Abd al-Karim, wanted—still at large
21. Nasir Matar Dahsh, 25—non-Kuwaiti, currently imprisoned at the central prison
22. Ahmad Abd al-Karim Niimah, 29—Iraqi, currently imprisoned at the central prison
23. Sharif Mutlaq Nasir, 44—non-Kuwaiti, currently imprisoned at the central prison
24. Abd ar-Rida Dawud Madwah, 53—Kuwaiti, currently imprisoned at the central prison
25. Abd as-Samad Jawad Abdallah as-Saffar, 32—Kuwaiti, currently imprisoned at the central prison

On December 12, in various parts of the city, the indictment sheet said: The first nineteen accused, as well as another person who died while causing one of the explosions, are charged with the premeditated murder of Ahmed Samara, Ali el Gamal, Mofid el Hakim, Mohammed Salam and Abdel Najeeb Ahmed al Rifai, and the attempted murder of others whose names are included in the list of witnesses for the prosecution, attached to the indictment sheet.

They also conspired to destroy the buildings of the American and French embassies, as well as the control tower of Kuwait international airport. Other targets included the control center of the Ministry of Electricity and Water, the offices of Raytheon Gulf System, the residential quarters of American experts in Al-Bida and the Shuaybah industrial area. Anyone found in these areas or nearby could have been killed as a result of the blasts.

The accused agreed among themselves on the roles to be undertaken by each and defined the means of imple-

mentation. They gathered a large number of gas cylinders and benzine and gasoline-filled containers which they acquired with the sole purpose of carrying out these explosions. With booby-trapped vehicles, the conspirators headed to their targets, and a twenty-sixth accused person perished in one of the operations when he attacked the American Embassy. The other accused drove vehicles loaded with explosives to the other targets.

Formal charges against defendants 1–19 were made under eight separate points:
—premeditated murder and attempted murder
—arson
—causing explosions
—damaging public property and installations
—illegal importation and possession of unlicensed explosives
—illegal importation and possession of unlicensed firearms
—illegal possession of unlicensed ammunition
—illegal importation of unlicensed ammunition

Specific charges were leveled at certain defendants according to the role they played in the incidents as revealed by security investigations:

Defendant 2 was specifically charged, along with others, of setting timers and detonators for the blasts. Defendant 6 was charged with driving a car to Kuwait airport to a place prepared by defendant 7 in order to cause the blast. Defendants 8 and 9 were charged with carrying out the Shuaybah explosion, while defendants 10 and 11 were accused of responsibility for the French Embassy incident.

Defendants 12–15 were accused of planting the bombs at the American offices and residential building, with two vehicles being used at each location to set off the blasts. Defendants 16 and 17 were specifically accused of responsibility for the explosion outside the Electricity and Water Ministry control center, although the indictment noted that in this case the coincidental absence of passersby meant that no one was killed or injured.

Defendants 20, 21 and 22 participated with the above-mentioned defendants in carrying out the eight crimes by agreeing with them on committing these actions, and the 20th defendant helped them by supplying his car to use in the explosives incidents. Therefore, the crimes had been committed with the complicity and help of those defendants.

Defendants 1–23 were accused of joining a group that aims at spreading principles calling for the destruction of basic systems through illegal means, including terrorism and force, and through using firearms and explosives with prior knowledge of the objectives of that group. The 10th defendant trained the 11th, 16th and 17th defendants in using arms and ammunition and in the aim of using their efforts to carry out illegal objectives. The 11th, 16th and 17th defendants were trained in using firearms and ammunition by the 10th defendant with knowledge that he was aiming to get their help to achieve illegal objectives as interrogations had shown. The 21st defendant possessed a gun and ammunition for that gun without licenses from the concerned authorities.

Defendants 24 and 25 were aware of the plan to commit murder and arson but refrained from reporting that to the authorities to enable them to prevent these crimes before being carried out.

The attorney general requested the State Security tribunal to punish the defendants in accordance with the penal code articles relating to their crimes, and gave a list of the witnesses for the prosecution.

Source: *FBIS-MEA-V–84–030,* 13 Feb. 1984, pp. C1-C2.

Document 25

State of Kuwait: Council of Ministers Report on the Hijacking

6 December 1984

The Council of Ministers resumed its meeting this morning Thursday, 6 December 1984, under His Royal Highness Shaykh Saad al-Abdallah al-Salim al-Sabah, heir apparent and prime minister, in the presence of Muhammad Yusuf al-Adsani, speaker of the National Assembly, to follow up developments of the hijacked Kuwait airliner, which has been at Tehran's Mehrabad International Airport since dawn Tuesday, 3 December. In this meeting, which lasted until late tonight, the council studied the developments.

The council heard that his royal highness the amir had telephoned Syrian President Hafiz al-Asad and that during this call views and consultations were exchanged on the hijacking and the efforts Syria can make to effect the release of the airliner and its passengers. The council also heard of the cable sent by His Highness Ali Khamenei, amir, to his excellency the president of the Islamic Republic of Iran, which includes his highness' request for the Iranian president to intervene in the release of the hostages. The council learned of the telephone call by His Royal Highness Hasan, crown prince of Jordan, to his highness the heir apparent and prime minister, in which he expressed dissatisfaction and condemnation of the hijacking incident. The council also learned of His Royal Highness Prince Saud al-Faysal's telephone call in which he expressed the Kingdom of Saudi Arabia's support for Kuwait's efforts to bring about the release of the hijacked airliner and its passengers.

The council reviewed the circumstances of the incident and its developments, and the attitudes of some states to this. It decided to send two more cables to the Iranian authorities: one from his highness the heir apparent and prime minister to Mir Hoseyn Musavi, and the other from the deputy prime minister, foreign minister and minister of information, to Dr. Ali Akbar Velayati, calling on them and

the Iranian Government to take the necessary steps and urgent measures to preserve the lives of all passengers. Also the ambassadors of Kuwait to Syria and Algeria were asked to contact the authorities in both countries and urge them to intervene with the Iranian authorities to prevent the deterioration of the situation. Another cable has been sent to the Pakistani Government for the same purpose.

The council learned of the return of the other Kuwaiti aircraft which was sent to bring back some of the freed passengers. At about 1030 in the evening his highness the heir apparent and prime minister received the Iranian chargé d'affaires who delivered a reply from Mir Hoseyn Musavi, prime minister of Islamic Iran, which included Iran's denunciation of the hijacking and its readiness to continue its efforts to preserve the lives of the passengers and the crew of the aircraft. His highness the heir apparent and prime minister thanked the Iranian Government for its efforts to bring about the release of the airliner, its passengers and crew. He confirmed the need to exert the utmost effort to bring about the release of the aircraft and maintain the safety of its passengers and crew.

The council will resume its meeting tomorrow morning to follow up the latest developments and take suitable measures in the light of these developments and we hope that God will make us succeed in bringing the aircraft, its passengers and crew safely back to the country, God willing.

Source: *FBIS-MEA-V–84–237,* 7 Dec. 1984, p. C1.

Document 26

Message from Shaykh Jabir al-Ahmad Al-Sabah, Amir of Kuwait, to President Khamenei of Iran

10 December 1984

Honorable brother, Your Excellency Seyyed Ali Khamenei, the President of Iran. God's peace and blessings be upon you. The ending of the hijacking tragedy of the Kuwaiti airliner in Mehrabad Airport and the release of the passengers provides me with an opportunity to express my most sincere gratitude and thanks for the attempts which were made by your excellency's government, under the wise guidelines of that brother, for achieving this end. I am confident that without doubt our cooperation and the cooperation of the international community under such sensitive conditions helps towards the implementation of sublime human goals which you are trying to achieve, and will prevent the recurrence of such events as the result of which a number of innocent people were killed and many others injured. While expressing my gratitude for the humane attempts of your excellency I wish for the health and well-being of your excellency and the success and progress of your nation and government.

[Signed] Your brother, Jabir al-Ahmad al-Sabah, amir of Kuwait

Source: *FBIS-MEA-V–84–239*, 11 Dec. 1984, p. C1.

Document 27

GCC Secretariat Statement on the Attack on Shaykh Jabir al-Ahmad Al-Sabah, Amir of Kuwait

26 May 1985

With extreme concern and strong bitterness, the GCC Secretariat followed the news on the criminal assassination attempt against His Highness Amir of Kuwait Shaykh Jabir al-Ahmad al-Sabah, which God almighty saved him from and blessed him with health and safety. While we thank the almighty God, we ask him during this holy month to give his highness a long life so that he can lead Kuwait's march to serve its people and to complete with his brothers—their majesties and highnesses, the leaders of the GCC countries—this good march, to serve the issues of the Arab and Islamic nation. While the GCC Secretariat strongly condemns this criminal attempt and all terrorist attempts and acts designed to threaten the security and stability of this vital region in the world, it affirms that this attempt will make Kuwait and its sister countries more determined to continue the march of welfare and construction to serve the issues of the Arab nation and Islamic solidarity, and to miss the opportunity of those who evilly and slyly lie in wait for the loyal sons of the nation. The Secretariat also affirms that only the enemies can benefit from this attempt at the time when the Arab nation is standing at a historic junction and is in extreme need of solidarity and unification of ranks in the face of those attempts. May God protect Kuwait, its amir and people, and bless this region and the rest of the Muslim countries with security, safety and stability. The almighty God has the power to do all things.

Source: *FBIS-MEA-V–85–102*, 28 May 1985, p. C1.

Document 28

State of Kuwait. Amiri Court Statement on the Motorcade Attack of Shaykh Al-Sabah

25 May 1985

At 0915 [0615 GMT] today, and while the procession of his highness the amir was going to his office at the Al-Sif Pal-

ace as usual, the procession of his highness the amir, God save him, was subjected to a sinful act of aggression. The Amiri Court would like to assure all the citizens that his highness the amir is in good health. It prays to almighty God to save his highness patron and leader of the dear homeland.

The Amiri Court will announce later statements on the details of this sinful incident.

God save Kuwait—amir and people—against all evils.

Source: *FBIS-MEA-V–85–102*, 28 May 1985, p. C3.

Document 29

State of Kuwait. Address to the Nation by Shaykh Jabir al-Ahmad Al-Sabah

25 May 1985

In the name of God, the merciful, the compassionate. Thanks be to God, the god of all peoples. God's prayers and peace be with the prophet.

Brothers and countrymen. Nothing will befall us except what God has destined for us. [Koranic verse]

You have heard what happened this morning. The faithful leaves his destiny in the hands of God almighty, for he is the protector and he controls everything.

I wish to reassure you all that, thanks be to God, I am well now. Whatever incidents I may be exposed to will not divert me or Kuwait from pursuing the road of seeking the good of all, and to do good for the Kuwaitis and for the Arab and Islamic nation.

I thank you all for the true feelings you have demonstrated. I pray to God, God almighty, to save you from all evil. I also wish to thank my brother presidents who contacted me to express their fraternal feelings, which I cherish. May God save all from all evil.

May God have mercy for the victims of this painful incident. May God bring healing to the injured.

God's peace, mercy and blessings be with you.

Source: *FBIS-MEA-V–85–102*, 28 May 1985, p. C4.

Document 30

State of Kuwait. Interior Ministry Statement on the Motorcade Attack of Shaykh Al-Sabah

25 May 1985

At 0915 today, the motorcade in which his highness the amir of the land was traveling was exposed to a sinful attack.

As his highness was traveling to his office at Al-Sif Palace, a car laden with explosives and parked on the central median of the road, tried to ram the motorcade. This led to an explosion and set fire to a number of cars in the motorcade and other cars in the vicinity. [*words indistinct*] and the killing of three people including Corporal Muhammad Qablan Muslih and Private Hadi Muhammad, both of whom belong to the Amiri Guard, and a pedestrian whose identity is not known. The culprit was also killed [*words indistinct*] the wounded as was mentioned in the official statements.

The security forces are exerting intensive efforts to discover the details of the treacherous plot.

We thank God for the safety of our amir and commander, whom we wish good health and safety. We wish our government and people all good, while praying to God to have mercy on the souls of the innocent and to grant their kin patience. May God save Kuwait and its people from all evil.

Source: *FBIS-MEA-V–85–102*, 28 May 1985, p. C4.

Document 31

State of Kuwait. National Assembly Statement on the Motorcade Attack of Shaykh Al-Sabah

25 May 1985

Say nothing will befall us other than which God has destined for us. Verily God has said the truth. [Koranic verse]

Let us start by thanking God almighty for the safety of the amir, may God preserve him and give him good health. We pray to God to save Kuwait and its people from all evils and afflictions and turn it into an oasis for security, stability, prosperity, and honorable work.

The National Assembly has heard the government's statement concerning the circumstances surrounding the treacherous incident which took place this morning directed against the life of his highness the amir.

The National Assembly, in the name of the Kuwaiti people, strongly denounces this treacherous incident and calls on the Kuwaiti people to rally together and destroy all opportunities for people with suspect aims, by asserting national unity and displaying the required vigilance needed in this critical state.

The National Assembly seizes this opportunity to appeal to the government to take all necessary measures to punish and deter all quarters responsible for this attempt and to acquaint the Kuwaiti people with all the facts pertaining to it.

We wish to affirm that the people, led by his highness the amir, who believes in democracy and nurtures it, will not be affected by such cowardly acts and that the Kuwaiti democratic march will continue relying on the unity of the Kuwaiti people.

Finally, the National Assembly affirms that the attack on his highness the amir was an attack on every citizen and resident and on democracy, freedom, and noble Islamic values.

The National Assembly stands by his highness and government in respect of all the measures it deems necessary to take. God is the granter of all success.

The National Assembly greets all those men who sacrificed their lives as they performed their national duty and offer the most sincere condolences to their kinsmen. The Assembly wishes the injured speedy recovery.

Source: *FBIS-MEA-V–85–102*, 28 May 1985, pp. C4-C5.

Document 32

State of Kuwait. Cabinet Statement on the Motorcade Attack of Shaykh Al-Sabah

25 May 1985

In the name of God, the compassionate, the merciful.

Dear listeners. Following the criminal attack this morning aimed at the life of his highness the amir, may God preserve and protect him, the Cabinet met at 1600 today, Saturday, 25 May 1985, under his highness the heir apparent, Shaykh Saad al-Abdallah al-Salim al-Sabah, and reviewed all the investigation results in this incident, and all the measures that have been taken in this regard.

In the name of Kuwait and its people, the Cabinet—while condemning and denouncing this criminal action—thanks almighty God on the saving of the leader of the nation's progress, his highness the amir, from this treacherous attempt on his life, and affirms to the honorable citizens that the government will not submit to blackmail, terror, or threat. The Cabinet also asserts that such cowardly actions will not impede Kuwait's good progress.

The government reasserts that it is determined to deter all those who are tempted to harm the country's security and stability, citing in this, God's words: In the name of God, the compassionate, the merciful. Those who attack you, retaliate against them in kind. Fear God and know that He supports the pious. [Koranic verse]

The government—on this painful occasion—conveys to the families of our virtuous martyrs, who sacrificed themselves to the homeland, its condolences and supplication to God, in this our holy month, to admit them into Heaven and grant their families patience and solace, and bless the wounded with rapid recovery.

Source: *FBIS-MEA-V-85-102*, 28 May 1985, p. C5.

Document 33

State of Kuwait. Address to the Nation by the Prime
Minister and Heir Apparent, Shaykh Saad al-
Abdallah al-Salim Al-Sabah

27 May 1985

In the name of God, the merciful and the compassionate.
Verily, God will defend those who believe. Verily, God lov-
eth not any that is a traitor to faith, or shows ingratitude.
God has spoken the truth. [Koranic verse]

   Brothers, citizens, faithful Kuwaitis: In your name, we
thank God ardently for his blessing and for looking after our
leader and the symbol of our unity—his highness the amir.
God's protection foiled the scheme of the aggressors, de-
feated their conspiracy, and taught us that God is the best
protector.

   The implications of the sinful incident that took place 2
days ago should not escape any of us. This attack was not
directed against the person of our amir, who has dedicated
all his life to good deeds and giving, and whose words still
carry a sincere invitation to everybody for compassion, solidarity, cooperation and reconciliation among brothers and
friends. This sinful attack was directed at what Kuwait represents: proud stances which do not compromise, or submit
to blackmail or terrorism. The attack was also directed
against the dearest of that which Kuwait was able to preserve during the darkest and most difficult of times, which
is to remain an oasis of security, stability, and freedom; it is
an oasis which opens its arms to any honorable guest who,
honorably and faithfully contributes to the construction of
the fort of progress, prosperity, and stability on its good
earth.

   We are used to dealing with domestic matters with patience and tolerance, and to think good of everybody. But
some people misunderstood and miscalculated; they
thought they could conspire against beloved Kuwait, commit aggression against it, and remain secure from deterrents
and punishment.

   It is now time for all of us to face the powers of evil in
order to block those who think that they could violate the
sanctity of this peaceful country, disturb its security, and
play with its interests and destiny. Brothers, it is the duty of
all of us to learn about the realities of the world in which
we live, and the nature of the realities around us; otherwise,
we will lose the ability to protect our rights, and to preserve
our freedom and the elements of our independence.

   The political, social, and religious conflicts which take
place around us have created a spirit of unlimited evil and
a tendency toward crazy violence in whose path values,
ideals, and feelings cannot stop. These conflicts, and what
they created, incited some of those who have no sense of
responsibility whatsoever to violate the most sacred of sanctities, and to disregard all rights and liberties, thinking that
terrorism would be able to switch off the light of right, that
blackmail could alter the stances of men, and that the

spread of chaos and disturbances could aid them to obstruct
the march of good, construction, and progress. If this is the
reality that surrounds us and the evil that is schemed against
us, then can any of us, whatever his position, doubt the
necessity of unrelentless firmness and unhesitating determination in confronting anyone who thinks of playing with
the security of the country and its citizens.

   Brothers, we have chosen democracy because of our
convictions and beliefs in its being the way and course for
us. We are constructing and seeking progress. Democracy,
in its essence, is participating in giving, being responsible,
and exchanging views and consultations when making decisions. But this democratic dialogue should not preoccupy
us from sensing the dangers that surround us; the reality of
the ambitions against us, our people, our land, and all we
have achieved in this land of construction, prosperity, stability, and progress.

   The government, together with the National Assembly,
will work as one to legislate the necessary laws for protecting
the supreme interests of the country, in order to deter the
schemers and the ambitions of the greedy.

   Brothers, I would like to tell you today, from the position
of responsibility, that the government intends, with unrelentless insistence, on opening a new book; we have no
other option. Represented by complete firmness in applying
laws, we will alter what needs altering in our laws; we will
put the supreme interests of society, which are related to its
security and stability, before any individual limited interest.
This may require that we all sacrifice some of our conve-
nience and abandon some measures to which we have become accustomed during the times of stable prosperity and
security. We all have to remember that any carelessness or
complacency we commit may mean we have to pay a high
price, because there is no way to restore lost security, stability, and interests. The government is confident that our
people have reached a high standard of maturity, consciousness and understanding, according to which they can
understand the dimensions of the evil directed against us,
and the aims of the good that we try to achieve. Let us all
arm ourselves with the spirit of firmness and determination,
without which we cannot protect our beloved Kuwait from
the evil of criminals and the harm of the aggressors.

   Dear brothers, faithful compatriots. People are not
tested during their times of prosperity; they are tested during
their times of difficulties and crisis. Now, during the march
of prosperity, which we are following, critical moments face
us. However, we can say to anybody: We are a small country, in area and population, but our belief in God, our commitment to our right, our solidarity with our leadership,
and our complete expression of our responsibility make us
always—with the help of God—able to give an example of
unity and our insistence of our right and commitment to
it, whatever the powers of evil, sabotage and aggression
might try against us.

Source: *FBIS-MEA-V–85–102*, 28 May 1985, pp. C6-C7.

Document 34

GCC Secretariat Statement Condemns Kuwaiti Explosions

13 July 1985

The GCC Secretariat has followed with great sorrow and pain the criminal explosions that took place in some popular cafes in the state of Kuwait and which were directed against innocent citizens. The GCC Secretariat strongly condemns such criminal actions and all forms of terrorism and affirms that such vile actions will only make Kuwait and its sister GCC states stronger and more solid.

The GCC Secretariat also affirms that it is fully anxious, and will make indefatigable efforts, to implement the resolutions of the 15th session of the GCC Ministerial Council that call for the unification and coordination of efforts of the various quarters in the GCC member states to confront and tackle such attempts.

The GCC Secretariat asks Almighty God to grant mercy and forgiveness to the martyrs and patience and fortitude to their families.

Source: *FBIS-MEA-V–85–136*, 16 July 1985, p. C1.

Document 35

Interview with Kuwaiti Interior Minister Shaykh Nawwaf al-Ahmad al-Jabir Al-Sabah

27 July 1985

[Excerpts] Question: Do you think that the democracy and freedom prevailing in Kuwait are the target of the terrorism we are currently witnessing?

Answer: Our democracy and freedom may not please some people, but I do not believe that they are the reason for the terrorist and criminal acts committed against Kuwait. The region we live in is a hotbed of tension, and we have adopted principled political attitudes towards national and Islamic issues, some of them fateful issues. I believe that these attitudes are the real targets of the terrorists and the criminals. Our policies are based on principles based on justice. We will never change our attitudes or abandon our policies, which are drawn up by our amir and leader Shaykh Jabir al-Ahmad, particularly because Kuwait's policies stem from right, faith, and justice.

Question: Do you believe that the security measures taken will prevent further acts of terrorism in Kuwait?

Answer: We realize that we are up against organized terrorism and we may not be able to put an end to terrorist acts on our territory because they are linked to political circumstances and what happens in the world. However, we are trying to prevent the intensification and spread of terrorism, which is foreign and alien to our society, which is characterized by true democracy.

Question: In addition to the security measures are you engaged in any foreign political contacts?

Answer: Kuwait has always stressed that it will never change its policies and will not back down from the positions it has taken on our national fateful issues. There are continuous contacts with the GCC states and with other fraternal and friendly states.

Question: One question being asked is why the security authorities were able to apprehend the perpetrators of previous terrorist acts, and particularly the 12 January 1984 explosions, within 24 hours but have been unable to find the perpetrators of recent incidents such as the attack on the motorcade of his highness the amir and the explosions in crowded cafes?

Answer: In past incidents we managed to get early leads which we exploited and, with the help of all our practical and technological equipment, we were able to arrest the perpetrators with dazzling speed. As for the recent incidents, I frankly and regrettably say that we have not had any leads. We have fingerprints of the person who carried out the sinful attack on the amir's motorcade but we do not have the identical fingerprints on our records. That strengthens the belief that the perpetrator must have either infiltrated into the country or entered on a visitor's visa.

Question: What is the extent of cooperation between you and the GCC states on matters of security and combating terrorism?

Answer: The fraternal GCC states have cooperated with us in every way. We are deeply touched by their recent attitudes towards the incidents which occurred in Kuwait. There is cooperation among the GCC states in all fields, including the field of security.

Source: *Al-Tadamun* (London), 27 July–2 Aug. 1985, p. 22, as translated in *FBIS-MEA-V–85–146*, 30 July 1985, p. C1.

3
Deterring the Spread of War

ANALYSIS

Created primarily to contain the contagion of the Iranian Revolution, the Gulf Cooperation Council struggled during the first five years of its existence to deter the spread of the Iraq-Iran war in the Gulf region. To be sure, the six monarchies perceived external threats to their security from a variety of sources, depending on their particular circumstances. For example, in 1981 Oman and Saudi Arabia considered South Yemen a greater threat than did the other four GCC monarchies. To cite other examples, Kuwait, and possibly the UAE, regarded the Soviet Union as less of a threat than did the other member states. And the Omanis and the Saudis were more alarmed by the creation of the so-called tripartite axis (August 1981) among Ethiopia, Libya, and South Yemen than were their GCC partners.

Yet, no other threat was so commonly perceived by the GCC states as the threat of the spread of the Iraq-Iran war to the rest of the Gulf region. To be sure, there was no uniformity in the perception of the various GCC states regarding this threat, but as opposed to other kinds of threats, there was a greater degree of commonality of security concern over it. No other single threat emerged so forcefully as the impetus behind the efforts of the GCC states to create a credible integrated defense and deterrent system in the Gulf region. Any attempt at understanding defense cooperation among the GCC states would, therefore, be inadequate without considering the challenge of the war and their response to it. In fact, the war should be considered not only the engine of their cooperation in defense matters but also the most influential catalyst of their military buildup.

The Iraq-Iran War and Defense Cooperation

Broadly speaking, defense cooperation among the GCC states went through four major phases in 1981–86. The first phase began with the start of the war in September 1980, before the birth of the GCC, and December 1981. There is little doubt that the war acted as a catalyst in creating the GCC, but the decisive factor behind its formation was the great concern of the GCC monarchies with the perceived threat of the contagion of the Islamic revolutionary fundamentalism. Bahrain, Kuwait and Saudi Arabia all had experienced various kinds of Iranian-inspired domestic upheavals during 1979–80. On 27 May 1981, the day after the first GCC summit meeting in Abu Dhabi, the UAE president said that the GCC leaders had hoped that the war would have ended by then, that they were "affected by this war," and that they and Iran were "linked by relations stemming from Islam and neighbourliness. Iraq is a fraternal country. Both are our brothers in Islam and Arabism."[1] Even six months later, when the second GCC summit was held in November 1981, the same conciliatory tone toward Iran was sounded. The Saudi foreign minister, Saud al-Faysal, for example, said that the relations of the GCC members with Iran "should be excellent and based on the basic pillars of international relations, that is, relations of fraternity, religion, and neighborliness."[2]

Yet, such remarks did not mean lack of security concern during this first, and earliest, phase of the war. Two developments in the war had already alarmed the GCC states. First, Iran launched its first offensive against the Iraqi forces in January 1981. Although it was unsuccessful, this action showed the prospective GCC states that, contrary to their perception, Iran was quite capable of undertaking such offensives despite the revolutionary chaos. Second, in September 1981 Iranian forces succeeded in compelling the Iraqi troops to lift the yearlong siege of the oil refinery city of Abadan. This successful military offensive was the first hard evidence of Iran's military challenge, despite the toll that the revolution had taken.

The second phase, between December 1981 and February 1984, saw unprecedented efforts at defense cooperation among the GCC members. As seen, the aborted Bahrain plot in December 1981 led to four security pacts between Saudi Arabia and its GCC partners and a draft agreement for collective internal security. But it took three major developments in the war to increase the concern of the GCC members with their external security. First, in March 1982 Iran launched an impressive offensive (*Fath al-Mubin*) against the Iraqi forces, starting at Dezful and ending with the recovery of 800 square miles of territory stretching to an area within seven miles of the international border.

The second event, the follow-up Iranian offensive ("Operation Jerusalem"), rang the alarm bell all the way from the Persian Gulf to Washington, D.C. The Iranian appellation, Khoninshahr ("bloodied town"), used for the city of Khorramshahr ("blooming town") dramatized the fierce fighting, often house to house and even hand to hand, that led to the defeat of the Iraqi forces and the recovery of the Iranian port city in May 1982. The victory demoralized Iraq and frightened the GCC members, while it raised Iranian morale to a fault, for it led to the bloodiest Iranian failure as a result of the third major event, another Iranian offensive ("Operation Ramadan"). Although this offensive, launched in July 1982, carried the war into Iraqi territory for the first time, it ended in a great disaster for Iranian forces. The massive attacks, which involved about a quarter of a million troops, resulted in nearly 30,000 dead without any significant territorial gains. So far as the GCC member states were concerned, however, this was no cause for comfort. The overall Iranian military successes during this phase outweighed the momentary disaster suffered in this one offensive.

The defense ministers of the GCC held their first meeting on 25 January 1982 in Riyadh. The secretary general of the GCC, Abdallah Bisharah, reportedly said that with their meeting "the ministers of defense laid the first brick in the foundation [of defense cooperation] and forged the tool for the edifice that will safeguard the security and stability of the Gulf with its own forces and without help from anyone."[3] In replying to a question about why the defense ministers' conference concentrated so much on the problem of security, whereas the first GCC summit in Abu Dhabi had focused on political and economic matters, Bisharah replied that "there was no alternative to cooperation in matters of security and defense."[4] The Saudi defense minister, Prince Sultan, said that the decisions of the ministers were secret "because they touch on the sublime interests of these countries." Reportedly, he denied that the Bahrain coup plot of the previous December had prompted "the great work" of the defense ministers at this, their first meeting. He added that the coup plot was "in the eyes of the area's people, no more than a childish move."[5] As has been seen, however, that plot was the first and foremost catalytical event that prompted Saudi Arabia to conclude security agreements with four other GCC partners. It was also the real reason for the first meeting of the chiefs of staff of the GCC states who did the preparatory work for the defense ministers.

In the same way that the Bahrain coup plot led to the first meeting of the GCC defense ministers, the successful Iranian offensives between March and June 1982 prompted emergency meetings of the foreign ministers between 15 and 31 May 1982. The final communiqué of 31 May confined itself to saying that the Ministerial Council hoped that Iran would respond to the call for "ending the bloodshed and the war in a manner safeguarding the legitimate rights of the two Muslim countries" (D72). The Kuwaiti foreign minister considered such a low-key statement a good one because the "circumstances in the area are dangerous and therefore any word uttered should always be well-studied to prevent any misinterpretation."[6]

From the GCC perspective, the milestone step toward defense cooperation among the six member states was their first-ever military exercises, which started on 11 October 1983. Symbolically, they were held in the UAE where the first GCC summit meeting had taken place in May 1981. Even the independent-minded Kuwaitis participated in the joint military exercises, named Peninsula Shield I. The Kuwaiti defense minister reportedly said that such exercises could bring army commanding officers together and "create a GCC rapid deployment force which can repel any external attack against any member-state of the council."[7] The Peninsula Shield maneuvers executed an attack operation using live ammunition against defined targets, including various weapons such as artillery, Mirage combat planes, and Al-Ghazal helicopters followed by the movement of columns of tanks and armored vehicles and then of the mechanized infantry.

The exercises were followed by a meeting of the joint chiefs of staff of the GCC. They considered the need for unifying the training methods in the armies of the GCC states. They also considered the need for unifying the curricula of the military colleges and for establishing a joint Gulf military command. At the time, Western sources reported that high-level contacts were taking place between GCC states and the United States, Britain, and France in attempts to reach an agreement on establishing "a huge radar defense network round the Gulf countries for defense against attacks." The same Western sources said that the plan would connect the GCC states with a comprehensive network of advanced radar and rocket systems, which would be linked to secret computer installations in each state and would be capable of detecting all air, sea, and land movements around the borders of the region.

The question of establishing a joint military force was left for the decision of the GCC leaders during their fourth summit meeting held in Doha, Qatar, in November 1983. After this summit meeting the GCC authorities spoke with optimism about the formation of a GCC rapid deployment force. According to the chief of staff of Bahrain, the force was "to be the first repellent of any aggression, playing the role of 'shock absorber' to prepare the groundwork for the participation of the main forces of the GCC countries." And yet, he viewed the defense of the strategic Strait of Hormuz as "the joint responsibility of all countries of the world."[8] The GCC countries would only give assistance to Oman if that part of the strait that is within its territorial waters was threatened.

Like the second phase, the third phase of GCC defense cooperation reflected the developments in the Iraq-Iran war. Between February 1984 and February 1986 the GCC states sensed the threat of the spread of the war most keenly. The two-year period was marked by three landmark events, each intensifying the fear of the GCC leaders and further encouraging cooperative efforts aimed at common defense. First, Iran launched a new offensive against Iraq on 24 February 1984. All the four previous offensives code-named "Operation before Dawn" (*Walfajr*) had failed, but this fifth attempt succeeded. The Iranian forces seized parts of the artificial oil islands of Majnoon inside the Iraqi marshes north of Basra, the vital Iraqi port city inhabited mostly by Shias. Besides sitting atop seven billion barrels of oil, the islands could be used as a jumping board for an offensive against the Baghdad-Basra strategic highway six miles distant.

The second development affected the GCC states directly for the first time. For three years before the spring of 1984, the Iraqis had attacked more than sixty ships, two-thirds of them commercial vessels from nations not involved in the war. But in April the Iraqis used French-made Super Etendard planes, instead of helicopters, to fire Exocet missiles at oil tankers in the Gulf. Ironically, Iraq bit the hand that fed it. Two Saudi oil tankers near the Iranian oil terminal at Kharg Island were hit, the first, *Safina al-Arab*, on 25 April and the second, *Al-Ahood*, on 7 May. But the Iranian attacks were the ones that really scared the GCC states. A Kuwaiti oil tanker, *Umm Casbah*, was hit on 13 May and another one the following day. And the Iranian attack on the Saudi oil tanker *Yanbu* on 16 May touched off unprecedented alarm among the GCC rulers.

Against the background of heightened tensions between Iran and Saudi Arabia, the third development may appear to have been an act of Saudi retaliation against Iran; it was not. On 5 June 1984 Saudi fighter jets shot down an Iranian F-4 plane. The Saudi action was in response to the perceived Iranian encroachment on Saudi territorial waters. The following day the Iranians protested the Saudi downing of their jet plane, claiming that the aircraft had been shot down in "international waters." Against the background of years of intensified military buildup, a successful Saudi dogfight in the air may indeed appear insignificant, but it was important in two respects. It showed the Saudi political resolve, and it boosted the morale of the smaller GCC states which depended primarily on Saudi military deterrence. The aftermath of the crisis was no less important. Both Iran and the GCC countries showed mutual restraint. Iran's "underresponse" was matched by the GCC's low-profile stance despite the obvious sense of satisfaction with this first, and successful, show of force.

The so-called tanker war further goaded the GCC states to seek to increase efforts for common defense. Secretary General Bisharah reportedly said that "the Iranian attacks on Kuwaiti and Saudi oil tankers have prompted the council's states to speed up unification of the military effort under a united command."[9] Although he left out the impact of the Saudi-Iranian air fight, there is no doubt that the increased self-confidence of the GCC leaders as a result of that single event encouraged them to forge ahead with bolder attempts.

Seldom before had the need for an integrated defense system been so commonly felt. The GCC chiefs of staff met on 23 June 1984 after they apparently decided to abandon the GCC foreign ministers' idea of 14 June for designating a sea corridor close to the shores of their states over which would be extended a GCC "air umbrella." They decided instead that air cover was the best means for protecting the navigation outside the Iraq-Iran war zone in the northern part of the Gulf. Such an aerial coverage system would be backed by an early warning system. The chiefs of staff further decided to recommend to the GCC leaders a grant of an estimated $2 billion to Oman to upgrade its air defense system and to increase the effectiveness of its nascent radar network in the Strait of Hormuz in order "to monitor Iranian activities aimed at obstructing navigation in the Strait." They also recommended the formation of a "semiunified command" for the armies of the six countries.

Follow-up developments were first hinted at by Secretary General Bisharah in September 1984 when the GCC defense and foreign ministers were to hold a joint meeting in Abha. With respect to the importance of this meeting, he reportedly said that "for the first time in modern history of the region a document is being drawn to determine the consequences of collective responsibility in preserving the independence and security of the member countries."[10] At the end of their meeting on 19 September, it was reported that the ministers "approved the defense policy paper and its principal outline as the document that will determine the course and philosophy of defense for GCC countries."[11] It was also reported that the ministers considered allocating an annual sum of $60 million to bolster air defense systems and communications in the GCC countries, the first step in a planned joint military strategy. The defense policy paper that resulted from this joint meeting was to be submitted to the GCC leaders at their fifth summit meeting in Kuwait in November 1984 for approval. In the meantime, according to Saudi defense minister Sultan, "no minister in the council's countries is able to disclose the contents of the paper in detail."[12]

Kuwaiti sources, however, revealed some details when in October 1984 Defense Minister Shaykh Salim al-Sabah spoke to an extraordinary session of the Kuwaiti parliament. He reportedly said that a two-brigade force would be based at the Saudi Arabian Shuayb al-Batin, 200 miles north of the Red Sea port city of Jidda. A Kuwaiti parliamentary source reportedly added that the projected force would be under the command of a Saudi officer, who would be assisted by officers from the rest of the GCC member countries. The force would be equipped with land and air weapons, with emphasis on air defense missile networks.[13] Subsequently, the Kuwaiti daily *Al-Qabas* reported that at their summit meeting in November 1984 in Kuwait, the GCC leaders would "adopt a common defence policy involving a five-year armament program and the creation of a 'dissuasion force.'"[14] For this program, they would allocate $60 million a year to boost antiaircraft defenses of the six member states.

Before the fifth summit meeting in Kuwait, however, a second round of joint military exercises took place in Hafr al-Batin, about 700 kilometers northeast of Riyadh. These joint military maneuvers, code-named Peninsula Shield II, were held in October 1984, a year after Peninsula Shield I in the UAE. According to Secretary General Bisharah, "the importance of the Peninsula Shield II maneuvers lies in that they constitute a translation of the willingness of their majesties and highnesses, the leaders of the GCC countries, to bear their responsibilities in defending this region and clearly shows the unity of destiny and the unity of vision and the determination to confront any aggression."[15]

According to the commander of the joint exercises, Brigadier General Abd al-Rahman al-Alkami, the maneuvers represented "joint training" of the forces from the six countries; only the troops of each country would defend it against attacks. In other words, although these forces would learn about the terrain and other logistical matters in each other's country, the aim of the exercises was not to train them to fight together in a battlefield. Rather, the exercises were intended to train commanders and staff in achieving coordination for various military operations. They also would train joint units to implement fighting defense operations, test the proficiency of the communications system, and assess the effectiveness of backup fighting methods. Such annual exercises are meant to prepare the forces of the six countries for participation in a GCC rapid deployment force once it actually comes into existence. According to the Kuwaiti Force commander Brigadier Riyadh al-Salih, the idea behind forming such a force was basically to create "a striking force to deter any designs to interfere in the GCC states' internal affairs."[16]

Despite the great secrecy surrounding the results of the fifth summit meeting, it would seem that the tanker war and the Saudi-Iranian dogfight in the air during the previous spring did indeed lead to more GCC decisions about security. Reportedly, Secretary General Bisharah (who was reappointed secretary general for another three-year term at this summit meeting) said that the GCC "for the first time formed a unified military force," through which the member countries would defend the region "against any foreign aggression and those intending to meddle with the region's internal security."[17] Shaykh Sabah al-Ahmad al-Jabir, deputy prime minister and minister of foreign affairs and minister of information of Kuwait, said that this force "will be a joint force of all the Arab countries of the Gulf, will have a combined leadership and will exist for a fixed period after which its existence will be reviewed." He added that the force would be formed from the GCC countries "and it is a force which is ready for any emergency in any Gulf country jointly with the forces of the country under aggression."[18]

The issue of a collective internal security agreement apparently was not taken up at this summit meeting, but from the statements quoted above it appears that the GCC leaders decided to form a unified force that could be used for internal as well as external security purposes. If so, the two major internal security problems that occurred in the GCC area did not occasion the deployment of such a force because it did not yet exist. The two terrorist acts that took place in Kuwait, the attempted assassination of the amir on 25 May 1985 and the twin explosions in Kuwait on 11 July 1985, both happened after the summit meeting in Kuwait.

This brings us to the fourth, and the last, phase of the impact of the Iraq-Iran war on defense cooperation among the GCC states. Two major developments marked this phase. First, in August 1985 Iraq escalated its attack on the Kharg Island oil terminal, and in retaliation Iran, on 6 September, escalated its stoppage, search, and sometimes seizure of vessels suspected of carrying arms and other supplies destined for Iraq. This strategy affected the ships of all countries so suspected, including those of the GCC states. Because Kuwait had been providing logistical support for Iraqi war efforts, Kuwaiti ships and other vessels destined for Kuwait were the natural targets of the Iranian retaliation. For example, the Iranian navy detained in September the container ship *Al-Watiyah*, which was owned by the United Arab Navigation Company and sailed under the Kuwaiti flag, near the Strait of Hormuz. Although Kuwait described the Iranian act as "a flagrant violation of all international norms and conventions," Western and Japanese sources considered such Iranian acts as "pretty correct" and compatible with "the rules of war."[19]

The second development was Iran's launching of a successful surprise offensive against Iraq on 9 February 1986. The Iranian forces, which for months had distracted Iraqi attention by nibbling at sectors of the war front to the north and east of Basra, suddenly hit the far-south sector by crossing the Shatt al-Arab and capturing the Iraqi oil port of Fao. Only fifty miles away lay Iran's main target, the highway linking Basra to Kuwait and the Gulf. Never before had an Iranian battlefield success shaken up the GCC states so badly. Although Saddam Hussein said that the Iranian bridgehead in the Fao Peninsula must be eliminated "at all costs," 30,000 Iranian troops had managed to defy the Iraqi efforts to dislodge them by the end of the first five years of the GCC's existence.

Like the terrorist acts in Kuwait, both these two developments in the war goaded the GCC states further toward defense cooperation. This is exactly why security became the overriding issue during the sixth summit meeting held in Muscat from 3 to 6 November 1985. The final communiqué of the summit meeting reaffirmed the United Nations resolutions on the freedom of navigation in the Gulf. More important, it also affirmed that any act of terrorism would be regarded as "a threat to all the GCC countries because the security of the GCC countries is indivisible" (D105).

With respect to the protection of freedom of navigation, apparent progress was made immediately after the sixth summit meeting. According to the Kuwaiti *Al-Qabas*, a specific navigational route had been defined for vessels, especially oil tankers. The GCC countries would take turns in monitoring their passage along this route, named "the leopard line" (*khatt al-fahd*). The monitoring would be done by helicopters in constant contact with their onshore bases.[20] If such monitoring did in fact take place, it was not possible to assess its effectiveness before the sixth anniversary of the GCC. By then Iran had stopped, searched, or seized more than 150 vessels. It also seemed to have every intention to continue to intercept ships of any flag that were suspected of carrying arms or other strategic materials to the coast of the GCC states.

In so far as the Iranian capture of Fao was concerned, Kuwait felt the greatest threat among the GCC states. Its close proximity to the war front, especially after the creation of the Iranian bridgehead on the Fao Peninsula, exposed it to potential Iranian military operations. Subsequent events demonstrated Kuwait's increased vulnerability. In March 1986 the defense minister of Kuwait told the Internal Affairs and Defense Committee of the Kuwaiti Assembly "about the Iranian helicopters which intercepted the Kuwaiti military vessel south of Kubbar Island inside Kuwaiti territorial waters."[21] He also told the committee that an Iranian civilian aircraft had approached some prohibited military locations, but apparently after being warned by the Kuwaiti air force pilots it had changed its course to Kuwait International Airport.

War and Military Buildup

The Iraq-Iran war acted as the primary catalyst for strengthening the GCC's defense and deterrence capability. The GCC leaders realized that the goal of defense cooperation would be unrealizable as long as military weakness was the lot of their countries. On paper the potential of the six in building up their military strength seemed quite impressive, especially in terms of their sheer financial prowess. As the richest small group of nations in the world, the GCC countries' defense budget amounted to around $40 billion a year, that is, about half the entire developing world's defense spending. The combined air power of the six also seemed impressive on paper; it included some 350 fighter aircraft and about 300 helicopters (see App. A, table 4).

Without implying that the military buildup by the smaller GCC states had no significance, it was the strength of Saudi Arabia that was pivotal to the whole idea of creating an integrated regional defense system. Saudi Arabia's military modernization began in the 1940s and 1950s. Nevertheless, before the revolution Iranian air power controlled the Gulf skies, just as the Iranian navy commanded the sea lanes in Gulf waters. Although Washington talked about Iran and Saudi Arabia as the "twin pillars" of Gulf security, in practice it was the shah's Iran that provided air protection for all the Gulf states, including Saudi Arabia.

By the time of the Iranian Revolution, however, the Saudis had begun to acquire the sophisticated F-15 interceptors. The purchase of these fighters was the outgrowth of Saudi Arabia's longtime military modernization efforts, not the eruption of the Iranian Revolution in 1978. While the shah was still in power, the strengthening of Saudi air power was viewed by the United States and Saudi Arabia in terms of Gulf security. But Israel and its supporters in Congress worried about the F-15's offensive capability, and the Saudis had to agree not to buy bomb racks or external fuel tanks in order to overcome the Israeli and pro-Israeli objections. They bought sixty F-15 interceptors before the outbreak of the Iraq-Iran war.

The war had a decisive effect on Saudi determination to acquire the most sophisticated air defense system that money could buy. The longtime Saudi awareness of its physical vulnerability increased as Iran and Iraq struck each other's oil facilities. The vital Saudi oil terminals at Ras Tanura and Jaymah, which handled more than 90 percent of the Saudi crude oil exports, could be reached by Iranian jets from the Iranian bases at Bushehr and Shiraz within sixteen minutes. Given Saudi Arabia's vast and exposed territory, air security for the kingdom had always been a major concern, as, for example, when the South Yemen air force struck at Saudi targets in 1973. But now it was no longer a matter of mere concern, it was an absolute necessity which impelled the Saudis to undertake an unprecedented military buildup for themselves and their junior GCC partners.

The Saudis accepted the deployment of four American Airborne Warning and Control System (AWACS) planes in their territory immediately after the outbreak of the war in September 1980 as a stopgap measure until they could create their own defense and deterrence capability. Then, miffed by the American sale conditions of the F-15s, the Saudis sought to enhance their capability by what finally emerged, after United States Senate approval on 28 October 1981, as the Air Defense Enhancement Package. By the time the war broke out, the F-15s were in Saudi possession, but the purchase of five AWACS in 1981 for later delivery was aimed at enhancing the Saudi military even further by combining the two systems.

The tanker war spurred the Saudi military buildup still further. Saudi Arabia asked the United States for emergency shipment of Stingers in May 1984, and over the Memorial Day weekend the Reagan administration supplied 400 shoulder-fired Stinger missiles and 200 launchers. Washington supplied the Stingers because, according to American military experts, it "is good against helicopters, . . . precisely the reason we think it is important for them [the Saudis] to have that capability in those coastal areas that are in range of the large number of attack helicopters the Iranians have. They have tremendous capability in that area."[22]

Toward an Integrated Defense System?

Although the Iraq-Iran war acted as the primary catalyst of defense cooperation among the GCC states during the first five years of the organization's existence, the GCC framework facilitated the development of a degree of consensus among the leaders of the six states on several principles and issues. The principle of indivisibility of the security of the six nations seemed to be accepted, as was the principle of collective self-reliance, that is, that the security of the Gulf region must be maintained by the littoral states.

The GCC leaders also reached agreement on a number of other issues: They agreed to create a joint command for a GCC Rapid Deployment Force (RDF), consisting of two brigades stationed at Hafr al-Batin in Saudi Arabia under the command of a Saudi officer. They began to assist Bahrain and Oman in building up their military strength. They held two Peninsula Shield exercises, which helped the ground forces of the six countries to learn about a variety of weapon systems and different terrains. They recognized the all-important need to create an integrated air defense system, especially after the AWACS aircraft demonstrated its capability during the Saudi-Iran aerial dogfight.

At the same time, however, there were numerous constraints on creating a common defense system. The RDF, for example, existed only in theory. It had only a headquarters staff at Hafr al-Batin without actual brigades on the ground as long as there was no emergency. Moreover, its mission seemed to be viewed differently by different GCC leaders and officials. Was it intended to become a counterinsurgency force permitted to intervene in any GCC country in an emergency situation or a common defensive force against external aggression, or both? In any case, in what kind of contingencies would the force be deployed, and against whom?

Another kind of constraint related to the role of the AWACS aircraft in an integrated air defense system. Only Saudi Arabia was attempting to own and operate the AWACS system. After the Saudi-Iranian aerial dogfight, the United States allowed the Saudis to share AWACS-based data with Kuwait on a more regular basis. But what about the other GCC states? Other than the Saudis, and to a much more limited extent the Kuwaitis, the GCC states depend exclusively on ground radar, which gives only two minutes' advance warning of an attack by low-flying aircraft. Will the UAE and Kuwait eventually acquire AWACS capability since the GCC leaders seem to agree that the air forces of the three countries constitute the core air defense of the GCC states?

The lists of constraints on creating a common GCC defense system can be easily extended, especially if societal and political as well as military impediments are considered. In fact, more serious than such military constraints as the diversity of weapons systems and military training are sociopolitical obstacles. In addition to the well-known problem of paucity of manpower, we have already mentioned in chapter 2 the large numbers of expatriates in the GCC societies, including some in the GCC armed forces such as those of Oman. Efforts to realize the goal of Saudization, Omanization, or "indigenization" of the military forces in the GCC states in general obviously will run into such societal problems. Furthermore, the process of sociopolitical alienation, partly because of the problem of demographic rejuvenation and partly because of the unsatisfied social and political aspirations discussed in chapter 2, will raise questions about the reliability of the armed forces. The collapse of the oil revenues in recent years may well be reversed in the 1990s, but before then its impact on military purchases may also pose unexpected problems.

Perhaps the key question is how durable will be the GCC efforts aimed at creating a credible defense and deterrence system. There is hardly any doubt that during the first five years of the GCC's history, the Iraq-Iran war acted as the primary engine of defense cooperation among the six. What will happen after the war when the common perception of the threat of the spread of war no longer exists? Will revolutionary Iran continue to be considered the paramount threat, or will Iraq also be perceived as a menace to the GCC states? In other words, who will be the enemy or enemies against which the GCC states will seek to create a common defense system? The same question may be raised about the durability of postwar GCC efforts aimed at economic integration and diplomatic coordination among the six.

Notes

1. *FBIS-MEA-V-81-102*, 28 May 1981.
2. *FBIS-MEA-V-81-218*, 12 Nov. 1981.
3. *FBIS-MEA-V-82-017*, 7 Jan. 1982.
4. Ibid.
5. Ibid.
6. *FBIS-MEA-V-82-106*, 2 June 1982.
7. *FBIS-MEA-V-83-116*, 15 June 1983.
8. *FBIS-MEA-V-84-026*, 7 Feb. 1984.
9. *FBIS-MEA-V-84-122*, 22 June 1984.
10. *FBIS-MEA-V-84-178*, 12 Sept. 1984.
11. *FBIS-MEA-V-84-184*, 20 Sept. 1984.
12. *FBIS-MEA-V-84-185*, 21 Sept. 1984.
13. *FBIS-MEA-V-84-196*, 9 Oct. 1984.
14. *FBIS-MEA-V-84-216*, 6 Nov. 1984.
15. *FBIS-MEA-V-84-205*, 22 Oct. 1984.
16. *FBIS-MEA-V-84-202*, 17 Oct. 1984.
17. *FBIS-MEA-V-84-242*, 14 Dec. 1984.
18. *FBIS-MEA-V-84-232*, 30 Nov. 1984.
19. *Washington Post*, 11 Nov. 1985.
20. *FBIS-MEA-V-85-220*, 14 Nov. 1985.
21. *FBIS-MEA-V-86-044*, 6 March 1986.
22. U.S. Congress, *Developments in the Persian Gulf, June 1984*, Hearing before the Subcommittee on Europe and the Middle East of the Committee on Foreign Affairs, House of Representatives (Washington, D.C.: U.S. Government Printing Office, 1984), pp. 31–32.

Documents

Document 36
Interview with Sultan Qabus of Oman
1 May 1982

[Excerpts] [Question] Talk about the military facilities given to the United States in the Sultanate of Oman has become a rich topic in the Arab and foreign press and a subject of comment and analysis. What is the truth about this subject?

[Answer] In fact, we must make clear that the question of facilities has been overblown and given different interpretations. Some have even gone as far as saying they are bases in the guise of facilities. This is unthinkable from the outset, and we refuse to discuss it in any way. However, because of the conditions created in the world, and our area in particular, it was necessary to have some kind of understanding between us and our friends, without specifying a particular state. Also, while the United States is on one side of the international scale, it has become necessary for the area that there be a balance because the opposite side has become heavy and the Eastern camp's presence has become large, whether in the sea or the ocean, particular in South Yemen and Ethiopia as well as in Afghanistan in the north, which is only 300 nautical miles from here. As for the U.S. naval presence, Oman has nothing to do with it—it is in the Indian Ocean and not under the sovereignty of a particular state.

It is in our interest that there be an understanding with the other superpower, because in the case of extreme necessity, God forbid, the area will need the United States. Therefore, there must be arrangements facilitating the rendering of U.S. aid.

The United States is prepared to develop our airfields and ports. It would be of no avail to lose such an opportunity to develop the facilities. As for the use of such facilities for anything, this will be by our request. On this basis, the sultanate has welcomed giving facilities to the United States. That is all there is to it. However, there has been a big hullabaloo. This uproar was expected, because any U.S. aid, whether military or economic, must pass through Congress, where there will be a reaction that will be reported in the media. Should there be an intrinsic power in the area through which we can confront any potential danger ourselves, then the need to seek U.S. help will end.

[Question] Doesn't the sultanate's stand with regard to

U.S. military facilities run contrary to the foreign policy agreed upon in the GCC?

[Answer] This question can be answered briefly. Before this council came into being, its six member states had their own individual policies and relations with other countries. Oman's relations with any country existed before the council was established. There are no bases or commitments involved in these relations that jeopardize Oman's sovereignty or the sovereignty of the area, because this is out of the question. What we have arranged with the United States is an understanding as a precaution against certain exigencies. In any case, there are different trends in the GCC, but these are differences in interpretation, not opposition. I believe the time will come when, as a result of experience and interpretations, there will be a unified foreign policy stemming from all trends and it will be possible to reach a middle ground acceptable to all and satisfactory to the desires of the peoples of the area. When I, in Oman, feel my people want a particular course, then I will pursue it. If I notice my people do not desire such a course, then I will avoid it.

[Question] It is being said the facilities given to the United States have indirectly strengthened the Soviet position in Aden, and that the ultimate result will be to involve the area in the conflict between the United States and the Soviet Union.

[Answer] I must reject such talk, because the U.S., or rather the Western, presence in the Indian Ocean and the surrounding area is in order to create some kind of balance with the Soviet presence. It must be said we have nothing to do with the U.S. presence in the Indian Ocean. It must also be said there is not only a U.S. presence in the Indian Ocean but a Western presence in general. Even Australia has a presence. The question is: Why? In fact, all this has come about because the Soviet presence in the area has become so substantial that the Europeans cannot ignore it. The Western presence is a result of the Soviet presence, which necessitated a Western presence in order to strike a balance.

[Question] From time to time we hear about efforts to mediate between the Sultanate of Oman and South Yemen. Do you believe some kind of political rapprochement can be achieved between the two countries, and on what basis should this rapprochement be, if at all?

[Answer] Plainly, the matter concerns the principle of interference in the affairs of others. We reject this interference and always say that any relations between Oman and any foreign state must be on the basis of noninterference, noninterference in internal affairs, mutual respect and equality. There is nothing between us and our brothers—and I say brothers--the Yemeni people. All problems and disputes are with the PDRY leaders, who are still interfering in other people's affairs and importing and training saboteurs and inculcating in them their ideologies and beliefs. I believe there will be no more disputes between us when they stop doing this.

[Question] What is your answer to South Yemeni President Ali Nasir Muhammad's recent press statement that Oman is trying to drag the GCC states into a confrontation with South Yemen?

[Answer] The Sultanate of Oman has not sought and will not seek to drag anybody into confrontation with anybody else. Our principles are sound throughout, but at the same time we must be cautious and ready to repel any aggression. Of course, we will not attack anybody. Oman will not drag any sisterly country into aggression or confrontation. If Oman is attacked we expect our brothers to support us. In the event of an attack on a Gulf State, we will help this state. We mean what we say. I believe all their attempts in Aden aim at one particular thing: preventing any military, defense or security understanding among the GCC states. Such understanding is fundamental and important because we cannot preserve security and stability and protect all that God has bestowed upon us without strength. The world today respects only the strong. I thank God the GCC states are well aware of their interests.

[Question] There have been calls by some Gulf officials for the establishment of diplomatic relations with the Soviet Union and East European countries. What is your view on such calls?

[Answer] We have not received an official invitation in this regard. We have heard talk about the trend to be more open toward the Eastern bloc, but the idea has never been proposed officially, neither at the GCC nor at the GCC Ministerial Council. It has not been put forward, not even as an idea or anything of this sort.

[Question] Do you have any particular views regarding the efforts being made to stop the Iraq-Iran war? What is the truth about the Sultanate of Oman's role in the purchase of military spare parts for Iraq from Egypt?

[Answer] Whenever there is an opportunity, the Sultanate of Oman always loves to contribute to any good efforts. We are in favor of any effort by any Arab, Islamic or non-aligned state to try to resolve a problem between two Muslim neighbors, uphold right and stop bloodshed among Muslims. We are prepared to make any efforts to this end. As for being a go-between in the purchase of weapons for Iraq, we do not hesitate in rendering a service to any Arab state when we are asked to do so.

[Question] There are questions about the ultimate aim of the GCC. Will it lead to the establishment of political unity among the member states or will it lead to a confederation or what?

[Answer] This question has not been brought up yet. The GCC is still in its infancy and feeling its way. It has taken big strides in certain aspects. As for the question of integration, we must not rush things, so that when integration comes it will be on a firm and solid basis and stem from the people's desire. We would like this to happen exactly as it happened with the birth of the GCC—in response to a need and to the desires of the people of the region. This will come with evolution, and the time will come when the GCC states will decide the best formula for integration and unity desired by the members. It would be premature to discuss details now. Moreover, the GCC has not yet completed 1 year. In any case, we are one people in the area.

[Question] You recently set up a consultative council that advises the government on matters of development plans and the sultanate's foreign relations. Do you intend to develop this political experiment so council members are elected rather than appointed, as is the case now?

[Answer] This is a first step toward people's participation in government. We have begun with what is of interest to the citizen in his daily life. As for taking further steps, this will be done at the appropriate time. I must stress that every step we take must stem from our heritage. We will not import ideas and beliefs from abroad but will seek what is beneficial from those who are ahead of us in this field. We will take what is good and leave what is not good.

Source: *Al-Majallah* (London), 1–7 May 1982, pp. 12–17, as translated in *FBIS-MEA-V–82–089*, 7 May 1982, pp. C2-C4.

Document 37

Interview with Lieutenant General Shaykh Khalifah ibn Zayid Al-Nuhayyan, Deputy Commander in Chief of the UAE Armed Forces

24 October 1983

[Excerpt] [Al-Muhanna] Some observers have interpreted the holding of the "Peninsula Shield" maneuvers at this time as a direct response to Iranian threats to close the Strait of Hormuz. What is your comment on this?

[Al Nuhayyan] The idea of creating a unified defense system for the GCC was not born in the past few weeks. Indeed, it has been the subject of long studies since the GCC was established, and its aim is to pool the real sources of strength of the Arab Gulf states in accordance with a strategy that ensures the maintenance of peace and defense of the people and the land. The "Peninsula Shield" maneuvers are a step toward the realization of this strategy and have absolutely nothing to do with current developments in the area.

With regard to the threats to close the Strait of Hormuz, the policy proclaimed by the GCC states and to which they adhere is the rejection of any military intervention by the big powers in the area. There is no doubt that the threats to close this waterway will give the powers that are eager to intervene in the area the opportunity to realize their dreams and to spread their influence—something that will have serious consequences for the security of the area and will threaten stability in it. For this reason we sincerely appeal to all sides to realize the facts of international conflict in the area and the dangers involved.

Closing the Strait of Hormuz will not benefit any party in the region. Moreover, it is an international waterway that should remain navigable and open to international shipping. We do all we can within the GCC framework to ease tension in this area and to strengthen regional peace. We hope that the parties concerned will change their stands for the sake of their own interest and the common interest.

We believe that it is our duty in this part of the world to contribute to world prosperity without making threats. This can be achieved only through the continued flow of vital oil supplies through the Strait of Hormuz, which has been kept open for thousands of years. This underlines the need for the world community to intensify its efforts to stop the Iraq-Iran war. We hope that the combatant parties will respond to those efforts in order to overcome the causes that led to this war.

[Al-Muhanna] The GCC has asserted its rejection of military alliances and axes. It has also affirmed that it is not a bloc against any party. In the present circumstances of heightened conflict the situation calls for more military cooperation and defense coordination. How far have efforts toward this end been made, and will military cooperation culminate into the establishment of a unified military force to defend the Gulf?

[Al Nuhayyan] The GCC's achievements in the short time since it was established are reassuring, because it was established on a firm basis and not as a result of an emotional outburst. The GCC is the realization of an existing reality whose elements are derived from a nature, common history, religion, and language that bind the people of the area together.

In fact what has been achieved in the past 2 years in laying the foundation of Gulf cooperation is tremendous; but this has been carried out quietly and with the help of thorough research and studied steps, and the results of it all have become evident in all fields. Steps toward military cooperation will continue to be taken in accordance with the study plans, whose ultimate aim is to establish a joint military command.

During the next month there will be joint air maneuvers by Saudi Arabia and Kuwait as a first stage, and joint air maneuvers by Oman and the UAE as a second stage.

Source: *Ukaz* (Jidda), 24 Oct. 1983, p. 6, as translated in *FBIS-MEA-V-83-210*, 28 Oct. 1983, pp. C5-C6.

Document 38

GCC Ministerial Council: Fourth Emergency Session Statement

17 May 1984

The GCC Ministerial Council held an extraordinary meeting today, Thursday, 16 Shaban 1404 of the Hegira corresponding to 17 May 1984 at the headquarters of the GCC's Secretariat in Riyadh and reviewed the recent developments in the area relating to the Iranian attacks against navigation from and to the ports of the GCC member countries consisting of the shelling of the Kuwaiti oil tanker *Umm Casbah* on 13 May 1984, the Kuwaiti oil tanker *Bahrah* on 14 May 1984, and the Saudi oil tanker *Yanbu* [*Pride*] on 16 May 1984. They also reviewed the threats these aggressions pose to the vital interests of the GCC member countries and the violation of international law and the UN Charter they entail, as well as their infringement on the Law of the Sea and the heightened tension in the area they cause.

The Ministerial Council recalled the decision taken by the Supreme Council considering any aggression of any member country as an aggression on them all. In line with the stand, the Council expressed its denunciation of these attacks.

The council also decided to submit the matter to an emergency meeting to be held by the Arab League in order to adopt a unified Arab stand. The council also decided to submit the matter to the UN Security Council in view of the threats these aggressions pose to international peace and security.

Source: *FBIS-MEA-V-84-097*, 17 May 1984, p. C1.

Document 39

Interview with Kuwaiti Minister of State for Cabinet Affairs, Abd al-Aziz Husayn

25 May 1984

Al-Hawadith: Kuwait recently carried out civil defense exercises. Can Kuwait face a foreign attack? In other words, would it, in the event of a foreign attack, rely solely on its Armed Forces, seek help from the GCC forces, or let Arab or foreign forces take part in repulsing such an attack?

Husayn: We in Kuwait have been giving civil defense the attention it deserves. One of the reasons for that is perhaps the fact that at the beginning of the war we suffered some damage because of our proximity to Iran and Iraq. Kuwait City is a big city and civil defense is therefore of special importance. We are building our Army. It is one of the good, small armies in the region. We do not expect war from one direction or another but we are building our army because it is a symbol of legality and sovereignty. We are always proud of our Army and its men and officers because, as I have said, it epitomizes the country's independence and unity, just like the country's flag. At the same time we have special relations with the GCC. We have carried out successful joint air and other exercises and we consider any aggression against any GCC member state to be aggression against all member states, and this is more reassuring to us.

Al-Hawadith: Some Western observers claim that the Gulf states, while outwardly distancing themselves from the United States, are actually willing to accept U.S. military assistance in repulsing foreign aggression. What is your comment?

Husayn: I can only speak for Kuwait. Here in Kuwait we have always held the view that the presence of superpower forces in the Gulf is tantamount to an open invitation to other forces to come in, which would turn the Gulf into a zone of superpower conflict. That is why we are against any superpower military presence in the Gulf.

Al-Hawadith: Why has Kuwait not yet signed the GCC's general security agreement, and what precisely are the articles to which Kuwait objects?

Husayn: A security defense draft agreement has been submitted to the GCC. Kuwait, taking into consideration its own Constitution and laws, decided that this agreement cannot be implemented in Kuwait because of the current laws in our country. When Kuwait conveyed this view to its brothers in the GCC they welcomed it and they showed understanding. It was agreed to reconsider the agreement with a view to harmonizing it with the laws of all the Gulf states.

Al-Hawadith: How would you describe Kuwaiti-Iranian relations at present, and what is Kuwait's attitude toward Iran's continuous media campaign against the Gulf and its regimes?

Husayn: There are relations between Iran and Kuwait. There is diplomatic representation between the two countries. Iran's continuous radio, television, and press campaign against Kuwait is perhaps an infringement of international courtesy, but Kuwait's policy is not to respond to these media campaigns. We avoid doing that with Iran and others because we are sure of ourselves and we believe in the political line we are following. We wish Iran would refrain from such campaigns against Kuwait. Otherwise, the relations between the two countries are normal.

Al-Hawadith: Do you believe that the amir of Kuwait will uphold the death sentence passed on those found guilty in the case of the recent explosions?

Husayn: Only his highness the amir has the power to commute this sentence, which is regarded in Kuwait and the Arab countries as a well studied sentence passed in accordance with the Constitution and current laws, and supported by documented evidence.

Al-Hawadith: Has the explosions incident led to restrictions on the [non-Kuwaiti] Arabs residing in Kuwait, and if so to what extent and why?

Husayn: The explosions that occurred in Kuwait were a surprise to us. Perhaps the stability, freedom, and our good relations with all Arab states without exception had led us to relax our security measures. When the explosions occurred we tackled the matter openly without hiding anything from the pubic or the world at large. We only tightened the noose around the suspects. Not more than 200 Arab residents of Kuwait were asked to leave Kuwait. The Arab residents constitute half the population of Kuwait and they live in peace, love, and harmony with their Kuwaiti brothers. In fact, the Arab brothers in Kuwait were even more upset than the Kuwaitis by the explosions. Each one of them was worried that one of the culprits might have been one of his own fellow countrymen. There is a common interest in the continued residence of these Arabs in Kuwait. They are working, and Kuwait wants them to stay. They were not forced on Kuwait. They are needed here because they are building Kuwait with us. They are welcome here. None of them has felt that he is being restricted in any way. Naturally, when the explosions occurred some security measures regarding movement, travel, and entry were introduced. Without these measures we would not have been able to arrest the entire gang which planted the explosions.

Al-Hawadith: Let us talk about Egypt's return to the Arab fold. Why, in your opinion, has Egypt's return to the Arab League been delayed? It has been claimed that the Gulf states are opposed to such a move.

Husayn: Egypt is a part of the Arab nation. There can be no doubt about that. The disagreement was over Camp David, which took us all by surprise. The Arabs agreed in Baghdad to exclude Egypt from the Arab League. In Baghdad we did not say that Egypt was no longer Arab. On the contrary, there were recommendations hailing the Egyptian people and welcoming cooperation with them. The boycott decision was a decision against As-Sadat's regime at the time. In Kuwait we believe that since that decision was taken by an Arab summit conference it is up to another summit conference to reconsider the matter and adopt a different decision on it. The circumstances in Egypt have changed and it may be appropriate that a new summit conference should be held to study this matter thoroughly.

Source: *Al-Hawadith* (London), 25 May 1984, pp. 28–29, as translated in *FBIS-MEA-V–84–106*, 31 May 1984, pp. C3-C4.

Document 40

Speech by Bahraini Foreign Minister Muhammad ibn Mubarak Al-Khalifah to the United Nations Security Council

29 May 1984

May I congratulate you for assuming the chairmanship of the council this month and praise the experience and efficiency which we have witnessed in you, wishing you all the success in your supreme task. On this occasion, I would like to praise the positive stance of your country, the Soviet Union, on the Arab issues. The issue which is raised by the six member countries of the GCC can be summed up by saying that there is a threat to the freedom of international navigation in the Gulf caused by Iran's flagrant and firm aggression against the four Saudi and Kuwaiti tankers—*Al-Ahud, Yanbu Pride, Umm Qasbah,* and *Bahrah*—during the 7–16 May period. This is a glaring violation of international law and freedom of navigation and trade from and to the ports of the Gulf countries. Bahrain adheres to its firm policy on ending this war, which has brought numerous disasters to the warring countries and which is aggravating daily. We have always desired for our region to remain a region of peace, neighborliness, and permanent stability. We have always shown our desire to purify the atmosphere with our neighbor, Iran, but it has adopted numerous stances which are full of fabrication and harm. The most recent of these is the expansion of the fighting instead of responding to the peace efforts which are based on law, legitimacy, each country's sovereignty on its own territories, implementation of the principle of noninterference in the domestic affairs of other countries, and keeping the region removed from the international conflicts. We have repeatedly warned against the continuation of this war, the seriousness of its expansion, and the threat to international peace and security. It has been proved that this war is wasting the human and financial energies of the two warring countries in vain and that its continuation does not only threaten the security and interests of the Gulf countries, it also threatens all the countries in the world.

As my country is one of the six GCC countries which are threatened by the continuation of this serious situation, we demand that the esteemed Security Council adopt the necessary quick and effective measures to stop this aggression and put an end to the Iran-Iraq war, the continuation of which augurs the explosion of the situation in the Gulf and the Middle East region. We demand the adoption of the draft plan presented to the esteemed council by Bahrain, the UAE, the Kingdom of Saudi Arabia, the Sultanate of Oman, Qatar, and Kuwait.

Source: *Akhbar Al-Khalij* (Manama), 30 May 1984, p. 3, as translated in *FBIS-MEA-V–84–106*, 31 May 1984, pp. C1-C2.

Document 41

GCC Resolution on Gulf Tanker War Submitted to the United Nations Security Council

31 May 1984

The Security Council

1. Reaffirms the right of free navigation in international water and sea lanes for shipping en route to and from all ports and installations of the littoral states that are not party to the hostilities;

2. Calls upon all states to respect the territorial integrity of the states that are not party to the hostilities and to exercise the utmost restraint and to refrain from any act which may lead to a further escalation and widening of the conflict;

3. Condemns these recent attacks on commercial ships en route to and from the ports of Kuwait and Saudi Arabia;

4. Demands that such attacks cease forthwith and that there be no interference with ships en route to and from states that are not party to the hostilities;

5. Decides, in the event of non-compliance with this resolution, to meet again to consider effective measures commensurate with the gravity of the situation in order to ensure the freedom of navigation in the area;

6. Requests the secretary-general to report on the progress of the implementation of this resolution;

7. Decides to remain seized of the matter.

Source: *FBIS-MEA-V–84–106*, 31 May 1984, p. C1.

Document 42

Interview with Kuwait's Deputy Prime Minister and Foreign Minister Shaykh Sabah al-Ahmad al-Jabir Al-Sabah

15 June 1984

[Dirgham] The Iraqi-Iranian war has been separated from the problem of the attacks on oil tankers. What will this separation, which you have advocated, achieve?

[Al-Sabah] First of all we are not a party to the Iraqi-Iranian war, so why should our problem be linked to it? We have separated the two issues because, where we are concerned, aggression has been committed against states not party to the Iraqi-Iranian conflict.

[Dirgham] But Iraq and Iran resent that separation for different reasons. Let us talk about Iraq, for example.

[Al-Sabah] I do not believe there is Iraqi resentment so much as Iraqi support.

[Dirgham] Iraqi statements say the war with Iran cannot be separated from the attacks on tankers.

[Al-Sabah] Both Iraq and Iran are in a state of war. We are not. That is why the attacks on oil tankers in international waters or territorial waters are attacks on the sovereignty of states not parties to the conflict.

[Dirgham] Your position on the separation of the two issues is strongly supported by the UN Security Council, that is, by all the big powers and most of the nonaligned states. What effect do you think this support will have, bearing in mind that Iran has rejected the resolution, thus refusing to separate the two issues?

[Al-Sabah] I see this support as an indication of respect

from world public opinion because these states represent world public opinion. All we want from these states is to listen to the voice of justice. Our states are not involved in the war, so why should our tankers be attacked? The attack on tankers is tantamount to attack on land installations. Our aim was to get this international support. It does not matter if 2 of the 15 member states express reservations. Each state has its own circumstances. We are very pleased with the international understanding of our cause.

[Dirgham] You have said you will treat other states according to their attitude toward your cause. What do you mean by that?

[Al-Sabah] It is not a threat. All states draw up their policies in light of the attitudes of other states toward them. This is natural among states. It is not condemned.

[Dirgham] The Soviet Union has very strongly supported your cause.

[Al-Sabah] All states appreciate the Soviets.

[Dirgham] There is an impression of an improvement in relations between the Soviet Union and the GCC states. Is that impression correct?

[Al-Sabah] I do not say it is correct or incorrect. This Soviet attitude, however, will bring the Soviet Union closer to being accepted in some GCC states.

[Dirgham] Let us go back to the tanker war and let us talk about the chances of containing the oil war. Iran's excuse is its oil is threatened because of the Iraqi attacks on Iranian oil installations; so it takes its revenge. Are there any attempts to contain the Iranian excuse itself?

[Al-Sabah] Resolution 540 tells the warring parties they should not attack each other's installations. That gives the two sides the right to export their oil. Regrettably, Iran has rejected that resolution. It has no right to wreak vengeance on states which are not parties to the Iraqi-Iranian conflict.

[Dirgham] Do you believe Iran has a right to defend its economic interests, including its oil interests? Is there a way to influence Iraq and persuade it to stop attacking Iranian oil installations?

[Al-Sabah] Is revenge by Iran on states not involved in the war the answer?

[Dirgham] I am not trying to link revenge to the defense of interests. I am just trying to find out why the tanker war broke out.

[Al-Sabah] Please do not associate our issue with the other one. I do hope a comprehensive solution can be found giving both sides the right to export their oil and guaranteeing freedom of shipping. I hope a solution can be found for this devastating war which has been raging for 4 years. We would be happy to see such a solution sought urgently.

[Dirgham] You have made efforts—you have personally pioneered these efforts—to reconcile Iraq and Syria in an attempt to have the Iraqi pipeline across Syria reopened.

[Al-Sabah] We have tried indeed. We are still trying and I hope we succeed on this score.

[Dirgham] What has become of the projects aimed at securing Iraq's oil exports through new pipelines across Saudi Arabia and Jordan?

[Al-Sabah] There are no projects, just contacts. The contacts some Arab states are holding with Syria and Iraq are geared toward overcoming the differences and ending the estrangement between the two states. I hope we succeed. The dispute is not a simple one. Circumstances should compel both sides to settle their differences and let amity replace estrangement.

[Dirgham] Do you believe that if Iraq's oil exports were secure it would not have to tighten the economic noose around Iran's neck and that subsequently Iran would stop wreaking vengeance on the tankers going to and leaving the Gulf states?

[Al-Sabah] Before we say "if" we should say: Let the war stop and let there be cooperation among the states on both sides of the Gulf, whether they are Arab or Iranian. What we mean to say is that continuation of the attacks on the oil tankers will only fuel the war. The interests of both sides can only be served if the war ends.

[Dirgham] You hope, naturally, but do you expect the war to end?

[Al-Sabah] Everyone hopes. As for my own expectations, I just hope that the war will not continue, particularly because there are international efforts to find a formula for ending the war. You will of course ask: What is this formula? I can only say this matter has been discussed with the permanent members of the UN Security Council. The current thinking is that something should be done. It is now up to the Security Council and what it can do, in view of the importance of this war issue to the member states.

[Dirgham] So we should expect the Security Council to embark on a new move regarding the Iraqi-Iranian war?

[Al-Sabah] That is what I believe.

[Dirgham] Are there any indications Iran is willing to cooperate with the Security Council?

[Al-Sabah] We wish Iran were willing to negotiate and show tolerance. The other brothers have already expressed a readiness to do whatever is required of them internationally or regionally. I wish and hope Iran would express the same feelings so the attempt to solve this problem would be collective.

[Dirgham] Do you support the theory that pressure should be brought to bear on both Iran and Iraq?

[Al-Sabah] How can I influence them if they do not listen? One side does not listen. Iraq has not laid down any conditions. It was asked to stop the war and it agreed, but there are Iranian conditions. It is difficult for Iraq or any other country to accept such conditions. One of these conditions is a change of the country's regime. This is unacceptable because it affects the country's sovereignty. If there is to be change, then it is up to the people to introduce it.

[Dirgham] The attitude of the Gulf states, which did not rush to accept the U.S. offers of direct aid, has been met with praise and satisfaction. Do you share the opinion that the Americans have tried and are trying to get facilities and military bases in the Gulf states?

[Al-Sabah] At any rate, we were not so much seeking praise from other countries as simply implementing our policy, which is that we do not accept intervention and we do not give facilities to any other state, be it Eastern or Western. This, however, does not mean we cannot seek the help of these countries by purchasing arms from all sides. This is our right. As a sovereign state we have a right to purchase the arms we need for self-defense.

[Dirgham] Washington circles say they prefer expansion of the circle of arms sellers to include the West Europeans. This followed what has been said about your request for Stinger missiles. What is your opinion of this American view, and why do you not seek arms from the Europeans?

[Al-Sabah] I have not heard about this personally or officially. The United States could adopt such an attitude, but I have not received anything official. Our arms purchases are not only from the United States. We have purchased and are purchasing arms from France, Britain, the Soviet Union, and other countries.

[Dirgham] Will this be an arms race summer in the region?

[Al-Sabah] I do not think it will reach that point, but every country must defend itself within its own capabilities. That is why I do not call it an arms race. I call it a self-defense race.

[Dirgham] Do you rule out the possibility of inviting direct U.S. assistance?

[Al-Sabah] I rule it out.

[Dirgham] What about the possibility of the Gulf states' providing the facilities sought by the United States if the situation deteriorated and reached crisis point?

[Al-Sabah] What facilities?

[Dirgham] U.S. officials have been quoted as saying direct U.S. assistance to the Gulf states would necessitate permission to use certain bases.

[Al-Sabah] I believe they do not need bases as long as their ships are in the Arab sea. In other words, the aircraft carriers and warships constitute bases for the Americans in the region. The aim of this kind of talk is to confuse. It is some kind of intrigue against the Gulf states. The United States and the Soviet Union are interested in obtaining military facilities, but that does not mean there is pressure on the Gulf states to agree to give facilities to the Americans.

[Dirgham] Is the current military coordination among the GCC states adequate to deal with possible developments if the situation deteriorates further?

[Al-Sabah] I believe we are capable. There is coordination, and it will continue.

[Dirgham] You said you would exercise self-defense through coordination. Are you prepared to retaliate inside Iranian territory if Iran continues to attack your interests or territory, or is self-defense restricted to intercepting the Iranians in the air only?

[Al-Sabah] We have not thought about taking revenge on anyone. We said we will defend ourselves against aggres-

sion. We hate war, and we have no intention of declaring it on anyone. All we ask of others is not to commit aggression against us.

[Dirgham] As a man who knows the region, its peoples, and its regimes well, how do you see Iran now and in the future?

[Al-Sabah] I really do not wish to discuss this because each country is entitled to its own policy. Iran inevitably has its own policy, and one should not interfere with it now or in the future.

[Dirgham] Do you believe the Iranian regime is still trying to export its revolution to neighboring states?

[Al-Sabah] This is regrettable. We had hoped Iran would not harbor such designs, but when we hear the statements coming out of Iran in Friday sermons and statements by Iranian officials, we discover they still harbor this idea of exporting revolution. I believe it is not in Iran's interest to do that because such an attitude makes it an enemy of the people before being an enemy of governments.

[Dirgham] It has been said that by rejecting U.S. aid you have deprived Iran of the excuse of U.S.-Gulf cooperation to turn the region's people against their rulers. Iran claims it is neither pro-East nor pro-West and that its concern is for this region. Do you agree you have deprived Iran of this excuse?

[Al-Sabah] We have not really considered this point. We just pursued our policy and will continue to do so. It is not a question of keeping Iran away or persuading it not to attack us. This is just our policy.

[Dirgham] The Gulf states maintain the situation is serious but some people, especially in the West, are trying to play down the seriousness of the situation. What is the reason for this difference?

[Al-Sabah] Does anyone think that the situation is not serious? Twenty-three percent of the oil comes from the Gulf. What would happen to the European and industrial states if their supply of oil were disrupted? Is this not a serious matter?

[Dirgham] In the meantime, what would you do if Iran continued to attack tankers in the Gulf?

[Al-Sabah] We will first exercise our right of self-defense. Furthermore, we must not forget the Gulf is international, and that is what makes it a serious matter. If Iran tries to block the Strait of Hormuz, it would in fact be giving others the opportunity to intervene.

[Dirgham] It has been said in Washington the Americans will not leave their ships in the region without military cover. Are they entitled to do that or would such a thing lead to a crisis?

[Al-Sabah] I hope it does not come to that—I mean to the point where a warship would accompany every tanker to our ports. If this must happen then let it happen on the open sea in the Gulf. We do not accept it in our territorial waters. We are prepared to protect our ships.

Source: *Al-Hawadith* (London), 15 June 1984, pp. 26–27, as translated in *FBIS-MEA-V–84–117*, 15 June 1984, pp. C1-C3.

Document 43

Interview with Kuwait's Deputy Prime Minister, Foreign, and Information Minister, Shaykh Sabah al-Ahmad al-Sabah

15 June 1984

[Question] There is information Iran will concentrate its future attacks on Kuwait in addition to its troop concentrations on the Iraqi front. Would you say this will escalate the war in a way that will harm the Gulf states, and how would you, as Gulf states in general and Kuwait in particular, reply to an Iranian attack against Kuwait?

[Answer] First, regarding Iran and its attack on Kuwait; this is nothing new because Iran has previously shelled Kuwaiti refineries 2 years ago. We were in New York, as I remember, and held a meeting of the Arab League which concluded with a condemnation, and stopped at that. We have also seen how the explosions that occurred at some Kuwait installations and foreign embassies had links with Iran, but we treated the matter as Kuwaiti only. Thanks to God we arrested many of those who carried out the explosion operations, except for two or three who fled to Iran. However, in the case of Kuwait's becoming the subject of Iranian attacks, Kuwait has the right to defend itself. The issue is not that of Kuwait's impotence; Kuwait will defend itself and will find its sisters, the Gulf states, on its side.

[Question] After agreeing to sell Stinger missiles to the Kingdom of Saudi Arabia, the United States refused to sell them to Kuwait. Do you think this attitude is aimed at reaching a stage where the United States will demand direct intervention to defend you?

[Answer] We have to remove the issue of direct U.S. intervention from our thoughts. We in the Gulf, and particularly in Kuwait, purchase arms from the East and the West, and what has been termed as rejection we perceive as preparation taking place in the Congress to sell the missiles to us. We will remain in contact with the U.S. Government to conclude the deal, and I hope that it will be concluded. But it will not happen with the speed we desire. Kuwait has enough Eastern and Western arms, and the equivalent of these missiles.

[Question] How does Shaykh Sabah perceive Saudi-Soviet relations, the Saudi request to the Soviet Union to support the resolution at the UN Security Council, and other events and signs?

[Answer] Saudi Arabia was the first Arab country to have relations with the Soviet Union. However, some kind of misunderstanding occurred, and relations between them were severed. I consider that these relations exist, but not through the exchange of embassies and ambassadors. We in Kuwait are among the countries that have diplomatic exchanges with the Soviet Union. Our contacts with the Soviet Union, in addition to the contacts made by our brothers in other Gulf countries, were made to ensure its support for the resolution, and this gives a good impression,

namely that in the future there is a possibility for diplomatic representation between the region's countries and the Soviet Union. We must not denounce this issue. It depends on the policy of each state. When we say we intend to re-evaluate our foreign policies, we mean we will include these matters among the points we will discuss in future meetings.

[Question] Not much has been announced about the visit by Syrian Vice President Abd al-Halim Khaddam to Tehran to mediate between it and Iraq. Have there been any positive signs?

[Answer] Before Khaddam embarked on his visit we raised the matter at the Arab League and issued a statement that any aggression against any Gulf country constitutes aggression against all Arab countries. Syria was one of those countries that voted in favor of this resolution. We appreciate this stand by Syria. According to my information, Syria has warned the Iranians that while it might have its differences with Iraq, when foreign armies enter Arab territories, including Iraqi territory, Syria would find itself obliged to side with its Arab sister states and with the collective Arab Defense Pact. This is the information I have obtained. If it proves anything, it is that no matter what difference its member countries might have among themselves, the Arab world would stand united in the face of danger. We must not forget there are Arab peoples. "We all are bound to die. All responsible officials will die one day. But the Arab land and peoples will remain," he added. Therefore I am fully hopeful that what has happened will bring us closer together—much closer than ever before.

[Question] You seem optimistic. This is a weapon which all the Arab peoples need.

[Answer] First, if I am optimistic it is because this is what our forefathers taught us. Besides, no responsible official will remain forever, but the people will. In view of this, I believe that the recent Arab unaminity in condemning Iran will have a great effect on the entire course of events in the region. We cannot deny that matters have reached a limit which demands we rally together in saying unanimously that any occupation of any Arab land is unlawful and we must stand by the side of anyone whose land has been occupied.

Source: *Al-Tadamun* (London), 16 June 1984, as translated in *FBIS-MEA-V–84–118*, 18 June 1984, pp. C2-C3.

Document 44

Interview with Kuwait's Deputy Prime Minister, Foreign, and Information Minister, Shaykh Sabah al-Ahmad Al-Sabah

17 August 1984

Question: Do you expect the Riyadh summit to be held on schedule despite the Arab differences?

Answer: We hope that the Riyadh summit will be held on schedule, unless circumstances arise leading to its postponement. It is no secret that events in our Arab homeland overtake each other, and we do not know what will happen tomorrow. But we hope that events will take their natural course.

Question: Do you have any ideas on how to solve Arab differences?

Answer: We have always worked and will continue to work to overcome all the differences among the fraternal Arab states. Yes, our idea on how to resolve the differences is to have a farsighted view of the damage these differences are causing, which reflect on all. Therefore, in my opinion, Arab differences can be eliminated if they are handled with wisdom and with sincere desire, avoiding personal whims and formalities, and if the general interest is placed above everything else.

Question: The acuteness of the Gulf war has abated, but it has not stopped. Do you think the present lull comes before the storm, or is it a phase paving the way toward ending this war?

Answer: We are still exerting efforts on all levels to end the Gulf war. We will continue to make efforts tirelessly. The damage caused by this war affects everyone. If its acuteness abates today, it will increase tomorrow, unless a radical end is put to it. You are aware that fraternal Iraq welcomes an end to this war, which has harmed the two warring parties, as well as the peoples of the region, who are bearing the greatest share of the damage. We will not rest until we can extinguish its flames with other sincere people.

Question: Is it possible to consider the UN Security Council's resolution with regard to the freedom of navigation in the Gulf as a factor that helped to stop the tanker war, or are the reasons due to the failure of Iran's military capabilities?

Answer: There is no doubt that the Security Council resolution has lessened the acuteness of the war and has also reduced the acuteness of the tanker attacks. It is a resolution from an international organization, and one must respect such a decision at all costs. Perhaps it will help to bring the views of the two warring parties closer, to end the tanker war, and then to reach an understanding on halting the war between Iraq and Iran and on satisfying the claims of the parties.

Question: Exercises to train special forces for the war in the Gulf region took place recently in the United States. What is your comment on this?

Answer: The exercises conducted by the United States or others do not concern us. The same applies to what they say and spread in the world. Our views are known, namely not to recognize and condemn any foreign intervention in our region.

Question: Is there any hope that Iran will accept the mediation of the group of Islamic states or others to stop the war?

Answer: If we lose hope then despair takes over; and if despair takes over it brings nothing but destruction. I say yes, despite Iran's intransigence and its rejection of numerous mediations. I am fully confident that the responsible officials in Iran will take into consideration the interest of the Iranian people. Indeed, without any doubt they do take such interest into consideration. Therefore hope is pinned on those men of wisdom and on those who have the final word.

Question: Could you assess the efforts of the Arab Foreign Ministers Committee? Was there international sympathy for such efforts?

Answer: Yes. The seven man committee found international sympathy for its good offices. Perhaps you are following up what the press agencies have reported about its continuous call for an end to this war, because it is harming everyone and is affecting the international interests in general. As to the evaluation of its efforts, this is left for the others who appreciate its role and what it had done. They also appreciate the damage this war is causing.

Question: Have the efforts succeeded in convincing Japan to reduce its dealings with Iran to compel it to accept negotiations to resolve the differences with Iraq by peaceful means?

Answer: I believe Japan has interests with both Iran and Iraq, and I believe that its dealings have been reduced because of the tanker war. As to the acceptance of negotiations between the two warring parties, in my view this cannot be done except by working to bring the viewpoints of the two parties closer and by narrowing the gap between them and by convincing them of the advantages to be gained for present and future generations. Iran and Iraq will always be neighbors. Therefore, a comprehensive agreement between them must be established. This must replace the dispute that does not benefit this generation nor future generations. Peoples and nations do not make progress and flourish except through understanding and cooperation in all areas of life.

Question: What is the attitude of Kuwait and the states of the GCC toward any direct U.S. intervention in the Gulf war?

Answer: As I have said, we are against any foreign intervention, whether direct or indirect, and whether this intervention came from the West or the East. Foreign intervention adds fuel to the fire and does not solve the problem. The only intervention we accept is the intervention to end the war, provided that it is acceptable to the two warring parties. In this instance we consider this intervention—if acceptable to the warring parties—as an intervention for the sake of good, otherwise it will be the evil we do not accept or agree to.

Question: Can one give the visit of the Kuwaiti Defense minister to Moscow a political significance. . . .

Answer: I say no; the buying of arms is not a policy, but business. I buy the weapons I need and pay for them. It is a business deal, whether it was concluded with the East or the West. The weapons I buy with my money are of no concern to others. It is my own affair, and it is purely a commercial affair.

Question: It has been reiterated that the weapons that will be purchased from the Soviet Union will bring with them Soviet experts to Kuwait and the Gulf region. Is this correct?

Answer: The weapons I purchase are for use and not for storing. There are weapons I purchase and know how to use; and there are new weapons I purchase and must learn how to use, whether it be in the country that sold these weapons or in my country. I purchase weapons only for my own use, and I will not allow another hand to use them on my behalf. I will be trained in the use of such weapons by the seller for a period of time, but I will never leave it to the instructors forever. Furthermore, who said I buy weapons along with the instructors . . . and how can I buy weapons and not know how to use them. . . . We are not concerned about the tendentious utterances that cast doubts on everything and portray things contrary to the facts.

Question: Was there a kind of coordination between Kuwait and the rest of the GCC states on this military turning toward Moscow?

Answer: It is no secret that we have long had friendly relations with the Soviet Union, since it stood beside us on our issues. We greatly appreciate such stances. Our turning to buy weapons that we are short of is a turning of friendship, a turning of interest between our two countries. This is not a question of coordination with the GCC states. This is a bilateral arms deal between us and the Soviet Union.

Question: It is being reiterated that Kuwait is experiencing an economic crisis because of the Gulf war, the limiting of oil production, and the shakeup in the stock market. What is the truth about this?

Answer: Economic crisis is being experienced all over the world. Kuwait's economy is not separate from the world economy. There is no doubt that the Gulf war, the limiting of the oil production and the shakeup in the stock market have had their impact on Kuwait. But let me assure you that Kuwait's economy is firm and strong. Perhaps you read 2 or 3 days ago about the strength of the Kuwaiti dinar and its strong position in the world markets. This indicates the soundness of the Kuwaiti economy and the soundness of our financial and economic policy. As for the shakeup in the stock market, as you put it, it is on the way of being resolved, after all the problem has been contained, and legislation has been enacted to solve it.

Question: Is it possible to define the important issues the next GCC summit in Kuwait will discuss?

Answer: There are many issues the Gulf summit conference will tackle in Kuwait. Some of them are connected with the GCC, and they are numerous. They form the nucleus of the comprehensive unity, the most important of which is economic cooperation among the states of the council. Naturally the Iraq-Iran war will be discussed and so will be the Arab differences.

Question: Do you think that the GCC has achieved its purpose, and do you think its existence is a pressing need for the region?

Answer: The GCC is proceeding on its course as planned. I am not saying that it has accomplished everything. But it is sufficient to say that it has successfully accomplished its first steps. The GCC was born and began to make its strides firmly; but the road is long, matters are complicated, and we do not want to treat them hastily. Rather we want to study them conscientiously so that they become a strong brick for the foundation of its unity. There are some matters in which we have made long strides, including economic and cultural, political and military matters. We are proceeding on the road, thanks to the cooperation and understanding of the leaders, and to their consideration of the interests of their peoples. We pray to almighty God to accomplish the hopes, and we hope that the GCC would be the strongest brick in the building of comprehensive Arab unity.

Source: *An-Nahar Al-Arabi Wa Ad-Duwali* (Beirut), 18 Aug. 1984, as translated in *FBIS-MEA-V–84–162*, 20 Aug. 1984, pp. C1-C3.

Document 45
King Fahd Speech at the Inauguration of the King Faysal Naval Base
21 August 1984

No doubt a day such as today will be remembered in the history of the Kingdom of Saudi Arabia with regard to the Kingdom's Naval Forces. We all know that many years ago the idea was formulated concerning the establishment of the Navy. We who are living in such an atmosphere may realize the effort which was made. Anyone who visits the naval bases could believe that they were established some 50 years ago. I can say that they were established during the past 10 years. They are the nucleus of something bigger and more comprehensive regarding the naval border of Saudi Arabia. It is known that the naval frontiers of the Kingdom of Saudi Arabia extend more than 1,000 kms into the Red Sea, and in the Gulf to several hundred kilometers.

It is known that the policy of the Kingdom of Saudi Arabia is always based on nonaggression against others. But at the same time it does not permit the violation of its territory—at sea, on land or in the air. When thought was given to the establishment of the Saudi Navy, this was based on the fact that a country such as the Kingdom of Saudi Arabia, having an important and strategic position, should inevitably have naval, land and air forces. Thanks to God, and praise be to him, that we see from time to time these establishments of the three branches of the Armed Forces at the highest of levels, particularly what has been prepared by His Royal Highness Prince Abdallah ibn Abd al-Aziz, crown prince of the Kingdom of Saudi Arabia, for the National Guard, which in all circumstances shares with the other forces in the defense of the homeland. When we saw on many occasions the organization and arrangements which have been prepared for the divisions of the National Guard, we and all citizens were very pleased with the fact that the officials responsible for this great development are led by His Royal Highness Prince Abdallah ibn Abd al-Aziz. We were also pleased with the preparations made with regard to the security forces, which in actual fact shoulder the responsibility of protecting the citizens day and night. Therefore there are forces, thanks to God, which are in good shape.

At the same time, anyone who wants to harm the Kingdom of Saudi Arabia should realize that there is sufficient preparation to check any aggression. The basic principle in actual fact is adherence of this country—government and people—to the fundamentals which made our country what it is today—the Islamic foundation with which God has honored this country and the entire world for the good and prosperity of mankind. I hope, God willing, to see all our military forces develop for the better. I was most pleased to see all officers in all these forces which I have mentioned—supervisors, trainers, commanders and soldiers—are from among the sons of this homeland. This is the biggest step that we could possibly have taken. I wish our forces success in all spheres. Their government will not withhold anything that will help to move these forces forward, God willing.

Source: *FBIS-MEA-V–84–164*, 22 Aug. 1984, p. C3.

Document 46

Interview with Kuwaiti Defense Minister Shaykh Salim al-Sabah al-Salim

23 March 1985

[Excerpts] [Al-Mutawwa] The Iraqi-Iranian war is escalating these days. From your position what is the information available to you? Do you think that the war has entered a new stage that is different from the previous stages?

[Al-Sabah] The recent developments in the war are a continuation of this war which is almost 5 years old. This war has become a war of attrition. This war of attrition gives a chance to each party to prepare and reorganize itself and make its plans in order to be ready to attack at any time. In my view, what happened recently is an escalation of the operation and has a political nature as well as a military nature. Any development in this escalation may lead to a more critical situation such as the continuation of the war.

Therefore, the last attack has significance for the world, especially the Gulf.

[Al-Mutawwa] Is there any possibility that the war may expand to the Kuwaiti borders? Are the Armed Forces prepared for such possibility?

[Al-Sabah] There is no doubt in that. Since the beginning of the war we have been studying all its directions and preparing our positions and air and ground defenses as a precaution for the consequences and we have been consolidating the locations which may pose a weakness for Kuwait. Therefore, as you can see we have prevented visitors from entering Bubiyan Island because it has become a military island equipped with antiaircraft weapons. There is a plan for Bubiyan Island and there are plans for other locations and sensitive centers in Kuwait. The compulsory recruitment is of a very great importance for these plans. I proudly say that compulsory service in the Army is not a picnic.

[Al-Mutawwa] Kuwait's speech at the recent meetings of the GCC ministerial council pointed out that the GCC bears the responsibility of warding off any danger to the region. What is the practical action taken for this purpose? What is the role of the joint forces which the last GCC summit decided to form? How far is the practical implementation of this decision?

[Al-Sabah] There is no doubt that you understand what is meant by warding off dangers. Brother Abu Nasir [Kuwaiti foreign minister] is an experienced politician who chooses precise words for the purpose intended and this is the nature of the Gulf citizen and the Kuwaitis in particular. We speak briefly.

When we say warding off dangers we mean that our country is not an aggressive country and that the Gulf countries are peaceful countries which do not harbor hostility toward anyone. But we will never forgive anyone who tries to play with the security of our countries internally or externally. Our principle in Kuwait and in the GCC as defense ministers is based on the fact that any attack on any Gulf country is an attack on us all and this is affirmed by the Arab League Charter too. Therefore, we have to make common arrangements and conduct joint exercises so that we can defend the Gulf by ourselves and foil the attempts of those who want to interfere on the pretext of defending us or assisting us to defend ourselves. I believe that when Brother Abu Nasir said this he meant it and meant that the sons of Kuwait and Gulf countries are the ones who will repulse any aggression against their countries.

There is no doubt that the joint forces are existing and are represented by the Peninsula Shield forces. The "Peninsula-1" and "2" exercises were carried out and the forces are still carrying out their exercises. One cannot melt all the Gulf forces together. It is necessary to form a homogeneous nucleus that can repel any danger on the spot and rapidly. This force should be rapidly deployed and should have clear tasks in defense. What is important is the principle of participation—the participation with a soldier, or a battalion or a brigade. All the Gulf countries will be one hand and will cooperate to deter any aggression against their territories.

[Al-Mutawwa] In this case and for armament specifically, don't you think that for the formation of this nucleus these countries should have unified training and homogeneous weapons and that there should not be any loopholes? Did you study this?

[Al-Sabah] There are two schools regarding the unification of arms, a school that believes in the unification of arms and a school that believes in the diversification of arms sources. Experience proves that the diversification of arms sources is better. The political matters and the ability not to be subjected to pressures when more weapons are needed are most important.

Experience in this regard has proved the validity of this. You may be surprised to know that even arms-producing countries use this method. Britain, for example, purchases arms from Europe and the United States also purchases some of its arms from Europe. Arms sometimes impose themselves on the state. This means that if I want to purchase a durable weapon, for example artillery, I have to seek what is best for me. As a Kuwaiti, I may find this kind of weapon in France, so France will be my source of this kind of weapon. If I want missiles, I may find that Soviet missiles have advantages which meet my manpower capability and individual competence. These missiles, therefore, will be suitable for me. This means that I may find the suitable fighter planes in the United States and the suitable tanks in Britain, and so on.

In this case, I choose what is best for me and at the same time I do not become tied to one party or authority. Out of this principle, diversification is better and it gives the opportunity for arms to complement each other. Weapons are almost similar in the region's countries because sources of weapons in the world are a few and if you do not purchase arms from one source you will have to purchase it from another. Therefore you find that our weapons in the Gulf are similar.

Saudi Arabia, for example, is using British and U.S. fighter planes; the UAE uses French fighter planes; we, in Kuwait, have French and U.S. fighter planes and some old British ones. There is cooperation and coordination in this field. There are no loopholes. If there are any, they can be filled. Something of this sort was experienced at the beginning during the "Peninsula Shield" exercises. In telecommunications, for example, some equipment did not fit on others. What we did is that one kind of Kuwaiti equipment was put in the command and control tent, and when there was a need to contact us, they did so through our equipment to give us instructions through coordination. This also was the case in tanks.

[Al-Mutawwa] The force which the Gulf summit has defined, where is it?

[Al-Sabah] The force was approved initially by the leaders. The formation was passed to the defense ministers who charged their technicians and directors of operations. The [Saudi] chief of staff and director of operations, Brigadier

General Salim al-Turki, was here a few days ago. He presented to me his visualization. This visualization will be submitted to the chiefs of staff to study and decide on. Their recommendations will be submitted to us, the defense ministers. When we meet, we will approve the detail and names. The commander will be Saudi, and his rank has been defined. Brother Sultan [ibn Abd al-Aziz] will choose the commander for this force. Saudi Arabia has been chosen to lead this force because it has more military personnel. There is an internationally acknowledged theory which states that command should be given to whoever has more military personnel. This brings me to talk about the Western nations. If we take the NATO, for example, we will find that its command is usually given to the countries which have more contributions. The diversification of weapons is also found in Europe. This proves my theory that diversified weapons is alright and does not necessarily affect others. On the contrary, it complements itself. German, French, U.S., British, and Italian weapons are ultimately homogeneous and fulfill one plan, each according to its task.

[Al-Mutawwa] Has the number of soldiers for each country been defined according to its army?

[Al-Sabah] No ratio has been defined. The thing was left to each country to give what it can. For example, some countries are not able to offer one brigade, but can give one battalion, or more. Kuwait, for example, has given two battalions. Saudi Arabia has given almost one brigade. The issue is of total strength. I think that is the question in your mind. Let me answer it before you ask it. The total of this force is about two brigades, or slightly less than that.

[Al-Mutawwa] Does this not raise questions regarding the force which participates more, or other questions on this matter?

[Al-Sabah] These are pessimistic questions—if you allow me, Brother Jasim, to use this phrase—and I hope they will not be posed even by Kuwait or Gulf nationals in particular, and Arab nationals in general. I wish to answer this with certain facts so that one can be clear with regard to the reader by talking to him through our esteemed *Al-Watan*. When Kuwait made a contribution with fraternal Syria and Egypt, the ratio of Kuwaiti military personnel with regard to the Egyptian Army was nearly nothing, and with regard to the Syrian Army, also nothing. However, the Kuwaiti soldier fought with a spirit that represents Kuwait and was motivated by Kuwait's belief in Arab causes. We offered martyrs. Then how about in the Gulf, his country? The individual must make contributions just as the group does. As I said at the beginning, it is a symbolic force representing Gulf solidarity and fraternity. Consequently, when I participate with two battalions, this does not mean that it stops at the limit of two battalions.

[Al-Mutawwa] Going back to the subject of arms diversification, we have agreed that this is proof of the country's independence. When a country is independent and its political decisionmaking is independent, it will be able to make its purchases anywhere and will not be at the mercy of a particular party.

[Al-Sabah] Your analysis is correct from the political point of view. I did not touch on this matter from the political point of view because I committed myself to talk with regard to the military side. However, your analysis is correct from the political point of view. This is what it means and what it proves.

[Al-Mutawwa] For this reason we find that Kuwait is free to choose its weapons.

[Al-Sabah] Kuwait's freedom is limited by the type and quality of the weapons. Kuwait is respected by the government with which we deal regarding the subject of arms because we always buy weapons from governments and through them. This is a policy laid down by his highness the heir apparent and which we have followed at the Defense Ministry. It has become Kuwait's policy. Kuwait's respect springs from its freedom of choice and direct dealing with the governments. I remember that in the case of a particular weapon, our experts had studied it and wanted to get it, but when we asked the [concerned] government, it declined. It said: Go ahead and make a deal with the company. However, we told them: "We are sorry," we do not want this weapon, and we chose the other. We actually asked the other delegation for a discussion. Suddenly the ambassador contacted us and said: "I want to discuss the matter with you." I said: If you have changes regarding acceptance, then you are welcome. He said yes. He came, and made the offer again. We brought them over, and discussed the matter with them and with the others and obtained a very large discount because they found we were serious in that matter, and that we were not bargaining. They believed that we would submit to them if they said no. However, the situation changed when I bade them off. Their government was compelled to make a pledge that the deal will be direct, without any go-betweens and without any arms dealers.

[Al-Mutawwa] I remember that during one of its meetings with you, *Al-Watan* posed a question on the attacks on tankers. You said that measures are being taken in the event there are attacks on tankers in the future. In fact, there has been attacks on tankers recently. Is there a way to protect our tankers from attacks in the light of the new developments?

[Al-Sabah] This question can be interpreted in several ways. However, what I want to say is this: Where were these tankers hit? They were not hit within Kuwait's borders. I am responsible for Kuwait's borders and its security.

If memory does not fail me, I said in one of my statements: If they are brave, let them come to my land and I am ready for a confrontation. I want now to repeat this statement. I have men of whom I am proud, whether in the ground forces, the Navy, or the Air Force. They also are more ready than I am for these matters. The tanker that you are talking about was hit outside the range of radar and was hit by Iran. This ship, as you know, is leased by the oil company and is not Kuwaiti.

[Al-Mutawwa] It is agreed that it is better to ensure full protection so that these tankers are not hit in our territorial waters or near it. Is it possible to reduce the danger to these tankers through coordination among the Gulf countries or by patrol ships or warships from the Gulf itself?

[Al-Sabah] There are technical problems regarding these questions such as the depth of the sea. The draft of the ship is big when it is loaded and needs deep waters. It is important in this case for the ship to pass through international waters. Here, the control over these international waters falls under legal and international questions. There are ways and methods for protecting these ships as long as they are within territorial waters, provided that their drafts allow them to pass, but they become out of control of the concerned countries when they enter international waters.

[Al-Mutawwa] Talks were held between Kuwait and the United States to develop an early warning network and to be connected with the AWACs. It was said that the United States has agreed to that. What are the steps which followed that? When will this system be implemented? Do we have enough defenses to protect Kuwait's airspace against any possible aggression?

[Al-Sabah] Allow me to clarify some points about these talks which many media men think were held. I don't intend to defend the U.S. Administration, but I only intend to clarify this point when I say that the U.S. Administration has to obtain permission beforehand from Congress for the purpose of selling any weapons to any friendly country which does not pose a threat to it or to its interests as far as security is concerned. What do the news agencies do? They monitor the news and circulate it by saying that the United States agreed to sell to Kuwait this or that, while the truth remains that Kuwait has not made any request. The U.S. Administration has a plan which states: If Kuwait surprises us with a request for F–16 planes for example, I cannot sell them immediately because I don't have permission from the Congress beforehand. Therefore, it is necessary to obtain a permission beforehand. If we then make the request for the planes they will have the chance of selling them to us and if we do not make our request they keep the planes. This happened.

One time we spoke with the United States about matters concerning air defense but we found that the French air defense is much more suitable for us and we signed an agreement with the French Government which, I say proudly, was studied by Kuwaiti technicians and officers both technically and tactically. They submitted to us clear memorandums. I spoke to them and asked them to be patient with me. I told them: We will bring to you experts from neutral countries to study the work which you carried out. I have no doubt in your work, but I just want to make sure, because I am entrusted with a great responsibility. I want to make sure that you are going in the correct way. When I find out that your report is identical to the report of the experts I will be more proud of you. I want to protect you as future experts. I want to protect you from any mistakes which may make you liable to a great responsibility in the future.

They accepted my advice with open hearts. Then we brought in the experts. I say proudly that these experts assured me that the reports of our experts were correct and that their style was correct and that the points they tackled with regard to air defense in low levels from zero to 10,000 feet were 100 percent correct. Therefore, I congratulated them and the heir apparent and chairman of the supreme defense council congratulated them. The amir also blessed their work. We signed the agreement on basis of Kuwaiti studies and experiences. The agreement is about to be finalized and we have begun installing some of the equipment which arrived.

[Al-Mutawwa] Regardless of this, are the defenses which we possess enough protection?

[Al-Sabah] They will be when they are completed. We did not have enough low level and very low level radars simply because at that time we did not need them; but now we need them. Therefore, we signed a contract with the French. Some equipment began to arrive and we began to install them. Everything will be complete and integrated after the arrival of the equipment.

[Al-Mutawwa] In case that all defensive preparations have been completed, does it mean that the coordination and the exchange of information with the GCC states will end or will Kuwait be in need of cooperation in this field?

[Al-Sabah] On the contrary, we must increase cooperation in this field. This does not mean that when we achieve such matters that we stop cooperation. No, there are more developments and better equipment which we change after some years. We still maintain direct lines of communication and exchanges of information with the GCC states. On the contrary, this equipment will be an active and contributory element in the development of communications and putting the brothers into the picture.

[Al-Mutawwa] Regarding military developments around us, you must have benefited from Gulf information. Has this information contributed to avoiding dangers and helped the defense system?

[Al-Sabah] There have been communications. They have two aspects: speed and extreme necessity. The second aspect has its own dangers but its importance is not very urgent. When we use to see some aircraft reported by some brothers in the Gulf. Our sightings have usually been confirmed. To explain further, the radar picks up the plane as a moving dot, then we observe it and plot its path. Later we receive information from the Gulf states confirming the credibility of our information and we reassure them that we will be in contact with them. Then the fighters intercept and keep it away from the region. We have benefited from our cooperation with the Gulf states in this field.

[Al-Mutawwa] Does our airspace allow such training? You know that our airspace is not that vast vis-à-vis the speed of various aircraft.

[Al-Sabah] Our airspace is suitable in the western and the southern regions and to some extent in the eastern re-

gion. We are coordinating with Saudi Arabia and Bahrain. There are aerial training zones. We inform civil aviation about the training zones to avoid the presence of civilian aircraft in these zones.

[Al-Mutawwa] Do you allow the GCC states to use these aerial zones in their training?

[Al-Sabah] Yes, without question as long as we are aware of it.

[Al-Mutawwa] How can we benefit from the military situation around us?

[Al-Sabah] The Kuwaiti Army has benefited from the responsibility and the present threat. It is alert evaluating the events, and following what is happening around it. The Navy is currently in the northern region. In the past when the Navy saw a launch they used to say it was a fishing boat but now things have changed and it will try to confirm it. It is a sort of caution.

In the past when the radar detected an airplane, they would say it was far from our airspace. But now they observe it carefully and issue orders to the operations room. The operations room alerts the base. The base acts even though the aircraft is far away. These are precautionary steps and the readiness for the state of war.

Source: *Al-Watan* (Kuwait), 23 March 1985, pp. 6, 7, as translated in *FBIS-MEA-V–85–058*, 26 March 1985, pp. C3-C6.

Document 47
Kuwaiti National Assembly Statement on Gulf Conflict
9 April 1985

The latest developments of the Iraqi-Iranian war have gone far beyond established human values and international norms with the destruction of cities and the killing of innocent children, women, and old people. All this urges us—being Muslim Arab people who seek an immediate end to this aggravating disaster—to call on "Iran" to positively respond to the calls made by fraternal and friendly countries in addition to the international organizations to halt the fighting and hold negotiations that lead to a reconciliation, since reconciliation is always good. "However, if the enemy is inclined towards peace, do thou incline towards peace and trust in God." [Koranic verse]

The killing of Muslims and shedding of blood is not only prohibited, but should be better directed to the cause of liberating our lands and sanctities, to defeating the forces of evil, and to aborting the plans machinated by Zionism and its agents. We, in the name of the Kuwaiti Arab people, pledge our support to any peace initiative designed to terminate bloodshed and to contain the war so that everyone does not go up in flames. We also call for an active international and Islamic role in supporting the efforts to end the war and establish stability—particularly the efforts of the UN secretary general.

The unity of the Arab and Islamic peoples, in addition to the elimination of factional and racial differences, are among the basic factors that will ensure stability and promote development in the region. This is a principled issue linked with the fate of the region and its people.

This bestial war enabled the Zionist enemy to tamper with southern Lebanon and with the entire occupied Arab territories. It also served as a pretext for a foreign presence in the region; moreover, it stopped and blocked all the region's development plans. We do not believe that any side will be satisfied with this. The continuation of the war will only serve the enemies of this nation. The time has come to bring this war to a moratorium so that the Arab and Islamic nations will consequently restore their power and unity.

Finally, the Kuwaiti National Assembly supports Iraq's rights to defend itself, and safeguard its territorial integrity and the safety of its people. The assembly emphasizes that the Kuwaiti and our Arab people in Iraq are bound by a common fate and destiny.

Source: *Al-Watan* (Kuwait), 10 April 1985, p. 6, as translated in *FBIS-MEA-V–85–071*, 12 April 1985, p. C1.

Document 48

Interview with Saudi Deputy Minister of Defense and Aviation Prince Abd al-Rahman ibn Abd al-Aziz

27 April 1985

[Excerpts] Al-Bunyan: What stage has the compulsory conscription project reached and do you believe that the next phase will require implementation of such a project?

Abd al-Rahman: We in the Ministry of Defense and Aviation call it flag service. The project is now at a very advanced stage. I do not want to anticipate events before the aims and objectives of the project are completely defined. All I can say is that we are at a very advanced stage.

Al-Bunyan: If implemented, will the project apply to all Saudi young men?

Abd al-Rahman: Certainly. There is no doubt about that. When it is promulgated it will be comprehensive and it will state who will be called up.

Al-Bunyan: Western sources are claiming that Saudi Arabia is doubling its arms purchases although there is no sufficiently qualified manpower to use their weapons. What is your answer to these claims?

Abd al-Rahman: These are deliberate prevarications, not claims. The truth is that the Saudi Defense and Aviation

Ministry has been trying to build on the ground and to do its duty to the Armed Forces by building military cities and airports, and providing all that is needed to enable the Armed Forces to do their duty.

The Defense and Aviation Ministry has also been giving some attention to the equipment itself. For example, last year there was nowhere to keep the equipment to protect it from the weather and damage. Now the ground installations are almost complete. Without doubt, most of the expenditure over the past few years was geared toward preparation. Not many years ago there was nothing on the ground to serve the Armed Forces.

As regards armament, the Kingdom is doubling the purchase of certain equipment that we never purchased before. When the circumstances became ripe on the ground such equipment became necessary for the Armed Forces. However, most of the expenditure which is claimed to have been earmarked for excessive arms purchases has in fact been also earmarked for implementation of Armed Forces projects that have cost billions.

The Saudi Defense and Aviation Ministry's current method is that it never purchases any weapons before sending Saudis abroad to train on them so that when the weapons arrive in Saudi Arabia the trained manpower is available at the same time. That is what happened in relation to the naval units purchased from the United States and France. They were piloted by Saudis who had received special electronics training.

Al-Bunyan: Does that apply to the other branches of the Armed Forces?

Abd al-Rahman: Yes, it applies to the Air Force and the ground forces. This is now our way at the Defense and Aviation Ministry, and it will always be—training before the arms arrive.

Al-Bunyan: Some Western sources emphasize that Saudi Arabia is giving military and economic aid to Iraq in its war against Iran. Is that true?

Abd al-Rahman: Iraq is a fraternal Arab country. There are Gulf states agreements and Arab states agreements providing for mutual assistance in times of war and peace.

Al-Bunyan: Are you referring to the Arab Joint Defense Pact?

Abd al-Rahman: Yes, there are agreements. Such a thing has been approved at meetings of Arab leaders.

Al-Bunyan: So, is Iraq getting military and economic aid from Saudi Arabia?

Abd al-Rahman: Naturally, in accordance with the agreements concluded by all the Arab states. That is a fact.

Al-Bunyan: The Americans are saying that they are studying an arms deal covering arms that Saudi Arabia is interested in purchasing. What types are these weapons and do you expect Congress to oppose the deal?

Abd al-Rahman: We have long been buying arms from the United States, we still are and we will continue to do so.

Al-Bunyan: However, recently a U.S. embargo has been imposed on the sale of U.S. arms to the Middle Eastern states. Does that embargo apply to the Saudi deal that was in existence before the embargo was announced?

Abd al-Rahman: I believe that what is needed, what has been decided and agreed between the United States and the Saudi Kingdom will be implemented. Whether Congress would support or oppose is a U.S. internal matter but what has already been agreed upon should be implemented.

Al-Bunyan: Do you believe that this particular deal will go through without objection?

Abd al-Rahman: Naturally there are bound to be difficulties, sometimes at U.S. domestic level, but when a state reaches agreement with another state that agreement is supposed to be honored. We do not know what will happen in the future but it is common knowledge that Saudi Arabia can buy arms from any source whose arms it considers to be useful and fulfill its purpose.

Al-Bunyan: How many foreign experts are there in the Saudi Armed Forces?

Abd al-Rahman (Immediately): What experts are you talking about?

Al-Bunyan: We hear that there are foreign experts.

Abd al-Rahman: We do not have a specific number of foreign experts. That depends on our needs. Sometimes, when there is need, there are more experts than other times. They are brought in for a specific period. When that period expires their services are terminated.

Al-Bunyan: What are your plans for strengthening security measures to protect Saudi Airlines planes against hijacking, particularly since there already have been two hijacking attempts?

Abd al-Rahman: Undoubtedly we do have plans. We had plans in the past. A plan requires time because the people we train are human and humans have a limited capacity; so, we give them time to enable them to perform their duties perfectly. You know that the recent attempt ended when the hijacker was promptly killed at Dhahran airport. That provides the evidence that Saudi planes' security protection capabilities are increasing. We have training and we have effective capabilities to repulse any aggression against our planes.

Source: *Al-Sharq Al-Awsat* (London), 27 April 1985, p. 10, as translated in *FBIS-MEA-V–85–084*, 1 May 1985, pp. C1-C2.

Document 49

Islamic Conference Organization: Islamic Good Offices Committee Statement on Gulf Affairs

2 May 1985

The Islamic Good Offices Committee held its seventh session in Jeddah in the Saudi Arabian Kingdom from 1 to 2 May under the chairmanship of the Gambian president,

Dawda Jawara, and in the presence of the PLO Executive Committee chairman, Yasir Arafat; the secretary general of the ICO, Sharifuddin Pirzada; and the foreign ministers and high-ranking representatives of the other member-countries of the committee.

Following a brief public session, during which the president of the Islamic Good Offices Committee and the secretary general of the ICO delivered short speeches, the committee held a closed session; during this session it heard a report from its chairman concerning the consultations he held with Iran and Iraq, the heads of state of a number of other countries, as well as with the PLO Executive Committee chairman, with a view to exploring ways and means for ending the Iran-Iraq war in accordance with the powers vested in him by the Islamic Good Offices Committee during its third session held in July 1984.

The secretary general of the ICO then delivered a report about his contacts and discussions with representatives of Iran, Iraq, heads of state and governments of the other countries, and with the PLO Executive Committee chairman, the UN secretary general, and the president of the Nonaligned Movement.

The Islamic Good Offices Committee expressed its complete appreciation of the efforts exerted by the President of the Islamic Good Offices Committee and the secretary general of the ICO, and decided that its president should continue his efforts for a speedy, peaceful and honorable settlement of the Iran-Iraq war in accordance with the power vested in him.

The committee expressed its concern over the recent escalation of acts of aggression between the two sides.

The committee also expressed its deep frustration and extreme concern over the continuation of the armed conflict between Iran and Iraq—a conflict that has not halted despite the repeated appeals and good offices exerted by the Islamic Good Offices Committee for ending the war.

The committee also expressed its profound regret at the continued preparations for launching further attacks across the borders, thereby threatening the region and the Islamic world in general.

The committee reiterated its call for an immediate cease-fire and the urgent need for the establishment of a just and honorable peace on the basis of Islamic principles and international law which govern relations among countries.

The committee took note of the reports on the use of chemical weapons in the Iraq-Iran war in complete violation of the Geneva Protocol for 1925 concerning the use of chemical weapons.

The committee denounced the violation of the provisions of the international law on human rights at times of armed conflicts, particularly the Geneva agreements on the laws of war and the treatment of prisoners, and the Geneva Protocol of 1925 which prohibits the use of chemical weapons, and the Chicago agreement on civil aviation. The committee called for the strict observation of these agreements and laws.

The committee noted with full regret the failure of the 12 June 1984 agreement which was achieved under the auspices of the United Nations and in which both sides agreed not to attack civilian targets in each other's countries.

The committee called on both sides to respect the international agreements and treaties aimed at preventing or alleviating human sufferings in wars.

In view of the importance of the information provided by the committee's chairman and the secretary general of the Islamic Conference Organization, the committee decided to refer their two reports to the heads of states of the committee member-countries.

The committee decided to hold its eighth session on the level of heads of state in Jeddah on 15 August.

The committee expressed its gratitude to the Bangladesh Government for offering to play host to the meetings of the Islamic Good Offices Committee and agreed to hold the future meeting of the committee in Dhaka.

The committee expressed its gratitude and thanks to King Fahd ibn Abd al-Aziz, the monarch of the Saudi Arabian Kingdom for playing host to its meetings and for providing it with all facilities.

Source: *FBIS-MEA-V–85–086*, 3 May 1985, pp. C2-C3.

Document 50

Interview with Bahrain's Prime Minister Shaykh Khalifah ibn Salman Al-Khalifah

30 June 1985

Al-Husayni: Is Bahrain concerned about the possibility of the Gulf war expanding?

Khalifah: Bahrain and all its sister countries are concerned. The Gulf war is very worrying. None of the Gulf countries are free from this worry.

Al-Husayni: What do you think about the escalation of the cities' war between Iraq and Iran? Do you think it will expand?

Khalifah: War is war. It cannot be confined to a specific place. Had the efforts exerted to end this war been effective, the war would not have expanded. War is like a fire in dry grass; it can expand to devour large sectors and can only be contained through good intentions. The war against cities is a natural matter, because so long as the war continues, the cities will be exposed to shelling.

Al-Husayni: What is Bahrain doing to stop this war?

Khalifah: Bahrain, like other fraternal countries in the region, has supported from the beginning and has contributed to peace efforts. The truth is that since the first week of the eruption of the war the brothers of Iraq have expressed their full readiness to stop the war and affirmed many times that they are ready to sit at the negotiating table and hold discussions. The GCC countries had hoped that both sides would respond, but regrettably only one side has done so. Nevertheless, we hope that we will not be affected by the irresponsiveness of the other side. However, we will continue our efforts to stop the war.

Al-Husayni: Is the visit by Saudi Foreign Minister Prince Saud al-Faysal to Tehran the beginning of new relations between the Gulf states and Iran?

Khalifah: As a matter of fact, Saudi Arabia has always played a leading role in bringing about an appropriate solution to end bloodshed among Arab and Islamic countries. The visit of Prince Saud is a part of this objective. The Kingdom's objective has always been noble. The Kingdom exerts its efforts so that the whole world can live in peace. Since peace in the region is necessary and concerns all countries, and since the Kingdom makes all its efforts on the basis of its good intentions, we should hope it succeeds in its moves. The latest move, whatever it may be, shows the good intentions of Saudi Arabia and the GCC states.

Al-Husayni: Bahrain has relations with Iran. Are these relations distinguished or tense?

Khalifah: Relations between us are neither distinguished nor tense. We in Bahrain, like the rest of our brothers in the region, support cooperation with our neighbors and respect what the neighbor does within his own country. There are things which should not exceed these limits, such as interference in the affairs of others.

As for our relations with Iran, I cannot say that they are tense in view of the fact that the situation is not clear yet. As you know, the existing war is not directed against one country in particular. We consider it a threat to all the region's states. Therefore, once Iran wishes to establish good relations with countries through deeds, not just words, then Bahrain, like its neighbors, will welcome this.

Al-Husayni: Can you describe Bahrain's relations with the United States?

Khalifah: I assure you that our relations with the United States are good and strong and are based on mutual respect. These relations have not been affected by anything. There is nothing more to add than what is existing between us.

Al-Husayni: Do you highly trust these relations?

Khalifah: Relations are the factor which governs confidence among countries. Our relations with the United States are old and nothing has taken place to change them. At the same time, the United States has done nothing to make us lose our confidence in it. We hope that these relations will continue as they are on the basis of mutual respect.

Al-Husayni: It has been mentioned that the United States agreed to sell two [*figure as published*] military aircraft to Bahrain. Do you intend to consolidate your military defenses?

Khalifah: We always support the development of our military defenses. Whether we receive our weapons from the United States or from any other country, this comes within the framework of our attempt to diversify and consolidate our weapons. This is our policy in the armament of our forces.

Al-Husayni: To what extent do you want to develop your relations with the Soviet Union?

Khalifah: At present, we do not have relations with the Soviet Union. I think that we in the Gulf region must reconsider our relations with countries, especially since the Soviet Union is a superpower like the United States. The Soviet Union had relations with the United States before it had relations with other countries, including the Arab countries.

As a matter of fact, a few years ago I did not recommend the idea of establishing relations with the Soviet Union, but now I think we must reconsider our policies. I think it is in the interest of the region's states to try to establish relations with all countries on the basis of mutual interests. Moreover, the Soviet Union is a superpower which has its place and political influence in the world.

Al-Husayni: Can Bahrain take the initiative in establishing relations with the Soviet Union?

Khalifah: Bahrain is a free country and can take the initiative in many matters. However, we have deep relations with our neighbors and I do not think that it is in the interest of any country to make a decision without considering its relations with its neighbors. Normally, the arrangement of any relations with any country is made through consultations. Praise be to God, there are continuous consultations in the GCC and senior officials exchange matters openly. Politically, we agree on our foreign policies. We always discuss our foreign relations when the major GCC leaders meet.

Al-Husayni: This means that the Kingdom of Saudi Arabia can change its views with regard to relations with the Soviets.

Khalifah: I cannot speak on behalf of Saudi Arabia, nor can I speak about the establishment of relations between it and the Soviet Union. The Kingdom has its own policy. However, in this regard the Kingdom always consults its neighbors regarding the adoption of resolutions and the approval of foreign policies, although it is a big country which has its political and economic influence in the whole world.

Al-Husayni: What is your advice to Kuwait after what has happened in it?

Khalifah: The Kuwaiti brothers do not need any advice. We consider what happened in Kuwait as something which happened to all of us. As I said, Kuwait does not need any advice, but like any other country it needs support. Praise be to God, Kuwait is supported by the region. It is a pity that such things happen in Kuwait repeatedly, especially since Kuwait has not harbored hostility toward any regime, any country, or any organization. Kuwait opened its doors for others to come and live in its territory. What has happened should not have happened, but these matters are not in our hands. I think that these acts are carried out by elements that are directed from outside our countries. If we agree among ourselves and coordinate in a better manner

those matters related to security, then we will ward off many dangers aimed toward us.

We as officials and countries are threatened like other countries in the world. The threat to the Gulf countries in particular may be due to our stability, which we consider an important element. Our development in recent years has been due to stability in the first place, and then due to the facilities and existing systems and legislations, from which anyone can benefit. For all these reasons, investment and construction projects have increased and everything that serves the interests of the citizens in the Gulf has flourished.

Al-Husayni: Are Bahraini prisons empty or full?

Khalifah: There are prisons in every country which hold prisoners of various types. Regarding your question, I say that our prisons are not full, nor do we hope that we will fill them. In this we depend on our policy which serves the citizen's interest. Those who rebel against us, such as some elements which create disorder, can be found in every country. If one is sent to prison for other offenses, he will be sent there temporarily because of certain violations or because of human mistakes, which we hope will dwindle with time.

Al-Husayni: Is there any internal threat to Bahrain, from sectarian strife for example?

Khalifah: I do not believe there is a threat of sectarian conflict in Bahrain. I believe that when internal threats take place in many countries, there are foreign and international policies and plots being implemented through internal tools. It is regrettable that laymen and many citizens in the Arab Gulf countries or other Arab countries, or even in the countries which have such problems do not understand this. That is why it does not bother me if internal problems occur in the Gulf region, because the Arab governments in the Gulf have provided everything the citizen needs. It is known to many Arab countries and Arab intelligentsia that the governments of these Arab countries adopt policies which serve the citizen's interest, and nothing else. Hence, I believe that internal matters which cause ideological friction or something similar are external plots which aim to shake Arab unity. Regrettably, these attempts have been successful in many countries throughout the entire Arab nation, and attempts are being made to implement these plots in this region.

Your question gives me the opportunity to talk about this issue in detail. You are a Lebanese. The Lebanese brothers are dear to us and we know what is taking place in your country and the policy your leaders are trying to implement there. We have been trying, together with our brothers in the GCC and our Arab brothers, to save Lebanon. We hope that our people in the region will learn a lesson from what is taking place in other countries so that these people will form the first defense line in the face of any possible discord taking place among them. If the citizen understands that this discord only serves the interests of foreign countries and not his own, the people will form the first defense line for the governments.

I say once again that I am pleased to have this question directed to me because this issue is critical and concerns all citizens, even though many of them do not like to indulge in it or talk about it because it concerns the fundamental beliefs of the people who are one nation. When we go to Europe or Western countries, we do not know whether a man is Catholic or Protestant. On the contrary, we find people who do not talk about religious disunity because this issue of religion only concerns one's self. On the other hand, when they talk about us with regard to this issue, they talk about discord; which faction this group belongs to and which one that belongs to? We are very hopeful that our people in the region will understand these matters before they are influenced by the discord some elements are trying to sow among them.

I thank God once again. I do not believe that this kind of threat exists among us. A threat exists when some people try to influence people's ideas by things which have nothing to do with religion. We are one people. This idea serves one people. We have the same interest and destiny.

Al-Husayni: Has Iran stopped insisting that Bahrain is a part of it?

Khalifah: The issue of Bahrain being a part of Iran is finished. Bahrain is a member of the United Nations. It is an independent and sovereign state. This issue has no value. I think that this file has been closed.

Al-Husayni: Are you able to defend yourselves without foreign support?

Khalifah: We have the capability to defend ourselves for at least several hours. No country in the world is capable of completely defending itself from any offensive. While it is true that we are able to defend, every country needs some support and assistance.

Al-Husayni: Are you in the Gulf worried that either Iraq or Iran will emerge more victorious and powerful at the end of the war?

Khalifah: I am talking about Bahrain. We did not want the war to erupt in the first place. I want to affirm that Iraq also did not want to enter this war. I had visited Iraq 2 weeks before the war broke out, and I saw development and construction which indicated their intention to maintain stability. This war was imposed on Iraq and the region. As to whether we are worried about who will win the war, the answer is no. We have great hopes that the bloodshed will stop and that the two Muslim neighbors will be reconciled. Iraq would like this most of all. I hope that those efforts exerted for halting the war will succeed. These efforts must be supported by all countries of the world. We do not boast of the one who will win or lose the war, because wars are only means for destruction.

The allies won the war because they cooperated among themselves. The countries against which they fought today are developed and civilized. They have their own policies, production, and exports. We are a Gulf state and Iran must realize this. We should review and revise our actions.

Al-Husayni: Let us shift to the Middle East. Do you support the Jordanian-Palestinian agreement?

Khalifah: We support whatever brings stability and solutions to the Palestinian people. We view King Husayn's efforts as beneficial for the Palestinian brothers, because of his long political experience and his contacts. He knows best the interests of the region.

We frankly support King Husayn's policy. We hope that the brother Palestinians will follow this road with King Husayn, for it is in everyone's interest. A solution to the Palestinian issue will benefit everyone. It will serve all the countries of the Arab world. We in the Gulf still consider the Palestinian issue as first priority. Of course, we support any initiative which will achieve positive results and any solution which will allow millions of Palestinians to live in stability.

Al-Husayni: Do you encourage the United States to recognize the PLO?

Khalifah: Of course we encourage the United States to recognize the PLO. This is because the PLO defends the legitimate rights of the Palestinians. We try to explain to the United States that the PLO and the Palestinian brothers who are affiliated with it are not terrorists, but an organization that defends the rights of the Palestinian people, and nothing more. The Palestinians, like any other people, are defending and demanding their rights. There are millions of Palestinians—not merely hundreds or thousands. Palestine was a country and a state. The Palestinians were not brought over from several countries to create an entity. The Palestinians mean Palestine, and Palestine was a country and a state.

Al-Husayni: Do you support the convening of an international conference to resolve the Palestinian question with, of course, the Soviet Union's participation?

Khalifah: I do not believe that international conferences resolve any issues. It is true that the United States and the Soviet Union are important elements, and Palestinian presence in any conference that deals with the Palestinian question is necessary, but I do not support the convening of international conferences to solve our own issues in view of what we have suffered from the results of such conferences.

I would support the convening of an international conference if there was any hope that such a conference would achieve results.

Al-Husayni: As the idea of an international conference is cast aside, there are those who propose direct negotiations among the Palestinians, the Jordanians, and Israel. What is your view?

Khalifah: I do not want to enter into the details of this matter. As you know, the Palestinian question is our principal cause. There is no Arab official who has not talked about this issue. There is no elected leader, old or new, who has not called for a solution to the Palestinian question. I believe it is better not to turn the Palestinian question into a scapegoat. I believe that the Palestinian question is important, but I do not want to add to what my brothers the Arab leaders have said. The efforts that we make and the efforts that are made by King Husayn and all those who are interested in the cause suffice.

I believe that Abu Ammar [Yasir Arafat] is a man who is being asked to do a lot of things: Everyone is asking him to do this or that. He has proven that he is a leader, and that he is active and flexible. We must support him. We must continue the efforts to find solutions that will safeguard a good living for our Palestinian brothers and protect their dignity.

Al-Husayni: What solution do you see for the Lebanese question?

Khalifah: The solution to the Lebanese question rests in the hands of the Lebanese. What is happening in Lebanon is painful for us. We have known Lebanon from the time we were young. I do not think that there is any person in the Gulf who did not visit Lebanon when it was stable and prosperous. Everyone feels that however much the Lebanese differ among themselves, they will not differ over Lebanon's interests. However, as I said in the beginning, it is external influences that have affected Lebanon.

There is no need to say much; the solution rests in the hands of the Lebanese brothers, and no one can impose any solution on them.

Source: *Akhbar Al-Khalij* (Manama), 30 June 1985, p. 5, as translated in *FBIS-MEA-V–85–127*, 2 July 1985, pp. C1-C4.

Document 51

Press Conference by Prince Sultan ibn Abd al-Aziz, Saudi Second Deputy Prime Minister, Minister of Defense and Aviation, and Inspector General, London

28 September 1985

Question: Will the aircraft deal that the Kingdom has signed with Britain constitute a major departure on the part of Saudi Arabia from dependence on the United States to obtain military equipment, or will it continue to seek to get U.S. F–15 planes and other U.S. defensive hardware?

Answer: The Saudi Government issued a statement before we departed the Kingdom which clarifies this stand. There are no restrictions on the arms that the Kingdom buys from any country for two reasons. The first is that Saudi Arabia pays the value of any arms that it purchases without borrowing from the country from which it purchases them. Hence, there is no reason to ask for permission from any country or for there to be objections from another country if we buy arms from whatever country.

The second reason is that we began considering this arms deal 2 years ago. Throughout this period we evaluated the arms found in the countries with which we deal. Purchasing this type of aircraft is within the plan of the Saudi Armed Forces. This explanation proves that the credibility

of the United States continues. [*sentence as received*] We will continue to purchase U.S. arms. As for the F–15 planes to which some newspapers have referred, when we request arms from a country we do not impose our will on it, nor do we impose conditions on when or how the purchase will take place. The matter is left up to the United States. When it finds that it is able to sell those arms to the Kingdom, then we will buy these planes.

Question: Does Saudi Arabia's plan to develop its Armed Forces include the acquisition of French Mirage–2000 planes?

Answer: Our relations with France are excellent. What the press has said regarding a difference between the Kingdom and France is not true. It is also untrue that there are complications with regard to purchasing these aircraft. His Highness said: I would like to assert that French arms are excellent. We are still carefully considering these planes and when the appropriate time comes and when our Armed Forces need this type or other types of aircraft, then we will not hesitate.

Question: You have stated that the deal you have signed with Britain will not affect your relationship with the United States. Does this mean that you have not given up hope that it is possible to make an arms deal with the United States which will be the equivalent of the one you have signed with Britain?

Answer: Actually the requests which are made by the Kingdom to friendly countries are made according to our needs and their ability to sell. If the United States is abler to sell us F–15 planes or other weapons which we need, then we will purchase these weapons. If we request arms from any country and it refuses because of its circumstances, we might appreciate these circumstances, but we will seek arms elsewhere. Diversification of arms is one of the bases of the Kingdom's policies. This is not new. We now have British, U.S., and French planes; French missiles; and French and U.S. warships. The Kingdom imports from its friends as long as they agree to supply us with what we require to defend our country and our Arab nation. We will continue to do so. Regarding any country that has certain circumstances that govern it or has problems, we never like to provoke any problem for any person or country. [*sentence as received*]

Question: What benefit does the Kingdom get from this exchange? Does this deal create a problem for the Kingdom with regard to OPEC?

Answer: Exchanging oil [for arms] in this deal is by agreement of the two countries on the principle of exchange. The decision depends on the Kingdom. A discussion will be held on this subject after 2 months. Saudi and British experts will have the opportunity to participate. If exchange is in the interest of the Kingdom, we will go ahead and the agreement will be approved within the limits of the Kingdom's production quota as approved by OPEC and within the limits of the declared price, this matter will be announced following the final agreement. As to whether there will be a disagreement between the Kingdom and the

OPEC countries, this is not expected, because the Kingdom is one of the founding countries of OPEC and will not do anything that harms OPEC. However, the Kingdom will not—as his majesty the king recently stated—remain silent with regard to the departure from OPEC resolutions by some OPEC countries. He said that the Kingdom does not want to be anyone's guardian, nor accept guardianship by anyone. If the Kingdom finds itself in certain circumstances, it will take the measures that it considers appropriate within the limits of its quota ceiling and the official prices of OPEC. What is without fault and controversy is that there are no conditions at all pertaining to the Kingdom's purchase of arms from whatever country, particularly this deal. The British defense secretary affirmed this in the press conference he held following the signing of the deal.

Source: *FBIS-MEA-V–85–189*, 30 Sept. 1985, p. C3.

Document 52

Press Conference by Prince Sultan ibn Abd al-Aziz, Saudi Second Deputy Prime Minister, Minister of Defense and Aviation, and Inspector General, Washington, D.C.

5 October 1985

I would like to thank my colleagues and brothers, the men of the Saudi media. We congratulate ourselves on the Kingdom's international standing, thanks to the Islamic faith adhered to by the Kingdom, its people, its government, and its leaders, and thanks to the continuous immense efforts made in service to Arabs and Muslims by His Majesty King Fahd and his crown prince. It is true that this prestige comes from a number of things, but the bases on which we depend is our faith. From this faith emanates development and stability. There is no life without stability. Stability is one of the bases and principles which every people, and all leaders are keen to attain. With God's protection we enjoy stability. In light of this, construction and progress has proceeded. It is worth saying that no one can claim to have done this country a favor. God, the almighty, granted this country the spiritual food needed for life by locating the house of God, the almighty, within the territories of the Kingdom, in addition to launching the prophesy and God's message from this land.

These were not given to any other country but this dear country, which reflects God's willingness to have his people ensure sincere worship in words and deeds. Moreover, the almighty granted us good things and gave us black gold—such gold no one else can claim to have given us. Social justice can only be accomplished when there are funds. The funds cannot be useful if there is no stability. Stability

cannot be useful when there are no principles. We live according to the Sunna of the prophet and under the umbrella of God's book.

Based on this premise, the [*word indistinct*] began, which is the correct citizenship, love, and allegiance to the almighty and to his sincere prophet. You know that education belongs to one person and history belongs to one person. [*as heard*] In our country, thanks be to God, education is independent of everything. The student can acquire education without being affected by anything except that which promotes the country's social and religious aspects. We have equality and equal opportunities among the son of his majesty the king, the son of the shepherd, and the son of the farmer. This is a privilege with which we are happy. We thank God that we have this kind of people. They are equal when they are at school, when they are in power, in stability, in justice, and in equality in rights. [*as heard*] How many times did his Majesty King Abd al-Aziz, the founder and the unifier of the peninsula—as did King Saud, King Faysal, King Khalid, and King Fahd—confer with those concerned to tackle general matters? These are parts of that to which we adhere. They are regarded as major concerns in other places.

As for the construction of society, each of us believes he was born here. Everyone believes that he is the brother of Abdallah. Each of us believes that he is a friend of the minister or any other person. There is no difference between the official and the citizen. The doors are open. In other words the simplicity and democracy—which the people call for all over the world—are applied habitually. I mention these things because we have to thank the almighty, who says: Proclaim the bounty of your God. Proclaiming God's bounties can be done by acknowledging it. We must thank God, the almighty, who bestowed on us this grace. From this premise, we have won world's respect.

The Saudi people do not ask for anyone's help. There are no countries [*words indistinct*], nor countries adopting our projects, nor countries granting us loans. On the contrary, we grant loans to people, and help them as much as we can, either with Islamic help, which is our duty, or with Arab and national help, which is a commitment to provide humane assistance for poverty, hunger, illiteracy, and sickness in various parts of the world. As you have heard, the United Nations has declared that Saudi Arabia is the only country that contributes everything required of it to the budget of the United Nations and its agencies and institutions.

Perhaps one of our faults, the faults that [*passage indistinct*] of an individual personally, but decreases the knowledge of the people on it, is propaganda. I do not say this to contradict my colleague the information minister, but the nature of the Kingdom is not to propagandize on what it spends, grants, or does. I believe this is an unseen good deed by which we should always abide, no matter what is said about us. Many countries issue propaganda against the Kingdom without result; they break on a rock called the Arab Muslim Saudi people.

I read your questions and found that they concentrate on four points. The first asks for the Saudi reaction to the Israeli raid on sister Tunis and our Palestinian brothers residing in Tunisia. As you know, his majesty the king has made a concentrated effort to contact all the Arab countries and to establish a decisive, rational stance. We here, as officials serving the Kingdom, upon instruction, were to contact the U.S. Government. The result of irrational decisiveness leads to failure and the result, laxity and complacency, is failure. However, the stance of the Kingdom—decisive, rational, and wise--was conveyed to us by his majesty the king, and I relayed it to friends at the United Nations.

As you know, 1 hour before delivering the address at the United Nations we were surprised by word of the raid. The response of his majesty the king was quick. We added a new closing to the address on the raid and the Kingdom's stance condemning Israel. It demanded that the entire free and civilized world, the world that serves peace, denounce and condemn this act characterized by the law of the jungle. We praise God that the resolution issued by Security Council was perhaps ideal within the context of the United Nations. It was not the resolution of the Kingdom of Saudi Arabia, but we are more proud of it than if it was our very own. It is the resolution of the world's countries.

It might be said that the United States abstained from voting. I believe that the United States took a big step by abstaining from the vote, which means support for the decision. The United States [*words indistinct*] and the infiltration of Zionism in U.S. establishments, particularly in the economic institutions, (?has nothing similar to it). The United States is not like other countries. The door to naturalization there is open. The U.S. citizenry is comprised of 200 world ethnic groups, all of them Americans. It means that a big country has attracted science and knowledge from all parts of the world. This has great advantages, but there is one disadvantage—solidarity is not 100 percent. A more hospitable people, like the Kingdom of Saudi Arabia, are one in origin and race, speak as one, and hold one opinion.

Three or four questions can be summed up in one: What is the Kingdom's view of the rash Israeli raid, which was an indirect shock? The Israeli rashness has been revealed day after day. I believe that the Israeli invasion of Lebanon, its defeat and withdrawal, and its raid on the Iraqi nuclear power plants and its failure [*words indistinct*]. It is true that Iraq lost a significant amount of money, but the solidarity of the Arab nation with Iraq reconstructed the power plants. Concerning Israel's raid on Tunis, it caused problems with European countries on the Mediterranean Sea, as Israel used an international passage for piracy [*words indistinct*]. Nevertheless, the result is bad for Israel.

The endeavors of his majesty the king toward Arab solidarity progresses. Arab solidarity has a great role in preventing harm to the Arab nation. There is nothing to keep harm from the Arab nation except solidarity and the unity of goals and fate. We should always keep this in mind. Despite this, we as Saudis are but a small nation compared to the Arab nation, yet big concerning targets and ideals. This is our belief and our call.

The second question for which you seek my reply asks what efforts the Kingdom has made to realize Arab solidarity. In reality the Fes summit, held 2 years ago, and the resolutions adopted by the entire Arab nation revealed to the world that we want right and justice. These are outlined in eight points in the Fes resolutions which stem from right, justice, legitimacy, and just peace. We do not seek war, but also we do not seek capitulation. We want a just peace which provides rights, legitimacy, and justice to the Palestinian citizen. Based on this, the Arab nation sent delegations, to contact the leaders of the Soviet Union, the United States, France, Britain, and the PRC—the five permanent member countries of the UN Security Council. The effectiveness and importance of these countries cannot be denied, without even looking at their mistakes, partiality, and desires. However, they are the five big countries that can move the world after almighty God. The Arab nation informed them of the Fes summit resolution, the concept of which was ridiculed, ignored, and violated by Israel. No matter how long it takes and whatever happens, Israel should submit to these eight points, because the points were drawn from comprehensive study and examination from all sides. The Arab nation adopted it unanimously; even those with extremist opinions and extremist concepts agreed on these eight points. Therefore, we must abide by them. This is the policy of the Kingdom, there is no alternative. On this basis the Casablanca summit was held in Rabat 2 months ago. On this basis, thank God, the brothers in Syria and Jordan came together in the Kingdom and a dialogue and fraternity began. We hope that these things will continue until we reach Arab solidarity, in light of which we will hold the basic Arab conference in Riyadh in a time [*words indistinct*] when the circumstances of the success are completed and the [*words indistinct*] of the Saudi people. We are ready to make sacrifices even if the conference fails. However, the success lies in the Arab nation. We do not want to say one day that a complete Arab summit has failed. We hope that the efforts of his majesty the king and his royal highness the crown prince and other Saudi efforts continue and bring about the success of this conference.

The third question asks what has been done about the arms deal? We have stated that there are plans that have been carried out by the Kingdom of Saudi Arabia. It is not in our interest to have the approval or disapproval of another country. We evaluate the needs of our Armed Forces. Our evaluation will be submitted to friendly countries. We give priority to any country which possesses such advanced arms. Naturally arms are similar in friendly European countries and the United States. For example, the Kingdom needs three types of aircraft: the modernized F–15E which means that the bomber [*words indistinct*] produced by the United States; the Tornado aircraft produced by Britain, which are of two types—long-range bomber aircraft and interceptor to support the bomber; and the French Mirage–2000, which includes bombers, and bomber interceptors. All three types of aircraft we gave as an example [*word indistinct*]. We ask for a detailed evaluation of each aircraft concerning its capability, armament, production, use, the possibility of obtaining it, flying range, and advantages and priorities.

I affirm once again that the studies have been in progress for 2 years. As a matter of fact, our youth in the Armed Forces, and particularly in the Air Force who work on the aircraft, may work more than 18 hours each day. I would like to affirm once again that for a year and a half they have not taken Thursdays and Fridays off at all, while they are entitled to take them alternatively. All this for only evaluation and study. The interests of the Armed Forces are based on this study. Everything studied was presented to the Armed Forces.

The studies clarified that there are but two bomber aircraft choices—the Tornado and the F–15E. This does not mean that our studies showed the Mirage–2000 aircraft to be of less use than those aircraft, but there were two reasons, which I mentioned earlier. I will visit France next week and meet with the president. I will also meet and hold talks with the new defense minister and the chief of staff. I would like to affirm that relations between the Kingdom of Saudi Arabia and France are significant, and not purchasing Mirage aircraft has had no effect at present.

However, concerning the F–15E aircraft, the Kingdom already has a large number of F–15 aircraft. We have spare parts, ammunition, high level training, and maintenance workshops, and hangars. Therefore, the addition of F–15E aircraft is 100 percent normal. This is why we made a request of the United States.

Concerning the Tornado aircraft, we have British Lightning aircraft. They were Lightning-II and the earlier Lightning-I, but they were worn out. Thus we had to either finally cancel it, which would cause the loss of tens of millions of pounds to the state, not millions but tens of millions. There are spare parts, ammunition, and aircraft, but more important there are hangars and maintenance workshops.

The military ideology of Britain is one thing, the military ideology of France or the United States is something else. Even the suits worn by the pilots are different. The suits from Britain, France and United States are all different. The same applies to the hydraulic equipment. You may talk to the Air Force personnel on this. The point was raised at the Finance Ministry when it asked why we should request 1000 uniforms from United States and the same number of uniforms from Britain. The uniforms for the Lightning aircraft are completely different from those of the American aircraft. Thus, the Tornado has its advantages. Britain will buy back all of our Lightning aircraft for an excellent price. This favors the Saudi treasury and the Saudi people. Millions have been spent on the hangars and workshops at four bases in the Kingdom,—no need to mention their names—and they are ready to immediately accommodate the Tornado aircraft. The Tornado aircraft will

arrive in the Kingdom in 6 months. They will be flown by Saudi pilots, maintained by Saudi technicians, and kept in Saudi hangars and workshops. Why? Because we have the bases for them.

One of the main reasons which made the Saudi Air Force assessor rule out the Mirage aircraft at present is that we did not have these aircraft before. However, we will proceed to hold joint coordination talks and study with the friendly French Government to ensure every possible improvement of this aircraft is made in the next stage. This period may last 2 years, or even 10 years. If things proceed well, we will make a decision to purchase the French Mirage aircraft without being influenced by any side. However, Saudi money is dearer to us than our own lives. No money should be spent uselessly. I have clarified that the Tornado aircraft which we have purchased from the United Kingdom were not purchased because the United States, as the press reports, rejected it or because some congressmen objected to Saudi Arabia's order for F–15E's. We planned to buy the Tornado whether the F–15E's were obtained or not. The Tornado aircraft has its own mission and tactics which differ from those of the various F–15 aircraft. Achieving a balance in weaponry is determined by Saudi Arabia's policy which is based on its own interests. When we decided to buy the Tornado we also asked for a Tornado interceptor, because a long-range Tornado bomber should have a fighter escort for protection. In order to ensure coordination between personnel of the Saudi air and ground forces with regard to equipment, communications, speed and maneuvering, we found it necessary to overcome financial problems and purchase two squadrons of Tornado interceptors, totaling 22 fighters. At present we have a complete, coordinated, and integrated set of aircraft. All Lightning aircraft currently in our possession, including weapons systems and ammunition which cost millions of pounds, will be returned to Britain. This deal is regarded as an act of Britain's friendship and good attitude toward us [*word indistinct*].

With regard to the F–15, naturally the United States has its regulations and rules as a superpower. We respect the American people with their democratic system and their rules. We also respect Congress and its members, whether they support us or do not. Hence, we respect the countries with which we deal, but the U.S. Administration is responsible in this case and not Congress. Congress is the concern of the United States and its administration, but dealings with us are the concern of the U.S. administration, beginning with the U.S. President down to the concerned ministers and the [*word indistinct*] who deal with us militarily. The United States has not rejected this request. We have not stated that the United States rejected or made excuses. We believe that actually the issue is the concern of their leaders.

I was appointed by his majesty the king to discuss this issue with the concerned sides upon arrival. Their answer was that they do not reject it at all and that they support all (?our requests) for aircraft, missiles, or advanced weapons.

I do not want to give more details on our weapons because it is not in the interest of the Saudi people for others to know about those details. Everything we requested from the United States was accepted. We agreed with them to leave the issue at present and to (?make) this deal with the Kingdom of Saudi Arabia at an appropriate time.

I would like to affirm that even if this deal is not made soon, it will in no way affect the defenses of the Kingdom of Saudi Arabia. However, if it is made, it will double the defenses of the Kingdom of Saudi Arabia. Thus, we are in need of them. The approval of the concerned U.S. parties is on its way, but the date is still open—it may be 1 month or 1 year, but the issue is making good progress.

With regard to the third question, which deals with the Air Force, aviation, and their (?fears), I have already talked to international media about this issue.

Please excuse me, my fellow pressmen, if I summarize the questions. The fourth question is about the GCC, and the significance of the GCC defense ministers meeting in Kuwait scheduled to convene on 20 October. The second part of this question is about the GCC military industry project and whether this project will be submitted to the GCC summit scheduled to convene in Muscat next November. The answer: The GCC defense ministers conference is an international conference. It is well known that the defense and foreign ministers are the basic powers of the GCC. The GCC summit must discuss military and political strategy. Respectively, security, the economy, and other issues must be discussed.

We thank God that for the first time in the Arab world, regional institutions are cooperating in six countries without any differences. They are cooperating further for the prosperity and the benefit of the people. We are working within the Arab League and the UN charters for international cooperation. These are countries of goodwill, not evil and aggressive countries. These countries work to achieve development and the aspirations of their people. The GCC defense ministers will hold a meeting in Kuwait on 20 October. The agenda actually consist[s] of three points. First, what are the achievements of the military committees formed by the joint defense and foreign ministers conference in Asir Region last year? We will evaluate every accomplishment.

We affirm that all decisions adopted by the joint defense and foreign ministers conference in Asir, and ratified by the GCC summit in Kuwait, were completely implemented. However, I feel that the details of these decisions must not be disclosed to the world, because they serve the security and the stability of the region. For example, the most important decision was to assemble the token forces, which began 15 days ago. The token forces are the GCC armed force currently assembled in King Khalid military city. These forces are to conduct exercises in harmony with each other. These forces are the nucleus for any deterrent rapid deployment forces from the GCC armed forces.

The GCC army chiefs of staff will convene next Monday in Riyadh to discuss military issues. They will submit to the GCC defense ministers conference in Kuwait the results of their evaluations as to what were the right and the wrong decisions. The right decisions will be passed on, the wrong decisions will be evaluated and corrected, in cooperation with our aides, the army chiefs of staff, the commanders of operations, and the commanders in chief of the GCC armed forces.

This is a summary of the forthcoming meeting of the GCC defense ministers to be convened in Kuwait. Concerning the military industry, a decision was made 2 years ago to establish a GCC military corporation. Of course the names of those involved and the location of the corporation has yet to be decided. However, we began to evaluate the military industry and the things needed by the GCC related to light and medium industries. We are looking ahead to heavy industry, but we must proceed gradually. A number of local military industry corporations have been formed in several GCC states. As you know, the Kingdom has established a general corporation for military industry, which includes forming its general secretariat. The corporation has an independent budget and a system similar to that found in military industries in the Kingdom of Saudi Arabia.

Among the budget goals is to establish a military institution in the Kingdom to replace the present military factories. It is to be a general institution with its own board of directors. Over the next few days the fruits of this project will be shown prior to the Arab summit. The Saudi military industrial corporation and the Saudi private sector are currently conducting consultations and exchanging expertise.

We have introduced a new element—economic balance. Economic balance stems from the peace shield project, related to the leadership and control of the air forces, which has assigned not less than 30 percent of the project to the private industrial sector in the Kingdom of Saudi Arabia, not necessarily to military industries, but to advance developed industries. For example, Saudi Airlines has contributed (?30) percent in this regard to manufacture machinery and equipment for Saudi Airlines, which previously purchased from abroad. In a few years they will be manufactured in the Kingdom. The Saudi investment corporation has contributed 5 percent. The Gulf Investment Corporation stemming from the GCC has contributed 28 percent, and other private sectors have allocated $500 million for the economic balance project. These form the basic nucleus currently participating in the Kingdom's military industries. When the general corporation is established and supervised by the Saudi industrial corporation, we will then present to the GCC an integrated organized industrial project. Hence, the GCC military industries corporation will be formed by GCC defense ministers, the army chiefs of staff, and the civil industry ministers. A military industry cannot be formed without the participation of civilian industries or national capital, and will be successful.

I think that we should end our fraternal talk because we might get involved in other issues and we do not have the time, we might begin repeating ourselves. Thank you.

Source: *FBIS-MEA-V–85–196*, 9 Oct. 1985, pp. C2-C5.

Document 53

Saudi King Issues Decree on War Industries Law

9 December 1985

In the name of God, the compassionate, the merciful.

No. 2/5 date: 20 Rabi al-Awwal 1406 of the Hegira [2 December 1985]

With the assistance of God, I Fahd ibn Abd al-Aziz Al Saud, King of the Kingdom of Saudi Arabia, following reference to articles 19 and 20 of the Cabinet law, issued by Royal Decree No. 38, dated 22 Shawwal 1377 of the Hegira, and following reference to the Cabinet decision No. 45, dated 28 Safar 1406 of the Hegira [11 November], have decreed the following:

1. Approval of the internal law of the general institution of military industries according to the accompanying text.

2. The deputy prime minister and ministers, each according to his concern, are required to implement this decree. It is effective from the date of issue.

Signed: Fahd ibn Abd al-Aziz

Source: *FBIS-MEA-V–85–239*, 12 Dec. 1985, p. C5.

Document 54

Interview with GCC Secretary General Abdallah Bisharah

14 December 1985

[Excerpts] *Al-Tadamun*: The latest GCC summit conference was characterized by a leaning toward moderation and balance in its approach to regional and international issues, but how successful was it in tackling Gulf controversial issues?

Bisharah: To be fair, it is too early to talk about the Muscat summit conference which ended only 3 weeks ago or about the resolutions it passed, particularly on issues of interest to the region. Ample time is needed for an assessment, but that does not mean that we should overlook the effects which the summit has had on the Gulf moves, which have actually gained more strength on regional, as well as international issues. All I can say for certain is that the summit conference studied the situation in the region from the angle of the delicate responsibilities which the Gulf states shoulder in ensuring their security. The question of balance and moderation is at the heart of the GCC policy. In essence the position of the GCC states has not changed. What matters is the purpose, not the sharp tone.

Al-Tadamun: The issue of security is still being raised urgently as the most fundamental issue for the states of the region. What is new in this connection?

Bisharah: Let me be frank with you. There is no courtesy in matters of security. There can be no ideological or economic development unless the security aspect is assured. There can be no question about that. We in the GCC are paying this matter great attention now that terrorism has found its way to our area. Terrorism, which has reached us, and the question of security reform in the region are closely related. I assure you that this matter has come to mean a lot to us after Kuwait became a target of terrorist acts aimed at undermining and destroying stability and security there. The attempt on the life of the amir of Kuwait and the blowing up of public places where people go with their children only mean killing innocent people to serve terrorist objectives. The Gulf states are not unaware of that they are trying to do what they can to avoid what is happening in other countries.

Al-Tadamun: What has become of the GCC contacts with Iraq and Iran aimed at persuading the latter to come to the negotiating table and why should not a policy of secret mediation be pursued?

Bisharah: We cannot be just spectators in the region. The fact that we do not resort to the method of secret contacts with Iran stems from our conviction that no sense of vacuum should develop. Our open contacts create the necessary movement toward reactivating the issue in the light of what we consider to be the responsibility of the GCC states to end the Iraq-Iran conflict. We must not despair. In this connection, the inclination in the GCC is that we should not reach the point where we throw up our hands and give up. We must go all the way until the matter is resolved.

Al-Tadamun: It seems that Iran's policy is to push the states of the region into the state of despair that you mentioned.

Bisharah: It is an unusual problem and should be tackled in an unusual way.

Al-Tadamun: Do you think that the calm on the Iraq-Iran war front indicates a change in the Iranian attitude or is what we are seeing now the calm before the storm?

Bisharah: Judging by the Iranian statements and the attitude of the Iranian rulers, there is no change in the Iranian attitude. This is due to the superpowers' indifference toward this war. We believe that there should be international efforts to help us end the war. We attribute the international attitude to the fact that the war has not spread all these years.

Al-Tadamun: Do you mean that the superpowers' nonchalance is the result of their not wanting the war to spread or because there is little chance of it spreading?

Bisharah: It is a known fact that superpower interests are what matter most to them and these interests have so far not been affected because the war has not spread.

Al-Tadamun: It seems that the process of establishing diplomatic relations between the GCC states and the Soviet Union has begun. Could you explain to us the background of the Gulf-Soviet contacts and their timing?

Bisharah: We in the GCC have a formula for the cooperation of the six member states, but each state has its own views. Flexibility is a special characteristic of the GCC because we do not wish to lay down laws for contacts with other world states. What I mean is that we do not want to be faced with or to lay down set rules. That is why each state has its own national views.

Al-Tadamun: You have supported the idea of clearing the Arab atmosphere. At the Muscat summit conference did you support the possibility of efforts for the return of Egypt [to the Arab fold]?

Bisharah: That matter was not discussed collectively.

Al-Tadamun: It was noticed that during his visit to Muscat after the summit conference President Mubarak was treated as if that issue had been discussed. Was that treatment just courtesy or did it reflect a political attitude?

Bisharah: Quite frankly, that issue was not discussed. The decision on it was left to the efforts and contacts of the member states.

Al-Tadamun: You must have read the Egyptian president's recent statements. For the GCC, do you see these statements as an obstacle to better relations between Egypt and the Arab world?

Bisharah: We in the GCC pursue a constructive course. We are not interested in incitement, which only widens the gap in the Arab world. Our position is this: Do good or keep quiet.

Al-Tadamun: Were there any contacts between the GCC and Moscow and Washington after the Geneva conference?

Bisharah: There were no contacts at GCC level but there may have been bilateral contacts.

Source: *FBIS-MEA-V–85–242*, 17 Dec. 1985, pp. C1-C2.

Document 55
Statement on the Iraq-Iran War Issued by the Kuwaiti National Assembly and Government
11 February 1986

The National Assembly and the government have been following news of the Iranian attack on brotherly Iraq with great concern. The assembly and the government express their strong condemnation of and great concern over Iran's attempt to occupy part of the Iraqi territory and the repeated attacks on Iraq which are aimed at harming the independence and sovereignty of an Arab country, despite all efforts which have been and are being made for peace and fraternity between the two Muslim neighboring countries.

The assembly and the government believe that the latest Iranian attack is shaking stability and security and increasing tension in the Arab Gulf region, is providing greater opportunity for the superpowers to interfere, and is greatly harming the countries in the region.

On the basis of Iraq's continuing response since the Islamic conference in al-Taif to the call for a cease-fire and a peaceful resolution of the conflict, Kuwait is hoping that Iran will respond to the repeated appeals emanating from international and regional organizations to establish a just peace that would safeguard the rights of the two sides, and save the region from the evil and calamity of war, foreign interference, and harm in the interests of the countries of the region. Kuwait again urges international organizations, especially the UN Security Council to carry out their essential role to establish peace. It also demands that Arab countries adhere to the Arab League's charters and agreements, especially the Fes summit resolutions, concerning the issue of the Iraqi-Iranian war, and take all the necessary steps to establish peace and stability in the region in order to safeguard the rights of the two neighboring Muslim countries within the framework of international charters and the concept of good-neighborliness.

Source: *FBIS-MEA-V–86–028*, 11 Feb. 1986, p. C1.

Document 56
Kuwaiti Assembly Issues Statement on Gulf War
18 February 1986

After the National Assembly listened to the government's statement on the dangerous developments of the Iraq-Iran war, the assembly confirmed the contents of the previous statement issued by the National Assembly and the government on 11 February. While the assembly confirms support for the contacts currently being held by the government to contain this destructive war and prevent its evils and hazards from harming the region, the assembly stresses its denunciation of the recent Iranian incursions into the territories of fraternal Iraq, which constitutes a gross danger to the region as [a] whole and paves the way for foreign interference.

During the current critical circumstances which our region is passing through, the assembly affirms the need to ensure cohesion and bolster the internal front to ward off any danger that threatens the homeland. This can only be attained by making every citizen shoulder his responsibilities toward his country and preserve it from the dangers and the rumors designed to harm its power and cohesion.

As the assembly values the contacts undertaken by the government with the fraternal and friendly countries, it hopes that these contacts will continue to ensure protection and safeguard the region. The assembly and the government agreed to jointly follow up the developments in the region and to exchange views.

Source: *Al-Qabas* (Kuwait), 19 Feb. 1986, p. 4, as translated in *FBIS-MEA-V–86–035*, 21 Feb. 1986, p. C1.

4

Integrating the Economy

ANALYSIS

Just as the perceived threats to internal and external security of the GCC states impelled them to cooperate in coping with acts of terrorism and in deterring the spread of war, these threats drove them to cooperate in integrating their economies. Just as their quest for greater internal and external security dated back to the decade before the establishment of the GCC, their desire to integrate their economies emerged during the same period. In fact, as already indicated in chapter 1, the Gulf states had an easier time cooperating with each other in the economic field than in the political and military fields before the establishment of the GCC as shown by the example of the Gulf Organization for Industrial Consulting (GOIC), dating back to 1976.

Yet, even though security concerns were paramount, the GCC states also had some economic motives in setting for themselves the goal of economic integration. Perhaps the single most compelling economic consideration behind the move to integrate the economy of the six countries was, and continues to be, the threat of depletion of their oil resources. The specter of the disappearance of these finite and nonrenewable resources looms larger in the GCC countries than in the relatively developed oil-rich countries. The GCC economies are extremely dependent on their oil revenues as the single most important source of income and foreign exchange, lacking significant productive capacity in the non-oil sectors.

Unlike some other economically underdeveloped oil-rich countries such as Iran, the GCC states as a whole have larger oil reserves and have, therefore, a longer time to develop their non-oil productive capacity before the oil runs out. That fact does not, however, affect their basic desire to reduce their dependence on oil as soon as possible. Moreover, there is a considerable discrepancy in the longevity of the GCC countries' oil reserves. According to one source, "oil in the GCC will run out in the lifetime of present generation (Qatar, Bahrain, Oman), its children (UAE), or its grandchildren (Saudi Arabia and Kuwait)." According to the same source, conscious of the risks of accumulating oil revenues in an inflationary world, the GCC countries are "no longer satisfied with their role as just the residual suppliers of the world crude oil requirements. Now they are contemplating the creation of an advanced and integrated industrial base and the expansion of their sphere of control over the transportation, processing and marketing of their oil and its derivatives."[1]

Perhaps this basic economic concern of the GCC countries accounts for the swiftness with which they adopted a concrete framework for integrating their economies. As early as 8 June 1981, the GCC states adopted the Economic Agreement that their leaders ratified during their second summit meeting in November 1981 in Riyadh (D57). This twenty-eight-article agreement provided for activities in a wide variety of economic sectors, including trade, movement of capital and people across the borders, coordination of economic development plans, cooperation in the transfer of technology, linking of transportation and communication, and financial and monetary cooperation. This agreement formed the basis for integrating the economies of the six countries in all sectors including the transit system (D61).

And yet, the GCC states accorded economic cooperation a lesser priority than security and political cooperation. In the words of Secretary General Abdallah Bisharah, "political and security coordination are pre-requisites to economic integration."[2] They are prerequisites because the perceived threats to internal and external security of the GCC states loomed so large in the wake of the Iranian Revolution and the Iraq-Iran war. One could argue that by pooling their economic resources the GCC countries would strengthen the economic base of their political and military security and, therefore, that economic integration should be accorded a higher priority. But from the perspective of the GCC leaders, the survival of their regimes could not await the so-called spillover effects of economic cooperation into the political and security areas.

In any event, the cooperation of the GCC states in the economic field seemed much less susceptible to the vicissitudes of the Iraq-Iran war. Although various joint economic plans were considered in direct reaction to the effects of the war, by and large most of the joint economic projects were unrelated to the developments in the war. The economic cooperation of the GCC states embraced the whole gamut of areas during the first five years of the GCC's history. The principal areas, however, revolved around cooperation in the hydrocarbon sector, the non-oil industrial sector, and the trade sector of their economies.

Integrating the Hydrocarbon Sector

The GCC states' efforts to integrate their economies partly involved their oil and gas resources (see App. A, table 5). They command the world's largest pool of proven oil reserves and one of the world's largest pools of gas reserves. With the exception of Bahrain and Oman, they are all members of the Organization of Petroleum Exporting Countries (OPEC), whose decisions affect, and are affected by, the four GCC states, especially Saudi Arabia. The GCC was born in the twilight of a dramatic change in the world oil market. From a seller's market it was transformed into a buyer's market. In the wake of the second oil shock in 1979, Saudi Arabia had produced more than 10 million barrels of oil a day. By 1985 it produced only about 2.5 million barrels. When the GCC was established, the member states altogether earned about $450 billion a year. Less than two years later, their combined oil revenues dropped to about half that amount.

This meant that the oil shock was in reverse. From the first oil shock in 1973–74 to the second one in 1979, oil consumers had paid for a fifteenfold rise in prices. Beginning in 1981 it was the turn of oil producers to suffer from diminishing oil revenues because of a glutted market. This momentous turn-around in the international oil market produced two milestone decisions by OPEC, one on 20 March 1982 and the other on 14 March 1983. For the first time in the history of OPEC, its members decided to set a formal limit on the level of their oil production, at a total daily output of 17.5 million barrels a day, in order to reduce the worldwide surplus of oil and boost oil prices. The second decision resulted in a cut in overall oil prices down to $29 from a high of $34 per barrel. By the end of the GCC's first five years, the price per barrel was about $12 and OPEC faced an unprecedented disarray in its ranks.

Under the circumstances, the Economic Agreement's call for a common oil policy meant that the GCC members had to cope primarily with the problems of production and prices in the oil sector. There is no need to survey numerous frantic meetings of the GCC to show how these issues preoccupied its members throughout the first five years of their experience. It is sufficient to cite a few examples of the GCC's discussions around the time of the two decisions of March 1982 and March 1983. More than a month after the March 1982 meeting on cutting production, the GCC oil ministers were still optimistic about their ability to hold on to the price of $34 per barrel. This optimism was voiced by the Saudi oil minister, Ahmad Zaki Yamani, at the end of an emergency meeting of the GCC oil ministers held on 24 April 1982.[3] But the continuing oversupply of oil and declining prices showed that whatever the nature of their joint "resolutions and recommendations," they had hardly any effect on the market situation.

Mutual recriminations between the hard-line and soft-line OPEC producers over cheating on production quotas marked the atmosphere between the March 1982 and March 1983 OPEC decisions. Before the latter meeting, even Oil Minister Ahmad Zaki Yamani did not believe that there was anything the GCC oil ministers together, or with the support of Iraq, or in consultation with other OPEC producers, could do to reverse the downward trend in oil prices. He said in February 1983 that "the cutback in prices is inevitable."[4] Dr. al-Utaybah, the UAE minister of petroleum and natural resources, even implied a GCC threat by saying, "We hope the OPEC ministers will agree to a new price below the current basic price of $34 a barrel. Otherwise we, the Arabian Gulf states, will take another path."[5] OPEC reduced the price of its oil for the first time on 14 March 1983 by $5 per barrel amid rumors of a "price war" and "production cheating."

The glutted oil market had weakened the oil power that Saudi Arabia and its junior partners had enjoyed in the OPEC ever since 1973–74. Nevertheless, the Economic Agreement provided a useful framework for coordinating the oil policies of the GCC states at a crucial juncture in the history of the international oil market. Outside OPEC, the four GCC producers managed to coordinate their oil policies with Oman, a non-OPEC GCC producer, with Iraq, an OPEC non-GCC member, and sometimes even with Libya and Iran. Inside OPEC, led by Saudi Arabia, they still formed the most powerful block of producers whether or not Saudi Arabia was the "swing producer."

Besides seeking a common policy on oil prices and production, the GCC members tried to coordinate policies on other issues concerning their hydrocarbon resources. One such issue related to the utilization of gas. The GCC region is believed to be rich in both natural gas reservoirs and the gas associated with oil production. Flaring of gas had been a common practice of the foreign companies that controlled Middle Eastern oil resources. But beginning early in the 1970s the increasing control of decision making by oil-producing countries had been associated with an ever-diminishing burning of gas. Qatar, the UAE, and Bahrain are believed to be the GCC nations that have gas. One of the earliest signs of the GCC's concern with the efficient utilization of gas was the possibility of integrating Qatar and Kuwait into Saudi Arabia's extensive gas grid. As oil production fell off, the need for associated gas increased because its production inevitably dropped too. Kuwait, Saudi Arabia, and Abu Dhabi faced shortages. The interest of the GCC in adopting plans for developing Qatar's offshore North Field increased. These plans would provide for the export of natural gas to these other three GCC countries. In 1983 Qatar was expected to move ahead with developing its North Field in the first half of 1984 in order to meet domestic demand. The production from the field would also be enough to sustain a regional gas grid as well. By the end of the first five years of the GCC's existence, however, proposals for a regional gas grid were still being considered. Reportedly, the GCC governments were reluctant to fund such schemes at the time. But they wished to do so eventually in the hope of reducing their dependence on Gulf oil terminals.[6]

Another issue was the construction of a GCC refinery in Oman. The GCC states have thirteen refineries (see App. A, table 6). Refined products could satisfy a great variety of economic and social needs ranging from pharmacological to petrochemical products. (The oldest refinery in the Gulf is located in Abadan, Iran. The oldest refinery within the GCC region is located in Bahrain; others are in Kuwait and in Saudi Arabia's Ras Tanura.) The GCC experts considered plans for building a gigantic refinery in Oman. The GCC states were not simply thinking of prestige; rather, they believed that an indigenous refining process was a necessary first step for developing downstream fuel and non fuel uses. The idea for building a 250,000-barrel-a-day refinery in Salalah, Oman, surfaced early in the life of the GCC. It had to be dropped later, however, because of the adverse effects of the oil slump. According to Abdallah al-Kuwaiz, the GCC assistant secretary general, the joint project for the construction of the refinery would be feasible, but it had to be shelved because of the collapse of the international oil market. The refinery was intended to give GCC producers an export outlet out of range of the Gulf war; traffic from the refinery would bypass the Strait of Hormuz.

This brings us to a related GCC project, the construction of a 1,700-kilometer oil pipeline to link the GCC states with Oman while bypassing the Strait of Hormuz. At the third meeting of the GCC oil ministers in October 1982, the Saudi oil minister, Shaykh Zaki Yamani, made public that this project was under study as a means of exporting oil via Oman.[7] The projected pipeline would connect with a terminal in one of three points in Oman: Salalah, Sur, or Kuria Muria Bay.[8] In November 1983 Omani petroleum and minerals minister Said Ahmad ash-Shanfari said that the proposed pipeline had become "a pressing matter under the current circumstances." The Iranian Speaker of the Majlis, Hojatolislam Hashemi-Rafsanjani, had threatened that Iran would stop oil exports from all Gulf states through the Strait of Hormuz if more than half of Iranian oil exports were disrupted for a period of more than six months.[9]

Although the idea of such a GCC pipeline seemed enticing, technical and other difficulties made its realization impossible. For example, the governor of the Saudi Petroleum and Minerals General Corporation was quoted as saying on 16 January 1985: "Oilfields are not similar and the quality of oil is also different, so we could not build one pipeline to transport all kinds of crudes since each oil has its own specifications. . . . We should distinguish between the heavy, medium and light crudes, one variety for export and another for other issues."[10] Meanwhile, Saudi Arabia awarded contracts to build a new pipeline from its eastern oil fields across the desert to the Red Sea port of Yanbu in a move to increase the security of its oil exports. But even five years after the establishment of the GCC, there was no joint GCC pipeline.

The fear of oil disruption because of the Iraq-Iran war also triggered the idea of creating a GCC-wide stockpile of oil, but like the pipeline idea it had not yet been realized by the end of five years of the GCC's existence. In late 1983 and early 1984 Saudi Arabia had built a floating stockpile of at least 50 million barrels of crude oil outside the Gulf. Kuwait was also planning on its own to build a floating storage facility because a severe disruption of gas supplies and oil products could cripple Kuwait's vital power and desalination plants. The GCC oil ministers reportedly reached an agreement on 23 October 1985 to ensure emergency oil supplies to member countries whose oil production or export installations were jeopardized. The agreement would involve loans to member countries in difficulty. The ministers also agreed to create a forty-five-day national strategic oil reserve in each GCC state.[11] It remained to be seen whether these plans, like those for the pipeline to, and refinery in Oman, would survive the financial constraints imposed by the fall in oil revenues.

Integrating Non-Oil Industry

Despite, or because of, the richness in oil and gas resources, the GCC states have not developed much in the non-oil sector of their economies. Industrial development, particularly outside the oil industry, is vitally important for independent, sustained, and productive growth. The Economic Agreement sets forth the aspirations of the six members for development in industry and agriculture. During its first five years of efforts at economic integration, the GCC, on the whole, paid more attention to industrial development in the non-oil sector of the economy than to agriculture.

The best place to start this discussion of industrial development is with the Gulf Organization for Investment (GOI). Over the years it has been called by such other names as Gulf Investment Authority (GIA) and Gulf Investment Corporation (GIC). The basic statute of the GOI was approved on 19–20 June 1982 in Riyadh by the GCC finance and economic ministers. At the time it was mistakenly reported that the Bahrain finance minister, Ibrahim Abd al-Karim, had said that the capital of the organization would be "2000 million" shared by the six member states and that each state was entitled to offer 49 percent of its share to its own citizens.[12] Other sources reported that no final decision on capital had been made. The GOI statute was endorsed by the GCC's Supreme Council during the third GCC summit held in Bahrain in November 1982. It was finally decided that the GOI would have a $2.1-billion capital with shares equally divided between the six member states, that it would be headquartered in Kuwait, and would be used for investment rather than for direct funding of joint ventures or industrial projects.[13]

Before the end of the first five years of the GCC's economic activities, some progress seems to have been made by the GOI. A board of directors had been appointed. The board approved GOI's future plan for investing in petrochemical, industrial, and livestock projects. The board also selected a number of limited schemes that would be jointly held with the private sector with a view to studying them as a prelude to execution.[14] By April 1985 $420 million of the GOI's capital had been paid up by the members. It was also believed that the GOI would involve itself in project finance, direct investment, and securities transactions. Priority would be given in the GCC region. Bahraini bankers suggested that the GOI would be active in capital markets, especially in floating-rate notes, but the *Middle East Economic Digest* (MEED) reported no confirmation of this information.[15] The GCC members were to contribute to the total $2.1-billion capital over a period of five years. Nevertheless, some believed that this key institution for economic integration would perhaps have a quicker takeoff because of the effects of international and regional economic developments.

Energy savings was another major concern of the GCC states. They asked Dhahran's University of Petroleum and Minerals and the Kuwait Institute for Scientific Research (KISR) to submit proposals for integrating member states' electric power networks. This was one of the schemes for energy saving that was recommended by the GCC electricity department heads in February 1983 at a meeting in Doha. It was believed that such a grid system would lead to a more rational use of electricity, as well as providing cheaper power overall, and a more reliable service to consumers.[16] The linking of the six power systems, some officials believed, would include high-voltage connections between Oman and the UAE, Saudi Arabia's Eastern Province and Bahrain, and the kingdom's Hofuf oasis area and Qatar. To encourage conservation, a three-tier electricity tariff structure was supposed to be introduced beginning on 1 October 1985. While the study for regional power integration was still under consideration, there were also talks about the establishment of a GCC industry producing electrical equipment.[17]

In the areas of capital and personal movement and ownership, the GCC states seemed to make some headway in the first five years of their cooperation. The establishment of separate passport control counters for GCC nationals at the airports of various member states reflected free movement of GCC nationals among the six countries despite strict security restrictions. In attempting to free economic activity in industry, construction, agriculture, fishing, and dairy and poultry production, theoretically local ownership requirements (usually 51 percent of any business) were to be no longer applicable in the case of GCC nationals. In practice, however, these requirements proved difficult to lift throughout the GCC area. A new draft bill in Kuwait specified conditions of ownership that fell short of total deregulation. Reportedly, GCC nationals could buy only one piece of land, of limited size and for residential use only.[18]

Insofar as the movement of capital in the GCC region was concerned, the GCC nationals were permitted to work in each other's states, and a company could be started in any member country on condition that a national had a 25 percent shareholding in it. Furthermore, after five years, the company could operate without any local participation. The example of Oman in issuing implementation regulations for this purpose is instructive. By a ministerial decision, the government of Oman decreed on 26 April 1984 that GCC citizens in Oman would be allowed to operate hotels and restaurants through companies in which Omani shares would not be less than 25 percent of the shared capital; after five years from the date of that decision the activity in these areas would be unconditional. Other provisions allowed professionals from the GCC countries to practice their professions in Oman under certain conditions (D62). The variety of interest rate structures and exchange rates, however, seemed to call for common interest and currency policies that were yet to be achieved.[19]

Two closely related problems of economic integration that also received the attention of the GCC policymakers were communication and transportation. On 15 January 1986 it was announced in Doha that the GCC communications ministers had agreed to unify prices and fees for telex, telephone, post, and telegraph services. However, the individual states would decide whether or not to implement them, depending on circumstances. The ministers also agreed to set up an integrated GCC communications network using light cells and coaxial cables. Standardization of charges for telephone calls meant a substantial reduction, although Oman would not be party to the new charges at first and would be expected to bring its costs into line at a later date. The usual tariff for calls between GCC states would be 2.3 gold francs a minute, equal to about $0.40. Although the GCC still had a long way to go before it reached the "sophistication of its European counterparts," Edmund O'Sullivan of *MEED* believed in 1984 that development in the communications area "has probably been the most concrete result of the GCC's first 54 months."[20]

Although as early as November 1983 the GCC commissioned a study for a proposed "peninsular railway" to tie in with the British Transmark, as late as 1986 there was no sign of progress. The line reportedly would link five GCC countries with Iraq—Oman, the UAE, Qatar, Saudi Arabia, and Kuwait. The railway would give the five countries access to both Eastern and Western Europe by connecting major cities along the line from Muscat to Umm Qasr in Iraq.[21] Bahrain, an island state, was left out of the scheme; however, before the sixth anniversary of the GCC in May 1987 the Bahrain–Saudi Arabia causeway probably would be in full operation. One of the main advantages of the $564-million causeway would be to link Bahrain to Saudi Arabia and other Arab lands by road. The economic and social advantages and disadvantages were being debated in Bahrain in 1986 before the causeway was fully opened to traffic.

No other single question symbolized the drive for industrialization in the GCC countries as much as petrochemicals. Most chemicals are produced from hydrocarbons derived from the petroleum and natural gas with which the GCC region is abundantly endowed. During the first five years of the GCC's drive to industrialize, Saudi Arabia's gigantic plants had already started up or were about to do so. The Saudi Methanol Company's 600,000-tonne-a-year complex (Ar-Razi) came on stream in February 1984. Methanol is one of the basic petrochemical products. In June that year the European Economic Community (EEC) imposed a 13.5 percent duty on Saudi methanol imports because they had climbed to twelve times the EEC ceiling of $191,870. This almost touched off a trade war between the GCC and the EEC, and as late as March 1985 it was believed that the dispute between the two could take up to three years to resolve.[22] Given a number of gigantic petrochemical plants, such as the ones at al-Jubail and Yanbu that have not yet come on stream (see App. A, table 7), the dispute will probably heat up rather than cool down in the near future. Petrochemical production eventually will be transferred from the EEC to the GCC area, and as a result many plants in the EEC region will "have to be closed down," according to European observers.[23]

Creating a Common Market

The GCC states also have tried to cooperate in the area of trade. The aspirations of freeing trade among the six by abolishing internal customs on regional products and of establishing a common tariff on nonregional imports seem to have received more attention than did some other economic sectors. After the 19–20 June 1982 meeting of the finance and economic ministers of the GCC, it was believed that customs duties on the products of the GCC states would be abolished, effective 1 December 1982, marking the first phase of implementation of the 8 June 1981 comprehensive Economic Agreement. But this step was put off until March 1983 for the officially stated purpose of further study. Oman stood to lose significant income from customs, for it was thought to be the major importer of GCC-made items; in the interval Oman sought and got agreement that eight unspecified Omani products would be exempted from the GCC measures for five years from 1 March 1983.[24] According to Secretary General Bisharah, the implementation of this first part of the Economic Agreement was "the birth of the first organism of the GCC." Reportedly, he also said that the fusion of the GCC countries was regarded as "the backbone," a vehicle that would "drive us close to our goals wherein the remaining activities are regarded as protection for this vehicle." He added that this economic fusion would lead to "the establishment of a Gulf common market."[25]

The GCC free-trade area was thus created, but it was not regarded as a major advancement toward economic integration. Little trade complementarity existed among the six countries. Like most developing regions of the world, the GCC area consisted of countries with similar economies that produced essentially competitive rather than complementary goods. Nevertheless, the move to free intraregional trade had a symbolic importance. In an area of the world which ordinarily is identified with tribal, nationalistic, and dynastic rivalries and feuds, this was no mean achievement. Furthermore, the abolition of internal customs could be regarded as advantageous in the future when the drive toward diversification and industrialization made it possible for the six to produce less similar products (see App. A, table 8).[26]

What proved more difficult to achieve in the trade sector was the establishment of a uniform external tariff system. The GCC finance ministers decided in a meeting in May 1983 to impose a unified levy [of ... pe]rcent on foreign imports from 1 September. The UAE announced on 16 May its intention to raise customs duties from 1 percent to the GCC's minimum of 4 percent. The ministers, however, exempted from this levy such items as food and medicine. The implementation of the decision seemed to run into trouble. Some member states of the GCC failed to impose new rates on 1 September as scheduled. Although the UAE had declared its intention to do so earlier than some others, the federal government was reportedly under pressure from "the influential trading community, whose members believe the new levy will not serve their commercial interests: trading is depressed in the UAE at present." It was even surmised that the government may "indefinitely suspend the implementation of the GCC ruling."[27]

While the UAE and Oman were holding back, Saudi Arabia and Qatar announced an increase of their duties to 4 percent. The Saudi increase from 3 to 4 percent applied to selected commodities amounting to half of its imports, including vehicles and spare parts, clothes, power tools, and canned food. Duty-free commodities included basic foods, raw materials, and industrial, agricultural, and health equipment.[28] By the end of 1984 all GCC states were observing the rule that tariffs on specified goods should be no less than 4 percent, rising to a maximum of 20 percent. But "variations from country to country remain, creating profitable trading possibilities for companies that import through a low-tariff state for sale in a high-tariff one."[29]

Despite the slow pace in approximating the ideal of a common GCC external tariff during the first five years after the establishment of the organization, the prospects did not seem too dim. The driving force behind achieving a common external tariff was the dispute with the EEC, a major exporter to the GCC region. A common external tariff would arm the GCC countries with a significant bargaining chip in dealing with the EEC states, particularly in trying to achieve a negotiated settlement of the dispute over EEC duties imposed on GCC petrochemical exports.

Recession and Economic Integration

Given the vital importance of economic development to economic integration in the GCC region, the drastic fall in oil revenues naturally concerned the promoters of regional economic integration. Within the first five years of the GCC, Saudi Arabia sank to the level of an economy with a deficit second only to that of the United States. Given the pivotal importance of the kingdom in the GCC community, the Saudi financial retrenchment caused concern not only in the kingdom but also in the other GCC communities, which faced more or less a similar predicament. The surprise deferral in March 1986 of the Saudi budget for 1986–87 because of, in King Fahd's words, "the present oil market situation and the implications of the current world economic crisis" showed the extent to which the economy seemed to be in trouble.

The dramatic collapse in oil prices seemed to have a similar effect on Kuwait. For the first time in Kuwait's modern history there was a real deficit in its 1986–87 budget. But substantial reserves were believed to ensure that the country would absorb the deficit more easily than most of its GCC partners. Other GCC states such as Qatar, which did not enjoy the cushioning effects of financial reserves, seemed to be in much worse shape. *MEED* forecast in May 1986 that "for the first time in more than eight years, there will be current account deficit in 1986. If the oil price averages $15 a barrel and Qatar maintains present production levels, the deficit will total roughly $600 million. This compares with surpluses of $1,000 million in 1985—and of a record $2,650 million in 1980."[30]

Those who argued that recession in the GCC region might turn out to be "a blessing in disguise" did not impress those GCC visionaries who wished to see a faster pace of economic development and integration. Even if the collapse of oil revenues reduced waste, induced more rational economic planning, and limited corruption, the GCC policymakers feared that the disadvantages of losing the momentum of economic integration might outweigh any such socioeconomic advantages. The aspiration to achieve economic productivity in order to reduce the overwhelming dependence on oil revenues was one of the main driving forces behind the very idea of economic integration in 1981. Paradoxically, the oil bust today may slow down the process of economic integration just as the oil boom of yesterday in part triggered the movement for economic integration. It is doubtful, however, that what was accomplished during the first five years of the GCC experience in integrating the economies of the six monarchies will be undone in the second five years, despite economic recession.

An Uneven Path to Economic Integration

All said, the efforts of the GCC states to integrate their economies were uneven in the three main sectors. In the hydrocarbon sector, the GCC states coordinated their policies on oil price and production issues as far as could be expected. The collapse of the oil market was partly the result of their pre-GCC policies of the 1970s when OPEC, no doubt led by the Gulf producers, increased oil prices fifteenfold. In 1981–86 the GCC producers had no choice but to jointly face the consequences of the oil slump within and outside OPEC. With or without the GCC, they would have had to do so, but the GCC framework probably facilitated the coordination of their oil policies, for what they were worth.

In nearly all other areas in the hydrocarbon sector, the GCC ideas and plans did not get off the ground. The plan to integrate Qatar and Kuwait into Saudi Arabia's extensive gas grid was still on paper. The plans for building a 250,000-barrel-a-day refinery in, and a 1,700-kilometer oil pipeline to Oman were shelved. To be sure, the GCC oil ministers reached major agreements on emergency aid for the member states whose oil exports were disrupted as a result of the Iraq-Iran war. They also agreed on creating a forty-five-day national strategic oil reserve in each GCC state. But by the sixth anniversary of the GCC these agreements had not yet been implemented. The Saudis managed to build outside the Gulf a floating stockpile of at least 50 million barrels of crude oil for themselves, but joint action was still an elusive goal.

In the non-oil industrial sector, perhaps the most notable achievement of the GCC states was the establishment of the GOI. It had plans for investing in petrochemical, industrial, and livestock projects. The member states had paid up about $500 million of its capital of $2.1 billion before the sixth anniversary of the GCC. It remains to be seen whether the GOI investment projects will concentrate within or outside the GCC economies. Other attempts in this sector, however, seem to have had an uneven record. Progress seems to have been made more on paper than in practice in freeing economic activity through the movement of capital across GCC borders. In regard to business ownership by GCC nationals, theoretically the 51 percent local ownership requirement was removed. But, in practice, the issue seems unresolved.

In the trade sector, the abolition of internal customs in fact was the first major step toward creating a GCC common market. At the moment, however, the lack of competitive goods in the GCC trade area seems to cast doubts on the real importance of this concrete step. It may prove to be significant in the distant future when as a result of diversification and industrialization the GCC states perhaps will produce less similar goods. The establishment of the common external tariffs was another major step toward creating a GCC common market, but some trading companies take advantage of remaining variations from one GCC country to another by importing through a low-tariff state for sale in a high-tariff country. The establishment of a common external tariff system may nevertheless prove to be significant. In its stiff negotiations with the EEC, for example, the GCC can use it as a bargaining chip in an effort to beat down the levies imposed on the GCC export of petrochemical products to European markets.

In the economic field the toughest question about the future is the same as in the security field. Will the momentum for cooperation among the six GCC states diminish if the current perception of the common threats of revolution and war no longer holds in the future? Before addressing this question, we should next consider the GCC efforts in the field of diplomatic coordination.

Notes

1. Atif Kubursi, *Oil, Industrialization, and Development in the Arab Gulf States* (London: Croom Helm, 1984), p. 43.

2. *FBIS-MEA-V-82-177*, 13 Sept. 1982.

3. *FBIS-MEA-V-82-080*, 26 April 1982.

4. *FBIS-MEA-V-83-038*, 24 Feb. 1983.

5. Ibid.

6. *Middle East Economic Digest* (hereafter *MEED*), 30 Sept., 10 Dec. 1983, and 26 Oct. 1985; see also D60 below.

7. *FBIS-MEA-V-82-200*, 15 Oct. 1982.

8. *MEED*, 16 Nov. 1984, 12 April 1986.

9. For the text, see Ramazani, *Revolutionary Iran*, pp. 275–81.

10. *FBIS-MEA-V-85-012*, 17 Jan. 1985.

11. *MEED*, 26 Oct. 1985.

12. *FBIS-MEA-V-82-120*, 22 June 1982.

13. *MEED*, 12 Nov. 1982.

14. *FBIS-MEA-V-85-016*, 24 Jan. 1985.

15. *MEED*, 5 April 1985.

16. *MEED*, 11 March 1983.

17. *MEED*, 26 April 1985.

18. *MEED*, 16 Nov. 1984.

19. *MEED*, 16 Nov. 1984.

20. Ibid.

21. *MEED*, 18 Nov. 1983.

22. *MEED*, 15 March 1985.

23. Ibid.

24. *MEED*, 12 Nov. 1982; see also *FBIS-MEA-V-82-237*, 9 Dec. 1982.

25. *FBIS-MEA-V-83-046*, 8 March 1983.

26. Kubursi, *Oil, Industrialization, and Development*, p. 2.

27. *MEED*, 9 Sept. 1983.

28. *MEED*, 7 Oct. 1983.

29. *MEED*, 16 Nov. 1984.

30. *MEED*, 3 May 1986.

Documents

Document 57
The Unified Economic Agreement of the
Cooperation Council for the Arab States of the Gulf
8 June 1981

With the help of God Almighty;

The Governments of the Member States of the Gulf Co-operation Council;

In accordance with the Charter thereof, which calls for closer rapprochement and stronger links; and,

Desiring to promote, expand and enhance their economic ties on solid foundations, in the best interest of their peoples; and,

Intending to coordinate and unify their economic, financial and monetary policies, as well as their commercial and industrial legislation, and customs regulations; have agreed as follows:

Chapter One
Trade Exchange
Article 1

1. The Member States shall permit the importation and exportation of agricultural, animal, industrial and natural resource products that are of national origin. Also, they shall permit exportation thereof to other member states.

2. All agricultural, animal, industrial and natural resource products that are of national origin shall receive the same treatment as national products.

Article 2

1. All agricultural, animal, industrial and natural resource products that are of national origin shall be exempted from customs duties and other charges having equivalent effect.

2. Fees charged for specific services such as demurrage, storage, transportation, haulage or unloading, shall not be considered as customs duties when they are levied on domestic products.

Article 3

1. For products of national origin to qualify as national products, the value added ensuing from their production in member states shall not be less than 40 percent of their final value. In addition, the share of the member states citizens in the ownership of the producing plant shall not be less than 51 percent.

2. Every item to be exempted hereby shall be accompanied by a certificate of origin duly authenticated by the government agency concerned.

Article 4

1. Member states shall establish a uniform minimum customs tariff applicable to the products of the third countries.

2. One of the objectives of the uniform customs tariff shall be the protection of national products from foreign competition.

3. The uniform customs tariff shall be applied gradually within five years from the date of entry into force of this agreement. Arrangements for the gradual application shall be agreed upon within one year from the said date.

Article 5

Member states shall grant all facilities for the transit of any member state's goods to other member states, exempting them from any duties and taxes whatsoever, without prejudice to the provisions of Paragraph 2 of Article 2.

Article 6

Transit shall be denied to any goods that are barred from entry into the territory of a member state by its local regulations. Lists of such goods shall be exchanged between the customs authorities of the member states.

Article 7

Member states shall coordinate their commercial policies and relations with other states and regional economic groupings and blocs with a view towards creating balanced trade relations and favorable circumstances and terms of trade therewith.

To achieve this goal, the member states shall make the following arrangements;

1. Coordinate import/export policies and regulations.

2. Coordinate policies for building up strategic food stocks.

3. Conclude economic agreements collectively when and if the common benefit of the member states is realized.

4. Work for the creation of a collective negotiating force to strengthen their negotiating position vis-à-vis foreign parties in the field of importation of basic needs and exportation of major products.

Chapter Two

Movement of Capital, Citizens and Exercise of Economic Activities

Article 8

The member states shall agree on the executive rules which would insure that each member state shall grant the citizens of all other member states the same treatment granted to its own citizens without any discrimination or differentiation in the following fields:

1. Freedom of movement, work and residence.

2. Right of ownership, inheritance and bequest.

3. Freedom to exercise economic activity.

4. Free movement of capital.

Article 9

The member states shall encourage their respective private sectors to establish joint ventures in order to link their citizens' economic interest in the various spheres.

Chapter Three

Coordination of Development

Article 10

The member states shall endeavor to achieve coordination and harmony among their respective development plans with a view to achieving economic integration between them.

Article 11

1. The member states shall endeavor to coordinate their policies with regard to all aspects of the oil industry including extraction, refining, marketing, processing, pricing, exploitation of natural gas, and development of energy sources.

2. The member states shall endeavor to formulate unified oil policies and adopt common positions vis-à-vis the outside world, and in the international and specialized organizations.

Article 12

To achieve the objectives specified in this Agreement, the member states shall perform the following:

1. Coordinate industrial activities, formulate policies and mechanisms aimed at the industrial development and the diversification of their productive bases on an integrated basis.

2. Standardize their industrial legislation and regulations and guide their local production units to meet their needs.

3. Allocate industries between member states according to relative advantages and economic feasibility, and encourage the establishment of basic as well as ancillary industries.

Article 13

Within the framework of their coordinating activities, the member states shall pay special attention to the establishment of joint ventures in the fields of industry, agriculture and services, and shall support them with public, private or mixed capital in order to achieve economic integration, productive interface, and common development on a sound economic basis.

Chapter Four

Technical Cooperation

Article 14

The member states shall collaborate in finding spheres for common technical cooperation aimed at building a genuine local base founded on encouragement and support of research and applied sciences and technology as well as adapting imported technology to meet the region's progress and development objectives.

Article 15

Member states shall set rules, make arrangements and lay down terms for the transfer of technology, selecting the most suitable or introducing such changes thereto as would serve their various needs. Member states shall also, whenever feasible, conclude uniform agreements with foreign governments and scientific or commercial firms to achieve these objectives.

Article 16

The member states shall formulate policies and implement coordinated programs for technical, vocational and professional training and rehabilitation at all levels and stages. They shall also upgrade educational curricula at all levels to link education and technology with the development needs of the member states.

Article 17

The member states shall coordinate their manpower policies and shall formulate uniform and standardized criteria and classifications for the various categories of occupations and crafts in different sectors in order to avoid harmful competition among themselves and to optimize the utilization of available human resources.

Chapter Five

Transport and Communication

Article 18

The member states shall accord means of passenger and cargo transportation belonging to citizens of the other member states, when transiting or entering their territory, the same treatment they accord to the means of passenger and cargo transportation belonging to their own citizens, including exemptions from all duties and taxes whatsoever. However, local means of transportation are excluded.

Article 19

1. The member states shall cooperate in the fields of land and sea transportation, and communication. They shall also coordinate and establish infrastructure projects such as seaports, airports, water and power stations, and roads, with a view to realizing common economic development and linking their economic activities with each other.

2. The contracting states shall coordinate aviation and air transport policies among them and promote all spheres of joint activities at various levels.

Article 20

The member states shall allow steamers, ships and boats and their cargoes, belonging to any member state to freely use the various port facilities and grant them the same treatment and privileges granted to their own in docking or calling at the ports as concerns fees, pilotage, and docking services, haulage, loading and unloading, maintenance, repair, storage of goods and other similar services.

Chapter Six

Financial and Monetary Cooperation

Article 21

The member states shall seek to unify investment in order to achieve a common investment policy aimed at directing their internal and external investments towards serving their interest, and realizing their peoples' aspirations in development and progress.

Article 22

The member states shall seek to coordinate their financial, monetary and banking policies and enhance cooperation between monetary agencies and central banks, including an endeavor to establish a common currency in order to further their desired economic integration.

Article 23

Member states shall seek to coordinate their external policies in the sphere of international and regional development aid.

Chapter Seven

Closing Provisions

Article 24

In the execution of the Agreement and determination of the procedures resulting therefrom, consideration shall be given to differences in the levels of development between the member states and the local development priorities of each. Any member state may be temporarily exempted from applying such provisions of this Agreement as may be necessitated by temporary local situations in that state or specific circumstances faced by it. Such exemption shall be for a specified period and shall be decided by the Supreme Council of the Gulf Arab States Cooperation Council.

Article 25

No member state shall give to any non-member state any preferential privilege exceeding that given herein.

Article 26

a. This Agreement shall enter into force four months after its approval by the Supreme Council.

b. This Agreement may be amended by consent from the Supreme Council.

Article 27

In case of conflict with local laws and regulations of member states, execution of the provisions of this Agreement shall prevail.

Article 28

Provisions herein shall supersede any similar provisions contained in bilateral agreements.

Drawn up at Riyadh on 6 Shaaban 1401 Corresponding to 8 June 1981.

Source: *American-Arab Affairs*, no. 7 (Winter 1983–84): 177–82.

Document 58

GCC Imigration, Passports, and Labor Committee of Directors Meeting: Concluding Statement

27 April 1982

The GCC Immigration, Passports, and Labor Committee of Directors met in Muscat 26–27 April 1982. The committee studied the agenda presented to it by the GCC General Secretariat. Following discussion of all topics on the agenda in sincere fraternity, the committee decided to make the necessary arrangements for the unification of all regulations adopted by the GCC member states, including immigration, passports, residence, labor, and naturalization regulations, in order to reach a standard system which will illustrate the spirit on which the GCC is based and for which the GCC leaders strive. The committee also decided to take measure to furnish the GCC citizens with all facilities to guarantee the freedom of labor, residence and travel among the GCC member states. The committee charged the GCC General Secretariat with examining the regulations currently accredited by the GCC member states, and with forming competent technical committees which will present their recommendations to the ministers of the interior at their upcoming meeting for setting forth a system which provides further measures to guarantee the safeguarding of the security and stability of the GCC states and the strengthening of their different security organs by including the adoption of the most advanced systems of the developed world's countries.

The committee also decided to send a thank you cable to His Majesty Sultan Qabus ibn Said of Oman expressing the committee's sincere thanks and gratitude for the intensive care the committee received and the facilities with which it was furnished, which highly affected the success of this committee, and wishing his majesty perpetual health and success and his government and the Omani people perpetual progress and prosperity.

Source: *FBIS-MEA-V–82–082*, 28 April 1982, p. C3.

Document 59
GCC Oil Ministers' Third Conference: Final Statement
14 October 1982

The GCC oil ministers in Salalah tonight concluded the meetings of their third conference. The ministers began their meetings yesterday.

During their meetings, the oil ministers approved a study presented by Petromin pertaining to treatment of air pollution in the gulf and formation of a committee consisting of Saudi Arabia, the UAE and Qatar to consider this issue and to expand efforts to protect the environment against oil industry pollution. The ministers also approved the establishment of a refinery for heavy Omani oil to make it light and increase the possibility of having it marketed in the international market. The conference also formed a special committee to study the factors linked with this project in order to put it into effect since it is important to GCC oil coordination and cooperation.

The GCC oil ministers also approved a recommendation that the GCC countries that produce natural gas should provide countries that lack it with the needed quantities for the latter's electrical stations.

The oil ministers also approved a report by the oil company directors calling for further flexibility in establishing oil-related industries and establishing refineries commensurate with all kinds of crude oil produced in the GCC member countries. The report also calls for cooperation among the GCC member countries in the areas of training, exchange of information about production, investment,

and the no-priority conditions to crude oil buyers from the GCC member countries in addition to the employment of technical cadres and expertise available in the GCC member countries in the establishment of oil-related industrial projects.

The conference formed a special committee comprising officials in charge of training in the member countries in order to develop a comprehensive plan among the countries in the field of training. The conference reviewed a special report presented by the GCC General Secretariat on transportation of freshwater from various parts of the world to the Gulf region aboard oil carriers that anchor in the region's ports to load crude oil.

The ministers discussed the significance of taking such steps and the usage of transported water. They decided to form a committee consisting of Saudi Arabia, Kuwait and Qatar to do further studies regarding the economic viability of the plan. The minsters also approved the minutes of their first and second meetings held in Riyadh last January and April.

The GCC oil ministers praised OPEC and its wisdom in deciding last March to protect oil price levels. In a statement issued tonight following the conclusion of their meetings in Salalah, Oman the ministers said the OPEC decision protected both consumers and producers. The ministers noted that some countries have exceeded the permitted production ceiling and have sold their oil for less than the agreed upon price in addition to taking other measures to reduce prices. The ministers affirmed that the continued difference in the current prices between North African oil and light Arab oil will aggravate the problem. The ministers' statement said the North Sea and Mexican producers who are selling their oil freely and for any price have caused the prices to fall. The ministers called upon the oil-producing countries to bear their responsibilities and warned that the GCC will not protect these countries from the consequences of their erroneous acts should they continue.

Source: *FBIS-MEA-V–82–200*, 15 Oct. 1982, pp. C3-C4.

Document 60
GCC Oil Ministers' Emergency Meeting: Final Statement
15 January 1983

First: The committee studied a report by one of the subcommittees on securing the supply of natural gas to consumption points in the GCC states. The report calls for linking the gas network with power stations in two divisions, northern and southern, provided that the two divisions will be linked through a continuous network in the future.

The second issue discussed by the committee was a report on the refining potential of the GCC states by the end of this decade. Due to the presence of a surplus in the quantity of refined oil, the council requested a study on the heavy part of a barrel—that is, the fuel oils—and whether they can be lightened, consumed, or converted into light oil products.

The third issue studied by the committee was finding petroleum products required by industries in the GCC States. The committee concentrated on two main issues: The first is finding black carbon for tire manufacturing in the future, and prospects for obtaining it. There is a study on the types of crude oil suitable for this industry. The second is finding coal for the aluminum industry.

The meeting was short. The subcommittees and the General Secretariat prepared well for it. Hence, the reports were available beforehand and the members were able to study them and adopt resolutions on them.

This is what was achieved during this meeting. The committee will hold its forth meeting in 3 or 4 months. It may be in April or May, pending notification of the secretary general.

Source: *FBIS-MEA-V–83–011,* 17 Jan. 1983, p. B3.

Document 61

GCC Transit System Regulations

1 March 1983

Regulations governing Transit Goods in the Cooperation Council for the Arab States of the Gulf.

These regulations were approved by the Financial and Economic Cooperation Committee in its second meeting on June 19-20th, 1982, for implementing the Fifth Article of the Unified Economic Agreement.

These regulations were effective from the first of March 1983 and were applied to commodities coming by land, sea and air.

First:

The shipment of commodities by means of transportation through the lands of all the countries signatory to the Unified Economic Agreement shall be permitted without delay, restriction or discrimination on the type of the containers.

Transit containers must meet the following conditions:

1. They must be designed for shipping commodities according to the Customs Seals System.

2. It must be possible to take the Customs Seals to be stamped easily and effectively.

3. It must be impossible to take out any commodities from the stamped part, or put anything in it, without leaving a clear spot or breaking the Customs Seals.

4. They must not contain unseen cavities that would make it easy to hide any commodity in them.

5. The uncovered means of transportation must be packed with tight covers, tied with ropes and wrapped with a wire from outside, allowing the stamping of the Customs Seals, to ensure the safety of the load.

Second: Wrapping Requirements:

1. The cover must consist of a single untorn piece that would make it impossible to reach the load.

2. The whole truck box must be covered completely on both sides.

3. The cover must have certain rings fixed inside and around the cloth.

4. The rope must consist of one piece, in a length that would allow gathering the two sides after passing through the cover's rings, and the box to be stamped by lead.

Third: Customs Seals:

Customs Seals must be clear and carry the word *CUSTOMS* and the country's name in Arabic.

Fourth: Transit Manifest:

Means of transportation must be accompanied with a transit manifest according to the layout approved by the GCC countries.

Fifth:

Exceptional shipments such as the commodities which can not be wrapped but can be examined and counted are excluded from the condition provided for in paragraphs 1, 2, and 3 shown above.

Sixth:

There shall be an exchange of signatures of the Customs officials who are authorized to sign clearing documents, and of the official Customs Seals for this purpose.

Source: *American-Arab Affairs,* no. 7 (Winter 1983–84): 183–84.

Document 62

Oman: Ministerial Decision on GCC Investments

26 April 1984

Ministerial Decision No. 25/84

Ministry of Commerce and Industry Decision dated April 26, 1984 and effective March 1, 1984.

According to the GCC Unified Economic Agreement signed in Riyadh on 11/11/81;

To implement the decisions of the fourth session for the High Committee of the GCC, which was held in Qatar from November 7–9, 1983;

According to Article 6 of Royal Decree No. 4/74, concerning foreign investment, and governmental decisions for implementing the Unified Economic Agreement,

It is decided:

Article 1. GCC Citizens in the Sultanate of Oman will

be allowed to operate hotels and restaurants and engage in their maintenance in accordance with the Unified Economic Agreement, through companies established and registered in the Sultanate according to Omani Law, where the Omani shares should not be less than 25 percent of the share capital. After five years from the date of this decision, the activity in these areas will be unconditional.

Article 2. Qualified citizens of the GCC countries are allowed to practice the pharmaceutical profession in the Sultanate of Oman on condition that they obtain the license and registration usually required for the citizens of the Sultanate in a similar profession. They are only allowed to import medicine through the approved national agent.

Article 3. Professionals from GCC countries may practice their professions in the Sultanate of Oman on the following conditions:

1. They are professionally qualified.

2. They practice the profession themselves.

3. They are permanent residents in the Sultanate.

4. They complete all required license and registration procedures.

Article 4. This decision is effective as of March 1, 1984 and will be published in the Official Gazette.

Issued on 24 Rajab 1404 H.

(Corresponding to April 26, 1984)

Salim Bin Abdulla Al-Gazali

Minister of Commerce and Industry

Source: *Middle East Executive Reports*, 7, no. 11 (Nov. 1984): 27.

Document 63
Saudi Planning Ministry Statement on 5-Year Plan
21 March 1985

1. Main features of the development plans in Saudi Arabia.

2. Socio-economic planning started in Saudi Arabia at the beginning of 1390 H, during which the first development plan was prepared. Most of its programs concentrated on construction of basic infrastructure, public utilities and development of manpower. The second development plan provided the first major thrust to development. It concentrated on provision of modern infrastructure, the diversification of non-oil economy. The third development plan emphasized diversification and focused on the producing sectors such as agriculture, industry and mining and the completion of the associated infrastructure.

Four plan themes:

Although the objectives of the fourth plan are mostly continuations of the principles and policies of the third plan, there are four broad themes which characterize and differentiate it from its predecessors. These are:

1. A greater concern with the efficiency of operations and usage of the Kingdom's resources and facilities and with the discovery and development of renewable alternatives;

2. A stronger focus of the diversification strategy on manufacturing, agriculture and finance;

3. A commitment to reduce the number of unskilled and manual foreign workers in the Kingdom by more than half million;

4. A clear and definite emphasis on promoting the private sector's involvement in economic development.

2. Elements of the 4DP:

2.1 Objectives: In its Resolution No. 36 date 24.2.1404 H, the Council of Ministers specified eleven objectives for the fourth plan as follows:

1. To safeguard Islamic values . . . duly observing, disseminating and confirming Allah's Shariah;

2. To defend the faith and the nation, and to uphold the security and social stability of the realm;

3. To form productive citizen—workers by providing them with the tributaries conducive thereunto—ensuring their livelihood and rewarding them on the basis of their work;

4. To develop human resources thus ensuring a constant supply of manpower and upgrading and improving its efficiency to serve all sectors;

5. To raise culture standards to keep pace with the Kingdom's development;

6. To reduce dependence on the production and export of crude oil as the main source of national income;

7. To continue with real structural changes in the Kingdom's economy through continuous transformation to produce a diversified economic base, with emphasis on industry and agriculture;

8. To develop mineral resources and to encourage discovery and utilization thereof;

9. To concentrate on qualitative development through improving and further developing the performance of the utilities and facilities already established during the three development plan periods;

10. To complete the infrastructural projects necessary to achieve overall development;

11. To achieve economic and social integration between the Arab Gulf Cooperation Council countries.

2.2 Basic strategic principles:

In its previously mentioned resolution, the Council of Ministers specified eight basic strategic principles to achieve the objectives mentioned in the said resolution. They are as follows:

1. Emphasis should be laid on improving the economic productive standards of the services, utilities, and products which the government provides for citizens—both directly (such as education and security services) and indirectly (such as electricity, transport and basic commodities);

2. Adopt policy giving the private sector the opportunity to undertake many of the economic tasks of the government, while the government would not engage in any economic activity undertaken by the private sector;

3. Rationalize the system of direct and indirect subsidies on many goods and services provided by the state;

4. The consideration of economies should predominate in many government investment and expenditure decisions;

5. Continue development of Saudi manpower, through the evaluation of educational and training programmes and curricula as well as by further development or modification of these in conformity with the Islamic Shariah, the changing needs of society, and the requirements of the development process;

6. Attention should be given to the development of Saudi society, to the provision of social welfare and health care for all, and to the support given to society's participation in the implementation of the programs of the plan as well as reaping the benefits of development;

7. In order to carry out the second objective the defense and security authorities shall plan their strategy in order to ensure the defence at the nation, and shall submit that strategy to the National Security Council preparatory to presenting it for consideration to the Council of Ministers;

8. Adopt a fiscal policy which keeps the level of expenditure in line with the government revenues through the fourth plan period.

These basic strategic principles include a total of 61 detailed policies which as a whole form a comprehensive policy framework to provide a base for government expenditure and development operations. Most of the policies have a close relationship with each sector, and have been summarized in the following sections. Some of these policies are more applicable to the government agencies and some to the private sector:

Reducing production costs of public services and utilities;

Ensuring that services are appropriate and not excessive, e.g. by limiting specifications for constructing or operation of projects to what is actually required;

Utilizing technology in all public service sectors through mechanization and the use of advanced technology;

Judging the economic feasibility of projects (of all types) by including operational and maintenance costs (including management cost) and not only capital cost;

Developing appropriate administrative organizations to serve the new needs of the community;

Giving the private sector the opportunity to operate, manage, maintain and renovate many of the utilities currently operated by government provided that this results in lower costs, better performance, and employment opportunities for Saudi citizens;

Reconsidering some of the prevailing methods, policies and regulations so as to allow the private sector to operate more freely and more flexibly and to assist it in becoming more creative and developed;

Reduce subsidy rate in ways that will rationalize consumption without significantly affecting low income consumers;

All government departments which administer public services should make economic efficiency a fundamental objective by adopting two basic principles. First, the cost of producing such services to the Saudi Community should be reduced, and second, the price of such services should not be less than production cost, except in rare areas and with the proviso that the price should be periodically reviewed.

The fourth plan has been prepared at a time of new economic conditions which have been gradually developing since the end of the second plan. These are:

1. Completion of the greater part of the basic infrastructure;

2. Considerable progress made in the diversification of the economy;

3. Increased capabilities and efficiency of Saudi manpower;

4. More efficient government administration;

5. Lower levels of oil revenues;

6. Increased oil production by non-OPEC countries;

7. The world economy began its recovery from the longest economic recession period in its recent history.

4. Planning approach to the 4DP:

The fourth development plan introduces a new planning methodology—the program approach. It is derived directly from the 8th basic strategic principle. As well as stipulating fiscal balance, this principle includes a policy directing that all authorized projects must comply with development objectives and principles as summarized above.

The "program approach" has introduced certain new emphases in planning government expenditure: on whole programs rather than on individual projects, on structure of expenditure rather than the component items, on responsibility for priorities and proportions than detailed commitments.

The program based method has also introduced other major changes in the planning process and in the allocation of government expenditure for the plan. It provides increased flexibility for the government agencies to select projects within the specific allocations for the program, taking into consideration the objective of the coordinating regional development.

5. The role of the private sector during the 4DP:

The 4DP introduces a major change in the respective roles of the government and the private sector. Many of the key goals and objectives of the plan will be achieved through the private sector, in particular great reliance is placed on the private sector to continue the strategy of economic diversification through the development of agriculture, industry and mining, and to improve the efficiency and productivity of existing economic units.

To facilitate this, financial provision has been made within the total 4DP expenditure to support and encourage the private sector to increase its contribution to development.

6. Civilian expenditure during the 4DP:

In light of the Kingdom's recent experience the importance of Saudi Arabia's strategy of diversification away form oil has been underlined. Government expenditure in the 4DP will reinforce this strategy.

The total government expenditure has been determined at SR 1000 billion (in current prices). Of this SR 500 billion is to devoted to development expenditure. The largest share of development expenditure 27.1 percent (SR 135.3 BN) will be allocated to human resources development, economic resources will receive 26.1 percent (SR 130.7 BN), health and social services 17.9 percent (SR 89.7 BN), transport and telecommunications 15.4 percent (SR 76.9 BN) and municipalities and housing 13.5 percent (SR 67.4 BN).

The amount allocated for the economic and human resources and health and social services will be more than the actual spending on these sectors during the 3DP. The percentage increase ranges between 28.9 percent for health and social services and 8.6 percent for economic resources. However, the basic infrastructure allocation will be lower. The reasons for this are first, conformity with the strategic principle that emphasizes development of the producing sectors; second, most of the infrastructure projects are already completed and third it is expected that project cost will be reduced through the implementation of programs concerned with the modification of construction specification, reducing the scope of projects and through higher competition in the market.

The number of projects to be implemented over the plan period total 3226 of which 1444 are new, and 1782 under construction are scheduled to be completed during the 4DP period.

The development sectors include natural resources, producing sectors, human resources, social development and basic infra-structure.

Also included are other sectors such as services which although not classified as development sectors support the development sectors.

7. Natural resources:

Natural resources include water, energy (oil), gas and solar energy and minerals. Main objective of the national resources sector:

To meet the present and future water needs of society:

To limit the development of water resources and conserve and rationalize the use of water;

To conserve and manage hydrocarbon resources and so achieve maximum benefits in the long run—develop solar energy as one of the alternative sources of energy in the Kingdom;

Investigate and explore mineral resources to determine occurrences in the Kingdom;

Explore and evaluate promising mineral deposits, develop them if economically feasible;

Encourage both the public and private sectors to develop and utilize mineral resources.

Main achievements envisaged in natural resources;

Desalination capacity will be increased by 364.4 thousand cubic meters of water per day, and by 603 megawatts of electric power generation. By 1409/10 the total capacity will be 1.8 million cubic meters of water per day and 3,748 megawatts of electricity capacity. Other programs include the implementation of national and regional water plans, regular assessment of water and agricultural policy, definition of maximum pump rates, and the establishment of a new tariff system. Greater emphasis is to be given to developing reclaimed water and surface water for direct use and for recharging aquifers. New supply networks will be constructed to improve access to water by small towns and rural areas;

Establishment of 675 water projects of various sizes in a number of towns and villages throughout the Kingdom. These will include drilling of 750 wells, the erection of 60 new dams and the installation of 480 pumping units all over the Kingdom;

Completion of the gas gathering and distributing system. Development of four major refineries, bulk storage plants and petroleum pipelines and also the implementation of a new project for hydrogen production through solar energy;

Production of geological maps for the Arabian shield and phanerozoic rocks;

Exploration of 30 gold deposits, 5 silver deposits, 20 copper deposits, 12 tin-tungsten deposits, 12 niobium and 3 chrome/nickel deposits;

The Saudi-Sudanese joint commission will implement pioneer mining projects in Atlantic Deep 2.

Government expenditure on natural resources sector 4DP:

	SR million	percent
Water	31,789	58
Energy	18,821	34
Mining	4,427	8
Total	55,037	100

7.2 Producing sectors: The non-oil producing sectors include: agriculture, industry, electricity, construction and the royal commission for Jubayl and Yanbu. Main objectives of the producing sectors:

To realize an acceptable increase in agriculture production using least possible costs and critical water resources;

The improvement of efficiency in the producing and marketing of agriculture products and attracting the private sector to invest in the agriculture sector;

Contribute to the Kingdom's growth of diversification through the continuation of the industrialization programs;

Development and utilization of hydrocarbon and mineral resources to increase the added value of these resources;

Provision of reliable electricity services for all population growth centers;

Conservation of energy and rationalization of electricity consumption;

Improvement of productivity of electric power utilities;

Supporting and encouraging Saudi construction industry;

Increasing the productivity and capabilities of Saudi contractors;

Reducing construction and associated maintenance cost;

Provision of necessary infrastructure for industry and residential communities;

Increasing private sector investment.

Main achievements envisaged for producing sector;

Projects include: the surveying and classification of 1,250,000 hectares of land, improvement of the irrigation network to cover more than 5,000 hectares, cultivation of 8,000 hectares of pasture, protection of 2.5 million hectares of cultivated land. Veterinary services will be established at Saudi ports for 37.5 million animals and the production of 600,000 tonnes of crops and 800,000 tonnes of fertilizers will be subsidized. Disbursements of SR 350 million of subsidies will be made for the production of dates and palm offshoots. Distribution of 300,000 tonnes of various improved seeds and 250,000 of improved seedlings will be made;

As part of Savic's activities five major projects are scheduled to come on stream during the fourth plan. These are the production of methyl tertiary butyl ether (500,000 tons/yr.), budtadiene (128,000 tons/yr.), vinyl chloride monomer (300,000 tons/yr).

Other Savic projects under evaluation are polypropylene, propane dehydrogenation, downstream propylene derivatives, compound fertilizers, additional ammonia capacity, single cell protein and rolled steel mill with one million tonnes annual capacity.

Programs for other manufacturing are broader and more supportive of the private sector initiatives. New industrial cities will be completed in Medina, Asir, Mecca, Hail, Tabuk, Jizan and Najran. A comprehensive industrial extension service and a new small industry loan facility are being evaluated. Greater emphasis is to be given to project identification and investment promotion and a program aimed at promoting manufactured exports is to be introduced that will include an export insurance and supplementary credit scheme. A pre-investment service is planned which will assist potential investors in the selection of projects and guide them in the procedure for applying for assistance.

The capacity of grain silos will be increase from 955,000 tonnes per year to 1,855,000 tonnes/year capacity, the capacity of flour mills form 748,000 tonnes/year to 979,000 tonnes/year and fodder from 336,000 tonnes/year to 480,000 tonnes/year;

The electric power network will be expanded to serve about 828,000 new customers, in so doing the long-standing goal of full electrification of the Kingdom will be realized;

Encouragement will be given to construction companies to diversify into new activities, especially servicing and maintenance, through the implementation of the 30 percent rule and opening tendering.

Government expenditure on the producing sector:

	SR million	percent
Electricity	41,932	48
Royal Commission for Jubayl and Yanbu	30,000	35
Agriculture	10,810	12
Industry	4,241	5
Classification of Contractors:		
Total Expenditure	87,054	100

Service sector: The service sector includes commercial services, banking and finance, environmental pollution control, specifications and standards and statistical information services. Main objectives of services sector:

To increase the contribution of the private sector in the activities currently undertaken by the government;

To increase the export of Saudi industrial products, and to improve trade relations with other countries particularly with the GCC states;

To maintain high standards of product supply and consumer protection;

To grow in accordance with the requirements and needs of the national economy and to encourage the private capital into domestic investment;

To improve the health, safety, and living conditions of the citizens of the Kingdom through the provision of meteorology and environmental protection services in the Kingdom;

To protect the environment of the Kingdom and its natural resources, from pollution, desertification and environmental deterioration;

To provide precise and reliable statistical data to support planning operation.

Principal achievements envisaged for service sectors.

The emphasis of the commercial service program is on ensuring business regulations keep pace with development needs, extending the consumer protection activities and assisting the business community in investment and export promotion initiatives. The financial sector will be also a leading growth sector. Considerable development of the Kingdom's financial structure is to be encouraged, the need for a formal stock exchange examined, and the longer term lending by the commercial banks stimulated. The government credit institution will provide the following loans during the fourth development plan.

Institution	fourth plan total in SR million
Saudi Arabian Agricultural Bank	10,150
Saudi Credit Bank	1,250
Saudi Industrial Development Fund	7,500
Real Estate Development Fund	21,000
Specialist funding programs	1,500
Public Investment fund	18,700
Total	60,100

Government expenditure on services sector:

Sector	SR millions	percent
Commercial services	825	1
Banking and finance	60,100	93

Meteorology and environment protection	/	2,831	/	4
Standards and specifications	/	507	/	1
Information and statistical data	/	558	/	1
Total	/	64,821	/	100

Social and cultural development:

This sector includes, social, cultural, health services, information, judicial, religious affairs, youth and sports development. Major objectives for social and cultural development sector:

1. To safeguard Islamic values, duly observing, dissemination and confirming God's divine law;

2. To continue providing integrated health services, particularly primary health care and increase coordination and operating efficiency;

3. To expand integrated social development in coordination with other agencies which provide such services and to encourage the participation of the local community in social development;

4. To improve and upgrade cultural levels, guide and orient members of the community to match the development process in the Kingdom.

Major achievements expected for social and cultural development:

About 45 hospitals will be established providing an additional 8,944 beds and increasing the total number of hospitals by the year 1989/90 to approximately 138 with 27,857 beds. Numerous primary health care centres will be established throughout the Kingdom to bring their number to about 2,187 by the year 1989/90 against 1,306 in 1984/85; in addition to about 100 maternal and diagnostic centres will be established in different areas of the country;

Approximately 50 classes for handicraft training will be open as well as 50 benevolent societies of which 20 will be concerned with women. There will be an expansion in pensions and also in social support to accommodate about 95,000 cases. Also 20 new social security offices will be opened;

The surrounding areas of the Holy Mosque at Mecca will be expanded to accommodate about 1.5 million pilgrims. The Prophet's Mosque in Medina will be expanded and renovated. Services provided to pilgrims will be improved.

Government Expenditure on social and cultural development sectors:

Sector	/	SR million	/	percent
Health	/	62,239	/	57
Judicial and religious sector	/	18,501	/	17
Cultural, information and youth	/	13,617	/	13
Welfare services	/	14,280	/	13
Total	/	108,637	/	100

Human resources: the human resources development sector includes general education for boys and girls, higher education and training in other government sectors, private

sector manpower development, training programs and science and technology. Main objectives:

1. Improving the efficiency and quality of education, and the elimination of the incidence of illiteracy among Saudi adults;

2. Ensuring that education is in conformity with Islamic values and Allah's shariah (God's divine law);

3. Provision of competent manpower required to achieve the objectives of national development;

4. Developing and improving internal training, on-the-job training programs, increasing coordination among training programs under the government supervision, achieving saudization goals in both the public and private sectors, provision of competent cadre for the public sector and the identification of employment opportunities for women in a manner which would not be contrary to Muslim faith;

5. Taking necessary action required for the implementation of proper strategies to increase saudization rate and productive efficiency;

6. Facilitation of the application of science and technology in support of the objectives of long-term development in the Kingdom.

Expected main achievements of human resources:

The number of male students in various levels of general education will increase from 914,000 in 1404/1405 to 1,168,000 in 1409/1410. The number of female students in general education will increase from 655,000 in 1404/1405 to 937,000 in 1409/1410. The total number of students will increase from 1,569,000 at the beginning of 4DP to 2,105,000 at the end of 4DP;

The number of male students in higher education will increase from 51,000 in 1404/1405 to more than 69,000 in 1409/1410. The number of female students in higher education will increase from 29,000 in 1404/1405 to more than 39,000 in 1409/1410. The total number of students will increase from approximately 80,000 at the beginning of the 4DP to more than 108,000 by the end;

The number of male graduates from secondary level will increase from a 3DP total of 70,076 to approximately 109,500 during the 4DP. The total number of graduates of secondary levels will increase form a 3DP total of 132,284 to approximately 215,000 during the 4DP;

The number of male graduates from higher education will increase from a 3DP total of 41,000 to approximately 60,000 during the 4DP;

The number of enrolments at technical education schools will increase from 12,000 in 1404/1405 to 16,000 in 1409/1410, and the number of graduates from technical education will increase from approximately 5,239 to 18,942 by 1405/1406. The number of enrolments at vocational training centres will also increase from 37,576 to 43,255 during the 4DP.

Government expenditures on human resources: 4DP

		SR million	/	percent
General education	/	85,232	/	62
Higher education	/	40,291	/	30

Technical education and voca- tional training	/	6,586	/	5
Institute of public administra- tion	/	1,053	/	1
Manpower development	/	1,195	/	1
Science and technology	/	1,816	/	1
Total expenditures on human resources	/	136,173	/	100

7.6 Physical infrastructure sector includes transport facilities, postal service, telecommunications, housing, municipal and public works services. The objectives of infrastructure: Expansion as necessary to cope with the gradual increase in demand on transport services:

Greater equality in the provision of physical infrastructure and municipal services throughout the Kingdom, increased efficiency of operation and improvements in services in villages and urban areas;

Improving the quality of housing and efficient utilization of the existing housing stock;

Supporting private sector housing construction through the real estate development fund;

Expansion of an improving of postal services and telecommunications particularly in areas where coverage is yet to be fully completed.

Expected main achievements:

The first stage of the new international airport at Zahran [Dhahran] will be completed by the end of 1410 (*as recieved*). New roads will be constructed to bring the total length of road network to 116,000 km which will comprise 20,000 km main roads, 15,000 km secondary and feeder roads and 81,000 km or rural roads;

The postal service will be expanded to cover a further 1,200 villages and local telephone networks will be enlarged to give 250,000 new subscribers access to installed exchanged capacity. Network switching capacity will be increased to 300,000 lines;

The following municipal projects will be implemented: 185 water projects, 78 sewage, 11 water drainage, 57 flood protection, 47 markets, 152 public utilities, 341 urban streets, 42 governmental buildings, 6 environmental improvements, 24 planning studies, 11 training, 215 other municipal projects.

Government expenditure on physical infrastructure:

		SR million	/	percent
Transport	/	45,851	/	36
Postal service and telecommun- ications	/	28,581	/	19
Municipal and public works	/	63,500	/	42
Housing	/	3,828	/	3
Total of physical infrastructure	/	150,760	/	100

8. Labor force and GDP in 4DP:

8.1 Labor force: The plan target is to increase productivity by 4 percent per annum. As a result the total civilian labor force will decline by approximately 1 percent leading to a reduction in employment of 855,000 compared to employment in 1404/05. Simultaneously, the target growth in non-oil economy of 2.9 percent per annum will create new employment opportunities for 630,000. Moreover, the numbers of Saudis in the work force will increase by 374,777 during the 4DP. AS a result, there will be an over all reduction in non-Saudi manpower of 600,000.

8.2 GDP: It is expected as a result of following the strategy approved by the Council of Ministers that GDP will grow at annual average rate of 4 percent P.A. The absolute value will increase from SR 284.1 billion in 1404/05 to SR 354.9 billion in 1409/1410 (constant 1399/1400 prices). The oil sector will grow at 5.6 percent P.A. and non-oil sector at a rate of 2.9 percent P.A.

The most important sectors expected to contribute to this growth are industry which is expected to grow at (15.5 percent per year), finance and business services (9 percent per year), agriculture (6 percent per year).

Growth in other sectors will be lower, construction 2.8 percent P.A., commercial services 2.5 percent per annum, oil and gas 3.8 percent per annum. In real estate and government there will be no growth.

Nonetheless, although these growth rates are lower, they do approximate those achieved in the 3DP and remain high by world standards.

Source: *FBIS-MEA-V–85–056*, 22 March 1985, pp. C2-C7.

Document 64

Saudi Ministry of Petroleum and Mineral Resources Statement on Oil Policy

22 February 1986

There has been an increasing number of talks and prophesies recently about the true Saudi petroleum policy and its alleged role in the current deteriorating situation. It has become a duty to issue a statement that will explain this policy's true nature and dot the i's.

First, we have to recall that the continuing fall in consumption, as a result of large price increases for many consecutive times accompanied by continuing annual increase in the production of oil exporting countries outside OPEC, has led to a continued drop in the OPEC share of the petroleum market. Thus, the financial situation of OPEC member-countries was affected and they were forced to give discounts on the specified price of their petroleum in order to [*words indistinct*].

Other OPEC member-countries were forced to disregard the shares allotted to them by giving bigger discounts; average prices began to collapse; and the Saudi Arabian Kingdom was the only member of the organization whose production fell to half and exports fell to one-third due to its adherence to official prices. Other member-countries marketed their petroleum either by discounting prices, owning refineries to refine their petroleum and selling it as products not subjected to OPEC pricing or because some of their petroleum production is not subject to OPEC pricing.

The Kingdom of Saudi Arabia was open with its colleagues in the organization regarding the difficulty of continuing with the aforementioned situation and on numerous occasions (?pointed out) in various and clear ways that it would be forced to follow suit unless all situations were rectified. When the majority of OPEC member-countries were unable to stop their aforementioned behavior due to the pressure of their difficult financial circumstances, and the refusal of the rest of producers outside the organization to give part of their share of the market, there was no alternative to adopting a selling policy that conformed with market prices, and enabled us to sell our share or close to it. We regarded this as a cautious and firm policy aimed at safeguarding prices from a collapse from which no one would have been spared its dire consequences. Nearly 3 months have passed after selling at market linked prices without the Saudi behavior having any negative effects on prices which maintained their levels and even continued rising.

When the OPEC ministerial council adopted a unanimous decision calling for the organization's adherence to a fair share of the market during its conference in Geneva in early December 1985, speculation started to push prices down. Everyone became convinced that unless producers outside OPEC amend their policy and abandon some markets which they took away from OPEC, there will be a surplus in the market and this will push prices down.

Some newspapers and articles began to forget all the clear facts and tried to portray the situation as the work of the Saudi Arabian Kingdom. Others were even more exaggerated by stressing that the Kingdom had an interest in what was happening and that it was conspiring in collusion with some major industrial powers against the market. And because of all this, it has become imperative to issue a statement which confirms the following facts:

One: What happened was the result of circumstances imposed on all for reasons which we explained in the past and which are beyond the control of any government which finds its revenue rapidly declining, causing a budget deficit that cannot be accepted or tolerated.

Two: What happened will cause harm to all the oil exporting states including the Kingdom of Saudi Arabia and its fraternal GCC states. It will also cause consumers short and long term harm.

Three: For there to be an end to the deteriorating situation, producers from outside OPEC must cooperate with the OPEC member-states, because it has become clear that the latter cannot, on their own, bear the burden of defending the price structure.

Four: The kingdom will not abandon its policy adopted since the early seventies which rejects quick upward and downward fluctuations in oil prices. Our past positions are known when we opposed the repeated price rises that led to our present situation. Our subsequent positions are also known when we agreed to cut our production down from 10 million barrels to about 2 million barrels, and as a result the wheels of economy nearly stopped in our country.

It would not be fair for the Kingdom to distort facts and present an incorrect picture of the situation and perhaps what was said by the Venezuelan Energy Ministry and chairman of OPEC to Saudi television, during his excellency's recent visit to Riyadh, is the best proof to the truth of our positions.

Five: The Kingdom is strenuously striving to correct the situation and to return prices to their acceptable and just levels. It puts its hand in the hand of anyone who is sincerely seeking to protect the economies of our peoples from great damage, and protect the international community from yet another energy crisis in the near future.

Source: *FBIS-MEA-V–86–037*, 25 Feb. 1986, pp. C3-C4.

5
Coordinating Diplomacy

ANALYSIS

A final area that remains to be examined is the GCC's diplomatic coordination. During the first five years of its existence, the GCC became the principal forum for the conduct of collective diplomacy by its member states. As an entity, the GCC concerned itself with many international issues that affected the interests of its members. The Arab-Israeli conflict, the Lebanon war and its aftermath, and the Palestinian question all absorbed a great deal of time and energy of the GCC members. Given the difficulties in the way of holding summit meetings among the Arab states, the GCC became the principal and regular forum on Arab affairs. As such, it dealt with the EEC, OPEC, Organization of Arab Petroleum Exporting Countries (OAPEC), Arab League, Organization of the Islamic Conference (OCI), Nonaligned Movement (NAM), United Nations, and other entities to protect and promote the interest of its members. It also expressed views on all kinds of international issues, whether they concerned small powers, medium powers, or superpowers.

Yet, the record shows that the problems of war and peace in the Persian Gulf absorbed most of the collective diplomatic efforts of the GCC. No matter how important the Arab-Israeli conflict, the Iraq-Iran war posed the most immediate and the largest threat to the GCC states. As already seen, the perceived threat of the spread of the Iraq-Iran war was the principal driving force behind the efforts of the GCC for defense cooperation among its member states. But the GCC efforts for containing the war were not confined to creating a credible military deterrence; they involved significant diplomatic activities as well.

A Tilted Neutrality

During the first five years of its existence, the GCC managed to act as the world's greatest diplomatic tightrope walker. Officially, it took a neutral stand in the Iraq-Iran war, but unofficially it tilted toward Iraq without forming an alliance against Iran. Its tilt toward Iraq stemmed from perceived common interests between the six and Iraq. Saddam Hussein decided to invade Iran avowedly because of Iranian provocations. As seen in chapters 1 and 2, the 1979–80 period was marked by the ever-increasing fear of the Gulf monarchies about the contagion of the Iranian Revolution. Bahrain, Kuwait, and Saudi Arabia, in particular, perceived serious threats to their political stability and security as a result of Iranian-inspired Shia upheavals and unrest. During the same period, the Baathist regime in Iraq shared the same kind of concern, but on a much larger scale. In absolute terms, Iraq has the greatest numbers of Shias of any Arab state; there are eight million Shias among a population of about fourteen million. More critically, Iraq has the best organized and the oldest underground Shia dissident movement in the entire Arab world, the *Dawa* party, which dates back to the period after the 1958 Iraqi Revolution, aims at creating an Islamic state in Iraq, and has clandestine cells in other Gulf states.[1]

In April 1980 Saddam Hussein began to prepare for the war with Iran. On the first day of the month, the first anniversary of the Islamic Republic of Iran, the Iraqi government charged that various "terrorist" acts were committed by Iranians and even by "some Iranian diplomats" in Baghdad, including an assassination attempt against the life of Tariq Aziz, then a member of the Iraqi Revolutionary Council and a deputy prime minister and later a foreign minister. The Iraqi government also charged that the *Dawa* party leaders planned to "overthrow the Iraqi Government, through subversion, sabotage, and terrorism" with the "blessings" of the Ayatollah Khomeini in Qom.[2] Whether or not these charges were valid, it is clear that during the crucial 1979–80 period the Gulf Arab monarchs and Saddam Hussein shared the common perception that revolutionary Iran was a threat to their regimes.

This perception was shared particularly by Saudi Arabia, Kuwait, Bahrain, and Oman. But only the first two of these states were in any position to aid Iraq when the war broke out. They wished to help Iraq because they believed that it invaded Iran at least in part for the purpose of containing the contagion of the Iranian Revolution. They shared this Iraqi objective without approving the war as an appropriate means to that end, but they felt that they had little choice other than to help Iraq. Short of committing their troops, Saudi Arabia and Kuwait aided the Iraqi war efforts both financially and logistically. As the principal paymasters of Iraq, they spent anywhere between $20 to $40 billion on Saddam Hussein's war machine. Logistically, Kuwait was the lifeline for Iraq, a distinction for which the Kuwaitis paid dearly in the form of Iranian "accidental" air raids on Kuwait twice in November 1980, once in June 1981, and once again in October 1981. At least in the early years of the war, Saudi Arabia quietly made three Red Sea ports available for the transshipment of military equipment to Iraq. Whether this kind of logistical aid continued later is not known; in any event, the Iranian search and seizure of vessels suspected of carrying strategic materials to Iraq seems to have slowed down the traffic, especially after September 1986 when the Iranian search strategy was put in high gear.

The obvious discrepancy between the GCC's official neutrality and the siding with Iraq in practice, however, did not signify all-out support of Iraq. First of all, until the Iranian Revolution the Gulf monarchies had felt threatened by subversive activities of revolutionary Iraq. If Iraq was to win the war, that threat, it was feared, would return with a vengeance. Second, if Iran was to win the war, the GCC states feared, then Iran would turn on them.

Despite this essentially ambivalent attitude of the Kuwaitis and Saudis toward Iraq, at the time the Iranian threat seemed the greater of the two evils. This predicament was reflected in the tilted character of the neutrality of the GCC states. The secretary general of the GCC reportedly told a Qatari newspaper on 16 January 1982 that all Gulf countries had become a basic party in the Iraq-Iran war. He also asked: "How can we be mediators in an issue in which we are a major party?"[3] Although some Gulf newspapers challenged the secretary general's frank remarks on the ground that the GCC's position had been neutral as evidenced by the statements issued at the first and second summits in Abu Dhabi and Riyadh respectively, Bisharah's remarks revealed the anomalousness that the GCC leaders felt over their tilted neutrality, a limited tilt that ebbed and flowed in tandem with the vicissitudes of the war.

Diplomatic Containment of War

Nine months and three days after the Iraqi invasion of Iran when the GCC began its first summit meeting, there was no sign of any serious GCC concern with the spread of the war. Nor was there any sign of diplomatic panic on the part of the GCC states. Although the Iraqi forces were bogged down in Iran, the Iranian forces were still on the defensive. The rather complacent attitude of the GCC at the time was reflected in the remarks of the UAE president, who said, on behalf of the GCC, that the

GCC leaders had "hoped that there would be no war. However, this is God's will."[4] The GCC attitude did not seem very different at the time of the second summit meeting of the leaders of the member states in November 1981. Although the Iranian forces had gone on the offensive for the first time in September 1981 and had compelled the Iraqis to lift the yearlong siege of the refinery city of Abadan, the Iraqi forces still occupied some 800 square miles of Iranian territory, including the major port city of Khorramshahr. At the second summit meeting held in Riyadh, the GCC states followed the same essentially neutralist position that they had adopted at their first summit about six months earlier in Abu Dhabi (D9). They "discussed the conflict between Iraq and Iran and the resulting threat to the security and stability of the region as a whole, and expressed the hope that the efforts stemming from the Islamic conference [OCI] and the efforts of the nonalignment and the United Nations would be successful" (D67).

The GCC's heavy reliance on third parties to seek an end to the war reflected more than its inability to play an effective role itself. By relying on the OCI, which the Saudis led and the Iranians mistrusted, the GCC states sought to maintain their own officially neutralist stand. The same was true of their reliance on the Nonaligned Movement and on such perceived impartial states as Algeria and Japan. They also hoped that the developments in the battlefield would not shift the balance of military power in favor of either of the two belligerents in such a way as to threaten their security. The discovery of the allegedly Iranian-supported coup plot in Bahrain, rather than developments on the war front, for the first time triggered an anti-Iranian Saudi campaign, in which Prince Nayif dubbed the Iranians "the terrorists of the Gulf." Although clearly startled by this event, the GCC leaders continued their essentially neutralist position in public until the spring of 1982.

The earliest tilt away from fence-sitting began to occur in reaction to the impressive Iranian offensive in March 1982 and especially the follow-up offensive in May. Seldom had the GCC capitals experienced so much diplomatic activity. A flurry of behind-the-scene meetings was followed by several extraordinary meetings of the Ministerial Council of the GCC. The council reviewed the contacts that Saudi Arabia and Kuwait had initiated with Iraq, Syria, and Algeria. With its back to the wall, Iraq was then asserting its readiness to withdraw to the international border, an assertion that the council believed would create "opportunities for a negotiated solution of the Iraq-Iran war—a solution that would safeguard the legitimate rights of both sides." The council also believed that the circumstances required an intensification of mediation efforts to end the war. In anticipation of the Israeli invasion of Lebanon, the council tried to seize the opportunity to find common ground with Iran "at this historic and decisive turning point in which the Islamic nation is the target of a fierce Zionist onslaught aimed at the entire Islamic entity" (D72).

Revolutionary Iran resented the GCC's implied approval of the Iraqi offer to withdraw forces to international borders. It saw no basis for making common cause with the GCC states when Israel invaded Lebanon. Ayatollah Khomeini saw this invasion as an American plot to divert Iranian attention from the war against Iraq at a time when Iran had turned the tide of war against Iraq. Single-mindedly, the Iranian forces followed up their May success at Khorramshahr and finally carried the war into Iraqi territory in July 1982. The GCC then dropped all pretensions of impartiality. It depicted the Iraqis as the peace seekers and, at first by implication, the Iranians as the real obstacle to a negotiated peace settlement. The Iranian July offensive proved to be a disastrous failure. The Iraqi forces showed an impressive determination to defend themselves, and the Iraqi citizens ignored Khomeini's call to rebel against the Baathist regime. Nevertheless, the GCC leaders felt threatened by the specter of an unconditional Iranian victory. This perception lay behind their successful diplomatic efforts at the Fez summit in September 1982. They secured an Arab League resolution which declared that "in case Iran fails to respond to the peace efforts and continues its war against Iraq" its actions could be viewed as "an act of war against the Arab nation" (D75 and D76).

Armed with this Arab League resolution, the GCC began from then on to depict the Iranian offensives as acts against the whole "Arab nation." A couple of months after the Fez meeting, in their third summit meeting held in Manama, Bahrain, between 9 and 11 November 1982, the GCC leaders declared their "great anxiety" over the developments in the war. The most serious development, they believed, was the crossing of the international border by Iran, which posed "the great threat to the safety and security of the Arab nation" in violation of its sovereignty (D81). In his closing statement at this meeting, Bahraini foreign minister Shaykh Muhammad ibn Mubarak al-Khalifah emphasized that the GCC stance on the war was based on the Fez summit resolution, trying to magnify the theme of the oneness of the GCC states and the Arab nation. "We are," he said, "part of this nation and our Arab stand is clear, open and committed" (D82).

The GCC efforts to generalize its concerns over the war, however, went beyond the Arab world. Once the news of the French sale of Super Etendard planes to Iraq surfaced, revolutionary Iran threatened to cut off the oil exports of all the Gulf states. Judging by the words of Hashemi-Rafsanjani, the Speaker of the Iranian Majlis, this was not a wild threat. He said on 14 October 1983: "We will block the Strait of Hormuz when we cannot export oil. Even if they [the Iraqis] hit half of our oil, it will not be in our interest to block the Strait of Hormuz. When we do not have oil, when we are unable to export oil, the Persian Gulf will be no use to us since we will have no money, and the Strait of Hormuz will be of no use to us. That is when we will enter the arena and do what we like, although I consider such an eventuality to be very unlikely."[5]

Likely or unlikely, the GCC states managed to generalize this threat as a threat to the interest of the international community in the uninterrupted flow of Gulf oil supplies to world markets. The United Nations Security Council passed a resolution on 31 October 1983 which the GCC latched onto about a week later at its fourth summit meeting held in Doha, Qatar. The GCC leaders supported the resolution, which "calls for an end to all military activities in the Gulf and for refraining from attacking cities, economic installations and ports and for an immediate end to all hostilities in the Gulf area, including all sea routes and waterways." They then called on Iran "to respond positively to this resolution and not to threaten the freedom of navigation in the Gulf and its straits." They also called on the United Nations Security Council and its permanent members in particular "to shoulder their responsibilities in taking the necessary measures to implement the resolution" (D90).

Once the Iranians began to strike oil tankers in retaliation for the Iraqi attacks in the spring of 1984, the GCC for all practical purposes publicly sided with Iraq, despite its declared policy of neutrality. But even before the Iranian attacks on the Saudi and Kuwaiti oil tankers in May 1984, the GCC states had decided to go on a diplomatic offensive against Iran for another reason. Not since the incursion of Iranian forces into the Iraqi territory in July 1982 had the GCC states felt so threatened as in February 1984. During this interval all Iranian offensives had failed, but on 24 February the war of attrition came to an end, at least momentarily, as Iranian forces seized parts of the artificial oil islands of Majnoon inside the Iraqi marshes north of Basra. With unusual speed, the foreign ministers of the six states met in Riyadh, mapped their strategy, and flew to Baghdad in March, when the Arab League tried to force Iran to the negotiation table by, in effect, calling on all countries to stop furnishing arms to Iran. More critically, the GCC leaders managed to get the Arab League in the meeting of 20 May 1984 to characterize the Iranian attacks on Kuwaiti and Saudi oil tankers as acts of aggression. They also managed to get the United Nations Security Council to adopt Resolution 552 on 1 June 1984, which Iran considered one-sided. Without mentioning Iran by name, the resolution criticized it for attacking oil tankers traveling to and from Kuwait and Saudi ports but made no reference to Iraqi attacks on tankers traveling to and from Iranian terminals. The discrepancy was cloaked in technical legal language.

The Saudi shoot-down of an Iranian fighter plane on 5 June 1984 appeared to bury all that was left of the GCC neutrality in the war. In retrospect, however, it marked the beginning of unprecedented GCC efforts to play the role of a mediator in the war. First of all, the mutual restraint of Iran and Saudi Arabia after the incident helped to improve the political atmosphere between Tehran and Riyadh.

Second, the GCC members all seem to have been convinced that they must try much harder than before to end the war because it very well might spread. The "forgotten war" now was on everybody's mind and an all-out effort to terminate it seemed vital. Not that the GCC had not tried to mediate between Iran and Iraq before; in 1983 and again in April 1984 the UAE and Kuwaiti foreign ministers visited Tehran and Baghdad, but the mediatory efforts had been stalled. To revive them, the GCC leaders took up the matter openly and vigorously during their fifth summit meeting in November 1984. Their increased fear of the "dangers" of the spread of the war was coupled with the readiness of the GCC states "to carry out any direct endeavor which could achieve progress towards dialogue and negotiation." "The council had laid down," said their final communiqué, "certain conceptions in this regard," and "it hopes they will meet the required response" (D95). These conceptions were never made public. At the time it was reported that Bahrain might have presented a plan for "peace in stages," neutralizing first Gulf ports, then larger areas. It was also reported that the UAE president had proposed a "Marshall Plan" to reconstruct the destroyed Iranian and Iraqi areas.[6]

Whatever the exact nature of the discussions on the war in closed sessions at the fifth GCC summit meeting in Kuwait, the determination to make all-out mediatory efforts was unmistakable. The GCC determination was further reinforced as a result of the "war of cities" in 1985 when Iraq and Iran struck each other's population centers. The destruction and casualties caused by the shelling of civilian targets were taken up by the GCC Ministerial Council on 17–19 March 1985 as a basis for the most explicit offer of mediation for ending the war. The council, the six foreign ministers said, "stresses its readiness to exert all efforts and to intensify endeavors to put an end to this devastating war, including sending a delegation to Tehran and to Baghdad to discuss without any delay the quickest way to stop the war" (D98). During the course of the council's meeting, the Kuwaiti deputy premier and foreign minister, Shaykh Sabah, left for a "lightning visit" to Baghdad for talks with Saddam Hussein. Reportedly, the UAE state minister for foreign affairs, Rashid Abdallah al-Nuaymi, was ready to fly to "Iran at any moment if he receives the green light from Tehran."[7] Whether or not the minister ever visited Tehran, the Ministerial Council continued to stress the readiness of the GCC to mediate between the parties during all its subsequent meetings in July, September, and October before the upcoming sixth summit meeting in Muscat, Oman. On 29 October 1985 the Oman minister of state for foreign affairs, Yusuf Alawi Abdallah, revealed that the GCC had assigned two envoys to visit Baghdad and Tehran, but "our efforts did not succeed."[8]

Yet, it is difficult to believe that the conciliatory attitudes of the GCC toward Iran displayed during the fifth summit in November 1984 and during the Ministerial Council meeting in March 1985 had been all in vain. The breakthrough in Saudi-Iranian relations in May 1985 may well have been a result. Saudi foreign minister Prince Saud al-Faysal visited Iran on 18 May, becoming the first Saudi minister to visit Iran after the Iranian Revolution. The visit appeared to be in response to an invitation by Iran's foreign minister, Ali Akbar Velayati, who paid a visit to Saudi Arabia starting on 7 December 1985 at the invitation of Prince Saud. The prince believed that his visit to Iran provided a "precious opportunity" for "serious and constructive" talks with Iranian leaders. According to Foreign Minister Velayati, he and Prince Saud discussed "an expansion of relations in the political, economic, trade and cultural fields. . . . It also was agreed that further trips should take place in both directions."[9]

No positive move toward ending the war resulted from this exchange of visits. But Saudi Arabia and the GCC as a whole seemed to temper their tilted neutrality, and the Iranian leaders responded positively. President Ali Khamenei told Prince Saud, "The Islamic Republic offers a friendly hand to all her neighbors as well as all the Muslims throughout the world and proposes to coexist with them in a spirit of unity and friendship."[10] The Iranians seemed overjoyed, especially with the conciliatory stance of the GCC at its sixth summit meeting held in Muscat in November 1985. Although the final communiqué referred to the stance assumed by the Supreme Council at its fifth session in Kuwait in November 1984, its language and the statements of the GCC leaders together were interpreted by impartial observers to signal a move by the GCC toward a "more neutralist position" (D105–D109). Speaker Hashemi-Rafsanjani reportedly said, "For the first time they [the GCC states] did not praise Iraq, and did not say that Iran does not want peace but Iraq does. Rather, they emphasized that they must better their relations with Iran. And this is the sort of realism which emerged in the GCC."[11]

Although five years of direct and indirect GCC attempts at ending the war had no effect whatsoever, they may have helped contain the war by maintaining a dialogue between the GCC states and Iran. The GCC's determined efforts to complement its military deterrence against the spread of the war with collective diplomacy utilized both disapprobation and dialogue. This twofold characteristic of its diplomatic containment of the war in part reflected the vicissitudes of the fighting. The GCC states blew hot and cold depending on the perceived threat of the war to their interests. Their behavior also reflected a degree of convergence of interests between the GCC states and Iran on a number of issues, including opposition to superpower military intervention in the Gulf, anticommunism, a basic distrust of Iraq, and mutual economic benefits, particularly between Dubai and Sharjah on the one hand and Iran on the other.[12]

Mediating between Oman and South Yemen

The GCC's principal efforts aimed at diplomatic coordination during the first five years of the life of the organization extended beyond the confines of the concerns of its member states over the Iraq-Iran war. These efforts involved two other types of diplomatic coordination as well. One concerned the relationship of a GCC state and a non-GCC state in which the organization as a whole had a major stake. The other pertained to intra-GCC relationships.

At their second summit meeting in Riyadh in November 1981, the GCC leaders specifically set "the elimination of disputes among sister Arab countries" as one of their main goals (D67). The inter-Arab dispute that at the time loomed largest in the minds of the GCC architects was the longtime conflict between Oman and South Yemen. The core of the conflict was the South Yemeni support of the

Popular Front for the Liberation of Oman and the Arabian Gulf (PFLOAG), founded partly with the aid of George Habash, the leader of the Popular Front for the Liberation of Palestine (PFLP). The PFLOAG, which was designated the Front for the Liberation of Oman (PFLO) after a splintering in its ranks in 1973, waged a war against the regime of Sultan Qabus with the material and moral support of not only South Yemen but also—through South Yemen, with the aid of the Soviets—Cuba and East Germany. Jordanian, Pakistani (Baluchi), British, and especially Iranian forces, on the other hand, helped the Omanis. According to Sultan Qabus, the Omani army, "massively aided by the Iranian expeditionary force," finally crushed the Dhofari armed rebellion by 1975. But as long as South Yemen provided sanctuary for rebels within its territory the threat of the resumption of guerrilla warfare continued. The rebels had used, among other things, Soviet-made Katyusha rockets to hit the Omani coastline near Salalah airport from mountaintops, according to Sultan Qabus, and they could do it again.[13]

Faced with fifteen years of unremitting hostility between South Yemen and Oman, the GCC was determined to seek a settlement between the two countries, which had never established diplomatic relations with each other. The GCC sponsored mediation by Kuwait and the UAE as early as July 1982 when several meetings of experts were held in the presence of delegations from South Yemen, Oman, and Kuwait. Other meetings were held later in October, and finally the Omanis and the South Yemenis signed an agreement on 27 October for the settlement of their long-standing conflict. The GCC mediation resulted in the parties' commitment to exchange ambassadors, to refrain from interfering in each others' internal affairs, and to negotiate on the future of military facilities for foreign powers.[14] On 6 November 1982 South Yemen's Supreme People's Council, in an emergency meeting, endorsed the reconciliation agreement of principles, stating, among other things, that it considered the agreement "to be a practical translation of the PDRY's [South Yemen's] foreign policy toward the region's states, aimed at establishing equal and normal relations on the basis of nonintervention in internal affairs, mutual respect of national sovereignty, good neighborliness and the achievement of fruitful cooperation, security and stability for the region's peoples and states" (D78).

Five days later, at their third summit meeting in Manama, Bahrain, the GCC leaders reviewed the results of what Secretary General Bisharah called "the great achievement" of the leaders of South Yemen and Oman. The Supreme Council praised the good offices of Kuwait and the UAE in ending the dispute between the two countries and said "it salutes the positive stands adopted by the Sultanate of Oman and the PDRY and their sincere desire to eliminate all causes of disagreement and alienation between the children of both countries and both fraternal peoples" (D81).

Given the longevity of the conflict between the two countries, the speedy rapprochement between them surprised most observers. Regarding Oman, however, there was little cause for surprise. Sultan Qabus's regime had been afflicted by the South Yemeni–supported armed rebellion within Omani territory for years. Furthermore, twelve years after the crushing of the rebellion, the PFLO's "Voice of Oman Revolution" still broadcast daily anti-Omani propaganda with the blessings of the Marxist regime in Aden. Under these circumstances, any pledge of nonintervention by South Yemen in Omani internal affairs obviously would be welcome. But speculation about the motivation of South Yemen is slightly more difficult. The desire of the Marxist regime to abandon its long-standing support of the rebels and to normalize relations with Oman may be attributed to the fact that Ali Nasser Muhammad, who seized power in 1980, was not as doctrinaire as his predecessor, Fatah Ismail, who had come to power through a coup in 1978. Without necessarily contradicting this explanation, one could also suggest that Nasser Muhammad was motivated primarily by economic considerations. One of the world's poorest countries, with a population of perhaps two million, South Yemen had tried ever since 1969 to built a communist paradise in a tribal society plagued by personal, clannish, and ideological rivalries. As the only Marxist state in the Arab world, it repelled its oil-rich conservative Arab neighbors such as Saudi Arabia and Oman politically and deprived itself of their largesse economically. In April 1982 South Yemen was hit by the most disastrous floods in forty years, devastating its agricultural base. The GCC states generously rushed to its aid, "a tempting glimpse of the reward for a political settlement with Oman."[15]

With money, the GCC facilitated a political settlement which redounded to its strategic advantage beyond the frontiers of Oman. Ever since the British forces withdrew from Aden and the Persian Gulf region, South Yemen had become the Soviet Union's sole ally in the Arabian Peninsula, providing a useful base for Soviet ships and nuclear submarines and an air base for Soviet long-range surveillance of the American base at Diego Garcia some 2,000 miles away in the Indian Ocean. Only 200 miles away from the South Yemen's shore is its island of Socotra, the Soviet Union's main base in the Arabian Sea and a strategic thorn in the side of Arab states from North Yemen to Saudi Arabia and Oman. The GCC's success in securing a political settlement between Oman and South Yemen could aid the objective of its member states to keep the Soviet-American rivalry from their doorstep. Even the Omanis who agreed to the American use of Omani facilities believed that "it is in the interests of all parties to see that both sides [United States and the USSR] keep their hands off this area."[16]

Speculations about the durability of the rapprochement between Oman and South Yemen intensified after the bloody coup against President Ali Nasser Muhammad, beginning on 12 January 1986. From the perspective of such hard-line Marxists as Abdul Fatah Ismail, whom Nasser Muhammad had deposed in 1980 and who supported the coup in 1986, the rapprochement with the GCC conservative monarchies must have seemed an unforgivable deviation from the Marxist path. But the outcome of the coup is unclear. Neither Abdul Fatah Ismail's faction nor that of the deposed Nasser Muhammad seems to have taken power. Months after the coup it was not certain whether the former was alive or dead and the latter's whereabouts were unknown. Haydar Abu Bakr al-Attas seems to have taken the leadership, but there was still talk about Soviet mediation between the rival political factions in South Yemen as late as May 1986.

When the foreign minister of the new regime in South Yemen visited the GCC countries in March 1986, Oman was conspicuously absent. Foreign Minister Abd al-Aziz al-Dali carried messages from Haydar Abu Bakr al-Attas to the leaders of the UAE, Bahrain, Qatar, Kuwait, and Saudi Arabia dealing with bilateral relations, local, Arab, and international issues. The principles of peaceful coexistence, nonintervention, etc., from which the foreign minister said his discussions with the GCC leaders proceeded were identical with those which were announced at the time when South Yemen's Supreme People's Council approved the agreement of 27 October 1982 with Oman.[17] This agreement was reaffirmed finally at the end of the visit of Omani foreign minister to South Yemen during 15–17 June 1986 (D122). It remains to be seen, however, whether the relationship between Oman and South Yemen will return to what it was before the coup of January 1986.

Containing Bahrain-Qatar Disputes

In part, the diplomatic coordination efforts of the GCC during the first five years of its existence concerned intra-GCC relationships. In the decade between the withdrawal of British forces from the

Gulf region and the birth of the GCC many disputes between the Gulf Arab states had been settled, but a number of others remained. Two of these were between Bahrain and Qatar. One concerned the Zubarah question. The Bahraini ruling family claimed a piece of land on the northern coast of the peninsula of Qatar, a claim based in part on the fact that the area had been the ancestral home of the Khalifah family before their conquest of Bahrain in 1783. The claim was also based on the grounds that the area was inhabited by the Nuaim tribe, which owed the ruler of Bahrain their allegiance.[18]

The other dispute concerned the claim of Qatar to Hawar Island. This island is ruled by Bahrain, but Qatar contends that since it is close to the Qatar peninsula it should be regarded as part of it. When in 1965 a United States company explored for oil in the area, with the permission of the British, Qatar protested the operation and it was abandoned. After the British withdrawal from the Persian Gulf in 1971, the Qatar claim continued against Bahrain, which had gained its independence from Britain. Even after the formation of the GCC the dispute continued. In fact, the tensions increased until 1982 when Saudi Arabian mediation, coupled with efforts of the GCC, prevented the escalation of the dispute.

During its meeting on 7–9 March 1982, the GCC Council of Ministers reviewed the dispute over Hawar Island and asked Saudi Arabia to continue its good offices. More critically, Bahrain and Qatar committed themselves "to freeze the situation and not to cause an escalation of the dispute," an agreement which was registered at the GCC Secretariat General. The two countries also agreed to halt propaganda campaigns against each other and to resume "fraternal relations" (D70). Whether Saudi Arabia continued its good offices is not known. Furthermore, the dispute over Hawar Island never was settled.

As if these two longtime disputes were not enough, a new one arose after the eruption of a crisis on 26 April 1986. This conflict, which had been simmering, concerned a reclaimed coral reef by the name of Fasht al-Dibal, located, according to Qatari sources, 12 miles northeast of the mainland of Qatar and 18 kilometers from Bahrain's Muharraq Island according to Bahraini sources. The Qatari forces invaded the Fasht, occupied it, and arrested thirty people (twenty-five from the Philippines, two from Britain, two from Thailand, and one from the Netherlands) who were engaged on a contract to build a small "coastguard station." The men were the employees of Ballast Nedam, Gray Mackenzie and Muharraq Engineering, whose tugboat was shot up when its captain attempted to flee. Their detention by Qatar for seventeen days touched off an international crisis. In the meantime, Bahrain increased its military presence on Hawar Island. Qatar did much more. It landed heavy artillery and antiaircraft guns, declared the maritime regions of Fasht and Hawar islands to be restricted naval and air zones, and suspended Bahraini workers in, and deported Bahraini students from Qatar. This Qatari muscle flexing reflected in part its three-to-one superior firepower vis-à-vis its fellow-GCC member Bahrain.

There seemed to be some confusion about the type of construction project involved and the identity of its sponsors. A number of newspapers said that the building of a small "coastguard station" was disrupted, while other sources indicated that "the installations were built as a center for surveilling ships in the Persian Gulf" so as to notify them of possible air attacks by Iran. Was it a Bahraini or a GCC project? *MEED* reported that according to a Ballast Nedam official the station was "being built with GCC approval and with GCC money, including some from Qatar," but diplomats in Doha questioned whether Qatar would have attacked the station if it knew it to be a GCC project.[19] My own investigation reveals that the plan was a GCC project, but it had not been approved by Qatar.

The official positions of Bahrain and Qatar emphasized different issues. Bahrain played up the fact that Qatar had resorted to the use of force against "Bahraini territory." It regretted this resort to violence, which was a "departure from the principles of good neighborliness on which the GCC is based." And it stressed the importance of its own self-restraint and the sympathy of the other fellow-GCC members for its position (D118). Qatar, on the other hand, charged that Bahrain had insisted on violating "the sovereignty of the State of Qatar over its maritime province" by such actions as "transforming Fasht al-Dibal into an industrial island." It asserted that any action that changed the status quo contradicted the "principles of mediation" carried out by Saudi Arabia and that one such principle had been adopted by the GCC Ministerial Council in 1982 (D120). As seen above, however, the principle in the 1982 case involved Hawar Island specifically rather than the new dispute over Fasht.

The GCC, led by Saudi Arabia, arrested the escalation of the dispute within a month from the eruption of the crisis. Although the other GCC leaders played important parts in defusing the crisis, King Fahd's role was decisive. Behind-the-scene efforts by the United States were also important. As a result of the king's mediation, an agreement was reached between the leaders of Bahrain and Qatar to restore the situation on Fasht to "the status quo ante" (D119). The exact date of the agreement is not known, but its existence was first announced in Riyadh on 19 May 1986. The GCC Secretariat subsequently issued a statement on the agreement, announcing that the supervising and monitoring commission for implementing it would begin its work on 25 May. The commission consisted of members of the GCC Secretariat, Saudi Arabia, Kuwait, Oman, and the UAE and was headed by General Saad al-Muwayni.

Apparently, the Qatari forces were dragging their feet in withdrawing from Fasht. King Fahd's hint during an interview of the possibility of resort to "binding international arbitration" if the parties failed to implement their agreement in "the current dispute" seems to have goaded Qatar to evacuate the island, starting on 5 June 1986.[20] If the agreement was fully implemented, the situation in and around Fasht and Hawar islands would return to what it was before 26 April when the crisis erupted. In addition, the two countries reportedly pledged in writing that they would not resort to force again as long as efforts were being exerted to achieve a solution to satisfy both sides. Nor would "symbolic Gulf forces" be stationed at Fasht al-Dibal.[21]

Given the perceived threat of the spread of the Iraq-Iran war, once again the two neighboring states seemed able to de-escalate their old and new disputes as a result of Saudi Arabian mediation and the implementation of their agreement by the GCC. Five years after the inception of the GCC, the Gulf Arabs themselves viewed the Fasht crisis with alarm for its adverse effects on the cohesion of their nascent organization for regional cooperation. The outspoken *Al-Khalij* of Sharjah reported that diplomatic sources in the area believed that the Qatari-Bahraini dispute "threatens the very existence of the GCC."[22] Foreign Minister Shaykh Sabah al-Ahmad al-Jabir of Kuwait regretted "what occurred among brother members of one council, the Gulf Cooperation Council," and described the Fasht dispute as "a passing cloud."[23] It remained to be seen whether it would be "a passing cloud" after the return to the status quo ante.

Tightrope Walking at Its Best

Of all the strategies pursued by the GCC states during the first five years of their cooperation, diplomatic coordination was the most ambitious. What could be more ambitious than trying to contain the spread of the Iraq-Iran war, to settle the protracted Oman–South Yemen conflict, and to arrest the expansion of the Bahrain-Qatar disputes? Iran itself, to be sure, was not interested in expanding the war for a variety of reasons, including that of preserving its firepower for the war with Iraq and denying the superpowers the opportunity to intervene in the Gulf region by military means. But to some extent, the collective diplomacy of the GCC states may have also contributed to the containment of the war.

The GCC's diplomacy was marked by flexibility. No official neutrality stood in the way of the GCC's active, flexible response to the state of armed hostilities. The logistical and financial tilt toward Iraq was not allowed to impede a dialogue with Iran. The GCC's rather strict fence-sitting during 1980–82—before the successful Iranian offensives in the spring of 1982—was changed to a vigorous diplomatic offensive against Iran in 1982–84. In turn, this was changed to an unprecedented conciliation with Iran and a brief cooling of relations with Iraq in 1984–85 when the Iraqi escalation of the tanker war subjected the Kuwaiti and Saudi oil tankers to Iranian retaliatory attacks.

In terms of its principal ingredients, the GCC's collective diplomacy from 1981 to 1986 consisted of three tactical moves. These were disapprobative, mediatory, and conciliatory in nature. When the GCC states felt threatened by the armed hostilities between Iran and Iraq—as at the height of the tanker war—they went on a diplomatic offensive. By using the Arab League medium, they generalized the threat to them as a threat to the whole Arab world, as evidenced by their success in acquiring a favorable resolution on the war at the Fez summit in September 1982. By using the United Nations Security Council, they internationalized the threat to them as a threat to the international community, as demonstrated by their success in securing the 31 October 1983 and 1 June 1984 resolutions emphasizing the principle of freedom of navigation in the Gulf.

Despite their official neutrality and actual partiality, the GCC states did make earnest efforts to mediate between the two belligerents. Indirectly, they tried to use the good offices of such international organizations as OCI and NAM and such countries as Algeria and Japan. Directly, they used the GCC medium to launch a campaign of mediation first during the fifth summit of November 1984 in Kuwait and then during the ministerial meeting of March 1985 and especially during the sixth summit of November 1985 in Muscat. There can be little doubt that the improved political climate as a result of these moves aided the exchange of visits between the Saudi Arabian and Iranian foreign ministers in 1985.

Despite their dwindling oil revenues, the GCC states made conciliatory gestures toward both belligerents by offering them financial aid. During the Iraqi oil-spill offensive in 1983 the mediation visits of the foreign ministers of Kuwait and the UAE to Tehran and Baghdad were accompanied by talks about the GCC's offer of aid to the two countries for postwar reconstruction. The GCC leaders tried to use the oil-spill problem to secure a temporary ceasefire ostensibly in order to cap the damaged oil wells but actually to extend it to an overall negotiated peace settlement. When the efforts for mediation were intensified in 1985, again the offer of financial assistance for rebuilding "institutions destroyed in the war" was renewed. At the time of the fifth summit, as mentioned, the president of the UAE proposed the adoption of a GCC "Marshall Plan" for aiding Iran and Iraq after the war.

No matter how effective the threat of American intervention against Iran may have been, the containment of the war must be attributed in part to the ability of the GCC states to exercise sustained restraint. While they kept their powder dry for a possible showdown with Iran, as in the aerial dogfight in 1984, they managed, against all odds, to intensify this dialogue with the Khomeini regime. To the annoyance of the GCC leaders, such Iranian officials as Prime Minister Musavi attributed their conciliatory stance to Iran's "firm stands," but, in fact, the mutual self-restraint prompted by self-interest helped maintain the GCC-Iran dialogue.

The GCC's role in the settlement of the old conflict between Oman and South Yemen was equally impressive. Here, as in the Iraq-Iran war, the principal mediators were Kuwait and UAE. Regardless of what motivated South Yemeni leaders to sign the agreement of 27 October 1982, whether financial need or ideological mellowing, the settlement of the conflict redounded to the advantage of both Oman and its GCC partners. More critically, the agreement seemed to weather the effects of the bloody coup in South Yemen, whose new leaders affirmed their commitment to the agreement with Oman signed by their predecessors. One factor that may well keep the relationship between Aden and Muscat from deteriorating in the near future is Oman's own new relationship with the Soviet Union. When the GCC was established, only Kuwait had diplomatic relations with the Soviet Union, whereas before the sixth GCC summit was held, Oman and the UAE also had established diplomatic relations with Moscow. If it wishes, the Soviet Union can pressure South Yemen not to resume its conflict with Oman now that Muscat has established diplomatic relations with Moscow.

Despite the simmering disputes between Bahrain and Qatar, the GCC leaders were surprised by the Qatari invasion of Fasht al-Dibal. Although as early as 1982 the GCC had become involved in the Bahrain-Qatar dispute over Hawar Island, it did not then try to settle the Fasht dispute. The Qatari government had in 1982 confined itself to protesting the Bahraini naval exercises near Fasht. Just as the role of Kuwait and the UAE was pivotal in the settlement of the Omani–South Yemeni dispute, the role of Saudi Arabia was decisive in containing the Bahraini-Qatari disputes.

Although the return to the status quo ante was the best possible solution to the Fasht crisis, the GCC leaders realized the need for a conclusive settlement. After all, the Fasht crisis was the sole challenge to the cohesion of the GCC itself during its first five years of existence. Undoubtedly the specter of the protracted Iraq-Iran war—especially the Iranian capture of Fao only a couple of months earlier—was used by the Saudis, and behind the scenes by the Americans and others as well, to impress upon the disputants, particularly the Qataris, the need to settle their differences in the face of the greater threat of the war.

This consideration once again brings up the wider and more crucial question about cooperation among the GCC states in the future. The Fasht crisis in 1986 was contained, as was the Hawar dispute in 1982, but neither has been resolved. In both instances, the threat of the spread of the Iraq-Iran war impelled restraint on the part of the disputants. But will such restraint continue after the war? This question may be better addressed in the next chapter which concludes this study.

Notes

1. For details, see Ramazani, "Shiism in the Persian Gulf," pp. 30–54.

2. See Ministry of Foreign Affairs of the Republic of Iraq, *The Iraqi-Iranian Dispute: Facts and Allegations* (New York, 1980), especially p. 28.

3. *FBIS-MEA-V-82-013*, 20 Jan. 1982.

4. *FBIS-MEA-V-81-102*, 28 May 1981.

5. *FBIS-South Asia-VIII-83-201*, 17 Oct. 1983.

6. *Middle East*, Dec. 1984, p. 15.

7. *FBIS-MEA-V-85-053*, 19 March 1985.

8. *FBIS-MEA-V-85-211*, 31 Oct. 1985.

9. For details, see Ramazani, *Revolutionary Iran*, pp. 97–100.

10. *FBIS-SA-VIII-85-098*, 20 May 1985.

11. *FBIS-SA-VIII-85-212*, 1 Nov. 1985.

12. For details, see Ramazani, *Revolutionary Iran*, pp. 139–43.

13. For details, see R. K. Ramazani, *The Persian Gulf and the Strait of Hormuz* (Alphen aan den Rijn, The Netherlands: Sijthoff and Noordhoff, 1979), pp. 75–80.

14. *Middle East*, Dec. 1982.

15. *Middle East*, Dec. 1982, p. 20.

16. See the text of an interview by an Omani official, ibid., p. 19.

17. *FBIS-MEA-V-86-053*, 19 March 1986.

18. For details, see Husein M. Albaharna, *The Arabian Gulf States: Their Legal and Political Status and Their International Problems*, rev. 2d ed. (Singapore: Trin Wah Press, 1978), pp. 247–50.

19. *MEED*, 3 May 1986, p. 23.

20. For the text of the interview, see *FBIS-MEA-V-68-107*, 4 June 1986; on the withdrawal of Qatari forces, see *FBIS-MEA-V-86-109*, 6 June 1986.

21. *FBIS-MEA-V-86-101*, 27 May 1986.

22. *FBIS-MEA-V-86-098*, 21 May 1986.

23. *FBIS-MEA-V-86-082*, 29 April 1986.

Documents

Document 65
Ethiopian-Libyan-Peoples Democratic Republic of Yemen Cooperation Treaty
20 August 1981

Mindful of the coordinated conspiracies of international imperialism, Zionism, racism, and reactionary forces to encircle, strang[l]e and reverse the revolutions of their three countries; mindful of these forces' continuous attempts to plunder their natural resources by bringing the African Continent and the Arab world under these forces' influence and control, and in the belief that the unity and cooperation of the three revolutionary countries to resist this conspiracy, to unite in the political, economic and other fields will further strengthen their anti-imperialist, anti-reactionary, anti-Zionist and antiracist stance; and mindful that the common struggle they wage in these fields will benefit not only to their peoples but also regional peace, the progressive forces of the world and all independence movements; and in confirmation of their strong desire to safeguard their territorial integrity against all aggression and to protect and safeguard their freedom, national unity and territorial integrity and their revolutions from counterrevolution, to closely forge their revolutionary experiences, to strengthen the experience of struggle of their peoples and to further promote their efforts to resist all kinds of oppression; mindful of the need to establish cooperation, friendship and coordination among the three revolutions in various fields; reaffirming that they will adhere to the charter and principles of the United Nations and the principles of the Nonaligned Movement and the charters of continental organizations of which the three countries are members, the three countries, socialist Ethiopia, the Socialist People's Libyan Arab Jamahiriyah and the PDRY have decided to conclude the following treaty:

Article 1: The three signatory parties shall cooperate in the political, economic and other fields to enable them to coordinate their anti-imperialist, anti-reactionary, anti-Zionist and antiracist stand.

Article 2: The three signatory parties shall cooperate in the political field to guarantee the common struggle of the three revolutionary countries.

Article 3: The three signatory parties shall cooperate in resisting and foiling the conspiracies of imperialism, Zionism, and reactionary forces that aim to strangle progressive forces and countries by strengthening their military forces as well as establishing and expanding military bases in countries located in the Indian Ocean, the Mediterranean Sea, the Red Sea and elsewhere in the region.

Article 4: The three signatory parties shall resist the conspiracies and alignment of the Camp David accords.

Article 5: The three signatory parties reiterate their solidarity with Arab, African and other national liberation movements, and in particular with the Palestine revolution and those of Namibia and South Africa in the struggle against imperialism, Zionism, reaction and racism.

Article 6: The three signatory parties shall exchange ideas to enable them to coordinate their stand on international and continental issues.

Article 7: The three signatory parties shall make every possible effort to strengthen and deepen their relations with the region's progressive countries and forces, as well as with socialist countries.

Article 8: A political committee consisting of the foreign minister of socialist Ethiopia, the secretary of the Foreign relations Bureau [*as heard*] of the Socialist Peoples Libyan Arab Jamahiriyah and the PDRY foreign ministers shall be established.

Article 9: The duties of the Political Committee are: to monitor the implementation of established political lines, to give opinions and ideas to the Supreme Council as to how political cooperation can be developed with confidence, to prepare for meetings of the Supreme Council and to carry out additional duties entrusted to it.

Article 10: The three signatory parties shall cooperate in the economic field to develop their national economies.

Article 11: The three signatory parties shall exchange material and financial assistance to enable them to implement their national development plans and to find solutions to their economic problems. They shall also strengthen their commercial relations.

Article 12: The three signatory parties, taking into consideration each country's material potential and on this basis, shall cooperate in formulating development plans that will strengthen their socioeconomic development.

Article 13: The three signatory parties shall make every possible effort to coordinate their stand on international and continental economic issues and to strengthen their relations with the region's progressive countries as well as with the socialist countries.

Article 14: An economic committee consisting of the economic minister of socialist Ethiopia, the Socialist People's Libyan Arab Jamahiriyah people's general economic secretary [*as heard*] and the PDRY planning minister shall be established.

Article 15: The duties of the Economic Committee are: to make plans to promote and coordinate economic relations among the three signatory parties, to formulate ideas and express opinions on ways of developing economic cooperation and to perform additional duties entrusted to it by the Supreme Council.

Article 16: The three signatory parties, in the event of aggression committed against any one of them, shall assist the victim of aggression in all necessary ways individually or collectively, since aggression against one shall be considered aggression directed against all the signatory parties.

Article 17: The three signatory parties, in accordance with agreements to be signed by them, shall make efforts to strengthen their defensive capabilities and promote their cooperation in the military and security fields to enable them to protect their freedom and territorial integrity.

Article 18: A supreme council shall be established consisting of: the chairman of the Provisional Military Administrative Council and of the commission for organizing the Ethiopian workers party and the commander in chief of the Revolutionary Army; the leader of the Socialist People's Libyan Arab Jamahiriyah; the secretary general of the YSP Central Committee, the chairman of the PDRY Council of Ministers and chairman of the Presidium of the Supreme People's Council and the chairman of the political, economic and other committees.

The Supreme Council shall have the following duties: it shall analyze the work of the political, economic and other committees and take measures to fully implement this work, and it shall establish other ministerial committees or secretariats as necessary.

Article 19: The Supreme council shall meet once a year in the capitals of signatory countries in rotation. If demanded by one of the three signatory countries, an emergency meeting shall be convened.

Article 20: The political, economic and other committees shall meet every 6 months in the capitals of the signatory countries in rotation. If demanded by one among the three signatory countries, an emergency session shall be convened.

Article 21: The Political Committee shall submit its work report to the Supreme Council. The other committees shall submit their work reports to the Supreme Council through the Political Committee.

Article 22: The Political Committee shall present an internal constitution that shall be ratified at the first meeting of the Supreme Council.

Article 23: The three signatory parties affirm that the articles of their treaty are not contrary to the international treaties and obligations entered into by the three countries. The three signatory countries also undertake not to enter into any kind of international agreement that runs contrary to the articles of this treaty.

Article 24: This treaty requires ratification by the three signatory parties. Documents of ratification shall be kept with the PDRY Government.

Article 25: This treaty shall become effective when the final document of ratification is lodged with the PDRY Government. The PDRY Government shall notify the other signatory parties of the arrival of each and every document of ratification.

Article 26: Other parties that follow the objectives and goal of this treaty as well as the provision of the UN Charter and the guidelines of the Nonaligned Movement can become members of the treaty upon full approval by the three signatory countries.

Article 27: The three signatory parties shall sign political, economic and other agreements and protocols that will facilitate the implementation of the articles of this treaty and that shall be part of the treaty concluded.

Article 28: If one of the parties desires to revoke the treaty, it may do so 1 year after written notification to the PDRY Government. The PDRY government shall in turn notify the other signatory parties of this development. This treaty has three copies, in Amharic, Arabic, and English. All the languages in which the treaty is written are equally acceptable.

[Signed] 20 August 1981, Aden

Source: *FBIS-MEA-V–81–170*, 2 Sept. 1981, pp. R1-R3.

Document 66
GCC Ministerial Council: First Session Statement
2 September 1981

The Ministerial Council of the Gulf States Cooperation Council held its first session from 31 August to 2 September 1981 in At-Taif, Saudi Arabia.

In accordance with the final statement of the first summit conference held in Abu Dhabi in the UAE on 25 and 26 May 1981, which stressed the determination of their majesties and highnesses to keep the Gulf area free from international conflicts and to entrust responsibility for security in the region to the states of the area, the first ministerial council session reviewed the political and security situation in the Gulf region in the light of current developments. The council reasserted that the security and stability of the Gulf are the responsibility of its states only. The council expressed opposition to the attempts by the great powers to interfere in the affairs of the area in view of the fact that this might result in involving the region in a conflict which does not conform with the interests of its states nor the will of its peoples.

The council also discussed all the attempts being made by other forces which are seeking to find position in the Gulf from which to threaten its security and sovereignty. The council declared its rejection of these attempts, which constitute a threat to the region and its people and which seek to ensure the influence of foreign forces in the region.

The council declared its intention to consolidate political and security coordination among the member states, so as to face the dangers encircling the region, and to increase contacts so as to eliminate these dangers.

The council also discussed the situation in the Middle East and reasserted its absolute support for the struggling of the People of Palestine for their established right to exercise self-determination and to set up their own independent state on their territory under the leadership of the PLO. The council reiterated the belief of its member states that there can be no just peace in the Middle East unless Israel withdraws from all the occupied Arab territories, including holy Jerusalem, and removes the settlements it is building on those territories. In discussing the Palestinian issue in all its aspects, the council reviewed the declaration of principles contained in the statement of His Royal Highness Prince Fahd ibn Abd al-Aziz, the Saudi crown prince, regarding a just and comprehensive solution to the problem. The council also reviewed the positive Arab and international reaction to these principles.

In view of the support these principles enjoy from the member states, the council decided to request that they be placed on the agenda of the upcoming Arab summit with the aim of bringing about a unified Arab stand on the issue.

The council also condemned the Zionist aggressions against the Lebanese and Palestinian peoples and the violation of the sovereignty and independence of Lebanon. It declared its support for Lebanon in its efforts to spread its legal authority over the southern part of the territory and to preserve its safety in the region and its political independence and sovereignty.

The council also discussed the conflict between Iraq and Iran and the threat it constitutes to the security and stability of the entire region. It expressed the hope that the efforts of the Muslim states, as initiated by the Islamic summit conference, will be crowned with success. It also expressed its support for those efforts and its readiness to participate in anything that might contribute to their success.

The council also discussed the detention of a ship which

had been sailing in the Gulf waters, a matter which violated international law. The council condemned this behavior so as to reassert the freedom of navigation in the Gulf.

The council reviewed the situation in Afghanistan and the dangers this situation constitutes, not only to the security and independence of the region but also to world peace. It stressed its adherence to the resolutions of the Islamic congress in this respect. It also expressed its adherence to Islamic solidarity and the policy of nonalignment and its objection to the attempts by the great powers to set up military bases in the region and in the Arabian Sea, the Red Sea and the Indian Ocean. It reviewed the economic agreement which was initialed by the ministers of finance and economy in Riyadh on 8 June 1981.

In accordance with the resolutions of the first summit conference of the Cooperation Council held in Abu Dhabi, in line with the economic working paper which was approved by their majesties and highnesses, in realization of the wishes of the people of the region to remove the economic barriers among the member states of the Cooperation Council and in order to ensure the principle of equality among all citizens, the council approved the draft economic agreement and decided to put it before their majesties and highnesses at their upcoming conference in Riyadh.

While taking this important and blessed step, the Ministerial Council declares that economic cooperation among the member states of the council is the backbone for future actions to ensure the molding of the area into a framework which paves the way to unity.

The council also decided to invite the industry ministers in the member states to meet before the second summit so as to lay down the executive rules of industrial cooperation in accordance with the third chapter of the draft economic treaty. The council also endorsed the appointment of Dr. Abdallah al-Quwayz as assistant secretary general for economic affairs and of Ambassador Ibrahim Ahmud as-Subhi as assistant secretary general for political affairs.

The council recommended that the [*words indistinct*] 3 November 1981 be the date for the convening of the second conference of the supreme council of the Gulf Cooperation Council in Riyadh, Saudi Arabia, and that this conference be preceded by a meeting of the foreign ministers 2 days earlier.

The council expressed thanks and appreciation to the government of His Majesty King Khalid ibn Abd al-Aziz for his hospitality and patronage of the session.

Source: *FBIS-MEA-V–81–171*, 3 Sept. 1981, pp. C2-C4.

Document 67

Riyadh Supreme Council Summit: Final Communiqué

11 November, 1981

At the invitation of His Majesty King Khalid ibn Abd Al-Aziz, King of Saudi Arabia, with God's assistance, it was possible to hold the second session of the supreme council of the Cooperation Council of the Gulf Arab States in Riyadh from 10–11 November in the presence of their majesties and highnesses.

The council reviewed the political, economic and security situation in the Gulf in the light of current developments and expressed its readiness to continue coordination in these fields in order to face up to the dangers surrounding the region, and to increase the contacts between member states in order to ward off these dangers. The council also discussed all the attempts by other forces aimed at establishing positions in the Gulf in order to threaten its security and sovereignty, and announced its rejection of these attempts which constitute a danger to the region and its people and which are aimed at securing influence for foreign forces in the region. It confirmed once again that the security and the stability of the Gulf are the responsibility of its states. It expressed opposition to the attempts by superpowers to interfere in the affairs of the region with the resulting involvement of the region in a conflict which is not in agreement with the interests of its states and the will of its people.

It also confirmed the need to keep the region as a whole away from international conflicts, especially the presence of military fleets and foreign bases, in its interest and the interest of security and peace in the world.

The council also discussed the situation in the Middle East and confirmed anew its absolute support for the struggle of the Palestinian people for their indispensable right to self-determination and to set up an independent state on their land under the leadership of the PLO. The council renewed its belief that there is no way to achieve a just peace in the Middle East without the withdrawal by Israel from all the occupied Arab territories, including holy Jerusalem, and the removal of Israeli colonies being established on Arab land.

The council reviewed the Arab and international reactions to the principles of peace announced by the Kingdom of Saudi Arabia regarding the just and comprehensive solution to the Palestinian problem. The council decided to ask the Kingdom of Saudi Arabia to place it on the agenda of the 12th Arab summit conference to be held in Morocco with the objective to crystallizing a unified Arab attitude to the Palestine problem.

The council reviewed the current Arab situation and the shouldering of national responsibilities, including the need to achieve Arab solidarity and the elimination of disputes among sister Arab countries, the rejection of disunity, and the confirmation of unity of efforts in line with the principles outlined in the basic statute to the effect that the [Gulf] Cooperation Council is an indivisible part of the Arab nation. The council decided that member countries will make real efforts to achieve unity of Arab ranks.

The council discussed the conflict between Iraq and Iran and the resulting threat to the security and stability of the region as a whole, and expressed the hope that the efforts stemming from the Islamic conference and the efforts of the nonaligned and the United Nations would be (?successful).

The council reviewed the situation in Afghanistan and the dangers it constitutes not only to the security and independence of the region, but also to world peace. It confirmed its adherence to the resolutions of the Islamic Conference in this respect.

The council reviewed the economic agreement initialed by the ministers of finance and the economy in Riyadh on 8 June 1981, which was discussed by the ministerial council in At-Taif from 31 August to 1 September 1981. The supreme council, by taking this important step [*as heard*] is adhering to the aspirations of citizens to see the removal of barriers between member countries and the strengthening of ties between the people of the region on firm foundations, leading to the unity of the region and the understanding that this is the ideal way of securing progress and prosperity for all member countries of the council.

The council also reviewed the issue of military cooperation among its states and decided to invite the defense ministers to meet in order to fix the priorities of the member countries in securing their independence and sovereignty.

The council decided that its third session will be held in Bahrain in the first week of November 1982.

The council expressed its thanks, appreciation and gratitude to His Majesty King Khalid ibn Abd al-Aziz and Crown Prince Fahd ibn Abd al-Aziz and to the government of the Kingdom of Saudi Arabia for the hospitality and warm reception accorded to the leaders and members of the participating delegations during their attendance. This had good effects on the success of the work of this fraternal meeting. It wished his majesty and the crown prince continued good health and wished the Saudi people continued prosperity and progress.

Source: *FBIS-MEA-V–81–218*, 12 Nov. 1981, pp. C4-C5.

Document 68

Ethiopia-Libya-PDRY (Aden Pact): First Summit Communiqué

18 November 1981

In accordance with the friendship and cooperation treaty signed between socialist Ethiopia, the Socialist People's Li-byan Arab Jamahiriyah and the PDRY on 18 August 1981, the Political Committee held an extraordinary meeting in Addis Ababa 15–16 November 1981.

Comrade Dr. Felleke Gedle-Giorgis, minister of foreign affairs of socialist Ethiopia and Commission for Organizing the Party of the Workers of Ethiopia Central Committee member; Brother Abd al-Ati al-Ubyadi, secretary of the Socialist People's Libyan Arab Jamahiriyah People's Committee for Foreign Affairs; and Comrade Salim Salih Muhammad, member of the YSP Central Committee and PDRY foreign minister, led the delegations of their respective countries to the meeting.

The Political Committee assessed the present situation in our region and examined in depth the situation created in recent months in the same region where the United States is actively trying to create rifts, misunderstandings and direct conflicts among neighboring countries in the region.

The Political Committee members stated they hold similar views in their analysis of international and regional situations and noted that imperialism's main objectives in the world in general, and in the region in particular, are to perpetuate its exploitation of the natural resources in the region, to establish its dominance over the countries in the region, to cut short their independent (?progress), to divert the international community's attention from the perplexing problems in the Middle East and southern Africa and to obstruct the efforts of the African and Arab peoples and countries for socioeconomic development.

The Political Committee also noted that, with a view to maintaining the Mediterranean, Africa, the Middle East, the Red Sea, the Persian Gulf and the Indian Ocean regions as areas of constant tension, the U.S. military arms in the regions have recently been further strengthened.

The committee (?repeatedly) pointed out that the acts of provocation and aggression being committed by the Reagan administration are directed not only against Ethiopia, Libya and the PDRY, which hold anti-imperialist, antireaction, antiracist and anti-Zionist stances, but also against peace-loving, democratic and progressive countries, as well as against national liberation movements in Africa and the Middle East.

The Political Committee also noted that U.S. imperialism, in collaboration with Egypt, Sudan, Somalia and Oman, as well as with the Zionist country, is conducting a major military exercise known as Bright Star 82 in the area from the southern Mediterranean to the Indian Ocean.

The Political Committee observed that U.S. imperialism, in collaboration with its reactionary, racist, and Zionist accomplices, is also deploying its Rapid Deployment Force (RDF) not only to threaten the three countries but also to confirm its hegemony in the region.

The Political Committee stated that the presence of U.S. military bases and institutions on the basis of permission granted to the United States by a number of countries in the region coupled with military cooperation is a source of very grave concern for the three countries, for stability in the region and world peace and security.

The Political Committee recalled that many of the African and Middle East countries attained their independence after a protracted struggle and great sacrifice and said that U.S. imperialism and its NATO collaborators are exploiting resources, trying to establish their domination and committing acts of provocation and aggression at a time when the African peoples, together with their Arab brethren, are striving to promote regional cooperation so as to utilize properly their natural resources for socioeconomic development.

The committee said that the NATO forces headed by U.S. imperialism are conducting major military exercises to prevent peaceful cooperation between independent countries in the region and to obstruct the struggles being waged by genuine liberation movements in Africa and the Middle East.

The committee noted that the supply of modern weapons to a few countries in the region is aimed at intensifying tensions and internal conflicts. Creating a military axis by building new military bases and expanding the existing ones, creating a strategic consensus and strategic unity and deploying the RDF are all part of the U.S. plan to create favorable conditions for its political and economic ends by destabilizing peace in the region.

The committee said that the aim of the current military exercise which ranges from North Dakota in the United States to Diego Garcia in the Indian [Ocean] and which includes the Atlantic Ocean, Europe, the Mediterranean, Africa, the Middle East, the Red Sea and the Persian Gulf regions and their inhabitants is to beat the cold war drum in preparation for a general international conflict.

In addition, it said that the ongoing U.S. military exercise is aimed at weakening the national sovereignty of the countries which are not willing to receive orders from the United States, at perpetuating the exploitation of the natural resources of the countries in the region by creating rifts, misunderstandings and direct conflicts between them and at misleading international opinion on the dangerous situation in southern Africa and the Middle East.

The committee said that to realize its objectives U.S. imperialism employs various methods such as interfering in the internal affairs of countries, committing direct aggression, creating rifts, intensifying existing conflicts between countries, establishing new military bases and expanding the existing ones, deploying the RDF, conducting intelligence operations by means of AWACS and other ultramodern methods and conducting military exercises such as Bright Star 81 and the ongoing Bright Star 82 from time to time.

The Political Committee, having examined the situation, and the situation created in the region at present, strongly condemned the acts of intimidation and the major military exercises being conducted by U.S. imperialism and its collaborators in the region. It also condemned the presence of those imperialist and reactionary forces which are opposed to the charters and principles of the OAU, the Arab League, the Nonaligned Movement and the United Nations.

It decided to adopt the necessary measures to counter the conspiracies of international imperialism, neocolonialism, racism, Zionism, and reaction aimed not only at suffocating the revolutions of the three countries and at subverting them but also at perpetuating the exploitative positions of imperialists and neocolonialists over the peoples and natural resources of the region.

The three countries reaffirmed their position to strengthen further their friendship, cooperation and solidarity with socialist countries. They call on peace-loving, democratic and progressive countries in general, and the countries of the region in particular, to condemn such acts of provocation and aggression, which entail grave consequences for the stability of the region and for world peace and security.

They decided to present the matter to the OAU, the Arab League, the Nonaligned Movement and the United Nations and to press these organizations to take steps commensurate with the danger of the situation.

The three countries reaffirmed their position of promoting goodneighborliness, peace and cooperation, something which is in conformity with the charters and principles of regional and international organizations.

Source: *FBIS-MEA-V–81–223*, 19 Nov. 1981, pp. R1-R3.

Document 69
GCC Interior Ministers: First Session Statement
24 February 1982

The GCC interior ministers held their first conference in Riyadh from 23 to 24 February 1982. The ministers reviewed the recommendations submitted by the experts committee which met on 20 and 21 February.

Inspired by the principles embodied in the GCC statute, enlightened by the statements and resolutions made by their majesties and highnesses during the first and second sessions of the Supreme Council, and in reaffirmation of the determination to secure the safety of the member states, to preserve stability in them, and to seek tranquility for the citizens and secure the firmness and strength of the region, the GCC interior ministers agreed to sign a comprehensive joint security agreement. This agreement stems from their belief that a strong Gulf means a strong Arab nation.

The interior ministers decided to commission the general secretariat to call upon specialists in the member states and to meet in order to prepare the draft agreement, taking into consideration the opinions that were presented and the bills that were submitted by some of the member states.

The ministers will meet in October to review the draft agreement.

The ministers also reviewed the documents submitted by Bahrain on the Iranian plot to undermine legitimate institutions, spread sedition and endanger security and stability. In this regard, the ministers expressed their full support for Bahrain to preserve its safety, security, sovereignty and independence on the basis of their belief that the security of the Gulf is inseparable, that aggression against any member state is aggression against the other states and that the responsibility of confronting aggression against any state is a collective responsibility to be shouldered by all of the member states.

The ministers stressed that intervention by any country in the internal affairs of one of the member states is considered to be intervention in the internal affairs of the GCC states.

The ministers expressed hope that the hostile stands adopted by some states against the GCC states will end by virtue of neighborly relations, unity of faith and known historic ties.

The GCC interior ministers expressed most sincere feelings of appreciation and gratitude to His Majesty King Khalid ibn Abd al-Aziz of the Kingdom of Saudi Arabia and to Crown Prince Fahd ibn Abd al-Aziz and the kingdom's government for their fine reception, pleasant preparations and sincere hospitality.

Source: *FBIS-MEA-V–82–038*, 25 Feb. 1982, p. C3.

Document 70
GCC Ministerial Council: Third Session Statement
9 March 1982

The Council of Ministers held its third session in Riyadh at the headquarters of the GCC secretary general from 7 to 9 March 1982.

During its meeting the council reviewed the dispute between Bahrain and Qatar. The council expressed its regret over this dispute and its anxiety regarding its effects on the region and the results of its continuation. It noted that this dispute is not in keeping with the principles embodied by the basic statute [of the council] and that it is not in accordance with the prevailing spirit among the GCC states.

The council stressed that the establishment of the GCC has provided a constitutional framework for settling disputes among member states, which is demonstrated in the decision of their majesties and their highnesses to form a body to settle disputes.

Following an exchange of views and adhering to the principles upon which the GCC is based, and guided by

the spirit which distinguishes relations among the member states, the council adopted the following decisions:

1. To ask the Kingdom of Saudi Arabia to continue its good offices to settle the dispute between the two countries.

2. The agreement reached between Bahrain and of Qatar regarding the commitment of both sides to freeze the situation and not to cause an escalation of the dispute is to be recorded at the GCC Secretariat General.

3. Propaganda campaigns between the two countries are to be halted and they are to refrain from stirring them up.

4. To confirm the continuation of fraternal relations between the two countries and to return to earlier conditions.

The council also reviewed the speech delivered by Col. Muammar al-Qadhdhafi. Council members expressed to Saudi rabia their strong regret and displeasure at Col. Muammar al- Qadhdhafi's stand vis-à-vis Saudi Arabia, a stand which is not in line with the spirit of Arab fraternity because it also escalates disputes among the Arab states, makes the realization of Arab solidarity remote and conflicts with the aspirations and hopes of the Arab nation for the harmony and rallying, solidarity and unity of the Arab ranks.

The council hopes the Arab nation will draw its conclusion and will avoid provocations and setting Arab peoples against one another, something condemned by those who work for the unity and solidarity of the Arab nation.

The council reviewed the interior minister's resolutions and agreed that the member states should sign a reciprocal general security agreement. In this respect the Secretariat General should prepare a draft agreement to be discussed by the interior ministers at their next meeting.

The council also adopted the resolutions adopted by the ministers of finance and economy and the oil ministers. The council expressed its sincere thanks and appreciation to His Majesty King Khalid ibn Abd al-Aziz and to the crown prince for their hospitality and for the Saudi Arabian Government's arrangements and facilities, which greatly contributed to the success of this session. The council wished the king, the crown prince and the Saudi Arabian people continuous success and prosperity.

Source: *FBIS-MEA-V–82–047*, 10 March 1982, pp. C1-C2.

Document 71
GCC Ministerial Council: Second Extraordinary
Meeting Statement
20 April 1982

In view of the events which the Arab region has witnessed recently; in light of the important developments on the Arab level and the uprising which the West Bank and the occupied Arab territories have witnessed in the face of Zionist obstinacy manifested by its occupation of the Arab territories and its denial of the rights of the Palestinian people; and in view of the consequences of these events such as the threat to security, stability and peace, the Ministerial Council held its second extraordinary session at the headquarters of the General Secretariat in Riyadh on Tuesday, 20 April.

After reviewing the situation, the council decided to use its good offices to bring about unity of the Arab ranks and to eliminate differences between brothers in order to confront all the challenges to which the Arab nation is exposed by the Zionist threat.

The council also expressed appreciation for the call His Majesty King Khalid ibn Abd al-Aziz, monarch of the Kingdom of Saudi Arabia and chairman of the Islamic Conference Organization, made for a total strike in the Islamic world in solidarity with the Palestinian people in the occupied Arab territories, and in condemnation of the desecration of the holy places by the Zionist enemy—a call which has met with great response from the Islamic world.

The council declared its support for all efforts being made to end the war between Iraq and Iran in order to stop the shedding of Islamic blood and protect the region's security and stability.

It was also decided to hold the fourth [*as received*] session of the Ministerial Council in At-Taif on 19 May.

Source: *FBIS-MEA-V–82–077*, 21 April 1982, pp. C1-C2.

Document 72

GCC Ministerial Council: Third Extraordinary Meeting Statement

31 May 1982

In continuation of the third extraordinary session that began in Kuwait on 22 Rajab 1402 Hegira, corresponding to 15 May, 1982, the GCC Ministerial Council resumed its meetings on Sunday and Monday, 7 and 8 Shaban 1402 Hegira, 30 and 31 May 1982. The council reviewed the results of contacts initiated by Kuwait and Saudi Arabia with Iraq, the Syrian Arab Republic and the Democratic and Popular Republic of Algeria. The council also reviewed developments that occurred since the third extraordinary session began, and Iraq's consistent assertion [of its readiness] to withdraw to the international border and what this entails in the way of creating opportunities for a negotiated solution of the Iraq-Iran war—a solution that would safeguard the legitimate rights of both sides.

The council believes the present circumstances require redoubling of efforts and intensifying mediation to end the war and the bloodshed that have exhausted the two Muslim neighbors in order to preserve their capabilities and rechan-

nel them toward domestic reconstruction and concentration upon rebuilding what the current war between them has destroyed.

The council believes the achievement of a united Arab stand is a basic factor for ending the bloodshed and the war in a manner safeguarding the legitimate rights of the two Muslim countries. In these efforts the council hopes the Islamic Republic of Iran will also respond to the achievement of this objective at this historic and decisive turning point in which the Islamic nation is the target of a fierce Zionist onslaught aimed at the entire Islamic entity.

The council reaffirms its belief that ending the war is an important factor in the region's stability and in consolidating its security while it is surging ahead toward making a positive contribution to Arab, Muslim and international issues.

The council reaffirms that security and stability in the region are the responsibility of the area countries alone, and that an important factor in averting foreign intervention is putting an end to the war between Iraq and Iran. In order to achieve this objective, the council has adopted decisions to strengthen the efforts of the ICO, the Nonaligned Movement and the United Nations. The council expresses hope that these efforts will be successful and will serve the interests of the two Muslim peoples, the region, and the Arab and Muslim nation.

In this regard, the council lauds the efforts of the Good Offices Committee set up by the ICO in Mecca and looks forward to seeing the results of the committee's endeavors. Out of concern for the consolidation of security and providing assurance to its countries, the council has reviewed the steps taken to safeguard the GCC countries' safety, independence and sovereignty. The council expresses satisfaction at the steps taken in this regard.

Source: *FBIS-MEA-V–82–105*, 1 June 1982, pp. C3-C4.

Document 73

GCC Ministerial Council: Fourth Session Statement

11 July 1982

The GCC ministerial council held its fourth ordinary session at At-Taif on 20 and 21 Ramadan, 1402 Hegira, corresponding to 11 July 1982 [*dates as received*].

The council expressed deep sorrow and grief for the death of King Khalid ibn Abd al-Aziz who passed away while following closely the developments of the Zionist aggression against the Palestinian and Lebanese people. The council remembers the magnificent work of the late departed and his role in the emergence of and care for the cooperation council, and it begs God to grant him mercy and let him rest in peace.

The council reviewed the region's present political situation, the conditions produced by the Zionist invasion of Lebanese territory, and the acts of annihilation to which the Palestinian and Lebanese people are being exposed at the hands of the Zionist invaders who have not respected international charters or laws, who have committed criminal acts in the war of annihilation they are waging and who were not deterred by the sanctity of women, by the innocence of children or by the resignation of the elderly. They have spread destruction and devastation and wreaked havoc in the land of Arab Lebanon, disregarding the international community, international values, charters and norms, and ignoring international public opinion.

The council denounces and condemns this barbaric invasion which violates human dignity and is further proof for the whole world of the real Israeli aggressive and expansionist intentions and plans. The council also warns of the consequences of the continuation of the Israeli occupation of Lebanon, saying this may lead to the disintegration of conditions in the region and to the creation of serious complications, the outcome of which will not be limited to this region alone, but will extend to a wider circle, threatening world peace and security.

The council, while affirming its backing for and its stand by the side of the Palestinian [and the] Lebanese people[s] in defending their rights and the independence and the unity of Lebanese territory, believes at the same time that confronting the Zionist enemy's invasion of Lebanese territory and lifting the siege of West Beirut and of the Palestine Resistance which is struggling to enable the Palestinian people to exercise their right to self-determination and to establish their independent state on their national soil, is an Arab, Islamic and international responsibility, the burden of which lies on the international community, particularly on all Arab and Islamic states, and is a matter demanding determination to unite ranks and mass resources at the side of the Lebanese and Palestinian brethren as an embodiment of their solidarity and to deprive the Zionist entity of the opportunity of realizing its aims against our nation.

The council also stresses its states' duty to defend Lebanon and affirm its independence and sovereignty and maintain the safety of its territory and national unity in order to preserve the Palestinian Resistance and its leadership represented by the Palestine Liberation Organization in its capacity as the sole legitimate representative of the Palestinian people, and to back the efforts exerted by the six-member committee set up by the Arab League council in its recent emergency session held in Tunis.

The efforts of the GCC states, together with the rest of the Arab brethren within this framework, are bent on regional and international moves directed at a political aim: withdrawal of the invading Israeli forces from Lebanon.

The council calls on the five permanent members of the Security Council to shoulder their legal responsibilities according to the UN Charter to maintain peace in the world and to adopt measures stipulated in the charter to implement section 7 of the charter to impose economic sanctions on Israel for its refusal to comply with Security Council Resolutions No. 508 and 509.

While the council strongly denounces the United States for using the veto against implementing UN resolutions aimed at adopting measures to deter Israel, and considers that this action conflicts with the principles embodied by the charter and contradicts legitimate Arab rights, it calls on the United States not to hinder the implementation of UN resolutions.

Moreover, these efforts were also bent on the need to reach a Lebanese-Palestinian position that will maintain a Palestinian presence and to realize agreement between them on a matter giving the Arab nation the opportunity to concentrate on dealing with the fateful issue, the Palestine question, in all its aspects with the purpose of establishing a just and comprehensive peace corresponding to Arab rights, ensuring the realization of security and stability in the region and sparing it any complications that would allow foreign intervention in its affairs or make it an arena for a conflict of interests among the major powers.

The council expresses its hope that accord will be achieved among the various sections in Lebanon in order that justice, equality, a spirit of cooperation and fraternity may be realized, and to provide stability in sister Lebanon.

The council is continuing its sincere efforts through numerous Islamic, Arab and international channels to reach a solution that will ensure the end of the Iraq-Iran conflict, the continuation of which will benefit only the Zionist entity and other enemies of Arabism and Islam.

The council expressed its appreciation of Iraq's posture in withdrawing its forces from Iranian territory to international borders and its readiness to settle the problem through diplomatic negotiations in a manner that will ensure the rights of both sides. The council also hopes Iran will respond to this initiative in a fraternal Islamic spirit to spare the region any escalation of the conflict or to expose it to division, disorder and instability which will only benefit outside forces who are concerned with neither the well-being of the states of the region nor their security or stability.

The council expressed its satisfaction with the results achieved by the various ministerial committees to implement the unified economic community. It noted with appreciation the steps completed to set up the Gulf Establishment for Investment which is considered one of the distinguishing points of cooperation among the states of the council, and as it approves what these committees have achieved it has decided to submit their results to the Supreme Council for approval in its third session. The council also approved the financial and administrative programs of the General Secretariat.

Source: *FBIS-MEA-V–82–135*, 14 July 1982, pp. C1-C2.

Document 74

Al-Anba Interview with Ibrahim as-Subhi, GCC
Assistant Secretary General for Political Affairs

22 August 1982

[Excerpts] [Question] Is it true there is a proposal to institute a unified press and publications law for the GCC countries?

[Answer] We will study the fields that require more cooperation, and at the same time reactivate and improve this cooperation to the level for which the GCC leaders are aspiring. This will take place first through cooperation in internal media and then through external media, because the latter is an important and not appropriate for individual and bilateral initiatives. It requires studies and scientific planning by examining the potentials and channels we can use to convey the true image of the GCC countries to the world, to the Arab and Islamic world, and to explain our policies as laid down in GCC statutes. All this will take place through efforts to achieve integration in all fields, including the media, which is an important apparatus of the GCC countries.

[Question] The GCC had a role in trying to end the Iraq-Iran war. Is the GCC continuing its efforts in this regard?

[Answer] All the contacts that have been held to end the Iraq-Iran war were made after contacts had been made by the GCC countries with the Arab brothers and with other parties which—due to their close relations with the GCC countries and the Arab brothers on the one hand with peace-loving and politically influential countries international issues on the other—showed a readiness [in this regard].

[Question] What about the GCC efforts to mediate between Oman and the PDRY?

[Answer] The role Kuwait and the UAE are playing was assigned by the GCC Supreme Council. Officials in Kuwait and the UAE made efforts to mediate between Oman—which is a GCC country--and the PDRY—which is part of the Arabian Peninsula.

These efforts were remarkable: A meeting was held recently in Kuwait between officials from Oman and the PDRY. Another meeting will be held in Kuwait. This is a good indication of the GCC's policy and its efforts to clear the air among Arab countries and to eliminate differences among the Arab brothers.

[Question] After the recent meetings of GCC Interior Ministry experts in Bahrain recently, can we say the unified GCC security agreement is ready? Will it be discussed by the interior ministers at their meeting in October?

[Answer] I attended the meeting of the experts on behalf of the GCC Secretariat to discuss a unified security agreement among the GCC countries. The agreement will be proposed to the interior ministers during their next meeting and it will be one of the main topics of discussion by the ministers.

Although there is some security cooperation among GCC countries at present, greater efforts and more scientific coordination should be achieved. Security cooperation among GCC countries preceded the creation of the GCC. The unilateral security agreements that had been signed previously were a minimum, but they were not an overall security agreement. There is emphasis on this now and an awareness among the GCC countries, because without security we cannot do anything. Interests should be protected; this cannot be done without strengthening internal apparatuses while also guarding the land, air and sea. This cannot be achieved without coordination among the GCC countries.

Source: *Al-Anba* (Kuwait), 22 Aug. 1982, p. 3, as translated in *FBIS-MEA-V-82-164*, 24 Aug. 1982, pp. C1-C2.

Document 75

League of Arab States. Excerpt from the Final Statement of the 12th Arab Summit Conference at Fez, Morocco

9 September 1982

III. The Gulf War and the Arab Stance Toward It
The conference has studied the situation in the Gulf and observed with great sorrow and pain the continuation of the Iraq-Iran war despite the repeated attempts for a cease-fire and despite the offers of mediation and good offices by the international community. While appreciating the positive initiative by Iraq in withdrawing its military forces to the international borders, on the basis of the principle of solidarity and unity of Arab ranks, and out of the conference's concern that amity, harmony, and goodneighborliness prevail between the Arab countries and their neighbors, the conference has decided to declare its commitment to defend all Arab territory and to consider any aggression against any Arab country as an aggression against all Arab countries. It calls on the two warring parties to adhere fully to Security Council Resolutions Nos 499 of 1980 and 514 of 1982, and to act for their enforcement. The conference asks all states to abstain from taking any measure that will encourage the continuation of the war directly or indirectly.

Source: *FBIS-MEA-V-82-176*, 10 Sept. 1982, p. A18.

Document 76

League of Arab States. Gulf War Resolution Issued at the End of the 12th Arab Summit at Fez, Morocco

9 September 1982

Their majesties, excellencies and highnesses the kings, presidents and princes now meeting within the framework of the 12th Arab summit conference in Fez, Morocco, while noting with deep regret and extreme sorrow the continuation of the Iraq-Iran war despite all the repeated attempts to cease fighting and despite the mediation efforts and good offices by international organizations;

While recalling the call made by the 11th Arab summit conference, which convened in Amman in November 1980, to the two parties to cease fighting immediately and solve the conflict by peaceful means; while recalling the conference's welcome of Iraq's response to the good offices to solve the conflict through negotiations; while recalling the conference's appeal to Iran to respond to such efforts; while noting the conference's call on the two sides to mutually abide by the principles of nonintervention in domestic affairs, respect rights and sovereignty and set up strong relations of good neighborliness;

While highly appraising Iraq's initiative to withdraw its troops to the international border; while expressing their deep apprehension that the continued fighting would surely intensify war ordeals including human victims and material losses, would stop or delay the implementation of development projects, would sap national wealth, would serve the interests of the Zionist-imperialist designs and would gravely harm the Arab nation's interests;

While stressing the need for Arab solidarity and unity of ranks; while realizing their commitments toward the text of Article VI of the Arab League's Charter and Article II of the collective defense pact and economic cooperation among Arab countries;

While recalling UN Security Council Resolutions No. 479 of 28 September 1980 and No. 514 of 12 July 1982; while proceeding from their faith that an atmosphere of friendship, serenity and good neighborliness should prevail between Arab countries and neighboring countries, they have decided:

1. To declare their collective commitment to defend all Arab land. They consider every attack on any Arab state as an attack on all Arab countries. They also consider that preserving the independence of the Arab countries, the safety of their territories and the inviolability of their international borders as a duty that all Arab countries must respect and work for with all means.

2. To express their deep regret and apprehension for the lack of response to international initiatives to cease fighting and solve the conflict through peaceful means and negotiations.

3. To stress the need that the two combatant sides must fully abide by UN Security Council Resolutions 479 and 514 and to implement these resolutions in a well-coordinated manner.

4. To declare the Arab countries' readiness to implement their commitments toward Iraq in accordance with Article VI of the Arab League Charter and Article II of the Arab collective defense pact and economic cooperation among Arab countries should Iran fail to respond to the provisions of this resolution and continue the war against Iraq and try to violate Iraq's international border and enter its territory.

5. To request all countries to refrain from adopting any measure bound to encourage the continuation of the war, be it directly or indirectly. They also request all Arab countries to exert the necessary efforts to facilitate the implementation of the resolution.

Source: *FBIS-MEA-V–82–176*, 10 Sept. 1982, pp. A20-A21.

Document 77

Agreement on the Normalization of Relations between Oman and the PDRY

27 October 1982

In the name of God, the merciful, the compassionate. The State of Kuwait and the UAE, at the request of the GCC, acted as mediators to resolve the dispute between the PDRY and the Sultanate of Oman in the interest of both countries.

In implementation of the common desire of the PDRY and Oman to consolidate bilateral relations, eliminate all causes of dispute and open a new page in their relations, providing for stability, security, and cooperation between them and for the region in general, several meetings were held at the expert level in July 1982 in the presence of delegations from the PDRY, Oman and Kuwait. During those meetings it was agreed to hold further meetings.

Meetings of experts were held on 23 and 24 October 1982. These were followed by meetings on 25, 26 and 27 October 1982 between a delegation from the Sultanate of Oman, headed by His Excellency Yusuf al-Alawi Abdallah, and a PDRY delegation, led by His Excellency Dr Abd al-Aziz ad-Dali, held in the presence of the head of the UAE delegation, His Excellency Abd ar-Rahman al-Jarwan, and his excellency the deputy prime minister, foreign minister and information minister, Shaykh Sabah al-Ahmad al-Jabir as-Sabah, leader of the Kuwaiti delegation.

All matters were discussed and defined formulas for each of them were reached. The talks were held in an atmosphere dominated by a spirit of openness, responsibility and a sincere desire to create normal relations based on good neighborliness and cooperation.

The fruit of these fraternal talks was the signing of the agreement of the declaration of principles between the concerned parties. It will be released after a ratification by each of the sister countries on 15 November 1982.

Source: *FBIS-MEA-V–82–209*, 28 Oct. 1982, p. C1.

Document 78

PDRY Supreme People's Council Communiqué on Reconciliation with Oman Issued by Chairman Ali Nasir Muhammad

6 November 1982

The Supreme People's Council this morning, 6 November 1982, held an emergency session to discuss a report submitted by the brother foreign minister on the results of negotiations between the PDRY and the Sultanate of Oman with the participation of the States of Kuwait and the UAE. The council endorsed the agreement of principles and commissioned the Presidium to adopt the necessary legal measures on it.

The Supreme People's Council sees that its ratification of the principles between the PDRY and the Sultanate of Oman represents an important contribution by the PDRY's Government and people in the constructive efforts aimed at creating the appropriate climate for achieving security and stability in the region, to save its peoples from the dangers of the hostile plots of imperialist powers that have been escalating since the declaration of the strategic alliance between the United States of America and the Zionist entity and what this alliance produced in the way of aggressive and expansionist practices, the most recent of which was the Israeli armed invasion of Lebanon that resulted in ugly bloody massacres and mass liquidation actions against the Palestinian and Lebanese peoples.

This matter necessitates a decisive confrontation of these dangers, as well as the deployment of all Arab efforts and resources to confront them.

The council expressed its profound satisfaction with the efforts the government experts to achieve security and stability in the region through wide scale political and diplomatic moves to keep this region away from the danger threatening it as a result of the imperialist military presence and for the region's peoples and states to live in peace and accomplish fruitful cooperation among them.

In this regard, the council affirmed the correctness of these efforts, (?including) the initiative of Brother Ali Nasir Muhammad, secretary general of the YSP Central Committee, chairman of the Supreme People's Council Presidium and chairman of the Council of Ministers, calling for a summit conference of the countries of the Arabian Penin- sula, the Gulf and the parties concerned with the aim of eliminating foreign military bases in the region.

As it currently evaluates the efforts made by the government in the correct application of the principle of coexistence on which our foreign policy depends, the Supreme People's Council considers the agreement of principles to be a practical translation of the PDRY's foreign policy toward the region's states, aimed at establishing equal and normal relations on the basis of nonintervention in internal affairs, mutual respect of national sovereignty, good neighborliness and the achievement of fruitful cooperation, security and stability for the region's peoples and states. The council hopes that the region's states will contribute to the reinforcement of security and stability and realize the dangers of foreign military presence.

On this occasion, the Supreme People's Council praises the efforts exerted by the fraternal States of Kuwait and the UAE at all stages in the negotiations between the PDRY and the Sultanate of Oman, which helped eliminate many difficulties and bring about the signing of the agreement of principles.

Source: *FBIS-MEA-V–82–216*, 8 Nov. 1982, pp. C4-C5.

Document 79

Ukaz Interview with Shaykh Isa ibn Salman Al- Khalifah, Amir of Bahrain

9 November 1982

[Excerpts] [Question] Your Highness, Shaykh Isa, some people still regard the GCC as a block against other powers. Others, without good will, see it as a secession from the Arab League and a blow to Arab Solidarity.

[Answer] Anyone who says such things either bears a grudge against the Gulf states and is therefore unhappy about the achievements of these states under this good body [the GCC] or is afraid of the strength of this entity, which is based on sound foundations and rejects all forms of connivance. This is why we must not pay any attention to such false claims.

[Question] There are those who claim that there is no full agreement among our states and who doubt that such degree of agreement can be achieved.

[Answer] As I said, those people base their claims on different experiences and make erroneous judgments on the basis of false evaluations of events and developments. What we know here in Bahrain is that what has been achieved is more than the length of the experiment might indicate. To be fair, we should not talk about any negative aspects of the experiment because it is unnatural for an independent state with a long history to merge with a new united entity in a few years, and it is unnatural to entirely dispense with the existence of a country with its characteristics and circumstances which might be somewhat different from the others. It is unnatural to ask the Gulf States to accelerate more than necessary their movement toward unity or federation because our objective is bigger and more far-reaching than just coming up with superficial formula to give the impression that the Gulf states are united and in agreement.

We have agreed within the GCC not to pay any attention to the time element as long as we take the right steps and work with confidence, cooperation and sincerity for the fulfillment of the collective objectives. We are not in a hurry and we do not want to come out with a statement tomorrow talking about unity among our states without any strong foundation. As we meet in Bahrain today, we emphasize to the world that we do not give so much thought to form as we do to thoroughly and carefully studying every step, taking into consideration all the circumstances and consequences. We do not care if the study takes a long time or a short time as long as we have real and effective cooperation.

What has been achieved so far confirms the opposite of what those people claim. Nobody knows of any similar experiment under which many difficulties were surmounted and several important steps taken in such a record time as in the case of the six Arab Gulf states.

[Question] What about the security and economic agreements?

[Answer] There is steady progress, as in other areas.

[Question] Do you not think, Your Highness, that the tendentious news agencies have given the impression that the GCC states are in disagreement over some fundamental issues?

[Answer] We are well aware of the motives of the tendentious media and their determination to distort or undermine any successful work. We also know that the aim of any efforts to unify the regimes of the GCC states is to ensure that there are sufficient grounds for getting together and achieving integration.

[Question] Your Highness, could you talk to us about the nature of the dangers the states of the region anticipate and seek to avoid?

[Answer] I want to explain an extremely important point. The GCC states are formulating an integrated and consistent strategy based on their knowledge of the needs of their people and the factors guaranteeing permanent security and stability. Therefore, looking left and right at what is around us should not give the impression that the Gulf states anticipate a particular danger and are trying to avoid it. No, the Gulf states are seeking to achieve intrinsic power enabling them to deal with any present or future danger. In other words, what we are doing now is trying to detect the dangers and to search for the best way to confront them. We are preparing ourselves for the worst.

So, linking developments in the region to our meetings is pointless, because it means that the Gulf states only react and do not move on the basis of specific principles and clear overall strategic long-term objectives. Those people do not understand our states and they do not know the people of the Gulf. They do not appreciate our interest in making a real and great achievement. We excuse them but we cannot excuse the people of the region.

[Question] What is the situation regarding defense coordination, especially in the field of armament?

[Answer] Everything is going well. The region's states should be pleased with this not because it is a cause for optimism, but because it is a clear indication that we have made up our minds to be strong and rightly so.

[Question] Your Highness Shaykh Isa, do the Gulf states expect any particular foreign threat, and, if so, from where?

[Answer] The Gulf states would be wrong not to expect such a threat because it would mean that they are living in a state of false security which could have grave consequences. However, what is important is not the expectation as such. What is important is to have done what our responsibilities dictate so as to be ready for immediate confrontation.

[Question] Your Highness, do you have any concept in mind regarding solutions to the Lebanese problems and support for the PLO?

[Answer] This is no longer the time for just concepts. It is our duty to do something to ensure Israel's withdrawal from Lebanon and to give the Lebanese authorities ample opportunity to exercise full control over Lebanon. We in the Gulf region support Lebanon and the PLO. These are two basic elements in the equation for the region's security and stability, that is if the others really want stability to prevail.

[Question] I would like to ask you about the GCC expectations regarding the current dialogue between the Arabs and the United States and the UN Security Council member states. Do you expect the outstanding issues to be resolved?

[Answer] The Arabs have made their statement in Fez. The seven-member committee is making great efforts to promote the Fez principles. At any rate, the efforts are continuing and we hope that they will result in something beneficial to the cause. We should wait a while to see the outcome.

[Question] Your Highness, are you optimistic on this matter?

[Answer] I tend to be optimistic under all circumstances. What is more important than optimism is that the momentum should continue, because optimism is meaningless if there is no movement. Anyway, the GCC is well aware of what is happening and we beseech Almighty God to grant this nation success.

Source: *Ukaz* (Jidda), 9 Nov. 1982, pp. 10, 11, as translated in *FBIS-MEA-V–82–223*, 18 Nov. 1982, pp. C1-C3.

Document 80

Manama Supreme Council Summit: Opening
Statement by Shaykh Isa ibn Salman Al-Khalifah,
Amir of Bahrain

9 November 1982

In the name of God, the most gracious, the most merciful.
Brothers, Your Majesties and Highnesses, honorable conferees: I welcome you with the most sublime meanings of
brotherhood and loyalty and with what is appropriate to
what Bahrain, your second home, shelters for you. From
the bottom of my heart, I present to you the most sincere
feelings of appreciation and gratitude for honoring us and
enabling us to embrace the third session of the GCC Supreme Council in a manner that will ascend to the heights
of our relations. Their inevitableness is strong and will exist
through the generations in order to embody the greatest
meaning of fusion among the brothers.

It is my profound faith that you have come to your land
and your own people—and how is it possible for a person
to welcome those who own the homes of his own tribe? My
brothers, Your Majesties and Highnesses, the emergence of
the GCC was equivalent to a shining star in the sky of our
region. It acquired its light from a genuine source in which
strong links that gather our peoples throughout history
fused. It was nourished by the wills of their leaders until it
became like a current flowing from the past to pour in the
present and irrigate the path of the future where it meets
with the streams of good and aspires for the coasts of glory
until it settles with its good nourishment on the banks of
our giving Gulf.

History had no alternative but to respond to this unique
accomplishment that was demanded by our peoples and
achieved by their leaders to affirm the extent of the faith of
our one region and its agreement on joint goals at the present that acquires its historic roots from an ancient past and
aspires for a brighter future until it has become a continuing movement toward a development that does not stop and
whose pillar is force, support is truth, essence is cohesion
and unity, basis is brotherhood and solidarity and slogan is
the peace and security it spreads across the earth. This was
a hope, and it has now been accomplished.

It is an essential event in the march of Gulf action by
the GCC states that converted its various small streams into
a single great stream that represents all aspirations and
works for their embodiment. This is testified by the
achievements of only 2 years in the life of the GCC. This
is a relatively very short period of time. Nevertheless, what
has been achieved in this short period has surpassed all expectations and won the admiration of the international
community living the age of world groupings. There is no
room for individual stands in international relations.
Hence, the [GCC] economic agreement, has become the
basis for the coordination of development plans and for integrated economic policies, which portend the achieve-

ment of many gains for our peoples. These economic
policies are accompanied and supported by other cooperation and coordination policies that are making steady strides
in social, cultural, industrial and security spheres so as to
achieve, God willing, the aspirations of our citizens toward
a prosperous and secure future.

My brothers, Your Majesties and Highnesses, the various frameworks of cooperation that have been completed in
that period in various fields have proved that we are taking
the correct path to meet with the (?desires) of the peoples of
our countries and with the hopes of their leaders in safeguarding the future of coming generations, leading our
peoples toward progress and growth and guaranteeing our
region's defense and security, [a guarantee] that stems from
the region and its capability and that relies on its citizens
who work in unison, each of them supporting the other.

Our meeting is another link in the chain of our constant
efforts to face the future and prepare for the challenges with
faith, determination and confidence. I hope that we shall
conclude our meetings having built new bridges through
which we achieve another hope that brings us closer to attaining our aspirations, strengthens the factors of our progress and contributes toward championing our Arab causes
and enhancing the prestige of our Muslim nation and contribute toward world peace and security. Let history be a
witness for it is the final arbiter.

Brothers, Your Majesties and Highnesses, our best provision in this situation is to turn to Almighty God and pray
to Him to grant us strength and wisdom and to light our
path so that we can achieve prosperity for our peoples and
spread peace and security throughout our region and extend
it to our nation, the Muslim community and the entire
world. God hears and is most rewarding.

Peace and God's mercy and benedictions be upon you.
[applause]

Source: *FBIS-MEA-V–82–218*, 10 Nov. 1982, pp. C2-C3.

Document 81

Manama Supreme Council Summit: Final
Communiqué

11 November 1982

At the invitation of His Highness Shaykh Isa ibn Salman
Al Khalifah, amir of the State of Bahrain, the third session
of the GCC Supreme Council was held in Manama from
9 to 11 November 1982. His highness Shaykh Zayid ibn Al
Nuhayyan, the UAE president; His highness Shaykh Isa
ibn Salman Al Khalifah, amir of the Sate of Bahrain; His
Majesty King Fahd ibn Abd al-Aziz Al Saud, monarch of
the Kingdom of Saudi Arabia; His Majesty Sultan Qabus
ibn Said of Oman; His Highness Shaykh Khalifa ibn Ha-

mad Al Thani, amir of the State of Qatar; and His Highness Shaykh Jabir al-Ahmed as-Sabah, amir of the State of Kuwait, attended.

During this session, the GCC Supreme Council reviewed the political and economic ties among the GCC countries. It also reviewed the political and security situation in the Gulf region in light of current events.

On reviewing ties among the GCC countries, the Supreme Council expressed its satisfaction with the level of coordination among the GCC countries in implementation of the provisions and spirit of the principles of the GCC statutes and the objectives of the efforts of the GCC member countries to strengthen cooperation and ties in order to achieve integration and the aspirations of their peoples for a better future.

The Supreme Council viewed with satisfaction the laying down of the bases and infrastructure of collective action, thus paving the way for joint Gulf action on its practical objectives and its lofty goals. The council urged the various cooperation apparatuses and committees to continue toward the second stage of collective action and to take the necessary steps to implement the cooperation program that was agreed upon to serve the citizens of the GCC countries and to consolidate their affiliation to the greater entity on the basis of equality among them in rights and duties, so that they will carry out their important role in continuing to safeguard the factors for the march of cooperation and in pushing forward this march toward the planned goal.

On reviewing aspects of military cooperation among the GCC countries, the council has approved the recommendations of the defense ministers of the GCC countries, which aim to build the intrinsic strength of GCC member countries and coordinate among them to achieve the self-reliance of the area countries in protecting their security and safeguarding their stability.

The council has reviewed the resolution of the interior ministers made during their meeting in Riyadh on 17 October 1982, on the comprehensive security agreement, and decided to agree to the interior ministers' request to complete discussion of necessary studies.

The council discussed with great anxiety the developments in the war between Iraq and Iran. While it follows the serious developments represented by Iran crossing its international border with Iraq and the great threat which these developments pose to the safety and security of the Arab nation and the violation of its sovereignty, and as it believes that these latest developments have taken place at a time when the Arab nation is striving to consolidate its solidarity and mobilize its forces to confront the escalating Zionist aggression, which requires the unification of the efforts of the Muslim countries, the council affirms its support for Iraq in its endeavor to put an end to this war by peaceful means and to safeguard the efforts of the committee stemming from the Islamic Conference Organization and the efforts of the nonaligned countries and the United Nations, and asks Iran to respond to these efforts.

The council also reviewed the results of the good offices efforts that were made by the States of Kuwait and the UAE to end the disputes between the Sultanate of Oman and the PDRY. As the council praises the efforts that were made by Kuwait and the UAE and the spirit of perseverance which characterized these efforts, it salutes the positive stands adopted by the Sultanate of Oman and the PDRY and their sincere desire to eliminate all causes of disagreement and alienation between the children of both countries and both fraternal peoples. The success of these good efforts is practical evidence of the constructive role the council plays in establishing peace in the region and in establishing fraternal and neighborly relations among its states.

The council also studied the developments pertaining to the Arab-Israeli conflict and affirmed in this regard its support for the decisions and the statements made by the 12th Arab summit that was held in Fez, Morocco. The council also reviewed the primary results of the contacts made by the seven-member committee which stemmed from the Fez summit under the chairmanship of King Hassan II of Morocco, and expressed its support for all efforts to achieve the Arab goals as defined by the Fez summit.

The council reiterated its belief that there is no way a just and permanent peace can be achieved in the Middle East region except through Israeli withdrawal from all the occupied Arab territories, including holy Jerusalem, the elimination of all the Zionist settlements that were built and are being built on the occupied Arab soil and the establishment of the Palestinian state on its national soil under the leadership of the PLO, the only legitimate representative of the Palestinian people.

The council also affirmed its full support for Lebanon in preserving its safety, sovereignty, independence and territorial integrity, and demanded an immediate and unconditional Israeli withdrawal from all the Lebanese territories.

The council also reviewed the developments concerning the implementation of the articles of the unified economic agreement and expressed its pleasure for the implementation of the first state of the agreement on 1 March 1983, when the citizens will experience the beginning of the economic integration that the agreement aims to achieve.

The council also reviewed the decisions of the committee for financial and economic cooperation concerning the Gulf Investment Corporation. It decided to approve the formation of this corporation with a capital of $2.1 billion. The council also approved converting the Saudi Arab Foundation for Specifications and Measures into a Gulf establishment that will standardize specifications and measures in the council states.

The council expressed its thanks, gratitude and appreciation to Bahraini Amir Shaykh Isa ibn Salman Al Khalifah and his government for their hospitality and the good reception extended to the heads and members of participating delegations during the meetings. This has had a good effect on promoting the success of the meetings of this fraternal conference. We wish his highness continued health and happiness and wish the Bahraini people continued prosperity, development and progress.

The council decided to hold the fourth conference in the State of Qatar in November 1983.

Issued in the State of Bahrain on 11 November 1982. May the peace and mercy of God be upon you.

Source: *FBIS-MEA-V–82–219*, 12 Nov. 1982, pp. C1-C3.

Document 82

Manama Supreme Council Summit: Closing Statement by Bahraini Foreign Minister Shaykh Muhammad ibn mubarak Al-Khalifah

11 November 1982

In the name of God, the most gracious, the most merciful. Ladies and gentlemen of the press: I welcome you on behalf of their majesties and highnesses and convey to you their profound appreciation for your participation in this meeting—this historic meeting that Bahrain was honored to embrace. We are proud that it was held in Bahrain's land because it represents another round of cooperation, cohesion and development among the brothers of this region. We started on the path of cooperation less than 2 years ago, which, in this age, is a short period of time; it is no more than a moment in history. We work at the speed with which we can achieve what we want through this region's method, thinking and conceptions.

The concluding statement that you listened to the secretary general read moments ago included all the questions that were on the agenda. These questions, as you know and as you have heard, branch into several articles: the political article; the economic article; the defense and security article; and the proceedings and administrative article.

As for the political situation, the Supreme Council dealt with the developments of the current situation in the Middle East region in general. The council's opinion of these matters is based on Arab summit resolutions, particularly the resolutions of the recent summit, the Fez summit. We are part of this nation and our Arab stand is clear, open and committed. We also reviewed the current serious situation in the Gulf region and the Iraqi-Iranian war. We had a previous stand and we have a stand now that is based on ending this war, based on returning peace to this region. Based on that, there is no interest for Iraq or Iran or for this region or for the Arab or Islamic nation [in this war], so we seek with all we can and with all the resources available to us to end this war.

There is another topic I wish to note, and that is the defense side. It is the establishment of the intrinsic power of the member states. This topic is important. There are

committees that have studied the foundations for the establishment of this intrinsic power. I believe that this is a new leap forward in the cooperation among this region's states. When we say that the security of this region is the responsibility of the region's states, this principle should be possible to implement. It cannot be implemented unless these states become able to implement this concept. We have started the march and I hope that we will implement these plans for the sake of the stability and safety of this region and in order to defend it from the blocs.

As for the economic sides, before I move to the economic side I wish to praise the important role played by Kuwait and the UAE in order to end the dispute between the Sultanate of Oman and the PDRY. This accomplishment represents the importance of the GCC, represents its method and the fact that this group of states does not work for the benefit of these states alone, but works for eliminating all blemishes that exist among the Arab states. This is the principle we agreed upon and this is one of its fruits. I hope that we shall be able to play similar roles for the benefit of this nation.

As for the economic side, the economic agreement as I know it is a comprehensive agreement that stems from several concepts and stages. Economic matters cannot be implemented within a day and/or a night, but we have started their implementation through several stages. The implementation of this agreement, as you know, will begin on 1 March. This postponement took place, and I shall explain to you why.

This was scheduled to take place on 1 December, but one of the fraternal states saw that it requires time to issue the necessary legislation for implementation of this agreement. For this reason it was agreed to give this time, because what matters is not the signing, but the implementation. This is the goal and I believe that postponing it 90 days is in the interest of implementing this agreement. I say this in order not to have to answer questions [on this matter]. It is easier to explain at the very beginning.

The establishment of the Gulf investment foundation is without a doubt a good and basic step. This is not the first [investment] foundation in the region. However, the significance of this foundation is different. We have decided to work together in this economic sphere—and I mean the investment sphere. These countries will invest collectively to develop the region and will invest in other spheres. The first fruits of the foundation will come into effect. For instance, there is a project to construct oil refineries in the Sultanate of Oman. There are other projects which will also be financed by the foundation.

I wish to say that we have begun to invest our funds to develop the region. The foundation in itself is not a new thing. What is new is the aim of establishing the foundation and the method of its establishment. The region's (?mainstay), the region's funds are invested for collective development. There is a point that may appear simple but I believe it is important: transforming the Saudi Arabian organization for specifications and measures into a Gulf organization that specializes in specifications and measures in GCC countries. When specifications and measures are unified and organized, we will have entered the age of unification in most things in our life. By this I mean that such a situation will help in many spheres—in industry or any other aspect of our daily lives. It will have an effect. It is a simple event, but I believe that the unification of such things yields a great reward.

You have no doubt heard the communiqué. I wish to clarify some things if they are not clear. With regard to the security agreement, the interior ministers' recommendation for further study has been approved. As I have said, we are in a hurry and at the same time we are not in a hurry. I'd like to clarify this response. I want to tell you a story. There was a wise man who was in a hurry and was going to an important meeting that would decide his political and economic fate. The driver was driving him with great speed and therefore endangering his life. This wise man said: "Slow down, I am in a hurry."

I want to say that we are in fact in a hurry, but these matters have to take time.

These briefly are the matters that were discussed. I say this and leave all comment to you. If you wish, I, the GCC secretary general and the assistant secretary generals are prepared to clarify. Thank you.

Source: *FBIS-MEA-V–82–219*, 12 Nov. 1982, pp. C6-C8.

Document 83

Manama Supreme Council Summit: Press Conference Held by Bahraini Foreign Minister Muhammad ibn Mubarak Al-Khalifah

11 November 1982

[Excerpts][Question—intercepted in progress] In the communiqué on studying the situation in the eastern flank of the Arab nation. It appears that developments are fast and the threat to the region is great. Another matter: On the other flank, Israel is continuing its bullying. I do not know, have the leaders, in their decision, relied on peaceful solutions? New steps need to be taken to implement peaceful solutions on peaceful efforts. It appears from the Communiqué that it has confined itself (?to) the efforts that have failed so far. There was a decision at the Fez summit conference to return to joint Arab defense. What is your view?

[Answer] Yes, thank you. The final communiqué included the GCC's view on this matter; the crossing of the Iranian forces over the Iraqi international border is a serious development. This matter concerns the Arab countries in general. There is an Arab League Charter and there are

Arab commitments. If this topic is going to be discussed it will be discussed on the Arab level and not on the GCC level. We share in the view that this is a serious matter and this is stated in the communiqué. However, the place for making a decision on this matter is the Arab League. When this takes place . . . . [*sentence left unfinished*] A clear resolution was adopted on this matter at the Fez conference, namely, the joint defense agreement. This is our view.

[Question] In the name of God, the merciful, the compassionate.

[Answer—interrupting] Yes.

[Question] Some papers today published reports on an agreement to allocate funds in support of Iraq. Is this correct?

[Answer] Such matters were not raised in the conference's agenda by any country. Issues of this kind are concluded on a bilateral basis.

[Question] One of the Gulf worries that can obstruct the mobilization of Gulf capabilities to achieve a common goal is the border issue. Was the issue of the border among the Gulf countries discussed—because ignoring these issues does not mean that we have solved them. Did the GCC summit discuss the border issue?

[Answer] The declared GCC aims are clear: The establishment of cooperation among these countries. The GCC determines the priorities and implements these priorities. We have in fact begun to implement these priorities. With regard to border issues, they exist. However, I wish to emphasize that the spirit that prevailed during the conference, the determination, the spirit of responsibility and brotherhood, will open great horizons toward the elimination of all such blemishes. The GCC course is the course that will help to solve these issues. I wish to say that we are working within the framework of enabling the region to solve all differences. This is my view.

[Question] [*Words indistinct*] there have been reports in the region that the Gulf countries have shown a readiness to compensate Iran in order to end the war. Was this matter discussed during the meetings among the six GCC countries in Bahrain?

[Answer] I wish to emphasize that (?we did not) discuss this matter. The countries of the region discuss all the possible ways to end the war. However, we wish to emphasize that this matter is not for discussion.

[Question] You talk about peaceful means. Iran now says that its objective is Baghdad. How can we, at a time when Iran openly declares that [*words indistinct*] to Baghdad, talk about asking Iraq to look for a peaceful solution to this matter? Will you on your part make contacts with Iran to discuss the peaceful means? Do you believe that the GCC six will be able to succeed where others have failed?

[Answer] There are two parts to your question: the mediation aspect, and the second part is the military aspect. With regard to the mediation, we in the Gulf countries are fully prepared to carry out any possible role to resolve this dispute peacefully. We are working through three channels: We have activated the task of the United Nations, we have activated the Islamic Conference Organization and we have helped the nonaligned countries. The GCC is working through these three channels—the mediation is through these channels. There are other countries that have special relations with the two sides that are carrying our their role. I wish to say that there are channels through which the GCC has been able to exert efforts. This matter has been covered. We are making endeavors and acting through a number of channels to reach a kind of acceptance or peaceful solutions. With regard to your reference to threats against an Arab capital, the place to discuss these threats is the Arab League, which represents the Arab community in general. We are prepared to study any matter in this regard within the framework of the Arab League.

[Question] Mr. Minister, regarding the recommendations of the defense ministers: Is it possible to shed light on these recommendations? Do they include the establishment of a joint Gulf defense command or council? With regard to the Gulf Investment establishment, will it also invest abroad, or will its activity be confined to the Gulf countries?

[Answer] It is possible to answer the second question; it is not possible to answer the first question. [*Words indistinct*] investment, yes, investment at home and abroad. It will carry out all forms of investment. We are talking about a large sum of $2.1 billion. The investments will be made locally and abroad on firm bases. As for the recommendations of the defense ministers, they concern te defense ministers and will be implemented by the defense ministers. We in the council do not talk about military details. This should be known to everyone. We discuss principles—we leave the details to the defense ministers to implement what they believe is appropriate in this regard.

[Question] Mr. Minister, I have two questions.

[Answer] Please go ahead.

[Question] Can you explain what is meant by building an intrinsic force [*al-quwwah had-dhatiyah*] at a time when most people expected the formation of a unified Gulf force? Does the intrinsic force mean separate forces or a united force? Second, how serious is the slogan that has been raised for the past several months that it is the people of the Gulf who will defend themselves by themselves. We have repeatedly heard you say—2 days ago and now—that you may resort once again to the joint Arab defense charter. The two issues overlap and I hope that one will not prevail over the other.

[Answer] With regard to building the intrinsic strength of GCC member countries, we call things by their name. We are in fact building up the intrinsic strength of the area countries. By this I mean: How can the countries of this region deal with each other? How can such a force be effective? These matters require time, require a political decision and determination. I believe that we in the Arab world have a big experience: We make a decision on defense and when the time for implementation comes, we find it difficult to act. When we talk about building our intrinsic strength, we mean exactly what we say. We do not want to

call it anything else because such an appellation would not be correct or realistic. This is one point. The other point, with regard to our stand on any external aggression, as I have said, there are the GCC countries and there is the Arab League. In answer to another question, I have said that the implementation of such a matter is left to the Arab League council—it is not the responsibility of the GCC. There is a difference between the two. Thank you. Is there another question? Please, go ahead.

[Question] Mr. Minister, with regard to the intrinsic strength of the GCC countries, can you clarify what are the sources of the threats to the region's security and stability? What are they in particular? Will this intrinsic force be sufficiently strong to defend the region's security and stability?

[Answer] First, it is the right of any country or group of countries to think about defense. This is a legitimate right. When we plan and announce [this means that] we are countries that do not have ambitions against others and we do not have expansionist aims. We are talking about the defense of the region. Against whom? I believe that you want me to specify the countries.

I believe that as a matter of principle, it is the right of these countries to establish the organizations and apparatuses they want for their defense. This is a legitimate right and we are exercising it because this will not only help this region but will help the Arab region in general. To strengthen this region--the eastern flank of the Arab nation is to strengthen the Arab world in general. Against whom? Against those who harbor ambitions in this region. Any state that has ambitions, we shall try [to defend ourselves against it]. You ask me: Will you be able to? I will try, and I will do all that I can. I believe that defense is a legitimate right, and we shall continue along this line and develop our intrinsic strength. I hope that the region will be able to say in word and in deed that the security of this region is the responsibility of its people. It is a political principle and we want to change this principle into a fact. This is the objective. I hope what I have said is clear.

[Question] As an extension of the intrinsic power of the region, have any ideas been proposed on the joint action of the Gulf industrialization foundation? What are the steps that have been taken on this matter?

[Answer] Thank you. I believe this is one of the issues that was discussed. There are many areas for cooperation and coordination and I believe that the area of industries, all forms in fact, such as military industries and others . . . [*sentence left unfinished*] There have been studies. A large sum of money has allocated in the GCC budget this year for these studies. I believe, yes, there is consideration and there are studies in this field.

[Question] The concluding communiqué mentioned the good efforts that are being made by Kuwait and the UAE to normalize relations between the Sultanate of Oman and the PDRY. Has the GCC made efforts to support the PDRY, so as not to fall under pressures that may hinder the efforts to normalize the relations?

[Answer] We talked about ending the disputes but did

not talk about relations between the GCC and the Arab states. This is a different topic. So I believe that eliminating this obstacle will facilitate the development of relations between the GCC and the PDRY. We believe that reaching this solution will help intensify and deepen cooperation. We are still in the first stage and hope that this agreement will go into effect and that it will be effective.

[Indistinct question on the Iraq-Iran war]

[Answer] In fact, we are talking about a complicated issue that has many dimensions; it has a political dimension, an economic dimension, etc. So it is in fact difficult to talk much about this issue. We do what we can in order to reach a realistic solution. What channels we have are those that you have mentioned. If other means or channels are available, we shall not overlook them. We shall renew our actions and continue. I would like to stress that we do all we can and this is how far we have come in this field. We discussed all issues and I don't want to talk about what we discussed in our meetings. We discussed all you may think of; we announced the things we found possible. But as for what is not possible . . . [*sentence left unfinished*] You may give me 20 assumptions, but there is a difference between the assumption and its implementation.

[Question] The first summit laid the foundation; the second summit put forward concepts, the third summit initiated the implementation. What are the stages or things that have been implemented, knowing that both the economic agreement and security agrement have been postponed?

[Answer] I believe that the GCC has made great strides during this short period. First, we have established priorities and our collective thinking on a definite plan, whether in the economic field, the political field or defense field. Today, we have put the economies of these countries on a single course, which will become effective as of 1 March, the economic agreement has placed the relations among these countries that I believe other countries will not reach for dozens of years. Second, the GCC has started emerging as a group of states that have a stand and a special way of thinking and a role in the Arab and international fields. In the defense field, we talk today about building the intrinsic power. All these matters, within the short period of the GCC age, are a great accomplishment I believe.

Whoever wants to invest something, let him have patience. And as I said at the beginning, we are not in a hurry. It is this haste which may undermine the march of cooperation. We proceed with these steps while being confident that we add a brick every day. These meetings alone, the third meeting—and in Doha there will be a fourth meeting, God willing—the meeting that took place in Bahrain 2 days ago among their majesties and highnesses, and the discussion that took place, the dialogue and the exchange of views—I believe all this brings the region closer in thinking and in action. There is no alternative to this action.

As for the tangible things, yes, there are tangible things that developed. There are also many other things that require time to develop and grow. In my view, these matters should not be underestimated. These are long-term strate-

gic issues. I hope that our view of this matter will be different from the way we view anything else. We talk about a region that is building an intrinsic entity in all fields. This issue is a big one and it is not similar to any internal establishment.

[Question—in English] What was the council's attitude on Oman's reported willingness to allow U.S. forces to land on its territory as part of an exercise next month?

[Answer—in English] Well, we have not discussed the bilateral relations. If it is true, it is the concern of the country concerned. We have not made any view on any such reports—the accuracy of which I am not sure of—but I assure you that this topic was not raised during our meeting.

[Question] Concerning reinforcing the military capabilities of the GCC states, there must be some concept of whom this military force is deployed against. Is there an idea as to who the likely enemies of the GCC states are?

[Answer] The answer to this question is that this region is one of the most sensitive regions in the world. As you know, there is an international conflict over this region and not a regional one. This region is important to the lives of many people in the world. If there is another region that is desired more than this region, I believe this is a mistaken evaluation. Since this region is one of the most sensitive regions in the world, the people of the region must prepare themselves to avoid becoming easy prey for whomever wishes to intervene in their internal affairs or desires to control the region's resources. Here, I don't specify, but I generalize. In my view, building the intrinsic power is meant to deter those who aspire to intervene in the affairs of this region or attempt to exploit it.

[Interruption by same journalist] The question is who are the likely enemies?

[Answer] I say whoever has ambitions in the region is [*word indistinct*].

Source: *FBIS-MEA-V–82–219,* 12 Nov. 1982, pp. C8-C13.

Document 84
GCC Ministerial Council: Seventh Session Statement
19 May 1983

The GCC Ministerial Council at its seventh session held on 18 and 19 May 1983 reviewed and studied the events witnessed by Lebanon in recent years and the ordeals to which the people of Lebanon were exposed, and acknowledges the free will expressed by Lebanon through its constitutional institutions, which deserve the respect of the GCC states.

The council confirms its eagerness to see the withdrawal

of the Israeli forces from Lebanon, in maintenance of Lebanon's safety, its sovereignty, independence, integrity, and its Arab adherence. From the premise that Lebanon's security is linked to that of the Arab nation and the unity of its fate, the council confirms its eagerness to see Lebanon adhere to the resolutions of the Arab nation aimed at not exposing its security and safety or the security and the safety of any Arab state to danger. From the premise of the eagerness to maintain Arab solidarity and to end disputes among the brothers, especially during this sensitive period which the Arab nation is experiencing, the relations existing between Syria and Lebanon require from them and from all the Arab states special care, through which increased Arab solidarity and cohesion of the Arab nation are achieved.

By expressing this attitude the council renews its appreciation of the steadfastness of Syria and Lebanon and their sacrifices in supporting the Palestinian people in their struggle to achieve their legitimate rights, self-determination and the establishment of an independent state on their own soil.

The council urges all the major powers, and particularly the United States, to play their role and make more efforts to enable the Palestinian people to recover their legitimate rights to return to their homeland and to self-determination on their own soil, which requires that they work for Israel's withdrawal from all the Arab territories occupied since 1967, thus giving an impetus to the march toward the desired just and lasting peace in the region.

Source: *FBIS-MEA-V–83–099*, 20 May 1983, p. C1.

Document 85
GCC Ministerial Council: Eighth Session Statement
24 August 1983

The Ministerial Council held its eighth session at At-Taif in the period 22–24 August, 1983 with the participation of the ministers of finance and economy of the Council's member countries. The GCC reviewed the progress of the implementation of the economic agreement that came into force in March 1983. The Council expressed its satisfaction at the progress made in the five fields of coordinated activity: industry, agriculture, livestock, fisheries and contracts.

It also expressed satisfaction at the progress made in the implementation of the agreement with regard to the agreed vocations: medicine, accountancy, law and engineering including engineering—economic consultation, management, technical, industrial—and fishing bureaus for the promotion of economic activities, and the exploration of new sectors for the benefit of the peoples of the GCC countries.

The council expressed its satisfaction at the positive steps

taken toward the application of the unified customs tariff on import commodities from the GCC member countries and the abolition of tariffs on goods of GCC origin. The GCC noted the increase in the volume of trade among the GCC member countries as a result of this measure. The GCC ministers exchanged views on the best way for moving into the second stage in the implementation of the agreement and agreed that the Committee on Financial and Economic Cooperation should meet in Riyadh next October for this purpose.

The council acquainted itself with the memorandums submitted by the secretariat general to deepen and unify attitudes among the GCC member countries, and adopted necessary measures to bolster coordination of stands among the member countries.

The Ministerial Council studied the Arab situation in all its aspects and affirmed its firm position with regard to the elimination of Arab differences and the discarding of division and the establishment of harmony and a favorable atmosphere to ensure the success of the forthcoming Arab summit conference.

The GCC studied the situation in the region in the light of recent developments and expressed its regret at the continuation of the war between Iraq and Iran. It reiterated its determination to exert all efforts to put an end to this war.

The council acquainted itself with the development of cooperation in the field of defense and affirmed the importance of the steps taken in this regard in the interest of the GCC's objectives and the peace and security of the region.

The GCC hopes that the efforts being exerted for the safeguarding of the PLO unity as the sole legitimate representative of the Palestinian people will meet with success so that the Arab capabilities will be saved for confronting the enemy.

Affirming anew its steadfast position on the question of the preservation of Lebanon's independence, sovereignty, and territorial integrity, the GCC appeals to all factions of the Lebanese people to work to realize their national unity.

Source: *FBIS-MEA-V–83–166*, 25 Aug. 1983, pp. C1-C2.

Document 86
Uman Interview with Ibrahim Ahmad as-Subhi,
GCC Assistant Secretary General for Political Affairs
14 September 1983

[Excerpts] [Al-Hawari] The GCC has played a great role by ending aid to those countries which restored relations with Israel. Does this mean that the GCC states will adopt a unified policy toward all Arab and international issues, and if so, what will this policy be?

[As-Subhi] In fact, the decision adopted by the GCC

Ministerial Council in its latest session did not refer to a specific region or certain side. We will end our aid to any country that restores relations with Israel. This is the general policy decision. This is the principle that is applicable to any country that restores relations with Israel. Of course, this is a nationalist attitude. We have always stressed that the GCC is an inseparable part of the Arab nation and that the Council is acting within this framework. There is also coordination between us and the Arab League. This decision was not adopted with a particular continent, region, or country in mind. It is a general policy decision that is applicable to any country that restores relations with Israel.

[Al-Hawari] The Iran-Iraq war, which is continuing, constitutes a threat to the security of the GCC States. What is your role in reaching a peaceful settlement to this war?

[As-Subhi] This question is raised repeatedly and has been asked by more than one party before. What has the GCC done in this regard? I say openly that since its establishment the GCC has been discussing this matter. The GCC has spared no effort in working with all parties, with all the organizations, and with the Islamic Conference Organization on this issue. There has been continuous and direct contact between us and the Islamic Conference Organization. We also made contacts through the United Nations and the Nonaligned Movement. We also made contacts with countries which we thought have influence such as Pakistan, India, Turkey and the major countries. Their leaders sent messages and envoys who travelled to Moscow, Washington, London, Beijing, and Paris, which are the capitals of the permanent members of the UN Security Council.

[Al-Hawari] What about the minor border differences between some of the GCC states? Does this silence mean that they have already been resolved?

[As-Subhi] Regarding the question of differences, I don't think that they are critical differences. We have gone beyond the talking stage and we are now at the stage of implementation and execution. These matters can be settled through bilateral contacts, and they are about to be settled. However, these differences do not at all delay, hinder, or influence the continuing march of the GCC. The good efforts being exerted by their leaders are capable of eliminating these minor issues.

[Al-Hawari] Will the joint maneuvers which will be conducted by the GCC next month be taken as a beginning for other such maneuvers? What do you think about the future of the Gulf military Cooperation?

[As-Subhi] I would rather call them joint exercises and not maneuvers. These are very ordinary training exercises like any training exercise carried our by army units. It is a training exercise for the infantry, the air force, and the navy units. The only difference here is that more than one army and more than one unit are participating in these joint exercises, which are aimed at testing the situation of the current stage of military cooperation among the GCC states and at determining the weak points in order to eliminate them and the points of strength in order to exploit them.

These exercises are also aimed at learning whether there is truly coordination in this field.

Source: *Uman* (Muscat), 14 Sept. 1983, pp. 5,10, as translated in *FBIS-MEA-V-83-181*, 16 Sept. 1983, p. C1.

Document 87
Al-Ray Al-Amm Interview with Saudi King Fahd
7 November 1983

[Excerpt] [As-Said] Your majesty, nearly 3 years after the GCC's establishment, and in view of the political and economic achievements accomplished ever since, how do you view the future of the GCC's role in this region?

[Fahd] The GCC is the culmination of long efforts and successive steps of coordination and cooperation among fraternal Arab countries which are homogenous in traditions, norms, and common interests. It is in my view a framework for achieving Gulf unity in various fields and a result of understanding, cohesion, and joint action. We have been able to make great accomplishments in various spheres. Through the GCC's role, I believe that the future of this region will be, God willing, more plentiful for the general good of our peoples and our Arab and Islamic nations.

[As-Said] Your Majesty believes, with other GCC leaders, that the Gulf region's security is the responsibility of its sons. However, some try to make this devoid of meaning and shake it by threatening to close the waterways, thereby making a plea for the superpowers to interfere. What is Your Majesty's view?

[Fahd] Threats are regrettable and we do not want any party to contemplate closing the Strait of Hormuz because this would harm all. This might open doors wide for foreign intervention and drag the region into international conflict. The region's peoples do not need that.

[As-Said] The West believes that balance of forces has been moving against its favor during the past years and that it should adjust this balance—as we see in the Western military presence in the Mediterranean and the Indian Ocean.

[Fahd] Relations between the world superpowers are governed by many considerations and each is trying in one way or another to preserve its influence and interests. To avoid our peoples being involved in the international conflict and to preserve our countries' independence and sovereignty, we always call for staying out of the areas of influence of the foreign powers, be they Eastern or Western.

[As-Said] Your Majesty, some say that the Kingdom can do much to effect a change in the U.S. stand toward Arab causes, but that it does not want to do so. Is this true?

[Fahd] The Kingdom spares no efforts in working for the supreme Arab interest. It devotes all its efforts in relations with the United States, Western European countries and others to explaining the Arab point of view and affirming our sincere desire for a durable and just peace. I believe circumstances have begun to change to a certain extent and that our view has begun to be conveyed in a better way through most of the available channels. Dealing with the United States in particular requires more understanding of the reality of political circumstances. There are encouraging signs indeed, and the core for us is that the Israeli forces must be withdrawn from Lebanon and a state set up for the Palestinians, with Jerusalem as its capital. We hope the United States will understand this and will work to implement it. We do not claim that we can achieve all that we need for the Arab nation's interests—he who claims this is ignorant—but we should exert all efforts we can.

[As-Said] Your Majesty, what can be said about relations between the Kingdom and the Soviet Union, particularly since Your Majesty and the Soviet leaders exchange congratulatory cables on national days and Foreign Minister Prince Saud al-Faysal's visit to Moscow within the Arab seven-member committee was an indication of establishing some kind of relations between the two countries?

[Fahd] The Kingdom's foreign policy is tied only to the Arab interest and the Islamic nation. What determines its relations with other countries is the common interest which does not harm its principles or the Arab nation's goals. The Kingdom deals with the current international reality and the Soviet Union is one of the world's two superpowers.

[As-Said] Your Majesty, in the game of balance of military forces, Israeli strategists call the Saudi Army the new worker in the region's force. How do you view this?

[Fahd] Every country has the right to build a strong army able to safeguard its security and peace. The Kingdom, out of its Arab and Islamic responsibilities, must do all it can to shoulder these responsibilities.

[As-Said] The Soviet Union denies having any intention to interfere in Gulf affairs and this contradicts the West's assumptions. This makes the region open as an area of conflict in light of the concentration of fleets and forces.

[Fahd] We are concerned about the region's independence and reject all foreign interference or influence. We also do not want the region to turn into a pivot point for international polarization or conflict in any way whatsoever.

[As-Said] Your Majesty, reports said the committee to clear up Arab atmosphere will meet in the Kingdom shortly. Has a date been set and what are your hopes for these meetings?

[Fahd] The committee to clear up the Arab atmosphere, which includes Saudi Arabia and Algeria, has put forth certain measures to govern bilateral relations among Arab countries. The committee's task is part of the continuing multi-Arab efforts to create the most favorable atmosphere for the strong Arab solidarity that our country needs to face the various challenges.

[As-Said] Your Majesty, do you believe it is possible for Egypt to return to the Arab fold in the next summit conference?

[Fahd] Egypt's return to the Arab nation is very important. As is known, resolutions were adopted by Arab leaders at the Baghdad conference. Therefore, the final decision rests with the Arab leaders who adopted this decision.

[As-Said] Are the GCC countries thinking of setting up a joint military industry, particularly in view of the successful maneuvers held recently by the region's countries?

[Fahd] Strengthening the GCC countries' forces and coordination among them is normal and within the framework of projects such as military industrialization and the consequent studies and preparations, which should be based on sound and objective foundations.

[As-Said] Your Majesty, the Kingdom's role in Arab action reaches beyond Arab limits through its political and economic relations with West European countries. How do you view the European stand on Arab causes and on the Palestinian cause in particular?

[Fahd] The Kingdom spares no effort to discuss all that is good for the Arab nation and its interests. I believe the Europeans can take a more active [role] on establishing a just and durable settlement in the Middle East by coordinating with the United States. The European role can be more effective in working to stop the current Iranian-Iraqi war by not viewing this war through its interests only. Western Europe can also play a role in pressuring Israel into withdrawing from Lebanon and keeping Lebanon free from international conflict.

[As-Said] The GCC countries, and mainly Saudi Arabia, are trying to diversify their sources of weapons. They are also trying to unify their defense systems and achievements through the GCC. However, these moves, together with the Peninsula Shield maneuvers, have been viewed as a show of strength and a threat to others. What is Your Majesty's view?

[Fahd] It is clear to all that the maneuvers were not tied to any particular events. Rather, they are a part of a firm and longstanding policy of the GCC to safeguard the Gulf's stability and prevent foreign interference. The success of the Peninsula Shield maneuvers is to enhance the defense capabilities and has nothing to do with the events going on in the Gulf.

[As-Said] Observers assert that you won the round with the FRG after Chancellor Kohl was convinced of Saudi Arabia's correct view in its request for the tanks deal and that the Kingdom is about to receive its requirements of German arms. Are there any other plans to follow this move?

[Fahd] I believe that the chancellor's talks in the Kingdom and his acquaintance with our view on events in the region uncovered many angles of the stand and the urgent need for a durable and just settlement to the Middle East conflict and the need for respecting the Lebanese people's will to regain their country's unity and to safeguard its sovereignty and independence. No doubt cooperation between the Kingdom and the FRG is expanding to embrace various spheres.

Source: *Ar-Ray al-Amm*, 7 Nov. 1983, pp. 20, 21, as translated in *FBIS-MEA-V–83–218*, 9 Nov. 1983, pp. C6-C7.

Document 88
Interview with Sultan Qabus of Oman
7 November 1983

[Text] Question: What prompted Oman to decide to establish diplomatic relations with South Yemen, and what hopes does Your Majesty have on the settlement of border issues and the development of bilateral cooperation between the two countries?

Answer: The policy of Oman is a peaceful one. We always maintained over the years that Oman did not want to be in a quarrel with South Yemen. As long as South Yemen did not want to be a good neighbor, we had no reason to have relations. But different things are done under different leaders. And when the present South Yemeni leadership extended a willing hand to us, asking for good neighborly relations, we said yes and reached out for it. This is because we believe in the peaceful settlement of differences. After all, we are of the same race, we share the same religion and we hail from the same area. Concerning the settlement of border issues, I don't think we would be facing major difficulties. I'm hopeful that minor details here and there on the border issue can be sorted out by our joint committees.

Question: How has the world oil glut affected Oman's economy in particular and that of the Gulf in General?

Answer: Thank God, Oman has been able to organize itself and its economy to amortize the effects of the glut. In our economic planning, we have allowed for such things to happen in the oil world. We just had to look at our plans and to readjust our priorities. Matters which were not urgent in nature were done without, but the overall development of the country was not touched. This is as far as Oman is concerned, but I can't speak for the other (Gulf) countries.

Question: Kuwaiti officials have recently warned against sectarian troubles in their country, and the Gulf in general is believed to live in fear of Ayatollah Khomeyni's "Islamic Revolution." In Your Majesty's opinion, how stable is the Gulf and what are the factors threatening this stability?

Answer: Now that six Gulf countries have organized themselves in the Gulf Cooperation Council, the chances of a stable Gulf are better than at any time before. We are thinking together; we are talking together; we are planning together; and we are seeing things together instead of individually. I don't see the threat as being great for the reasons stated. But this does not mean that we are dismissing the threats altogether. We remain alert and we continue to look ahead and in all directions because we don't want to be caught unawares.

Question: How does Your Majesty evaluate the recent Gulf Cooperation Council war games and, in more general terms, the military capability of the Gulf alliance?

Answer: The maneuvers were a good step in the right direction. It was essential for our soldiers to get to know each other and to familiarize themselves with the equipment and hardware at their disposal. That's why the maneuvers were a good step in the right direction.

As to the military capabilities of the Gulf alliance, my answer is this: we are not great military powers. We do not produce our own planes, tanks, and gunships; we buy them. With such limitations, military capability becomes limited.

But, having said that, we (in the Gulf Cooperation Council) are pooling our resources and cooperating together to be able to hold our own against forces that are not more powerful than us. But should we be confronted by greater powers, then we will need to rethink.

Question: Iran is threatening to block the Strait of Hormuz and cut off all exports from the area if Iraq uses French Super-Etendards to attack Iran's oil facilities. Does Your Majesty take the threat seriously, and how is Oman likely to react to closure of the navigation route?

Answer: In any war situation, there is the possibility of hostilities getting out of hand. That's why I believe every possible step—on the national, regional and international level--should be taken to stop the (Iran-Iraq) war.

I understand from the Iranian declarations that Iran will not follow through its threats with steps on the ground unless all its oil facilities are crippled or destroyed. In such a situation, the Iranians will have nothing to lose. I believe too that the Iraqis are wise enough to evaluate what they are doing.

In the event that the Strait of Hormuz is blocked by mines or by other means, Oman's position is that this becomes a collective responsibility of the Gulf countries. The Strait of Hormuz is the gateway for all the Gulf countries and the movement not only of their crude oil, but all other goods.

We have also said that, while Strait of Hormuz is in Oman, the responsibility of keeping it open as an international waterway for international traffic is an international responsibility. It is not the responsibility of one country alone. Hence Oman's international consultations and expectations on the matter.

Question: Baghdad will reportedly refrain from using the Super-Etendards if Syria reopens the Kirkuk-Baniyas pipeline. Does Your Majesty favor GCC mediation with Syria to reopen the said pipeline to help ease the Iraqi economic strain?

Answer: Mediation (between Iraq and Syria) has been ongoing. Formerly ministers, notably from Kuwait, tried to mediate with Damascus. Unfortunately, their efforts weren't very successful. Syria has its view and it has not changed it. But I don't think one should give up (these mediation efforts)—especially since we are talking about two countries of the same race, the same religion and the same aspirations. I am not in favor of giving up the mediation bid. The good offices must continue.

Question: What solution does Your Majesty envision to the Gulf war?

Answer: The only solution is for the two countries to sit together in a neutral place and talk face to face. That's the only way to end the war. Internationally, I believe that more pressure should be brought to bear for this to happen. I know from my Iraqi brethren that they are ready to negotiate. I hope the other side feels the same need to sit and talk.

Question: President al-Asad of Syria recently said that the Arabs have nothing to fear from Moscow since the Soviets never massed their troops against an Arab country or fired a shot against an Arab soldier. Does Your Majesty share this view? What is Your Majesty's comment on Syrian criticism of U.S. military presence in Lebanon?

Answer: Our view on the Russian question is known. What we want to prevent is the long-term expansion of (communist) influence and the bid to install—through coups d'etat and sabotage—people or governments loyal to Moscow. Everyone has his way of seeing things. As far as we are concerned, we have seen Russia's allies, the Cubans for instance, fighting in Ethiopia against Somalia.

Regarding U.S. military presence in Lebanon, I will say this: We, here in Oman, respect any country's decision when it comes to its own sovereignty, unity and territorial integrity. Oman respects the Lebanese government's decision to ask for the help of the Multinational Force in restoring peace and reestablishing its central authority.

Question: Does the GCC and therefore, Oman, support the May 17 agreement between Lebanon and Israel?

Answer: Again, Oman respects another country's decision if the said country feels that it is in its own interest to have such an agreement. Lebanon, in this case, knows better than anyone else what is in its best interest.

Question: How can Lebanon, in Your Majesty's view, extricate itself from the situation it is in today? Through national reconciliation talks such as are being held in Geneva this week, through joint U.S.-Saudi diplomacy or the United Nations?

Answer: We believe the Lebanese should be encouraged to sit together and solve their differences. If they think their constitution needs changes or amendments, that's entirely up to them. The important thing is that they sit together. It's for them to decide if they need help to reconcile their views.

I stress that the Lebanese themselves should sit together and solve their problems. That's the best guarantee for a lasting settlement.

Question: What is Oman's view of the struggle for power going on within the PLO today?

Answer: Any struggle anywhere amongst one people is a bad thing. One calls upon the Palestinians to stop their internecine strife, to pull themselves together and to realize that when they fight one another, they lose more than they gain in solving their problem. The world community cannot address itself to solving the problem of a people fighting among themselves. The power struggle within the PLO is making the Palestinians lose respect and credibility.

Question: Where does Your Majesty see a road to Arab-Israeli peace; in the Reagan initiative, the Fez plan, or a regional conference sponsored by the United Nations?

Answer: We believe that every effort should be made to solve problems—in this case, the Arab-Israeli conflict—by peaceful means. I think all these peace plans should be put together, scrutinized and revised until a formula for a durable settlement is reached that is acceptable to both (Arab and Israeli) parties. I would like to see the Arabs leave no stone unturned in their search for proposals that can be put to the Israeli side through the United Nations or any other third party. If such proposals are turned down, they should be revised, until a formula is reached which is acceptable to all.

Such an effort may take time. But the world community should witness a continuous and determined effort for a peaceful settlement by the Arab side that would leave the Israelis with no excuse to turn it down.

Source: *Monday Morning* (Beirut), 7–13 Nov. 1983, pp. 99–103, in *FBIS-MEA-V–83–219*, 10 Nov. 1983, pp. C3-C4.

Document 89
Statement by Shaykh Khalifah ibn Hamad Al-Thani, Amir of Qatar, at the Opening of the Fourth GCC Supreme Council Summit
7 November 1983

In the name of God, the merciful, the compassionate. Dear brothers, your majesties, your highnesses, your excellencies, gentlemen: I greet you and welcome you warmly among your kinsmen in your second home, Qatar, which harbors toward you the sincerest sentiments of love and appreciation, deep sentiments that express the nobility of our brotherhood and the strength of the close ties that bind us together, as well as our common goal and destiny.

How happy we are to meet with you in Doha today at this fourth meeting of our council, a meeting that provides us with a happy opportunity in which we together renew the memory of that historic event in which we achieved a dear hope that has been cherished for long by the leaders and people of our Arab Gulf region—the establishment of the GCC—in order to organize ways to integrate our natural and human resources so as to realize the prosperity, strength, and stability to which we aspire, under the canopy of our tolerant Islamic ideology and our lofty Arab values.

The course we pursued to achieve our integration was

based on the development of the means of such integration in a manner in which it gradually proceeds towards its objectives and in harmony with our circumstances and potential. We are convinced that this is the best course that ensures for our GCC stability, continuity, and success. With the help of Almighty God, and as a result of following this course, we have succeeded in the short period that has lapsed since the GCC's establishment to take positive and important steps in various fields. These steps were appreciated by the Arab world, the Muslim world, and the international community.

Dear brothers, we are meeting today in very critical circumstances in which our Arab nation is being threatened by great dangers. These circumstances require of all of us to restore our total solidarity in order to put an end to the continued treacherous Israeli aggression against our rights and Arab land and solve our issues of destiny that have resulted from this aggression, foremost among which are the Palestinian and Lebanese questions, in order to establish a just comprehensive peace in the region, a peace to which we and the international community aspire. However, instead of uniting our ranks to confront the challenges that surround us, regretfully divisions now prevail in our Arab world as a result of differences among some Arab countries. The situation has exacerbated and discord has split the sons of the same Arab homeland, resulting in their fighting each other in both the Palestinian and Lebanese arenas.

Out of their conviction that divisions are a very serious threat to the destiny of our nation, the GCC countries have exerted, and continue to exert, efforts within the GCC framework to put an end to such divisions through brotherly dialogue, in order to unify Arab ranks. The leaders and peoples of our nation believe that their total solidarity is the way by which our nation can confront the challenges posed by our common enemy who has been tempted by our disunity in persisting in his aggression. It is definitely high time to act in accordance with what we believe, and devote our united efforts to achieving the solidarity that alone can ensure that our nation achieves all its goals and enjoys the dignified, strong, and prestigious position among other nations which it deserves.

It is painful for every sincere Muslim to see the Iraqi-Iranian war entering its fourth year despite all Arab, Muslim, and international efforts that have been made to end it. The most recent such effort was the resolution adopted by the UN Security Council. The continuation of this war can lead only to the shedding of the blood of thousands of citizens of these two neighboring Muslim countries, dissipating their human and economic resources and exposing the region to the threat of foreign interference in its affairs. Therefore, in order to ward off these great threats and losses, we still hope that Iran will follow Iraq's example in responding positively to endeavors to end the war between them and to establish peace in the area, in observance of the teachings of our Islamic religion, which calls for peace and amity and turning away from divisions and hostility, and to achieve the hope of all of us that the human and economic resources of both Iraq and Iran will be a source of good to the peoples of the two countries and the peoples of the area and the whole world.

Dear brothers, the GCC member countries are agreed that the best way to achieve our goals is to rely primarily on ourselves and to lay down sound foundations for building our own strength, because, more than any other strength, it safeguards our ability to avert all interference in our affairs and to keep our area free of superpower conflict. I am confident that, as a result of the spirit of genuine brotherhood and sincere cooperation and deep sense of the responsibility we hold which always prevail in our discussions, we shall turn the product of our work in this meeting of our council, God willing, into a new important stage in our progress toward the realization of our lofty national, pan-Arab, and international goals.

I ask Almighty God to guide us in reuniting on what is right and to grant us success in furthering our noble Islamic religion and achieving all good for our countries, our nation, and for the whole of mankind. Peace and God's mercy and blessings be upon you.

Source: *FBIS-MEA-V–83–217*, 8 Nov. 1983, p. C1.

Document 90
Doha Supreme Council Summit: Final
Communiqué
9 November 1983

In the name of God, the merciful, the compassionate.

The final statement of the fourth session of the GCC Supreme Council held in Doha, State of Qatar, 3–5 Safar 1404 Hegira, corresponding to 7–9 November 1983:

At the request of His Highness Shaykh Khalifah ibn Hamad Al Thani, the amir of the State of Qatar, the fourth session of the Supreme GCC Council was held in Doha 3–5 Safar 1404 Hegira, corresponding to 7–9 November 1983, in the presence of His Highness Shaykh Zayid ibn Sultan Al Nuhayyan, president of the UAE; His Highness Shaykh Isa ibn Salman Al Khalifah, the amir of the state of Bahrain; His Majesty King Fahd ibn Abd al-Aziz of the Kingdom of Saudi Arabia; His Majesty Qabus ibn Said of Oman; Shaykh Khalifah ibn Hamad Al Thani, the amir of the Sate of Qatar; and Shaykh Jabir al-Ahmad al-Jabir as-Sabah, the amir of the State of Kuwait.

During this session the GCC Supreme Council reviewed the political and economic ties and coordination in defense affairs among the GCC member countries. The GCC Supreme Council also reviewed the political situation in the Gulf area in light of current events.

On reviewing the ties among the GCC countries, the Supreme Council expressed satisfaction with the level of cooperation attained by the GCC member countries in implementation of the principles of the GCC statutes. The Supreme Council noted that the steps that have been made to achieve political coordination and regular consultations to adopt unified stands on the international level have strengthened the GCC and consolidated the ties among the GCC countries.

On reviewing the situation in the region, the GCC Supreme Council discussed the continuation of the Iraqi-Iranian war and its effect on the region's stability. The Supreme Council expressed hope that the two countries will agree on ending the war between them in order to end the shedding of the blood of the two Muslim countries and the depletion of the resources of the two neighboring countries and so that they can harness their efforts to confront the enemies of our Arab and Muslim nation. The GCC Supreme Council expressed its support for the UN Security Council resolution of 31 October 1983 which calls for an end to all military activities in the Gulf and for refraining from attacking cities, economic installations, and ports and for an immediate end to all hostilities in the Gulf area, including all sea routes and waterways. The GCC Supreme Council noted with satisfaction Iraq's agreement to the Security Council resolution. It calls on Iran to respond positively to this resolution and not to threaten the freedom of navigation in the Gulf and its straits in view of the international importance of such straits and in accordance with international agreements that govern shipping in the straits.

The GCC Supreme Council calls on the UN Security Council, and the permanent members of the Security Council in particular, to shoulder their responsibilities in taking the necessary measures to implement the resolution. The GCC Supreme Council reiterates its readiness to resume the endeavors carried out by the State of Kuwait and the UAE on behalf of the GCC countries.

Out of its concern to end the shedding of Arab blood, the Supreme Council sent Shaykh Sabah al-Ahmad al-Jabir, Kuwaiti deputy prime minister and foreign and information minister, and Shaykh Ahmad ibn Sayf Al Thani, Qatari minister of state for foreign affairs, to the Syrian Arab Republic in an Arab endeavor--in cooperation with Syria and Algeria and the representatives of the Arab League—and within the framework of the intensive endeavors and efforts to end the current regrettable fighting on the Palestinian arena so as to heal the rift and stand united behind the PLO, the sole legitimate representative of the Palestinian people. The Supreme Council hopes that all the parties will observe the cease-fire as agreed.

The Supreme Council emphasized its support for the PLO's unity and cohesion and for resolving all differences through constitutional and legal channels. The GCC Supreme Council expressed the belief that there can be no peace in the Middle East unless the Palestinian people, under the leadership of their organization, are able to obtain their inalienable national rights, including their right to repatriation, self-determination, and to establish an independent state on their national homeland.

The GCC Supreme Council heard a detailed report from Shaykh Sabah al-Ahmad al-Jabir, Kuwaiti deputy prime minister and foreign and information minister, and Shaykh Ahmad ibn Sayf Al Thani, Qatari minister of state for foreign affairs, on their meetings in Damascus and on what was achieved. The GCC Supreme Council hopes that what was agreed upon will be implemented.

The GCC Supreme Council also emphasized its support for Lebanon and for safeguarding Lebanon's safety, sovereignty, stability, and territorial integrity. The Supreme Council expressed its support for the National Reconciliation conference in Geneva and expressed the hope that it will achieve the results to which the Lebanese people aspire. The GCC Supreme Council also discussed the development in the relations between the Sultanate of Oman and the PDRY. The GCC Supreme Council lauds the positive development represented by the declaration on the exchange of diplomatic relations between the two countries.

The GCC Supreme Council reviewed the progress of military coordination among the GCC countries in implementation of the resolutions adopted at its third session held in the State of Bahrain in November 1982—resolutions aimed at building the strength of the GCC member countries and coordinating among them so that the GCC countries will be able to rely on themselves in defending their security and safeguarding their stability. The Supreme Council expressed its satisfaction with what has been achieved in this regard. The Supreme Council also viewed with satisfaction the Peninsula Shield exercises held in the UAE and the results and significance of these exercises, which reflect the determination of the citizens of the region to defend it and consolidate its independence, and also reflect the cohesion among the citizens of the area and their readiness to shoulder their responsibilities in safeguarding stability and security.

The GCC Supreme Council reviewed the progress in the implementation of the unified economic agreement and decided to expand the scope of economic activities which citizens of their countries are allowed to carry out in other GCC member countries as of 1 March 1984. The Supreme Council also adopted decisions on completing the measures for the establishment of the Gulf Investment Foundation [*muassasat al-khalij lil-istithmar*], which will begin its work at the end of November 1983.

The GCC Supreme Council expressed its gratitude and appreciation to Shaykh ibn Hamad Al Thani, the amir of the State of Qatar, and to his government for the generous hospitality and warm welcome accorded to the leaders and members of the delegations taking part in the conference—which had a good effect in bringing about the success of this brotherly conference—and wish His Highness good health and happiness and the Qatari people continued prosperity, progress and affluence.

In response to the invitation of His Highness Shaykh Jabir al-Ahmad al-Jabir as-Sabah, the amir of the State of Kuwait, the GCC Supreme Council decided to hold its fifth session in the State of Kuwait in November 1984.

Issued in the State of Qatar on 5 Safar 1404 Hegira, 9 November 1983.

Thank you. [applause]

Source: *FBIS-MEA-V–83–218*, 9 Nov. 1983, pp. C3-C4.

Document 91

Press Conference Held by Shaykh Ahmad ibn Sayf Al-Thani, Qatari Minister of State for Foreign Affairs, and Abdallah Yaqub Bisharah, GCC Secretary General, at the Conclusion of the Doha Supreme Council Summit

9 November 1983

[Excerpts][*Al-Mustaqbal* correspondent] With regard to the delegation that went to Damascus, it was said that it achieved a cease-fire. However, the summit's concluding statement called on all parties to cease-fire, so the fighting continues. Can you brief us on the steps you will adopt after the summit in order to stabilize a cease-fire?

[Al Thani] As you know, we were commissioned by the summit leaders to go to Damascus. The delegation consisted of Shaykh Sabah, Kuwaiti deputy prime minister, foreign minister and acting information minister; myself; Brother Beji Caid es-Sebsi, Tunisian foreign minister; and the Algerian information minister. We went to Damascus and met with Brother Abd al-Halim Khaddam. He told us that we had better meet the Palestinian brothers and acquaint ourselves with the problems. So we met with members of the PLO Executive committee.

We sat together and discussed the situation. Then we met with the dissidents, Abu Musa and Abu Salih. The meeting lasted about 5 hours. We agreed with them on a cease-fire effective today at 1430 [1130 GMT] Doha local time. We told them we couldn't contact Brother Yasir Arafat, PLO chairman, except from Doha. They gave us time and when we returned to Doha we contacted Brother Arafat, who welcomed the idea of a cease-fire. We informed them that to start with a cease-fire is what we want, and then we shall think of the problems that can be solved or the problems that the PNC, which will meet in January, will be able to solve in addition to the differences in opinion.

We are surprised that the fighting erupted anew. This we regret and we are still trying and the brothers here in Doha and the brothers in Tunis are in continuous contact with Brothers Yasir Arafat, Abu Musa, and Abu Salih. The important thing is the cease-fire. There are differences in views. We listened to both sides and told them to cease-fire for 4 days and then it will be possible to meet in any Arab country you choose.

[BBC correspondent] During the talks held by the GCC delegation in Damascus, did the opponents or loyalists to Mr. Arafat set any specific conditions for a cease-fire?

[Al Thani] There were no conditions. The matter simply is a Palestinian-Palestinian disagreement in views.

[*Ar-Rayah*'s Babakr Isa] God forbid, if all efforts to achieve and maintain a cease-fire fail, what will the stand of the GCC be, and will any of its leaders be dispatched to continue these efforts?

[Al Thani] To start with, the delegation that had been to [Damascus] went on behalf of the Arab states as a whole. There were two members from the GCC and a delegate from the Arab League attended too. What we understood is that differences do exist but they can be resolved without resorting to arms. All of them understand this. Yesterday, we met with 24 PLO members representing all groups including those belonging to Abu Musa, Abu Salih, and the entire group as well as those belonging to the other party. We are optimistic. Since they all sat with us at the negotiating table yesterday, this makes us optimistic on the possibility of a cease-fire today or tomorrow, God willing.

[Samir Abu Zayd from *Al-Arab*] What if a new PLO were formed and if it were to turn its back on all the Palestinian institutions? Second question: The experience of the GCC is considered one of the most successful experiences in the Arab world so far because it has accomplished what no other unification experience in the Arab world has accomplished. What prevents the formation of a single Gulf state and a single Gulf army?

[Al Thani] Your question actually consists of two parts. Regarding the PLO, it is recognized by all the Arab countries since the Rabat conference. No one has predicted or thought that another organization will be formed. None of the brothers whom we met with yesterday referred to this matter.

[Bisharah] As for the second part of the question on what prevents the formation of a single army and a single united state, the reply is that the statute, which is the charter, of the GCC stresses on the unity of the region. However, it has pursued an unhurried step-by-step method that is based on study and on the concept of conformity. Thus, our steps may be characterized by a slow pace, but they are steps that bring comfort and render what may be difficult today easy tomorrow and what may be difficult tomorrow, easy later on.

[Khalifah al-Husayni from *Al-Ahd* magazines] Concerning Egypt's absence from the Arab political and strategic map, what is the role of the GCC in the resumption of Egypt's role? Will the Sultanate of Oman play a role in this regard, particularly since it still has diplomatic relations with Egypt?

[Al Thani] Brother Khalifah, you asked me this question last week. As I told you, we all hope Egypt will return to Arab ranks. However, this decision is to be adopted by an Arab summit conference.

[Khalifah al-Husayni] Pardon, but the Sultanate of

Oman, which still has diplomatic relations, is a member of the GCC.

[Al Thani] Oman has not submitted any motion requesting anything in this regard.

[Excerpts] Unidentified correspondent] Within the framework of coordination among the GCC states with regard to threats to the region, has any decision been adopted pertaining to the threat to close the Strait of Hormuz or the threat of expanding the Iraqi-Iranian war? Did the summit adopt any decisions on this?

[Bisharah] I cannot talk about what has been adopted, but the matter was discussed in detail. Precautions and measures to safeguard the security and safety of the GCC states were adopted. God willing, we will try to make the measures appear in a more tangible form in the future.

[Unidentified correspondent] Shaykh Ahmad ibn Sayf, I have a question: During your latest tour and the agreement on a 4-day cease-fire, was this agreement verbal or written?

[Al Thani] The agreement was recorded by all parties.

[Unidentified correspondent] With regard to the security agreement or Gulf security cooperation, this was not clearly discussed in the final statement. This is the first question. The second question: You said that you will continue efforts to resolve the Iraqi-Iranian dispute through peaceful means. Does this mean that you might contact Syria once more so as to exert certain efforts?

[Al Thani] As for the second question, the mediation efforts by Prince Saud [Saudi foreign minister] and Shaykh Jabir [presumably Shaykh Sabah al-Ahmad as-Sabah, Kuwaiti deputy prime minister] between Syria and Iraq are still going on. They were supposed to visit both Syria and Iraq prior to the conference, but the visit was postponed until after the conference. As far as I was informed by the brothers in Syria yesterday, they are waiting for the mission. And as for the security agreement . . . [Bisharah] We did answer this question during the last meeting. We said there is an exaggeration and a misconception regarding the term "security agreement." We also said that it is simply a formulation of a draft law to deter crime and not a security agreement in the conventional meaning. Relations and cooperation in the security sector among the GCC states have been growing and increasing every day. The GCC interior ministers will meet on 28 November in Riyadh and you may thus raise this question there.

Source: *FBIS-MEA-V–83–219,* 10 Nov. 1983, pp. C1–C2

Document 92

GCC Ministerial Council: Eleventh Session Statement

14 June 1984

The ministerial council held its 11th session 12–14 June 1984 in At-Taif. The council reviewed the current situation in the region in the light of the Security Council resolution. The council expresses its satisfaction with Security Council Resolution No. 552 issued on 1 June 1984, in which the international community expressed its condemnation of the aggression to which commercial ships heading to and from Kuwaiti and Saudi ports were exposed, and in which it expressed its resolution that the territorial integrity of states not party to the conflict should be respected.

The council denounces strongly the latest attack against the Kuwaiti ship *Kazimah* after this Security Council resolution condemning these attacks. The UN secretary general and the president of the Security Council were informed of the details of this aggression.

The member countries have decided to continue contacts with the UN secretary general for the implementation of this Security Council resolution.

The ministerial council has dealt with the attacks in the spirit dictated by the UN Charter of peaceful coexistence, good neighborliness, and in accordance with its traditions of faith in dialogue and the removal of tension by restoring normal conditions, and adherence to the nonuse of force or threat of force in solving of problems.

The council also reviewed the reports of the various ministerial committees and approved them.

Issued in At-Taif on 14 June 1984.

Source: *FBIS-MEA-V–84–116,* 14 June 1984, p. C1.

Document 93

GCC Ministerial Council: Statement on Summit Preparatory Talks Issued by Kuwait's Deputy Prime Minister, Shaykh Sabah al-Ahmad

21 November 1984

Meetings of the GCC's ministerial council in preparation for the fifth GCC summit [*words indistinct*] ministers discussed items on the agenda in a friendly spirit which was characterized by complete frankness and a desire to deal with all issues reflecting the importance of their highnesses and majesties' fifth session.

As you know, ministers heard the comprehensive report of his excellency the GCC secretary-general, which covered the functions and efforts of the secretariat since the convening of the fourth ministerial council. It was decided to reappoint the assistant secretaries for economic and political affairs.

Our meeting reviewed the general situation in the Gulf and Arab regions, including fraternal Iraq and neighboring Iran. We also studied the (?Arab) situation in its various aspects and its pivotal cause, the question of Palestine, including the critical and sensitive circumstances throgh which it is passing which demands from us the utmost concern, alertness and responsibility to safeguard this [*words indistinct*] as a basic axis for joint Arab action.

Also discussed are the complications surrounding conditions in fraternal Lebanon as a result of the continuing Israeli occupation of south Lebanon. Our council adopted the necessary recommendations in this regard to be forwarded to the Supreme Council's forthcoming meeting.

The council also studied the various aspects of cooperation in military fields, and heard a report on this issue. The council also reviewed with interest the strategy for development and integration of the GCC's member states, and (?discussed) developments concerning the [*word indistinct*] with the European community.

We reviewed the resolutions of the various committees on unifying charges for services. Ministers (?expressed) great interest in topics related to giving [*words indistinct*] priority in government projects [*words indistinct*] as steps to implement the joint economic accord and the issue of real-estate ownership. [*passage indistinct*] of ensuring the basic interest of Gulf individuals and (?citizens) to the greatest extent. As for financial issues, the council approved the General Secretariat's (?administrative report) in line with its responsibilities.

Specific recommendations were forwarded to the Supreme Council in the political, military and economic fields with a view to achieving the GCC's aims and safeguarding stability of its member-states.

A spirit of friendship, seriousness and objectivity prevailed in the conference's discussions of the above topics. It is our pleasure that Kuwait's amir, [*words indistinct*] the honor of hosting our leaders' supreme council. We will take [*words indistinct*] to make the conference as successful as possible [*words indistinct*] the good of the region and our Arab nation.

We pray that God Almighty enable our leaders at their forthcoming conference to fulfill the hopes placed in them.

Source: *FBIS-MEA-V–84–227*, 23 Nov. 1984, pp. C1-C2.

Document 94

Press Conference Held by Shaykh Sabah al-Ahmad al-Jabir Al-Sabah, Kuwaiti Deputy Prime Minister and Foreign and Information Minister

26 November 1984

[Excerpts] [*name indistinct*] of Qatar Radio. Your Excellency, it has been reported that the Gulf countries have prepared a GCC plan on the Iraqi-Iranian war. Can you give us the outlines of this plan, and has Teheran shown a willingness to respond positively, particularly as it had adopted a hard-line stand toward all other initiative and plans?

[Shaykh Sabah al-Ahmad al-Jabir al-Sabah] I thank the Qatari Radio correspondent. I wish to say that since the inception of the GCC and since the outbreak of the war the GCC states—and I have said this in my statement—have been working hard in this regard in order to end the war. I want to say that there is no specific initiative but there is great interest in the matter. If circumstances help us and if the parties concerned accept such an initiative then the GCC will be the first to take an initiative in finding any solution to end the war—a war that not only harms the interests of the two countries but also harms the entire region and undermines world peace. Thank you.

[Ziyad (*surname indistinct*)] Ziyad [*name indistinct*] from Omani television, Mr. Minister, the GCC countries have supported and continue to support the Palestinian people and the restoration of their legitimate and inalienable rights. What has happened recently among the members of the PNC adds further division to the Arab ranks. What will the stand of the GCC be on healing the rift, and will contacts be made or will a delegation be sent to reconcile the parties concerned, especially as the PNC is convening almost during the same period as the GCC summit? Thank you.

[Shaykh Sabah] I thank the Omani television correspondent. I wish to say that the Palestinians are a people, and just as we do not accept that anyone interferes in our affairs, equally the Palestinian people do not accept that anyone interferes in their affairs. The PNC has held a legal meeting in Amman and elected a chairman. My government and the Kingdom of Saudi Arabia—according to what I have heard on the Saudi radio—have recognized the new chairman of the PNC. This is their affair, and on this premise we do not question the legality of the meeting, we do not object to it—it is a Palestinian affair. All that I hope is that this matter will not aggravate divisions among Palestinian brothers but instead will be the right course for the Palestinian question. Thank you.

[Bassam Mansur] Bassam Mansur from *Kull Al-Arab* magazine. Mr. Minister, [*words indistinct*] steps by Gulf countries regarding the Gulf war. However, it is rare that someone talks about the offers made in such initiatives. Can you give us an idea on these offers?

[Shaykh Sabah] First I have told the ministry under secretary that I hope that questions will not be repeated. This question was asked by the representative of Qatar [Radio], and I said to him there is no initiative, but that there is interest on all levels—the ministerial council and the Supreme Council, which represents our leaders—to end the war. The matter depends on the agreement of the parties concerned. If there is a positive response on the part of the parties concerned, then we will have a role to play in this matter, God willing.

[Nabil Yaqub al-Hamar] Nabil al-Hamar, director of WAKH. [*words indistinct*] several meetings of defense ministers of GCC states have been held. During the past 2 years joint exercises were held by the armies of the GCC countries. An intention or a trend to form a unified military command for the GCC states has recently crystallized. Is this true? Is there a trend to set up a so-called rapid deployment force?

[Shaykh Sabah] Thank you, WAKH. With regard to this matter we are paying attention to the military aspect to defend our region, particularly against the threats we are facing. Therefore we had to hold these joint exercises among the brothers in the armies of the region. The [summit] agenda includes the discussion of some kind of coordination whereby the Qatari, Bahraini, Omani, Saudi, and Kuwaiti armies and all the armies of the region will be under one umbrella when any GCC country is subject to an external threat. Here I wish to emphasize an essential point: When I refer to the defense of the region against outside [threats], this has nothing to do with what is happening inside the country—it is devoted to the defense of the [GCC] states against external aggression. Thank you.

[Oliver (?Delan)] Oliver (?Delan) from Radio France Internationale. Mr. Minister, one reads in the newspapers that GCC countries will follow Kuwait's example in making a decision on the establishment of diplomatic relations with the Soviet Union. I believe that you [*words indistinct*] latest decision. Does this topic appear on the agenda of today's conference? [*Question posed in French*]

[Shaykh Sabah] It is true that Kuwait maintains relations with all countries of the Eastern bloc. However, there is nothing on our agenda that makes it mandatory for any GCC member-state to adopt the same decision as Kuwait with regard to relations with other countries.

[Simon (?Mani)] Simon (?Mani) from *Freepacia* magazine. Mr. Minister, Kuwait has (?tried) more than once to join a military alliance of the GCC countries. What is your view in this regard? The Western press reported that the military exercises which Kuwait held with Gulf countries mean that Kuwait is moving in that direction. What are the [*words indistinct*] which Kuwait is making in this regard?

[Shaykh Sabah] Thank you, Simon, for your question. I assure you that what exists among the GCC countries is greater than an alliance. Alliances are between dissimilar countries, but we are states that trust each other. We call what we are doing military coordination among the area countries. Our policy is that the defense of the region does not come from outside but is the responsibility of the countries of the region. We are not influenced by what is written in the Western press as much as we are influenced by ourselves and our determination to continue in this policy. God willing, this topic will be discussed by the forthcoming summit: It is not the alliance that will be discussed, because the alliance already exists—the alliance is a family alliance, it is the heritage and history of the GCC countries. There is military coordination to defend the area countries and to block the loopholes—it is said that the area countries cannot defend themselves. I want to emphasize that we are capable of defending ourselves, thanks to the will of our

youth and the will of our leaders. We shall continue in this course. Thank you.

[Abd al-Hay al-Wazar] Abd al-Hay al-Wazar for the Qatari newspaper *Al-Arab*. Mr. Minister, the GCC countries have more than once brought about a reconciliation between Syria and the PLO. Now following the convening of the PNC session in Amman, it appears that relations between Syria and the PLO have further deteriorated. Can we expect a joint effort by the Gulf countries to bring about a relaxation in Syrian-Palestinian relations?

[Shaykh Sabah] We must not say that the road between Syria and the Palestinians has completely closed. I have already said that the PNC has held a legal meeting and a quorum was obtained. We have welcomed the meeting and welcomed the new PNC chairman. With regard to Syria and the Palestinians, we shall try as much as we can. As I have said, the GCC is acceptable to all parties who are willing to accept its mediation in this matter. We shall try as much as we can to prevent differences from becoming worse than estrangement and causing a split.

[Name indistinct] of Paris *Liberation*. [*Question indistinct*]

[Shaykh Sabah] First of all, I wish to affirm that it is true that Iraq is always asking for a solution to the war. I have said in the statement which I read to you that with regard to which party started the war we are not a court to decide who started the war. It is left to history to judge who began the war. What concerns us is that the war stops. When the war stops it will be made clear who started the war. Therefore, I hope you will excuse me from saying now who started the war. Thank you.

[Ahmad Jasim Al-Hamar] Ahmad Jasim al-Hamar, deputy director of QNA. Your excellency, first of all I would like my colleagues the journalists to thank the Kuwaiti Ministry of Information for the facilities it has extended to the journalists who are in Kuwait to cover the GCC summit. My question is within the framework of the GCC's interest in Arab affairs: During the PNC meetings, King Husayn has proposed a plan for a dialogue, or an initiative, in which the Palestinian and Jordanian sides join in an attempt to solve some Palestinian issues. What is the GCC view on this matter? Another question: During the ministerial council meetings the development plans for the GCC states were discussed. What are the major aspects of these development plans? Thank you.

[Shaykh Sabah] I thank the Qatari representative. I am glad that all the means of comfort and facilities have been extended to you in our country, Kuwait. With regard to King Husayn's initiative, it was made at the PNC. This matter concerns the Palestinians: If they want to accept it then this is their affair. It will be accepted or rejected, and when it is referred to a full Arab summit, and the GCC—which is part of the Arab world—we will then take a stand on this matter. However, now it is difficult to give any answer to this initiative before it is studied by the Palestinians themselves.

[Sulayman Nasir] Sulayman Nasir from the Saudi newspaper *Al-Riyad*. Has Oman or Bahrain asked for military aid, particularly since the Abha meetings approved the principle of aid to Oman and Bahrain? The other part of the question is: What significance do Aden and Sanaa hold for you, especially [*word indistinct*] the economic installations for the Sanaa port project?

[Shaykh Sabah] Thank you brother. The GCC decided last year, indeed 2 years ago during the Bahrain summit conference, that there would be financial aid to brothers in Aden [*as heard*] and Bahrain and [*words indistinct*] reason for this aid. As for the Aden and Sanaa issue, we believe it is an extension of the GCC—a security and economic extension. Although they are not part of the GCC, they are an extension of the GCC. That is why we made efforts with regard to Aden port and the earthquakes which took place in Sanaa 2 years ago. Now everything is proceeding in the right direction [*words indistinct*].

[Nasri Nassar] Nasri Nassar from the BBC in London. Your Excellency, please allow me to ask you a somewhat frank question. Through exploring the stance of Iran toward the Gulf efforts, do you believe that Iran regards the Gulf countries an indirect side in the war? Can this explain Iran's rejection so far of Gulf mediation efforts? To what extent militarily or politically can the Gulf countries avoid playing a direct role in the war? Or can the war continue until it comes to an end no matter what the result? Thank you.

[Shaykh Sabah] First, we have to comprehend this subject. We are not partners in this war. We will never be partners in it. At the same time, we are trying as much as we can through diplomatic channels to nail down a solution to this war. As for Iran regarding whether we are in a state of war or not, we say that we are not party to the dispute or the war. Thus, when our ships were hit, we made a decision, like countries that are not within the range of military operations or the war region between Iraq and Iran, to resort to the United Nations.

As for ending the war, I hope that we, the nonaligned countries, the Islamic countries and the United Nations will be successful in reaching a formula that will help us to end this war. Nobody actually benefits from this war in as much as it weakens the region and weakens the Arab countries. It also weakens countries of the nonaligned movement. Some countries may benefit from this war. But such countries that do benefit from this war will also one day suffer from it.

Source: *FBIS-MEA-V-84-230*, 28 Nov. 1984, pp. C3-C5.

Document 95
Kuwait Supreme Council Summit: Final Communiqué
29 November 1984

The Supreme Council of the GCC held its fifth session in the state of Kuwait from 4–6 Rabi ul Awal 1405 H., corresponding to 28–29 November 1984 at the invitation of H.H. Shaykh Jabir al-Ahmad al-Sabah, amir of the State of Kuwait. The meeting was attended by their majesties and highnesses:

H.H. Shaykh Zayid ibn Sultan Al Nuhayyaan—head of the state of United Arab Emirates;

H.H. Shaykh Isa ibn Salman Al Khalifah—amir of the state of Bahrain;

H.M. King Fahd ibn Abd al-Aziz al-Saud—King of Saudi Arabia;

H.M. Sultan Qabus ibn Said—Sultan of Oman;

H.H. Shaykh Khalifah ibn Hamad Al Thani—amir of the State of Qatar;

H.H. Shaykh Jabir al-Ahmad al-Sabah—Amir of the State of Kuwait.

The council reviewed the developments of cooperation between member states and what it had achieved since the fourth session at Doha, and debated the Iran-Iraq war because of the threat it constitutes on the security and stability of the region as a whole. The council considered the Arab current situation and the effect that Arab disputes have on Arab vital issues. It also debated the role played by member states in the international arena.

The council expressed its profound appreciation of the steps which have been taken towards unifying, coordinating the attitudes of member states, and consolidating the ties in a way that deepens the feelings of belonging and reaffirms the citizen's faith and conviction that he is an integral part of one frame that aims at achieving unity among their countries.

The council had emphasized its faith in the necessity of realizing wider horizons in political, economic and social cooperation in a way that strengthens its march towards attaining its ends. The council had noticed that the achievements which have been accomplished under the unified economic agreement have constituted the first milestone on the road towards economic integration. The council, in aiming at opening wide spheres for cooperation had agreed on the formula which organizes the right of appropriation for citizens of member states.

The council reviewed the results achieved by specialized committees in security and defense sectors and emphasized the significance of their achievements, which seek to translate the principle of self-reliance into tangible reality, which secures for the peoples of the council states the shouldering of their defense responsibilities.

The council considered the situation in the area and the dangers that the continuation of the Iran-Iraq war had on its security and stability. It also considered the development of contacts and endeavor which are made for the sake of putting an end to the war which consumed the potentials of the two neighboring countries and their Muslim peoples, and expressed its states' determination to continue exerting efforts until a peaceful solution is found, and to support the efforts carried out by the United Nations and the Good Offices Committee, which was set up by the Islamic Conference Organization and the Nonaligned Movement.

It also reiterated the readiness of the states of the council to carry out any direct endeavor which could achieve progress towards dialogue and negotiation. The council had laid down certain conceptions in this regard which it hopes they will meet the required response. It also expressed its satisfaction at the positive attitude of the Republic of Iraq towards the U.N. resolutions and the efforts of the Islamic Conference and the non-aligned sates. The council calls upon the Islam Republic of Iran to participate in the efforts which aim at finding a solution based on attaining the rights of both parties.

The council also emphasized the importance and significance of the principles which were included in the U.N. Security Council's Resolution 552, issued on the 1st of June 1982, in which the international community had required that the safety of navigation in the Council's states waterways be respected and that its independence and regional safety be maintained.

At the Arab field, the council reviewed the current Arab situation and the negative results of continued Arab disputes on the Arab vital issues. And in response to the national obligation the council expressed its readiness to participate in a joint Arab effort which aims at eliminating tensions, narrowing the gaps of Arab disputes and to seek an Arab agreement which puts Arab interests above all other considerations, and asks the Arab brotherly states to bypass their disputes and devote their efforts for attaining Arab detente based on cooperation and understanding.

The council debated the Palestinian issue and its stages, and reiterated its support for the legality of the PLO as being the sole legal representative of the Palestinian people.

The council emphasized the continuation of its support for the unity of brotherly Lebanon and for preserving its stability, independence and national sovereignty over its soil.

In the economic field, the council had expressed its satisfaction at the steps which had been taken to implement the unified economic agreement which participated in increasing commercial exchange between the council states; it also entrusted the General Secretariat with studying the means which would lead to the encouragement of joint ventures.

It endorsed giving priority to national products in governmental schemes and it entrusted also the ministerial council with ratifying the strategy of development and integration for the states of the GCC in its coming session after completing its study by member states.

The council also expressed its appreciation for the efforts

of the secretary general and decided to renew the appointment of Abdallah Yaqub Bisharah as secretary general of the GCC for the Arab states. It also endorsed the budget of the General Secretariat for the fiscal year 1405 H.

The council appreciated the great effort of H.H. Shaykh Jabir al-Ahmad al-Jabir, the amir of the state of Kuwait and his government for making the session a success. The council also appreciated the true sentiments reflected by the people of the state of Kuwait and the outstanding meaning that their feelings carry and that which reflects Kuwait's faith and role in the march of the council.

The council expresses its profound gratitude and thanks for H.H. Shaykh Jabir al-Ahmad al-Sabah and his government for all the efforts and records its sincere thanks for the warmth of the welcome accorded to their majesties and highnesses and for the excellent arrangements which played a basic role in realizing the outcome of their meeting.

The council looks forward toward meeting in its sixth session in Muscat on Rabi ul Awal 1406 H., corresponding to November 1985 at the invitation of H.H. Sultan Qabus ibn Said, sultan of Oman.

Source: *FBIS-MEA-V–84–231*, 29 Nov. 1984, pp. C1-C2.

Document 96
Saudi King Fahd Comments on Fifth GCC Summit
29 November 1984

I am overjoyed that God enabled me to meet my brothers, their majesties and highnesses the leaders of the Arab Gulf countries, and that he crowned our work with success. The fifth session of the Supreme Council was one of the important stages of cooperation and coordination consolidating the GCC march toward wider horizons of integration and cohesion. It dealt with all the issues aimed at achieving a prosperous life and guaranteeing security and stability for our peoples. It has become clear to all that the methodical nature of the march of cooperation and coordination among our states during the short period of our existence since its creation in 1401 H., that is about 4 years only, has led to achievements which are a source of pride. We have made a great step in the various spheres of cooperation, something which makes us feel confident about the march of this council, God willing.

The achievement of economic integration among its members has been one of the top priorities, because economics is the backbone of any cooperation and because our cooperation in this sphere will serve the aspirations of our peoples for economic development. Following up what has been achieved within the framework of the GCC unified economic agreement, we find that the achievements in this sphere are a source of satisfaction. The agreement has made great strides toward implementation in the spheres of economic cooperation, something which makes our region a unified economic region and an example for economic integration.

In the sphere of defense coordination the council considered in this session all that consolidates the principle of collective security for members within the framework of each state's own forces, within the context of a joint assessment. This stems from a sincere feeling of responsibility toward our peoples and the Islamic and Arab nation. What I want to confirm here is that without boundless love for nations, peace and stability, it is necessary to build a defensive force to defend out homelands and countries, capable of defending our achievement and gains and resisting every aggressor and enemy; guarantee security and stability for our peoples; and maintain the independence of our states and region. This is our responsibility in the first place, stemming from the premise that the security of the Gulf is the responsibility of its states and peoples, and that there is no place in the gulf for any foreign interference or influence.

We do not forget that we are at the start of the road. But our objectives and aspirations are big and we shall work for their achievement, God willing, setting out from our sincere sense of responsibility toward peoples and our Arab and Islamic nation. At the same time we confirm that the GCC is a solid brick made to become a shield for the Arab and Islamic nation. We call with sincere belief for cooperation, mutual assistance and fraternity among the Arab and Islamic peoples. The GCC's clear and firm attitudes confirm our determination to strive for the elimination of differences and rejection of disunity, and to replace disunity and dispute between any parties in the Arab and the Islamic arena with harmony in consolidation of this arena and in order to maintain its strength and capabilities as supports for our jihad for the recovery of usurped rights and victory of our causes.

The war between Iraq and Iran and what is prevalent in inter-Arab relations benefit no one but our common enemy, who benefits from this clouded atmosphere and enables it to continue its aggressive policy against our Arab and Islamic nation, whether in Palestine or in Lebanon. The efforts exerted by the GCC aimed at the elimination of these differences, healing this rift, and building bridges of trust and solidarity, are basic premises arising from the council's belief in the inevitability of the common fate and the need to resolve our differences in the spirit that characterizes our Islamic morals and authentic Arab heritage. I beseech God to grant us success and help us achieve the good to which we aspire for our nation and provide us with the strength and determination to continue the march of justice, progress, the achievement of our objectives, and the prosperity and high rank to which we aspire.

Source: *FBIS-MEA-V–84–232*, 30 Nov. 1984, p. C4.

Document 97
Al-Majalis Interview with Saudi King Fahd
8 December 1984

I was honored by the projects which you have inaugurated recently in Yanbu, Mecca and other places.

[Fahd] When we established the petrochemical industries complex in Yanbu everything was ready. We sent a group of Saudi youths to study abroad and gain experience and master the language. When we inaugurated the complex in Yanbu the Saudi technicians were ready to handle matters in cooperation with some foreign experts. We are working to prepare national expertise in the agricultural and industrial field so that our sons can shoulder the main responsibility for administering our development and projects. Do you know that Jeddah has been presented with an international award by the Arab cities organization for its good organization and for having all the facilities?

[Correspondent] What about the prize awarded to the Kingdom by the FAO for achieving self-sufficiency in the field of cultivation and production of grain?

[Fahd] We have begun to export the surplus of grain. Our production within 8 years has increased more than 433 times. While we produced 3,000 tons of grain in 1976, we produced this year 1.03 million tons of grain. I can say the same thing with regard to industry, especially steel used in building construction. We export a part of our steel production to the Gulf countries. We, the leaders, agreed that there should be coordination in the industrial field in order to avoid duplication of industries in our countries. Since there is a steel plant in the Kingdom we should not establish a similar plant in any of the fraternal countries to avoid duplication of projects. For example, the dry dock in Bahrain should not be repeated in another country. This also applies to the other agricultural, industrial and oil projects so that coordination and integration becomes a reality among our countries.

[Correspondent] Do you have something to say through the pages of *Al-Majalis* magazine to your sons in Kuwait and to the sons of the Arab nation on the occasion of the meeting of the GCC leaders?

[Fahd] The only thing I want to say to our sons in Kuwait and the Arab nation is that we should unite our ranks because coherence is the basis of such success.

[Correspondent] Your Majesty, there has been much talk about Egypt's return to the Arab ranks and about the individual step taken by Jordan in this regard. Do you think, Your Majesty, that Egypt's return to the Arab ranks has become a necessity that is imposed by nationalistic circumstances? Will the GCC countries adopt a unified position in this regard?

[Fahd] First, we respect and appreciate Egypt's leaders and people. Egypt is part of us and we are a part of Egypt. As to Egypt's return, this matter belongs to the Arab summit. I hope that God will gather the peoples of the Arab nation in one framework because the strength of this nation lies in its unity.

[Correspondent] The media have reported about a new U.S. move to bring about a solution to the Middle East crisis. The U.S. envoy, Richard Murphy, has paid more than one visit to the Kingdom of Saudi Arabia during his tour of some of the region's states. Do you think, Your Majesty, that there are changes in the U.S. position toward a just and lasting settlement of this crisis?

[Fahd] We do not ask the United States to do anything more than give justice to the legitimate rights of the Arab issues, especially the rights of the Palestinian people. We hope that the United States, in particular, and all the peace-loving peoples of the world will back this legitimate right practically.

[Correspondent] Will the Gulf rapid deployment force which the GCC has decided to form be tasked to participate in maintaining security inside the GCC countries or will it be tasked only to interfere to protect the region's countries from any foreign aggression?

[Fahd] The philosophy toward which the military cooperation among the GCC countries is leaning is based on building the intrinsic force of every GCC member state and the integration of these intrinsic forces in a common framework for the purpose of protecting the GCC countries against any foreign aggression or intervention. There is no doubt that this cooperation is not directed against anyone because the region's peoples want to live in peace, security, and stability.

[Correspondent] Your Majesty, how do you assess the gains of the GCC states? What are the reasons which prevent the implementation of all the articles of the economic agreement? What are the reasons which prevented the approval of the security agreement?

[Fahd] With regard to the economic agreement, this agreement has taken its natural shape to achieve the aspirations of the GCC countries. The ownership of properties by the Gulf peoples in the GCC countries is something that pleases us. However, the other agreements depend on the circumstances of each country.

[Correspondent] Your Majesty, the Arab region in general and the Gulf region in particular are passing through one of the most critical stages in their modern history, for they are the target of aggression and occupation. How do the leaders of the area countries view the confrontation of such a situation?

[Fahd] There is no doubt that some Arab differences do exist. These differences are a result of the desire to search for better solutions so that the Arab nation will reach the standard it deserves. Ultimately the Arab nation is bound to agree on what serves our religion and our lives. The Gulf countries are working together with their Arab brothers to achieve their aspirations and retrieve their occupied Arab territories, and above all to bring about the repatriation of the Palestinian people and the regaining of their legitimate rights.

[Correspondent] The project to establish a Gulf organi-

zation for military industrialization is among the projects that aim to achieve military self-reliance. What steps have been completed by the studies on the project? With regard to military preparations, has the policy of diversifying the sources of arms succeeded in your view?

[Fahd] We have taken a serious turn toward industrialization. God willing, industrialization will take shape so that it will fill the requirements of the Gulf countries. More important, we will have constructive joint industrialization which, God willing, will meet the requirements of the Gulf countries and enable them to do without imports. All this will be achieved with joint Gulf funds. The industries of the Gulf countries must be developed so that production meets the needs of these countries. The aim is to avoid having the same type of factories in several Gulf countries.

[Correspondent] In his address to the PNC His Majesty King Husayn put forward a Jordanian plan to solve the Middle East question, a plan that is based on UN Security Council Resolution 242. What is Your Majesty's stand on the plan, bearing in mind that the Palestinian cause is not the cause of the Palestinian people only but is also an Arab cause? Does the plan conflict with the Arab plan that was approved by the Fez summit conference?

[Fahd] The only solution is that Israel withdraw from the Arab territories it occupied in 1967 and the Palestinian people return to their homeland. The Fez summit resolutions stand and all the Arab parties are committed to them.

[Correspondent] The Arab situation now is passing through a difficult state. Your Majesty, you have exerted efforts to heal the rift while the Arab nation saw a good sign in the decision to hold the Arab summit conference in Riyadh. What is Your Majesty's view of the present deterioration in the Arab situation? Do you have any hopes that the Arab summit which has been postponed for more than 1 year will be convened?

[Fahd] In fact the Arab situation to which you refer makes Saudi Arabia prefer to wait and defer convening the Arab summit conference. This is in order to make further efforts to create a favorable Arab climate so that the summit conference will achieve some results. I hope that God will grant success to Saudi Arabia and the other fraternal countries in their efforts to achieve this end. The Arab summit conference is scheduled to be held, and it will be held, God willing. Its convening can be delayed only by further consultations among the leaders of the Arab nation and only when this is in the general interest.

[Correspondent] Inter-Arab differences have always hindered the progress of the Arab League as a unionist Arab organization. Does Your Majesty believe it is now necessary to amend the Arab League Charter, in light of past experience to save it from its state of suspended animation? What is the GCC's stand on the proposed amendments to the charter?

[Fahd] The present Arab situation cannot be primarily ascribed to shortcomings in the Arab League Charter. The Arab League is a mirror of the Arab homeland, a mirror that reflects the positive and negative aspects of the Arab homeland which result from the respective stands of each Arab country. Naturally, Saudi Arabia supports all actions that will improve the Arab situation. In my view, any organization that has been existing for a long time should be reviewed. If such a review indicates that it should be wholly or partly amended then Saudi Arabia supports such an amendment.

[Correspondent] The aid extended by the GCC countries individually and collectively to Third World countries is undoubtedly pure humanitarian aid. Is there any intention among the leaders of the GCC states to unify the policy of aid to these countries in light of their stands on our national [*qawmiyah*] causes?

[Fahd] Saudi Arabia has extended aid to some countries that have been stricken by natural disasters. In extending such aid Saudi Arabia is acting from purely humanitarian motives and within an ethical framework. Saudi Arabia has extended a great deal of economic aid within the framework of the economic development of friendly and fraternal countries. When extending such aid Saudi Arabia attaches no condition and acts from altruistic motives. Such aid is extended within the framework of brotherhood, friendship, and cooperation with these countries which reciprocate Saudi Arabia's sentiments and which show the same spirit of cooperation in various fields. If it transpires that such aid is used against the interest of Islam or the interests of the Arab nation then of course Saudi Arabia will review such aid.

[Correspondent] Your Majesty has exerted great and intensive efforts to help in resolving the Lebanese crisis. There have been developments in the Lebanese crisis and Lebanon has entered into new negotiations with Israel. What is your stand on these negotiations, and what solution do you envisage for the Lebanese crisis?

[Fahd] We have contributed, together with President Hafiz al-Asad and President Amin al-Jumayyil, as much as we could in an attempt to end the Lebanese crisis. It is known that President al-Asad gave all his attention. There is no doubt that, God willing, Lebanon will return to normal and the Lebanese people will enjoy security and stability. This is one of the greatest hopes we cherish for the Lebanese leaders, foremost among whom is President Amin al-Jumayyil, and the Lebanese people. Lebanon is a part of us, and we are a part of it. There is no doubt that Lebanon knows that Saudi Arabia's stand is a good and constructive stand.

[Correspondent] Your Majesty, the Palestinian issue is currently passing through a stage which may be described as a stage of being forgotten on the international level, because the Arabs and the world are busy with other side issues, such as the Lebanese question, the inter-Palestinian disputes, and the Palestinian-Arab disputes. In Your Majesty's opinion, how can the issue be reactivated, and what is the position of Saudi Arabia on the PNC meetings in Amman?

[Fahd] I do not believe that the Palestinian issue has been neglected. On the contrary, all Arab countries are

committed to the return of the Palestinian people to their homeland. This is a duty of the Arab and Muslim nation. With regard to the Palestinians themselves, the Kingdom's stand has long been known: nonintervention in internal Palestinian affairs. The Palestinians must decide what is good for them. Doubtlessly, the association of all Palestinian organizations within one framework is one of the things which will serve their interests under the leadership of the PLO.

[Correspondent] The Iraq-Iran war has lasted a long time, and its continuation poses a danger to the Gulf countries. Will the GCC countries propose an initiative to end this war? In Your Majesty's opinion, what are the causes of the mediation efforts which have so far been made by the ICO, the Nonaligned Movement, and the United Nations?

[Fahd] The Gulf countries are performing good offices with the brothers in Iraq and Iran to end this painful conflict between brothers. From this premise any effort from any party whatsoever is a good effort.

[Correspondent] Your Majesty, you emphasized more than once that the GCC is an integral part of the Arab nation. Is there any intention by the leaders of the GCC states to develop the GCC so that it may assume some form of Arab unity which Arabs from the ocean to the Gulf aspire to, and do you encourage the establishment of regional groupings similar to the GCC, in the Arab Maghreb for example?

[Fahd] One of the fundamental principles on which the GCC was established is that it is an integral part of the Arab nation. This principle has not and will not be doubted, God willing, at any time. It is the most important source of strength for the GCC and the GCC will never abandon its sources of strength, under any circumstances. With regard to the question whether there is an intention to develop the GCC so that it will assume a form of Arab unity, I believe that the important thing in such matters is in the essence and not the form. What drove the countries of the GCC to establish it was the feeling of their peoples that they are similar, and their consciousness of their unity of religion, soil, history, geography, and language, and the unity of their aims and destiny. All these mutual and unified elements led to and brought forth the GCC as a fundamental truth, and in a natural manner. I hope and encourage that more than one cooperation council will be established on the Arab level because of the benefit that will come to the whole Arab nation, and a fulfillment of the aims of the Arab League Charter.

Source: *Al-Majalis* (Kuwait), 8 Dec. 1984, as translated in *FBIS-MEA-V-84-238*, 10 Dec. 1984, pp. C3-C6.

Document 98

GCC Ministerial Council: Fourteenth Session
Statement

19 March 1985

The Ministerial Council of the GCC during its 14th session in Riyadh from 26 to 28 Jamada al-Akhirah, 1405 AH, corresponding to 17–19 March 1985 AD, discussed the Iraq-Iran war and the latest developments which have occurred in this war, the continued shelling of civilian targets, the destruction it has caused, the casualties suffered by innocent civilians and defenseless inhabitants. The council expresses its sorrow and pain for the sufferings of innocent civilians and for the destruction caused by this war to the peoples of the two neighboring countries which are linked together by faith and neighborliness. It also studied the gravity of the escalation of the war to security and peace it will produce. [*sentence as received*]

The council has followed up the recent escalation with anxiety and it affirms its full solidarity with Iraq in preserving the sovereignty, safety, and integrity of its territory.

It calls on Iran to respond to the international efforts to find a peaceful solution to this war and demands it should not cross Iraqi territory and should respect the international borders between the two countries.

The council notes with satisfaction Iraq's stance which is backed by its acceptance of all the resolutions passed by the Security Council and all international initiatives and calls for a halt to military operations to find a peaceful settlement for the conflict between the two countries.

The council has decided in pursuit of the resolutions of the fifth session of the GCC Supreme Council held in the state of Kuwait in November 1984 AD, to intensify contacts with the sister Arab countries, to rise to the responsibility to implement the resolutions of the Arab Summit conference in Fez connected with the Iraq-Iran war, to exert their efforts to maintain the unity of Arab territory, and to endeavor to cooperate with them to reach a just solution that takes into consideration the legitimate rights of both Iraq and Iran.

The council stresses its readiness to continue to exert all efforts and to intensify endeavors to put an end to this devastating war, including sending a delegation to Tehran and to Baghdad to discuss without any delay the quickest way to stop the war. The council also announced its complete readiness to carry out its duty imposed upon it by the righteous Islamic faith and the rights of neighborliness and fraternity, and hopes for a response to this posture.

The council also announces its backing for the efforts of the United Nations, the Islamic Conference Organization, and the Nonaligned Movement and calls on the UN secretary general to exert more efforts to contact the two sides to find a peaceful solution for the dispute between them.

The council has decided to keep the present session open, realizing the gravity of the present stage, the speedy moves required and the manifestation of the positive roles it could play in ending the dispute.

Shaykh Sabah al-Ahmad al-Jabir, the Kuwaiti deputy prime minister and foreign minister, then delivered a speech after the conclusion [*as received*] in which, on behalf of the participants, he expressed appreciation and gratitude for His Majesty King Fahd ibn Abd al-Aziz for his support. He beseeched God to protect his majesty and to maintain security and stability over our region in general.

The Kuwaiti minister also expressed his gratitude and appreciation for the participation of the foreign ministers in this meeting and for the good efforts they exerted in these conditions to make the meeting a success.

He said that the ministers agreed that the 14th session should remain open to follow up the developments of the situation in the region.

Source: *FBIS-MEA-V–85–053*, 19 March 1985, p. C1.

Document 99

GCC Ministerial Council: Fifteenth Session
Statement

9 July 1985

The GCC Ministerial Council met for its 15th session in Abha on 20–21 Shawal 1405, corresponding to 8–9 July 1985. The council reviewed the situation in the region and the developments of the Iraqi-Iranian war. It also reviewed the latest contacts made on this war as a continuation of the policy pursued and set up by the Supreme Council, especially the resolutions passed by their majesties and their highnesses in the Kuwait summit. The council affirms its determination to continue the contacts with the concerned parties, the Arab countries, and international organizations to support the efforts which aim at bringing about a peaceful solution to this devastating war. The council also discussed the sinful aggression against the procession of His Highness Shaykh Jabir al-Ahmad al-Sabah, amir of Kuwait, chairman of the fifth session of the Supreme Council, and one of the leaders and pioneers of the GCC march. While it condemns this criminal act, the council calls on the concerned authorities to intensify their efforts to confront such attempts.

The council also discussed Iran's detention in international waters of the United Arab Shipping Company's tanker *Al-Muharraq* and what this step constitutes—a violation of maritime law and freedom of shipping in international waterways and a violation of international law. The council emphasizes its rejection of this act and calls on Iran to free this ship immediately and to adhere to international law.

In the economic field, the council reviewed recommendations by various ministerial committees. It also decided to hand over a recommendation to the Supreme Council allowing GCC producers to market their products directly, without need for local agents. It also decided to recommend approving the equalization of all GCC citizens working in the private sector in rights and obligations with regard to profession.

Source: *FBIS-MEA-V–85–132*, 10 July 1985, p. C1.

Document 100
GCC Ministerial Council: Sixteenth Session Statement
3 September 1985

The ministerial council held its 16th session in the city of Riyadh on 2–3 September 1985, under the chairmanship of His Highness Shaykh Sabah al-Ahmad al-Jabir, Kuwaiti deputy prime minister, foreign minister, and chairman of the current council session. The council reviewed the issues on the agenda, foremost of which was the situation in the region and inter-Arab relations following the convocation of the Casablanca summit conference. The council stresses the continuation of the adopted policy with regard to encouraging all the efforts designed to end this war through peaceful channels. The council also reaffirms its previous positions with regard to its preparedness to undertake any action that expedites the process of ending the devastation, ending the war, and leading to a peaceful solution—a solution that takes into consideration the legitimate rights of the two sides. The council also regrets Iran's continued refusal to respond to the efforts made to end this war through negotiation and reconciliation.

The council also reviewed the current Arab situation. The council reaffirms adherence to the policy mapped out by their majesties and highnesses during the GCC summit conferences on the need to ensure Arab solidarity, elimination of differences, solution of problems through reconciliation and negotiation, and making efforts among the good offices among the brothers in order to place the supreme Arab interest above all consideration. Therefore, the council gives special importance to the tasks of the Arab committees formed at the Casablanca Arab summit in order to attain reconciliation and solve problems among Arab countries. The council emphasizes its readiness to play its role in creating the best possible atmosphere and in backing the activities of these committees. The council also approved the minutes of the various ministerial committees. The council also decided that the sixth preparatory session will be held Sunday, 27 October 1985, in Muscat.

Source: *FBIS-MEA-V–85–171*, 4 Sept. 1985, p. C5.

Document 101
Joint Communiqué on the Establishment of Diplomatic Relations between the USSR and the Sultanate of Oman
26 September 1985

The USSR and the Sultanate of Oman, guided by the desire to develop friendly relations and cooperation between the two countries in various fields have decided to establish diplomatic relations as of the date of signing of this communiqué and to exchange diplomatic missions at embassy level.

Both sides affirm that relations between the USSR and the Sultanate of Oman will be based on the principles of peaceful co-existence: mutual respect for sovereignty and territorial integrity, noninterference in each other's internal affairs, and equality and mutual advantage in accordance with the UN Charter.

Both sides are sure that the establishment of diplomatic relations between the USSR and the Sultanate of Oman accords with the two countries' interests and will help to strengthen international cooperation and world peace.

The USSR and the Sultanate of Oman have agreed that the exchange of diplomatic missions will be effected in the immediate future. They will give each other the necessary assistance in inaugurating and fulfilling the functions of the diplomatic missions in their respective capitals on the basis of international practice and the principle of reciprocity.

For the USSR, G. Korniyenko, USSR first deputy foreign minister.

For the Sultanate of Oman, His Highness Sayid Haytham Ibn Tariq al Said, chief of the Sultanate of Oman Foreign Ministry European and American Countries Department.

New York, 26 September 1985

Source: *Izvestia* (Moscow), 27 Sept. 1985, p. 4, as translated in *FBIS-USSR-III–85–189*, 30 Sept. 1985, p. H1.

Document 102
Interview with the UAE President Shaykh Zayid ibn Sultan Al-Nuhayyan
2 November 1985

Question: Your Highness the President, a few days from now, the GCC Summit will be held in Oman. How do you view this summit? What are the important issues on its agenda? Do you expect that this summit will find successful solutions to these issues?

Answer: Our hope is always that in all the meetings with brothers we will enhance unity and links among brothers. Every time new things arise. Time will bring these matters to the surface. Such matters require assessment. All know that we all can benefit from them. We pray to the Almighty that we will achieve unanimity for the benefit of the entire Arab and Muslim nation in general, and the Gulf countries in particular.

Question: The Iraq-Iran war is still raging between the two Muslim neighbors. How do you view this war? What is your opinion about its escalation? Will there be a new GCC initiative during the next GCC meetings in Muscat to stop this war and reestablish stability in the region?

Answer: The truth is that many initiatives have been made to end this devastating war between the two Muslim neighbors. The initiatives included one by the GCC countries. This war is a setback to the Muslim nation and an advance for the enemies of Islam. So far there are no signs of an end to this war and for reconciliation and views between the two countries to be brought together. It is possible that during their meetings in Muscat, the GCC will propose new ideas that will be subject to study within the framework of the keenness of all to end this war and make good moves and avert war between brothers. This is a duty which every Muslim and every true human being is anxious for.

Question: How do you view peace in the Middle East in view of the recent events in the region? Do you think that without the PLO's participation in any settlement to the Middle East crisis this crisis can be settled?

Answer: Comprehensive and just peace in the Arab and Muslim world is impossible without unity and solidarity. So long as the current fragmentation continues, this peace will be dubious. There will be no true peace without the PLO's participation in any settlement to the Middle East crisis.

Question: Fraternal Kuwait recently witnessed many bombing incidents. Do you think that these acts of terrorism were directed primarily at fraternal Kuwait, or are they aimed at the region's countries? In your opinion, what is the stand toward these acts of terrorism?

Answer: In my view, acts of terrorism against Kuwait were directed against all the region's countries, like all the disasters in the Arab world this year and last year. Unity, solidarity, and abandoning fragmentation are needed to face acts of terrorism because there have been grave losses as a result of the fragmentation and disunity which continued in the Arab world for many years. If we do not try to avoid suffering more losses, our current situation will continue.

Question: There is persistant talk about Egypt's return to the Arab world membership, which it lost after it signed the Camp David accords. How do you view this issue? Is it time for Egypt to return and occupy its place among its sisters

and fulfill its mission or is it not yet time to propose this issue so that Arab differences will not be aggravated?

Answer: The current situation requires the entire Arab nation to be united. Arab and Muslim countries are in dire need of this.

Source: *Al-Ittihad* (Abu Dhabi) and *Al-Watan* (Muscat), as translated in *FBIS-MEA-V–85–213*, 4 Nov. 1985, pp. C4-C5.

Document 103

Interview with the UAE Minister of Defense Shaykh Muhammad ibn Rashid

3 Novmeber 1985

Question: What do you think of the security and defence coordination among the AGCC countries, and what are, in your opinion, the fruits of this cooperation?

Muhammad: I could say and affirm that the defence coordination among the AGCC states has come a long way and we have started implementing our resolutions and recommendations regarding collective defense. The Peninsula Shield Force at King Khalid Military City in Hafr Al Batin in Saudi Arabia is the first fruit of cooperation in the defence among the member countries.

Question: The Iran-Iraq war is still going on despite the efforts exerted by the AGCC states or the moves made on the international level. What are, in your opinion, the effects of this war on the Arab Gulf region? And do you expect this war to come to an end, and are there signs that it would expand and spread?

Muhammad: The Iran-Iraq war is a war between two Muslim neighbours, and no one benefits from it except the enemies of Islamic and Arab nations. The AGCC countries have been sparing no efforts to stop the bloodshed in this devastating war, whether at regional or Islamic levels in the framework of the efforts of non-aligned countries or the United Nations. We hope these concerted efforts would lead to positive results to save Islamic and Arab energies and turn them in the service of our just causes. The negative impact of this war does not affect only our Gulf region but it may extend to the Arab nation and the whole world, because the security of Gulf region is connected with the Arab security, as we are a part of Arab nation and our security cannot be separated from the Arab security and subsequently the Arab security is connected with world peace.

Question: In case this war spreads, what measures do you expect the AGCC states to take?

Muhammad: I think there is little possibility of the war expanding. And we, in the Gulf Cooperation Council, work with all available means in cooperation with Islamic and international organizations which exert their good offices to put an end to the war.

Question: Kuwait was recently exposed to many explosions. They were aimed to shake the security and stability in that Arab Gulf region and what important measures should be taken to face any similar incidents in any of the AGCC states?

Muhammad: The AGCC countries are linked in a joint defence policy based on a clear defence strategy which was endorsed in our fourth conference in Kuwait a few days ago. What happened in the brotherly Kuwait may happen in any member-country. We are, therefore in need, more than at any time in the past, to proceed forward in our unification march in the national Arab framework to protect the security and stability of our people and maintain the unity and independence of our lands.

Question: With regard to armament in the AGCC countries, is the UAE expected to conclude shortly any deals to import new arms?

Muhammad: We, in the UAE, purchase arms suitable to our region and do not rely on any specific body or source to import for our needs.

Question: In the context of diversification of the sources of arms, we would like to know your point of view on this matter. Is there any move to standardise and unify the quality weapons of the armies of AGCC states in the near future?

Muhammad: The AGCC countries pursue the policy of diversifying their sources of arms and do not depend on any specific sources. This policy protects our political action. I would like to point out that the use of different types of weapons by the armies of AGCC countries does not constitutes an obstacle in the way of unifying our forces, and the Peninsula Shield at Hafr Al Batin, which includes contingents from Saudi Arabia, the Sultanate of Oman, Bahrain, Qatar, Kuwait and the UAE using different types of arms.

Question: It has been frequently said that Kuwait has asked to raise the level of alertness in the AGCC countries after a number of its trade vessels were attacked or detained by Iranian Navy in the Strait of Hormuz. It was said these attacks were a threat message to Kuwait. What are your comments on this? Of late the cases of trade vessels being intercepted in the strait have increased and this constitutes a threat to international navigation. What measures should be taken in this connection to eliminate this threat?

Muhammad: The AGCC countries proceed on the correct path to coordinate their efforts and unify their ranks to protect peace and security of their peoples, and the AGCC states refuse to impair in any way the freedom of international shipping through the Hormuz which is an international strait. Nobody whosoever is allowed to impede navigation in it or close it.

Question: What is your opinion about the joint exercises which were conducted recently among the AGCC forces? What are the main benefits and lessons that emerged from these exercises—in relation to the combating spirit to the soldiers and preparedness of the AGCC armies in general?

Muhammad: The joint exercises aim at strengthening the spirit of cooperation among the cadres of our armies and translate this cooperation into reality, and to get acquainted with the systems operative in the armies of each country. Furthermore, the exercises raise the morale of our armed forces and strengthen the relationship between the officer and the soldier with regard to team work and their will to protect our countries and preserve our sovereignty and independence. They also offer him the opportunity to be briefed on the quality of arms used by the armies of different member-states.

Question: It has been said that there is a trend in the AGCC states to establish armament industries to meet their requirements. When do you think the nucleus of this industry will be started?

Muhammad: I said this in an answer to a previous question. The AGCC proceeds along the right path and in accordance with the method approved by the AGCC leaders. This means achieving the maximum levels of coordination and integration in the different aspects. The question of armament industry is among the actions which the leaders and defence ministers of AGCC countries have taken and, Insha Allah we will start implementing plans in this respect after completing the necessary studies. There are appropriate committees being formed for this purpose and we hope they will finish their work in the near future.

Question: What level has the combating ability of the UAE armed forces achieved?

Muhammad: The UAE is a member of the AGCC and draws its strength from the strength of the sister countries in the council. We consider this as a major factor of support to Arab nation.

Question: There are some rumours circulated by certain sources that about 200 nuclear heads were ready to be fixed on to missiles by the Zionist enemy and the range of these missiles covers the entire Arab homeland, and, of course, the Arab Gulf countries. The Zionist entity recently raided the PLO headquarters in Tunisia in an apparent effort to tell the Arab world and the PLO that is has a long arm capable of reaching any place in the Arab world. Doesn't that bring to the mind the issue of the Mediterranean security and the emphasis by all Arab countries on joint defence?

Muhammad: The Zionist enemy does everything possible to achieve its wanton goals which are represented in establishing a "grand Israeli state" with boundaries stretching from the Nile to the Euphrates. The continuous Israeli aggression against the Arab countries and the people of Palestine and the raid of Israeli planes on the PLO headquarters in Tunisia represent the climax of arrogance of the Zionist enemy and its aggressive and expansionist designs. All this is a bell of danger tolling at our doors and waking us up to be cautious and remain in full alert to build an Arab force to which all our energies should be directed, so as to be able to repulse all aggression against our lands and protect the Arabs from such dangers, and defend the cause of our glorious nation.

Source: *FBIS-MEA-V–85–213*, 4 Nov. 1985, pp. C5-C7.

Document 104

Muscat Supreme Council Summit: Opening
Statement Made by Oman's Sultan Qabus

3 November 1985

In the name of God the merciful, the compassionate. Your Majesties and Highnesses: On this auspicious day on which we are meeting in Oman it pleases us to extend to you fraternal and sincere welcome. We express our extreme love and appreciation to you and also the happiness of the Omani people for this joyous meeting and their pride in the strong bonds linking our peoples in our march toward prosperity and solidarity. Our meeting today comes as a new embodiment of our determination to advance with our march for achieving the objectives for which our peoples have been aspiring since we adopted our blessed step in establishing the GCC. We thank God who granted us success during this short period in gaining positive achievements, through which we consolidated the pillars of this entity and began to open scopes of cooperation to include the various fields. Thanks to God and due to our fraternal and sincere efforts, our council has had the opportunity to play its positive role as an effective tool for consolidating the links among our countries for the benefit and prosperity of our peoples.

While we are extremely satisfied with the cooperation that exists within the framework of our council in all political, economic, and security fields, today, relying on this strong ground, we express our increasing awareness of the need to devote the greatest attention in this stage to vital fields according to the degree of contribution of these fields to the basic interests of our peoples. In this regard, it also pleases us to praise our fraternal understanding of the pursuance of a constructive and practical course in tackling the various issues wisely and patiently, realizing the importance of the positive experiences of our countries in developing the level of cooperation among them in a way that will assimilate all their energy and contribute toward the translation of the ambitions of our peoples into a reality, of which the generations of the sons of our gulf family will be proud.

Your Majesties and Your Highnesses, we are meeting under very critical regional and international circumstances which require us to confirm the role our council is playing as a factor of stability in the region. We all have the great hopes that we will develop the level of defence and security coordination to a point which will contribute to strengthening the ties among our states so that they can perform their common responsibilities. While we commend the keenness shown by the GCC states to coordinate among themselves to protect the region against the phenomena of violence and terrorism and all acts aimed at undermining our security, we reemphasized the great importance of translating this keenness into strong solidarity that can en-

sure the stability of our people and protect their achievements and gains against all dangers and challenges.

Our council has shown great keenness to stop the Iraq-Iran war and expressed sincere desire to bring the two sides together; our states have made every effort possible. While we affirm the importance of the continuation of regional and international efforts and mediation, we call on the leaders of the two countries to show flexibility that will open the road to these good office efforts. We also call on the international society to show more keenness to help stop this war, which has continued for a long time and whose continuation and escalation jeopardizes the interests of the region's countries and threatens world peace.

We look to the day when amity and good-neighborliness between Iraq and Iran will dominate so that security will prevail throughout the region and its peoples will enjoy stability. Then they can devote their resources and attention toward achieving their aspirations—development and progress.

Regarding the current developments in the Arab arena, while we are all pleased over the eagerness to clear the air and unify ranks, we affirm the utmost need to rise above obvious minor differences and put our nation's supreme interest above all considerations so that it will be able to face the circumstances of this stage in a spirit of solidarity, which is indispensable, as a basic starting point for effective constructive action for the benefit of its fateful issues, foremost being the Palestinian people's issue. It is a source of satisfaction that our council has been able, praise be to God, to reflect the sincere eagerness of all of us for a sincere and constructive role on both the Arab and Islamic levels, and to express very clearly our continuing readiness to cooperate with all international groups which reciprocate the same desire based on equal interests. This will provide a good example of our joint efforts which aim at the good of our people and the international community.

Your Majesties and Highnesses, while we begin, with God's blessings and support, the meetings of the sixth session of our council, we are sure that our fraternal efforts will unite during this meeting, as they always have, in order to reach results which will ensure the advance of our march another step that will add to what we have achieved during our previous meetings—a new achievement that will express our eagerness at this stage and enrich our joint experience for the benefit of the present and future of our people.

In conclusion, we reiterate our welcome to Your Majesties and Highnesses and the members of the delegations. We wish you a good stay among your kinfolk in Oman. We affirm our eagerness to devote all our energies to contribute with you toward the success of this session, God willing. We also extend thanks to the ministerial council, the permanent committees of our council, the secretary general and his assistants, and to the secretariat for their efforts in preparing for this meeting. We pray to God to guide our steps on the road of fraternity and cooperation, grace our efforts with his full care, and grant us all support and success. He is all-hearing and responsive. Peace and God's mercy and benedictions be upon you. [applause]

Source: *FBIS-MEA-V–85–213*, 4 Nov. 1985, pp. C2-C3.

Document 105

Muscat Supreme Council Summit: Final Communiqué

6 November 1985

The GCC Supreme Council held its sixth session in the Sultanate of Oman from 19–22 Safar 1406 Hegira, corresponding to 3–6 November 1985, at the invitation of His Majesty Sultan Qabus ibn Said, the sultan of Oman. The meeting was attended by their majesties and highnesses: His Highness Shaykh Zayid ibn Sultan Al Nuhayyan, president of the UAE; His Highness Shaykh Isa ibn Salman Al Khalifah, the amir of the State of Bahrain; His Majesty King Fahd ibn Abd al-Aziz Al Saud, king of the Kingdom of Saudi Arabia; His Majesty Sultan Qabus ibn Said, the sultan of Oman; His Highness Shaykh Khalifah ibn Hamad Al Thani, the amir of the state of Qatar; and His Highness Shaykh Jabir al-Ahmad al-Jabir al-Sabah, the amir of the State of Kuwait.

The Supreme Council reviewed cooperation among GCC member-states and expressed satisfaction at what has been achieved as a result of such cooperation since the fifth session held in the State of Kuwait. The GCC Supreme Council discussed the Iraq-Iran war in light of recent developments and in light of the serious escalation [of the war], particularly in the Gulf waters, and discussed the threat this poses to the security and stability of the entire region and to the freedom of navigation in the Gulf.

With regard to the situation in the Gulf region, the Supreme Council recalled what was announced at the conclusion of the fourth session held in Doha in November 1983, which affirmed its adherence to UN Security Council Resolutions 540 of 1983 and 552 of 1984, which expressed the international community's support for the freedom of navigation in international waterways and for the freedom of passage of merchant ships from and to the ports of the GCC states. The Supreme Council calls on Iran to respect the principles mentioned in these two resolutions.

The Supreme Council also reaffirmed what it had declared in its fifth session held in Kuwait in November 1984 regarding the Iran-Iraq war, especially its emphasis on the need of the readiness of the GCC states to continue their endeavors with the parties concerned to end this destructive war in a manner that safeguards the legitimate rights and interests of the two sides in order to bring about the establishment of normal relations among the Gulf states.

On the Arab level, the Supreme Council discussed the Palestinian question and its various stages and affirmed its continued support for the PLO as the sole legitimate representative of the Palestinian people. The Supreme Council also condemned the Zionist attack on Tunisia and on the PLO headquarters there, and affirms its support for the fraternal Republic of Tunisia and the PLO.

The council affirms its continued support for the unity of fraternal Lebanon and for safeguarding its stability, independence, and its national sovereignty on its soil.

The council also reviewed the Arab situation and the results of the extraordinary Arab summit held in Casablanca and the work of the two committees for reconciliation and clearing the Arab atmosphere, and expressed its satisfaction with the results achieved by the committee. The council affirmed its support for the work of the committees and for the need to continue their efforts until their task is accomplished.

The council also reviewed the steps achieved in accordance with the economic agreement. Out of its desire to push forward the GCC's march toward the achievements of the goals underlined by the economic agreement, the Supreme Council agreed to the drawing up of a timetable to carry out the various activities of economic cooperation. The Supreme Council decided to charge the administrative council with the task of approving this program and to study the possibility of adding new activities to the economic activities which the citizens of GCC states are allowed to carry out, such as insurance, trade, and buying, exchanging shares of companies that have been authorized to carry out their activities, and drawing up regulations for such transactions.

In implementation of the states for achieving and coordinating integration and links among the member-countries in all fields and to strengthen the ties of cooperation, the council has approved the following:

1. The agriculture policy of the GCC countries.
2. A unified strategy for industrial development.
3. Education goals and methods.
4. Policies and general principles for protecting the environment.

The Supreme Council was also informed of the progress of the initial contacts made with international economic bodies and countries, and has decided to continue these contacts. The council has approved equal treatment for students from GCC countries at the elementary, intermediate, and secondary levels as those students resident of the country in which they are studying; it also approved equal treatment of study certificates issued by the GCC countries as those issued from the country in which these certificates are needed.

The council reviewed the security situation in view of the escalation of terrorism in the region and the terrorist attempts carried out against some GCC countries in a bid to undermine their security and stability. While condemning all acts of terrorism, the council affirms its support for the solidarity with any member-state subjected to such acts and considers this a threat to all the GCC countries because the security of the GCC countries is indivisible.

Out of the determination to preserve the solid unity of the internal front and in order to achieve stability and security in the member countries, the council approved the goals of the security strategy and emphasized the need to quickly realize them.

In reviewing defence cooperation, the council expressed full satisfaction over the accomplishments achieved. The council also approved the strategic concept of defence cooperation among the GCC countries.

The council expresses appreciation for the great efforts of His Majesty Sultan Qabus ibn Said of Oman and his government to ensure the success of this session; it also expresses appreciation for the sincere feelings demonstrated by the people of the Sultanate of Oman and the great meanings of these overflowing feelings which reflect the Sultanate of Oman's conviction for and its positive role in the GCC march. The council reiterates sincere thanks to His Majesty Sultan Qabus ibn Said for the warm welcome their majesties and highnesses have been accorded and for the preparations and excellent organization which had a key role in reaching the good results achieved by the Supreme Council.

The council looks forward to its meetings during its seventh session in the UAE in Safar 1407 Hegira, corresponding to November 1986, in response to an invitation from UAE President His Highness Shaykh Zayid ibn Sultan al Nuhayyan.

Issued in Muscat on 22 Safar 1406 Hegira, corresponding to 6 November 1985.

Thank you, Your Majesty, the chairman. [applause]

Source: *FBIS-MEA-V–85–215*, 6 Nov. 1985, pp. C1-C2.

Document 106

Muscat Supreme Council Summit: Closing
Statement Made by Oman's Sultan Qabus

6 November 1985

In the name of God, the merciful, the compassionate. Your Majesties and Highnesses:

As we conclude the sixth session of the GCC, we would like to express our profound appreciation for this propitious opportunity that brought us together in Oman in the framework of the GCC. We also express our profound appreciation for the brotherly atmosphere that dominates our meetings and reaffirms our keenness to work in the direction of solidifying cooperation among our states and consolidating rapprochement among their peoples to guarantee their security and stability and help attain their aspirations, which are represented in progress and flourishing development. While we thank the Almighty who enabled us to

attain success in this meeting, we would like to convey thanks and gratitude to you for all the sincere efforts you exerted which enabled our council to attain positive resolutions and results. These results will have a positive effect and tangible result in accomplishing the noble goals of our brotherly procession. Your Majesties and Highnesses, the important consultations which we held with regard to military and security cooperation among our countries, in addition to the confrontation of terrorism, have participated in making further progress. Such progress would have a positive impact in preserving security and stability in our region. God willing.

Our sessions, which took place during this summit, have provided a new step that mirrors our firm desire to develop our common experience in a way commensurate with every stage and in a way that serves the vital interests of our countries and peoples and enhances solidarity among them in confrontation of the challenges.

What has been achieved in the framework of our council—through the Almighty's guidance and the massing of our fraternal efforts in all the meetings we held—affirms that if we continue our processing with the same sincere momentum it will have a shining future, God willing.

Today, as we conclude the sixth GCC session with absolute satisfaction for the positive step adopted during these meetings, we look forward to our next meeting in the UAE, where we will be the guests of Brother His Highness Shaykh Zayid ibn Sultan al Nuhayyan and his dear people. We hope that through our continuous meetings, we attain, God willing, all success for the best and progress of our peoples.

Your Majesties and Highnesses, we greet you and express to you once again our sincere gratitude and appreciation for these brotherly and propitious meetings. We also express bountiful thanks and appreciation to their highnesses and excellencies the members of the delegations, the secretary general and his aides, in addition to all those who work in the general secretariat who participated greatly in making our duties successful. We convey the loftiest expressions of gratitude and extolment to God, the almighty. We ask him, the Almighty, to bestow our efforts with His care and guidance. God will never cause dissipation of those who successfully fulfill their duties. God's peace and blessing be upon thee.

Source: *FBIS-MEA-V–85–216*, 7 Nov. 1985, p. C1.

Document 107

Muscat Supreme Council Summit: Closing
Statement Made by Shaykh Khalifah ibn Hamad Al-
Thani, Amir of Qatar

6 November 1985

I would like to express my complete satisfaction with the results of the Sixth Session of the GCC Supreme Council and the spirit of true fraternity and serious feeling of responsibility which prevail throughout our meetings and discussions toward all the issues which we discussed. I am confident that our firm solidarity and joint efforts will always be a strong support for us in implementing our resolutions. In every meeting these resolutions usher in a new phase which link it with previous phases on the path of our joint Gulf work in order to achieve further cooperation and closer ties among our peoples, who look forward to achieving their integration as the ideal method to obtain the national and pan-Arab hopes to which they aspire.

It pleases me to extol the great effort made by my brother, His Majesty Sultan Qabus ibn Said, in organizing our meetings, and the wisdom and ability with which he moderated our discussions. This has had the greatest effect on ensuring the success of the Sixth Session of the GCC Supreme Council.

I would like to express my thanks for the great welcome and generosity which we have found in this fraternal country during our stay.

I pray to God Almighty to guide us all in upholding the dignity of our religion and elevating our homeland and our nation. He is the best Lord and greatest support.

Source: *FBIS-MEA-V–85–216*, 7 Nov. 1985, p. C2.

Document 108
Muscat Supreme Council Summit: Closing Statement Made by Saudi King Fahd
6 November 1985

I am greatly pleased and happy to have met with my brothers their majesties and highnesses the leaders of the GCC Arab Gulf countries during the Sixth Session of the Supreme Council which was held in fraternal Oman. While departing my second country, Oman, I would like to express my deep appreciation and thanks to the dear brothers in Oman—the Sultan, government and people—for their good nature and hospitality and for their great efforts and energies which helped to ensure the success of the conference and to achieve the results expected from it and the hopes pinned on it.

As is the custom with the meetings of the Supreme Council, the goal was to find a general outlook and to achieve the dear aspirations of the Gulf people, represented through cooperation in various vital fields, and to establish an intrinsic strength which takes its roots from a glorious history and is based on a present in which they look for a bright future supported by hopes and strong determination.

The meetings of the Supreme Council in its sixth conference are considered one of the continuing stages with God's help, in the march of the GCC, which aim at holding consultations and coordination in order to reach further

cohesion and integration to preserve continued security, stability, and economic and social development in this dear region of our great homeland.

It should be noted that since the GCC was established, one of its priorities has been to realize economic integration among its countries, as economy is a great pillar for serving the ambitions of the Gulf people in implementing economic and social development plans in the near and distant future. To achieve this goal, the GCC has made marvelous and important steps in the fields of customs, property ownership, the movement of capital and persons, the encouragement of national products, and other means which lead to cooperation among the GCC countries. During this session, the GCC council reviewed issues which concern the security of the region's present and future amid the current international situations and circumstances, out of a responsibility for preserving the security of our peoples and region, and protecting their security and stability.

As we laud the achievements of the GCC since its establishment, we know that we are still at the beginning of the road and that the realization of our unlimited aspirations and ambitions requires more time and greater efforts. This will be easy, with God's help, as long as we realize this responsibility and undertake its execution with honesty and loyalty.

On this good occasion I affirm that the GCC has been and will always be, with God's permission, a firm pillar and a tool of goodness that works to embody the cooperation and fraternity between the Arab and Islamic peoples and endeavors to establish agreement in place of division and dispute due to the conviction that love and agreement are the basis of power and flourishment, and that division and dispute are the basis of the problems of nations and their weakening. For this reason, the war between Iraq and Iran and the negative atmosphere prevailing in Arab relations on some occasions are not in the interest of anyone, except our joint enemy who profits from these differences to continue its hostile trend against our Arab and Islamic nation in Palestine and in other places. The council's efforts aimed at eliminating the differences and uniting ranks stem from its belief in the inevitability of the joint fate. I ask God to grant us our wishes and ambitions for the good of our nations and to extend to us his strength so that we all will continue along the course of goodness and growth.

Source: *FBIS-MEA-V–85–216*, 7 Nov. 1985, pp. C1-C2.

Document 109
Muscat Supreme Council Summit: Closing Statement Made by the UAE's President Shaykh Zayid ibn Sultan Al-Nuhayyan
6 November 1985

My brother Your Majesty Sultan Qabus ibn Said; my brothers Your Majesties and Highnesses: In the name of all of you, I thank His Majesty Sultan Qabus for the generosity, respect, honor, and good hospitality that have been accorded to us. I also thank the Omani people for the generosity, joy, and jubilation with which they received us. We thank his majesty the sultan for his debate on the affairs which we reached resolutions on. He was the first to adopt these resolutions on such problems and their aspects. I also thank him for the wisdom he demonstrated in tackling all the issues which concern the GCC in particular, and the Arab countries in general.

Your Majesty, thank you for the welcome from you and your honorable people of Oman. Excellencies, I deeply congratulate the Omani people on your wise leadership and your care for the Omani people who are known for their goodness and high morals.

Your majesty, we are looking forward to your coming to us in the UAE next year. Your brothers and your sons there will be pleased to see you. Most of them know only good of you. In conclusion, peace, God's mercy and blessing be upon you. [applause]

Source: *FBIS-MEA-V–85–216*, 7 Nov. 1985, p. C1.

Document 110

Foreign Ministry Communiqué Announcing the Establishment of Diplomatic Relations between the UAE and the USSR

15 November 1985

As result of the exchanges of cables in December 1971 [at which time messages were exchanged in regard to establishing relations] between the chairman of the Presidium of the USSR Supreme Soviet and the president of the UAE, His Highness Shaykh Zayid ibn Sultan Al Nuhayyan, it was agreed by the governments of the two countries to establish diplomatic relations at the ambassadorial level as of Wednesday, 29 Safar 1406 Hegira, corresponding to 13 November 1985.

His Highness Shaykh Hamdan ibn Zayid, Foreign Ministry under secretary, has made a statement in which he said: In view of the development of the ties of friendship between the governments of the two countries, it was decided during the talks held in Abu Dhabi that the two countries would exchange diplomatic representation at the ambassadorial level. He said: The UAE views the countries of the world with respect and appreciation as long as these countries reciprocate such a view, and participate in its endeavors to establish world peace and achieve prosperity for the international community.

He added: His highness the president has defined the features of our foreign policy since our state won its inde-

pendence. His highness affirmed that our foreign policy is based on firm principles, foremost being the national interest of our people, who are part of the Arab nation and a member of the international family. Among the most important of these principles are the strengthening of world peace and friendship and cooperation with all states and peoples, based on mutual respect and consideration for the legitimate interests of all.

Shaykh Hamdan eclared: In light of these firm principles, we made our decision to establish relations with the Soviet Union. This affirms our nonaligned stands and our neutral policy, which we have always been anxious and are anxious to emphasize on all occasions.

In conclusion Shaykh Hamdan ibn Zayid said: The establishment of relations with the Soviet Union at this time will widen the scope of our international activity and our constant efforts to increase the number of our friends.

Source: *FBIS-MEA-V–85–221*, 15 Nov. 1985, p. C1.

Document 111

Interview with Oman's Sultan Qabus

7 December 1985

Q: The third five-year plan is to be introduced next year. The outline is understood to be in place. It is ready in details, and when exactly will it be implemented? Can you indicate overall expenditure and priorities, and the basis on which oil revenue is set?

A: The third five-year plan has to be announced at the beginning of 1986, but as I've said before, in this (current) five-year plan we've had to advance one or two things, rather than wait until the start of the third plan. The emphasis here will be on education and health, among other things; these two because they will never cease to be important and we must go on meeting the need for these. Communications such as roads, and electricity and water, are also priorities. Roads are the veins of the country, although we have made great strides in road development. There will be plans to see agriculture—and fisheries—get more attention, and industries too.

As for the revenue estimates, the greater part still comes from oil, but one-fifth of our national incomes comes from the non-oil sectors, and that is a good start. One has to take into account declining oil prices. This is expected and therefore we have to be realistic and calculate on $22–23 a barrel, and plan accordingly and then see how things go. We can increase oil production but we don't want to produce more oil than we should for various purposes of maintaining reserves. We are seeking a balance, and therefore to maintain production at 500,000 barrels a day.

Q: The 1985 budget deficit is estimated to be about RO

(Omani riyals) 200 million ($579 million). Can you confirm this? Will Oman be going to the international market for another loan? If so, when, for how much, and what it will be used for?

A: Yes, there is a budget deficit—it is no secret and no shame. In a developing country one sometimes has to do things which entail spending more, and when you compare it with other countries it is a drop in the ocean.

A loan? Over the five-year period maybe. Our finance people will be looking for various ways to cover the deficit, but at the moment our plans are stretched over the five-year period, and then they will see how (the deficit) will be handled. When the plan is completed and officially signed, it will include ways to cover the deficit, and in January or maybe after that they will think how to cover it.

Q: Three sizeable projects have been mentioned which might be brought forward to help maintain the momentum of development; construction of a regional hospital in Suhar, the Salalah sewerage scheme, and a dam near Qurayyat. Could you comment on these and identify other similar areas of important expenditure for the next year?

A: The dam (at Wadi Dayqah) is not an urgent matter, because it will be more a reservoir for drinking water and will not make any difference to the level of the water-table. Where we are always worried is in areas like the Batinah coast where we are concerned with building water re-charge dams. The Suhar Hospital will be looked at as a priority within the Ministry of Health's priorities. Hospitals vary within certain overall priorities, but Suhar is on the list. The Salalah sewerage scheme is only one of a whole series of sewerage problems which has to be looked at very seriously because towns are expanding. Again, it is on the list subject to overall priorities.

Q: In February 1985 the official gazette announced the dissolution of rural councils. Why was this done? Were they the only institutions in Oman directly elected by Omanis?

A: We dissolved the rural councils because we discovered they were not working properly. It is not because local councils were telling the government things it did not want to hear. The municipalities were given the job of looking at the problem and suggesting how best to deal with it.

Elections are part of the tradition of the country in so many forms in villages and towns. People even elect their own shaykhs, where people have a say within their own tribes, and if a shaykh is not a good man the tradition is they find another.

But to hear what people say is healthy. When it is not what the government wants to hear, then either they convince me or we convince them. But if I don't know what the people are happy or unhappy about, then how can I help them. But you know the State Consultative Council (a 55-member body of officials and regional representatives appointed by the government for two-year terms) is a real bridge between the government and the people.

Q: Many people seem surprised by the speed with which Oman established diplomatic relations with the Soviet Union. Can you say why the decision was taken, when embassies will be opened, and how many diplomats there will be on each side?

A: For two years we had contracts with the Soviet Union. They were saying they would like to have diplomatic relations with us and we said we would consider it, our principles being non-interference in each others' affairs. So on that basis we had talks at various levels and we found that they accepted these principles. Then we decided there would be a meeting between our foreign affairs ministers on neutral ground—at the UN in New York. Also we felt it was as good a time as any, with new faces in the Kremlin, to start a new chapter. The numbers will obviously be equal at both embassies and, for the time being, there will not be a resident ambassador because this must be taken slowly.

Q: On the Soviet presence in South Yemen?

A: Our relationship with South Yemen preceeded diplomatic relations with the Soviet Union. We had already had exchanged relations with South Yemen and we have nothing to say on that except they have kept a good neighborly relationship with us. We said (to the Soviet Union) the South Yemenis are your established friends and we don't interfere with their internal affairs and we do not allow other people to interfere with ours. They did so before, but not now.

Q: In your opening speech at the Arab Gulf Cooperation Council summit, it seemed you were putting Iran and Iraq on an equal footing—and not passing judgment on either side. The final communiqué did not seem to be so even-handed. Can you comment on this?

A: What I wanted to point out in my speech was that there was a war going on between two Muslim neighbors and I called on both of them to stop and solve their problems in a peaceful manner—stop this wastage of killing and crippling. My message was not to criticise either, but to make peace. This AGCC communiqué was an AGCC affair but one which had the same meaning as mine—it does not contain a criticism of either side. Oman has always said: 'We will put ourselves at the disposal of both countries if they want to use our good offices'. But I think things should be done quietly and not in the limelight of making a show of it. Better to seek where we can get through to both.

Q: In many countries graduates are coming on to the labor market with good degrees and high expectations, but with few opportunities because of the regional economic downturn. Is this a problem facing Omani graduates? Is the government concerned about a possible problem with unemployed graduates?

A: I am not worried now about the question of future unemployment of Omani graduates. In 20 years' time I don't know, but at this time, no. Our higher education is geared to technicians, scientists, doctors and engineers, and all these have places waiting for them in Oman—not arts degrees at the moment, although I respect these. But the whole policy of education is to guide students and for them to be useful when they come back. There are plenty of places and more, because we still have so many foreigners—so employment is tied up with Omanisation. I have ordered the Omanisation take place in every establishment and that every graduate must be given work which relates to his skills so that an engineer, for example, is not put to work where he cannot use his skills.

Q: On government officials' participation in private business.

A: Mistakes have been made in the past but these have now been corrected and this is now understood by everyone. Our religion does not tell us we can interfere in people's private lives, but I have said to ministers that your business must not interfere with your service to your government and your people, and if there is evidence that this is so then the minister will have no place. But we are not people who go just by rumors, and I like to have proper evidence. If business is above duty then they (the officials) will have no place.

Source: *Middle East Economic Digest*, 14 Dec. 1985, pp. 8, 11, and *Khaleej Times* (Dubayy), 14 Dec. 1985, p. 4, in *FBIS-MEA-V–85-241*, 16 Dec. 1985, pp. C2-C3.

Document 112
Interview with Oman's Sultan Qabus
10 December 1985

[Excerpt] Question: Your Majesty, Oman is an oil-producing country and now is considered to be in a very good financial situation. Why are you seeking loans from abroad?

Qabus ibn Said: The quick development plans needed money because the construction process in Oman is expensive by nature, especially when considering the rapid building of bridges, road construction, and other projects. Today the cost of construction has dropped slightly. Development plans currently follow priorities. In the future we may not need what we had needed previously. Now the national income is improving. Because of that we may not need foreign loans in the future.

Question: The festival atmosphere has projected a lively image of your country to the other countries of the region. It has also opened the eyes of investors in the Gulf region. Are you ready to accept investors in Oman?

Qabus: This depends on the feasibility of the investment. In Oman we do not allow industrial or economic investment unless we are convinced of its guaranteed benefit. We are convinced that without the feasibility of these investments, we would stumble very much. We do not want to stumble because to do so would frustrate both the investor and Omani sides. We also like to feel that the investment is useful to the Omani citizen and his national income. Thus we were cautious about the open-door policy. Now we will not close the doors as long as the policy is cautious and studied.

Question: Your Majesty, some think that you have performed a political and economic miracle over the past 15 years. Are you in a position relaxed enough to devote time to achieving more rapprochement with neighboring countries and other countries of the world?

Qabus: In the past we lived by ourselves for logical reasons. It is useless to have a comprehensive foreign policy without having an internal one, which was what we were avoiding. Our view is that, in order to deal with the world's foreign policies, the Omani internal security, economic, and social development fronts must be strong. Thus past years were completely devoted to internal Omani construction, from which emerges today's image. It is important that we are not against cautious and reasonable rapprochement with other countries, especially when terrorism and acts to undermine security escalate. I believe that we proceed within acceptable balances. The reasons for keeping close to ourselves in the past no longer exist. The internal Omani front is strong and well built. We have a respectable foreign policy. We have reached a good level of rapprochement with other countries.

Question: Your Majesty, the announcement of the establishment of diplomatic relations with the Soviet Union came as a surprise. Is this really a sudden decision to provoke surprise?

Qabus: The establishment of diplomatic relations with the Soviet Union came after initial contacts with the Soviet Union nearly 2 years ago. Both sides had reached similar views during the 2 months prior to the announcement of diplomatic relations. Contacts began at the diplomatic level. I have received Soviet envoys who conveyed to me messages from late Soviet leader Andropov. The Soviets have come to understand that they are dealing with a state which has basic principles in dealing with the world. We consider the Soviet Union a superpower within the international community. However we refuse to allow anyone to interfere in our internal affairs. The Soviet Union understands this. Therefore, there is no justification for not exchanging ambassadors as long as this country understands our demands.

Question: Your Majesty, what hinders the demarcation of borders with the PDRY as part of the current cordial bilateral relations?

Qabus: Relations with the PDRY are good. There is nothing to hinder the demarcation of borders. The delay is that such a mission would include other details which would take time to carry out. This is natural. Contacts with Aden in this regard continue. There is nothing unusual about that.

Question: Your Majesty, why did your foreign minister not visit Iran after his visit to Iraq?

Qabus: The invitation to the Omani foreign minister to visit Iran still exists. It is in fact open. That is what the officials in Tehran said. They said they welcome the visit at any time, but at Iranian request we decided it would be better for some sort of contacts to be made at a lower level before this visit, so that we can find common and acceptable grounds to ensure the objectives of the visit. For this reason, the visit was postponed. Nonetheless the visit may be made at any time.

The minister's visit to Baghdad was designed to explain Gulf views to our brothers in Iraq. After the Muscat summit we wanted to convey an idea about our objective to Baghdad so that it could understand our objective in detail. That is about it. The brothers in Baghdad understood the Gulf point of view.

Question: Your Majesty, is there any possible end to this war? I mean the Gulf war.

Qabus: Let me be honest with you. Nothing concrete concerning the end to this war is yet available. This war has passed through many turning points. During a recent meeting I asked the U.S. President's envoy Richard Murphy if the summit between the two superpowers in Geneva discussed the Gulf war. Murphy replied that the non-concern of the major powers over this war would contribute to putting an end to it. In his view, if certain attention is devoted to the war, many parties would be concerned about it, which would contribute to its expansion and increase its threats. This was Mr. Murphy's view. According to our information, there is a ban on the exportation of arms to Iran and there are serious attempts to prevent it from getting arms from the black market. Of course, this is due to the position of the Iraqi side which expressed its readiness for peace about 2 years ago. The Iraqi position has met with worldwide appreciation. At the same time, Iran is being blamed for continuing the war, according to certain internal calculations. Perhaps, the political regime there launched its revolution as part of certain calculations, including the export of the revolution and the continuation of the war until victory. The response to peace initiatives may lead to internal complications that Iran does not want. As Gulf countries, we want an end to this war, because it exhausts Iraq and Iran altogether and exhausts the region as well. We are looking forward to peace. In the end, Iran is a neighboring country and we want good relations with it. This is in its interest and in our interest. Therefore, we, as Gulf countries, wanted to take the initiative to create favorable grounds to put an end to the war.

I told some EEC foreign ministers and Japanese officials that the continuation of this war would not be useful and that real benefit could be achieved by ending it. The arms traders are benefiting from the war, but what the region would spend during peacetime would be more than what it spends during war. The EEC and Japan have interests with the warring sides. Their interests would increase when the war stops. The EEC and Japan have understood our views. Japan will send its foreign minister to Tehran early next year. This is what I have learned. We believe that the GCC countries together with the EEC countries can do something. However, there is nothing concrete now. Of course, under the circumstances of this war, which has lasted several years, we do not expect the two warring sides to sit at the negotiating table at the present time. We hope that military operations will stop and that the flames of war will be extinguished gradually until the war vanishes completely. Then, there will be favorable circumstances to understand the well-established fact that Iran, like the rest of the Gulf countries and Iraq, is situated in this region and that its situation in the region should be a basis for good and equal relations.

Question: Your Majesty, you discussed the issue of the Gulf war with the U.S. envoy. Did you discuss the Middle East issue with him?

Qabus: Yes I did. My point of view was that the United States should be flexible concerning Arab rights. If Israel is strengthening itself by its alliance and friendship with the United States, there are many Arab sides that have friendly relations with other superpowers. What I want to say here is that the genuine Palestinians should receive more care. By this I mean those who are suffering from hardships due to the Israeli occupation. I told U.S. envoy Murphy that the atmosphere of international reconciliation might encourage an end to this problem. Murphy presented his viewpoint and left for the confrontation countries to complete his tour. Recently, I heard that the U.S. envoy had achieved what was considered an encouraging position. This was reported by the news agencies. We believe that the current phase is, for the Arab world, a phase through which we should encourage peace efforts.

Question: Your Majesty, while you are talking about peace efforts, how do you view the Arab-Israeli conflict?

Qabus: I have said that care should be provided to the Palestinian individuals who are suffering from the occupation. In my view, they have a right to receive this care. It has been noticed here that the issue of Palestine is a paper over which various Arab regimes argue, while the Palestinians suffer from occupation and remain separate from the solution to the tragedy. Concerning the PLO, I believe that there are numerous sides which are dealing with the tragedy. Each is dealing with the tragedy from an angle that is far from reducing the pain of occupation. I believe that the recent Jordanian-Palestinian agreement is an excellent formula to end this conflict, that is, if the purpose is to restore the occupied territories of 1967 and to implement the peace formula approved internationally. Such an agreement can bear fruit. What concerns me personally about the end of this conflict are the Palestinian individuals in the occupied territories, who are far from an atmosphere which would end the Arab-Israeli conflict, even if Palestinian individuals realize what things should be like.

Question: Your Majesty, what about the restoration of relations with Egypt. There are those who believe that there should be Arab unanimity on restoring diplomatic relations with Egypt?

Qabus: Boycotting Egypt was not done with unanimity. It was a proposal and not a decision. Thus, we and other Arab countries did not boycott Egypt because of a political view beneficial to us which was later proven to be a sound view. Those who believe there should be Arab unanimity concerning Egypt's return may have intended to find an excuse. The truth is, because of political balances, they do not want to anger Arab countries that do not wish to restore diplomatic relations with Egypt or who might believe in the severance of those relations. Jordan boycotted Egypt but found that it should restore its diplomatic relations with Egypt. Those relations were restored without any need for Arab unanimity.

Question: Your Majesty, do you believe that it is necessary to restore diplomatic relations with Egypt?

Qabus: Relations with Egypt have not stopped. They have intensified, even in the atmosphere of the severance of diplomatic relations. The Arab people have not boycotted Egypt, particularly here in the Gulf countries where the boycott is official in form only. There are those who boycotted Egypt diplomatically. This boycott has caused a psychological burden on the Egyptian political administration. While Egypt is doing much for the Arab world, including readying its manpower to serve the issues of peace and war, it is still being boycotted diplomatically. This raises questions by the Egyptian people before the political administration. The people of Egypt are disturbed by this boycott, even if its political administration is not concerned with restoring diplomatic relations. Egypt's cooperation with the people of the Arab world eliminated the effect of the boycott. From my point of view, relations should be restored, because the Egyptian people feel hurt by the continuation of the boycott.

Question: Your Majesty, a question is asked by many people, not by me alone. Why hasn't an heir to the throne of the Sultanate been declared?

Qabus: According to the traditions of the Omani ruling family the post of heir apparent does not exist. When there is a need and when the qualified person appears, then the post of heir apparent will be necessary. Yes, I know that there are questions about this, but they are non-Omani questions. These questions are raised, especially by those who do not know the norms to which the ruling family here has been adhering.

Question: Your Majesty, some people think that the threats to navigation through the Strait of Hormuz have drawn attention to the Omani waters. Has the use of Omani waters been discussed by the GCC countries, so that these countries could abandon the use of the Strait of Hormuz in navigation?

Qabus: We did not discuss the matter during the Muscat summit, but the leaders might have discussed it individually. I know nothing about this matter.

Question: Your Majesty, in an interview, you affirmed that Iran would not close the strait due to certain difficulties. You were right in your assessment. How do you view the future situation in this vital and strategic strait?

Qabus: It is difficult for Iran to close the strait because that would require certain military and naval capabilities. Moreover, the countries using the strait have fleets in international Gulf waters. These countries would not permit

any harm to their trade. Yes, Iran can create tension in the strait, but the situation can be dealt with. I still affirm that it is difficult for Iran to close the Strait of Hormuz. I stick to my previous position. We are close to the strait and we know what is happening around it.

Question: Your Majesty, there has been much talk recently about terrorist operations. Some of these operations were directed against Egypt itself. What is the objective of that?

Qabus: There is no doubt that some want to create troubles and tension in Egypt due to the role played by the Egyptian president and due to the respected and appreciated role played by Egypt. To jeopardize this role they are causing disturbances in the internal Egyptian front. Some elements have been created to harm the Arab positions both internally and internationally. The Egyptian position was decisive in fighting against terrorism. Without this decisiveness we would give terrorists the chance to repeat their acts.

Source: *Al-Siyassah* (Kuwait), 10 Dec. 1985, as translated in *FBIS-MEA-V–85–239*, 12 Dec. 1985, pp. C1-C4.

Document 113

GCC Secretary General Abdallah Yaqub Bisharah Lecture Entitled "The Arab Gulf and the Two Superpowers," Delivered at the Second Seminar for GCC Diplomats on the Question of "Gulf Cooperation" Held at the Academy of Diplomatic Studies at the Saudi Foreign Ministry in Riyadh

24 January 1986

I will confine my words to discussing the attitudes of both the Soviet Union and the United States toward the GCC since its establishment in May 1981 and up to this day. I will not deal with the historical stands of the two countries toward the Gulf states because it is necessary, in view of our short time, to concentrate on one aspect of the subject so that the benefit will be greater.

The GCC and The Soviet Union

We cannot ignore the fact that the Soviet Union is a slow-moving superpower with its own international calculations or that its decision-making is complex and governed by several considerations, the most important of which is to avoid adventures and rashness. It would be correct to say that the Soviet Union is a conservative state whose actions and behavior are predictable; it does not take rash steps in order to obtain regional or international gains. It has its own calculations, and its strategy is tied to its all-embracing view.

However, this should not exempt it from criticism for being slow and hesitant in adopting stands. Therefore, it is our right to "blame" the Soviet Union for its "cool and in-different" attitude toward the GCC. The first official comment I heard from the Soviet leaders on the GCC was during an official meeting between the Kuwait deputy prime minister and foreign minister, Shaykh Sabah al-Ahmad al-Jabir, and the Soviet foreign minister, Gromyko in Moscow.

In April 1981, about 1 month before the official proclamation of the GCC, Shaykh Sabah al-Ahmad explained the objective behind the establishment of the GCC. Gromyko's response to this explanation was typical and predictable. He said that the Soviet Union knows nothing about the GCC and its philosophies. But, he added, the Soviet Union will be observing it and will declare its support for it. I was present at the meeting as a member of the Kuwaiti delegation. I was not surprised by this attitude since Soviet policy toward the GCC is influenced by traditional and inherited views—that this region includes Western strategic, economic, and political interests, and confrontation with the Western countries in the region is not part of Soviet plans. Although in the fifties and sixties Moscow was involved in a clash over the Middle East with Western countries, and particularly the United States, it was pursuing a different course in the Gulf that avoided a direct clash and mainly lent support to the nationalist forces resisting foreign influence.

During his visit to India in December 1980 Brezhnev announced a five-point peace initiative calling for neutralizing the region, guaranteeing its safety and security, and pledging not to attack the Gulf oil installations or shipping routes. In a speech before the Indian parliament he cited "Western allegations" about Soviet threats to the strategic oil-producing area.

The Soviet Union has put forth many proposals about neutralizing Latin America, Europe, or Africa. The objective of these initiatives is to score political propaganda points among these peoples and to portray the Soviet Union as their natural ally in their quest for liberation from Western or foreign influence.

Also, these principles cost the Soviet Union nothing as it has no traditional position in the region and the fleets to which Brezhnev's principle refers are Western, there for the purpose of defending Western interests and containing Soviet influence in the Indian Ocean or the Arabian Sea.

The Soviet Union's policy toward the GCC countries is to encourage the national trend toward self-reliance, keep the region away from the race for spheres of influence, and to neutralize it. This is the objective but the method has been traditionally futile; relying on a policy of caution, circumspection, and preservation; fearing confrontation, but not hesitating to applaud and openly support nationalist sentiments.

Following the establishment of the GCC and the crystallization of its foreign policy, on the basis of the stands defined by their majesties and highnesses the GCC leaders, and contained in the council's statements and documents, the Soviet Union did not seek to get acquainted with the new situation in the Gulf. Rather it was content with the traditional Russian method of watching from a distance with its traditional suspicious view. During the first 2 years of the GCC's establishment, the Soviet Union was influenced by its relationship with South Yemen and the dispute between Aden and Muscat and its desire to remain distant from Arab regional sensitivities.

Therefore, during the period from the GCC's establishment to 1984 I did not detect any direct interest by Moscow in the GCC or its course. I am not sure whether during that period the Soviet Union was seriously studying the experiment through its embassies in the area or the Arab capitals. It was content with keeping its distance and silence.

Also the Soviet Union, which portrays itself and is portrayed by Third World communist parties as the natural ally of the Third World peoples, is very sensitive to the attitudes of the GCC states toward the Soviet presence in Afghanistan.

There are certain Arab countries that support the Soviet presence in Afghanistan and have no reservations about it. Moscow and its ambassador get upset with the GCC countries' declared stands on this subject. The Soviet UN representative raised this point with me personally. I think he imagines that the attitude of the GCC countries is not spontaneous, stemming from certain beliefs and interaction with the Afghan people, but rather that this attitude is not entirely free of Western influence aimed at slandering the Soviet Union.

I believe that in this regard the Soviet Union did not seek to understand the causes of the attitude of the GCC countries and, instead, continued to ignore the matter and remained indifferent to its implications.

At a meeting between the Soviet ambassador to Kuwait and myself in 1984, the ambassador raised several points regarding the GCC. He did not show, however, that Moscow has ceased to be the captive of its own imagination. It appeared to me that the ambassador was surprised by the extent of the GCC's diplomatic flexibility when I suggested holding a dialogue with the GCC at any time or in any institute he suggested. But I have not heard from him since.

The Soviet Union attaches great importance to exchanging diplomatic representatives with the world's countries as it is impelled by the race with the United States to establish a diplomatic presence in all world capitals, especially in capitals of countries that have no historical ties with Moscow such as the Gulf states. Also, the Soviet Union interprets Muscat's and Abu Dhabi's decisions [to establish relations with the USSR] differently from the GCC countries, which see in them no more than subjective decisions beneficial to both sides.

Although the establishment of diplomatic ties with the Soviet Union elicited cautious praise from its press for the Muscat summit resolutions, which *Pravda* described as demonstrating these countries' resolve to preserve their independence and security based on self-reliance, the view of doubt and suspicion toward the council is still the stronger factor in evaluating the Soviet Union's policy toward the GCC countries. Obviously Soviet policy toward the GCC will not change and will continue to be based on the lack of conviction and belief in the interpretations and stands of the GCC countries regarding defense cooperation. Moscow believes that it has painful historical experiences with military blocs, particularly the Western countries' blocs, during the past two centuries, and that the Warsaw Pact bloc is defensive for the purpose of repelling what the Soviets term imperialist plots that continue to be hatched against the Soviet Union.

It is difficult to separate this wound from which Moscow is suffering from its view toward the GCC.

Moscow's Current Policy

Moscow's current policy toward the Gulf states can be summed up as follows:

1. Seeking to develop relations between Moscow and the GCC countries in all fields, provided that this effort remains confined to the bilateral framework.

2. Intensifying the Soviet diplomatic and economic presence without any change in the basic and fundamental attitude toward the GCC.

3. Seeking to contain the Western presence through supporting nationalist sentiments in the GCC countries, by isolating the area from the race between the big powers and by [fostering] self-reliance in ensuring stability and security. In this regard, to achieve its objective the Soviet Union depends on historical developments, a rise in national consciousness, and a serious inclination toward asserting national sovereignty and independence. Its method in the area is not much different from that which it has followed in other parts of the world, that is, to put the United States and the Western countries in a defensive position and to embarrass them.

It can be said that in this regard the Soviet Union has benefited and is still benefiting from the U.S. attitude toward the Palestine problem and from its attempts to exploit the negative feelings toward the United States in order to improve its own image and to pose as sympathizing with such feelings. This is evident in the activities of Soviet journalists and visitors in the area who have intensified their presence and journalistic meetings to an extraordinary level.

In my view Soviet policy toward the GCC countries, despite its recent development, is suffering from two basic elements. The first, and the more important, is that the GCC with its countries and institutions is a council for development and not change, a council that goes along with the march of history but which is not a mechanism for storms and hurricanes; it seeks adherence to heritage and to maintain the balance of power. It is a council for change through persuasion and not violence, a council in which there is no room for ideologies, philosophies, or theories.

The Soviet Union is not a state that stands for status quo. If it wants to pursue its philosophies, then neither the economic, nor the social, nor the political system in the GCC countries—to say nothing of the magnanimous Islamic religion—can accept the trends of this philosophy. Therefore, the GCC's pulse is not in rhythm with the Soviet pulse.

The second element is that, according to my impressions, the Soviet Union has not realized the strength of the GCC states' insistence on preserving their independence and ensuring their sovereignty and pursuing a foreign policy stemming from their beliefs. The Soviet Union's mistake is that it imagines that the GCC countries can be influenced by the stands of other countries, including the United States. This is evident in the Soviet Union's attitude toward the GCC and its belief that the GCC is a military alliance. This is probably due to the recent nature of contacts between the Soviet Union and the Gulf states as well as due to the justifiable historical Russian suspicion of the Western countries.

To sum up, the Soviet Union is not convinced of the GCC's pronouncements that the security of the area is the responsibility of its countries and that the Gulf states insist on keeping the area away from the big powers' presence. The Soviet Union interprets this as a shout against it although it has no bases and fleets in the area. The Soviet attitude toward the GCC will remain cautious and cool while Moscow will continue to seek to develop relations bilaterally.

The United States and the GCC

The GCC was established while Reagan's philosophy of opposing the Soviet Union, confronting it, and containing its influence was dominating the White House.

It is natural for this philosophy not to ignore the unique position of the GCC countries where 41 percent of the world's oil reserves exist. This percentage increases to 55 percent if we include Iraq and Iran in these calculations.

Also, the GCC came into being as the Iraq-Iran war was raging and the U.S. wounds incurred in the Iranian revolution were still sore and painful.

For this reason the U.S. attitude toward the GCC is to a large extent influenced by these two factors: chasing Soviet influence and infiltrating its legitimate positions such as in Eastern Europe, and the painful wounds caused by the Iranian revolution.

The United States understands the GCC philosophy which, as I have already said, does not agree with the Soviet trend and which rejects the Soviet dialectic about history, heritage, and religion. It also realizes that the GCC is a body that rejects ideologies and is a power that preserves the status quo and is opposed to political and partisan piracy and to change based on violence.

The United States also benefited from historical and traditional ties and continuous dialogue with the GCC countries on an individual basis. It also benefited from the cultural and academic bridges and human contacts between the GCC countries and both Europe and America.

It was with such a credit that the United States came to the GCC—giving support, asking questions, and showing openmindedness. The GCC has aroused its instinct of asking questions about the council, its bodies, its philosophy, and its objectives. While the Soviet Union showed a rigid reservation toward military cooperation among the member-states, the United States showed an interest in knowing more about the development of the GCC's work in all spheres.

The United States also submitted to the new reality by agreeing to deal with the GCC as an organization and an entity. This is evident in the annual meetings held in New York between the U.S. secretary of state and the GCC foreign ministers and secretary general during which the GCC's policy on world issues is discussed.

More important still is the fact that the United States acknowledges the GCC's legitimacy and its logic of self-reliance in preserving the security and stability of its member-states. It did not doubt these intentions; indeed, it felt that the logic of responsibilities makes it incumbent on the GCC countries to preserve their stability and security. It also felt that the sources of energy that its allies in Europe need can be protected and safeguarded only with the approval of the legitimate owners of these resources.

Therefore, the assertion of the policy of nonalignment, self-reliance, and building up intrinsic power is not only, in the final analysis, intended to serve the countries of the area and to achieve only their objectives, but also to secure and preserve the oil resources, keep away saboteurs, and safeguard resources in the interest of the world economy and for the benefit of association between the world's peoples. This is an objective that the world community is seeking to achieve.

This explains the U.S. attitude toward the GCC. To a large extent it is close to the GCC's philosophy of preserving the area and its security. However, the U.S. attitude toward the Palestine problem, its alignment with Israel, as well as its adoption of stands that do not accord with the national feelings in the GCC countries have affected its credibility in the Gulf and in the Arab world. It has also raised many questions about the integrity of its behavior.

Although the United States may have understood the GCC trend, may have gotten acquainted with it, and supported it, it failed to realize the strength of the GCC's links with Arab problems.

The Soviet Union did not hesitate to exploit this issue in order to embarrass Washington and to portray it as a power hostile to national feelings both in the Arab world and internationally.

The second and no less important factor is that the United States imagines that harmony can be created between the U.S. military presence in the Indian Ocean and the GCC's trends which express the true feelings of the area's people.

If the Soviet Union did not realize the strength of the GCC countries' independent spirit, the United States failed to realize the degree of seriousness about self-reliance and rejecting fleets in Gulf waters.

The Attitude of the Two Powers Toward Keeping the Gulf Away from Influence by Major Powers

Let us see how far the two superpowers respected the GCC resolutions to keep the area out of the race for spheres of influence. I believe that both sides appreciate the GCC countries' resolve to cooperate in preserving their security and stability by depending on their intrinsic power.

Both the Soviet Union and the United States realize that the GCC countries are capable of preserving and have resolved to preserve their security without resorting to foreign assistance. I have personally felt that this policy is appreciated. This question is different from that of a naval presence in areas near the Gulf where the two superpowers maintain tremendous fleets in their race for a military presence in the world's regions.

As a superpower the Soviet Union cannot withdraw from international waters simply because the United States wants it to do so. Nor can the United States turn its back on a Soviet military presence in new areas which it believes are traditional areas for Western fleets. Also, both powers are aware of the region's importance for the world economy as well as its strategic importance geographically and politically. For this reason, each side is convinced that the other side wants to consolidate its position, regardless of the feelings of the peoples of the area. This is contrary to the GCC's policies.

I would like to say that the emergence of the GCC with its tenets and trends has pulled the rug from under the U.S. allegation that there is a vacuum in the strategically, politically, and economically important Gulf region, that there is in a Gulf wealth without owners, or that there is a power vacuum that needs to be filled.

What has been proved is that there is an entity that is determined to deal collectively with security and defense matters and to tackle problems with a spirit of responsibility reflecting the Gulf peoples' realization of the characteristics of their region.

If defense cooperation caused the Soviets to imagine that the GCC has become a bloc influenced by the United States, the reality confirms that this cooperation has pulled the rug from under this and done away with Washington's ideas about volunteering, protecting, and keeping away the shadow of the red bear.

In my view, the Soviets have misread the GCC's policy of self-reliance, the policy that has "nullified" the U.S. pretext and given the GCC countries a great deal of international support and backing in keeping the area free of international influence.

The policy has also cut down to size the room for U.S. diplomatic maneuvering which, had it not been for the principle of self-reliance, security cooperation between the GCC countries, and the great efforts by the GCC to shoulder its responsibilities, would have led to the Gulf being filled with battleships and torpedo boats.

If the GCC has taken the Gulf out of the U.S. strategic

belt and its calculations, it gave no room for the Soviet Union to roam the Gulf waters with its fleets.

This is not only because it has done away with the idea of a vacuum, or because it has strongly resisted the policy of polarization and refused the easy way out and depended on the Third World's understanding of its difficult choice, but because it has sought to export the GCC's experiment outside the Gulf in the hope that it will be an example to be emulated in resisting the major powers' inducements inside the Arab world.

Source: *FBIS-MEA-V–86–030*, 13 Feb. 1986, pp. C1-C4.

Document 114

GCC Ministerial Council: Eighteenth Session Statement

3 March 1986

In the name of God, the compassionate, the merciful. The Ministerial Council held its 18th session in Riyadh at the General Secretariat headquarters in Riyadh from 1 to 3 March 1986, under the chairmanship of Yusuf al-Alawi Abdallah, Omani minister of state for foreign affairs.

The council reviewed the dangerous situation in the region in view of Iran's occupation of parts of Iraqi territory which is a violation of international charters and principles of good neighborliness and an assault against Iraq's sovereignty and the integrity of its territories. The council condemns this occupation and calls on Iran to immediately withdraw its forces to the international borders.

The council also reviewed Iran's threats against the GCC states, which leads to the expansion of the area of conflict. The GCC states have always abided by relations of good neighborliness based on mutual respect and non-intervention in the internal affairs of others. However, the Iranian threats have created a tense atmosphere. Thus, the council calls upon Iran to stop its threats which contribute to disturbing the security and stability of the region.

The council recalls the decisions their majesties and highnesses adopted during the previous sessions of the Supreme Council which affirm that maintaining the security and stability of the member countries is a collective responsibility of all countries inspired by the principles of the statutes. While recalling in particular the summit's decision to form the Peninsula Shield [Dira al-Jazirah] force and the duties assigned to it, the council affirms that the force is ready to move to any site which might be affected by the recent developments. The chiefs of staff will meet to adopt the necessary measures to face the possible threats. On the political level, the council decided to intensify its contacts with the fraternal Arab countries and all of the world countries to reach an Arab and international stand that would

contribute toward keeping the region away from the threats of conflict and removing tension from it.

The council affirms the member countries' adherence to the policy laid down by their majesties and highnesses to maintain the region's neutrality, resisting any action that might involve the Gulf in international conflict, and for commitment to peaceful coexistence among all of the region's countries, noninterference in the internal affairs of others, and the resolution of problems through peaceful means. The council also reiterates support for Iraq's acceptance of efforts to reach a peaceful settlement to the war going on between it and Iran. It calls on Iran to abide by the UN resolution and efforts by the ICO, the Nonaligned Movement, and other countries to reach a peaceful settlement to the problems between the two countries.

The council listened to a report prepared by the Secretariat on the implementation of the Supreme Council's economic decisions, took note of the minutes of meetings of a number of ministerial committees which met in the framework of the GCC and adopted the appropriate decisions on them.

The council discussed the contacts being made with international economic groups and decided to reactivate them to serve the GCC countries' interests.

Source: *FBIS-MEA-V–86–042*, 4 March 1986, p. C1.

Document 115

Interview with Shaykh Muhammad ibn Mubarak Al-Khalifah, Foreign Minister of Bahrain

5 March 1986

[Excerpts] Question: Throughout last week Bahrain was the center of activity. It was visited by the Algerian foreign minister and the Iranian foreign under secretary. What was the nature of these two visits?

Answer: Algerian Foreign Minister Ahmad Talib Ibrahimi's visit was within the framework of the continuing coordination between the state of Bahrain and the Arab brothers. Algeria has been and is still trying to play a role in ending this [Iraq-Iran] war. It is continuing to do so. The visit was aimed at learning the views of Bahrain and the Gulf countries regarding the recent developments. Bahrain had expressed its great concern over the recent escalation and the offensive on the territory of sisterly Iraq. The expansion of the war has given it a new dimension; its purpose is to affect shipping and the security situation in the area. For this reason we hope that the Algerian envoy's visit will give him a clearer view of the situation so that Algeria will continue with its good offices.

With regard to the Iranian envoy's visit, it was for a specific purpose. He has been sent by three countries—Libya,

Algeria, and Iran—to discuss an oil matter related to oil prices. They suggest holding a meeting in Geneva on 6 April between the OPEC countries and oil-producing countries outside OPEC, to lay down a new strategy to combat the deterioration in oil prices. With regard to the Iranian stand on the war, no change has been observed in it.

Question: Do we understand from this that you did not discuss the question of the war and the recent Iranian offensive with the Iranian envoy?

Answer: We certainly discussed the matter with him. We cannot ignore a vital and basic issue. We do not think that the energy crisis takes precedence over the issues of the Iraq-Iran war, which is the greatest threat facing the area. There is no doubt that the energy crisis is serious, but the war is the biggest of all the crises in the area. We believe that resolving this problem is a matter that concerns the Gulf states more than anybody else, whereas the question of oil is an international matter concerning both producing and consumer countries as well as other countries. Therefore, the Gulf states and the Arab and Islamic states should combine efforts in order to resolve the question of the war.

Question: Certain observers have linked the recent Iranian military move to the oil question. What is your view on this matter?

Answer: I do not think that this issue has anything to do with the question of the war. The war has been going on for 6 years, while the question of oil is a different matter. Although the question of oil concerns the sovereignty of each country separately, coordination on this matter is in the interest of all and calls for joining efforts and unifying views. The reasons for and the circumstances of the war are quite a different matter.

Question: What was the GCC countries' response to the Iranian reassurances given to them regarding the war?

Answer: Our stand is clear and declared. We are against the war and are seeking to end it. We do not accept aggression against the Iraqi borders. Iraq is an Arab country, and everybody is committed to an Arab stand when any Arab country is the target of aggression. We wish that Iran would revise its attitude of resolving disputes by force and instead resort to solving them through negotiations among brothers. We do not think that it is in the interest of Iraq or Iran or the countries of the area for the war to continue. We all are the losers, and the common enemy is the only winner. We have always urged that the war should end and that negotiations and a cease-fire should begin. We call for respect for international borders and for withdrawal. We do not wish the war to expand; rather we want to see it end. We have declared these principles time and time again at our meetings. I believe that Iran is aware of this stand, as are the other countries of the world. We are willing to help at any moment and have sent out delegations for this purpose.

Source: *Al-Majallah* (London), 5–11 March 1986, p. 17, as translated in *FBIS-MEA-V–86–047*, 11 March 1986, p. C1.

Document 116

Interview with GCC Secretary General Bisharah
21 March 1986

[Question] Mr. Secretary General, we follow continuously the developments of the war between Iraq and Iran and the dangers which these developments have brought, especially after the Iranian attack on the Al-Faw region where fierce battles are raging now. Is it possible to consider that your current visit to Morocco is linked with these developments?

[Bisharah] I would like to say how happy I am to be leading a delegation of the general secretariat of the GCC on a visit to Morocco at the generous invitation of the Moroccan Government. Frankly, it was by chance that the recent developments in the Gulf region coincided with my visit to sister Morocco. I did not come here because of these developments; rather, we are here in response to a generous invitation. [*words indistinct*] I found it an occasion for putting the officials of the sister Moroccan Government in the picture regarding the nature of the developments witnessed in the Gulf lately. I clarified the situation during my talks with the officials, and I acquainted the Moroccan officials with the nature of these developments and their dangers. I also acquainted them with the measures taken by the GCC countries to confront these developments. It pleases me to say we are proud and happy and appreciate the attitude of Morocco toward these developments, the attitude which was clarified by His Majesty King Hassan II during his press conference.

[Question] Yes, we learned that some newspapers in the United Arab Emirates have called for the holding of an Arab-Islamic summit to hear the views of Iraq and Iran and draw up a plan to end the war between the two countries. Has the GCC studied a proposal of this kind?

[Bisharah] In the GCC we believe that diplomatic action should not be confined to one channel; rather, it should be diversified and should reach the widest scope, benefiting from every channel. I cannot say whether such a proposal was studied in detail. What was studied in light of the latest developments is how to find a means of dealing with the latest events. We have not excluded any channel possible of benefiting us, be it bilateral relations, or traditional diplomatic means. We must not hesitate to benefit from any possible channel in order to contain the effects of the Iraqi-Iranian war and to deal with it. Let it be clear that the GCC ministerial council has not studied this issue in detail [*words indistinct*]; rather, it studied the possibility of using all the channels in order to deal with the latest developments.

[Question] Mr. Secretary General, how much understanding, cohesion and coordination is there among the GCC members for confronting future developments in the region, especially since the dangers of the war have become an open threat to Kuwait, a neighbor of Iraq. We notice that the Iranian Navy is carrying out piratical operations against Kuwaiti merchant ships in the Gulf.

[Bisharah] I say to you frankly that the Gulf countries are facing a situation which is not ordinary; an unusual situation should be dealt with by unusual means. Therefore, security is the top priority now in the coordination among the members. They have adopted coordinated, protective measures to deal with the latest developments. Also, they took coordinated steps in the diplomatic context. The GCC members strive for solving problems through peaceful means [*words indistinct*] and aim to live in peace and respect charters, including international law and the UN Charter. They also resort to diplomacy in its capacity as an effective way of dealing with problems. Inevitably, the GCC has escalated its diplomatic contacts. It is possible to say that the GCC members up to now have dealt wisely with the latest developments [*words indistinct*] and with effective methods which for the past 2 weeks have facilitated the reduction of tension. We have great trust in our good intentions, credibility and the contacts we have achieved throughout the world.

In short, there is coordination on the latest developments. We hope, God willing, that the Gulf region will witness stability and calm, which will deliver it from danger and the specter of foreign intervention—which would not be useful to any of us. Thank you.

Source: *FBIS-MEA-V–86–057*, 25 March 1986, pp. A3-A4.

Document 117

Interview with GCC Secretary General Bisharah
9 April 1986

[Jibril] During your tour of Morocco and Algeria you said that the purpose of the visit was to hold consultations and explain developments in the Arab Gulf region. We would like to know exactly what is the purpose of the consultations and what has this to do with the situation in the Gulf region?

[Bisharah] The purpose of the visit was to acquaint officials in Morocco and Algeria with the developments in the situation in our area and the implications and dangers of these developments, particularly with regard to security, and their effect on the Arab world and Arab solidarity. The other purpose of the visit was to acquaint officials of both countries with the GCC experiment and explain its features and dimensions. This is because we would like, at every possible opportunity, to explain this experiment on both the official and popular levels. In fact we have drawn great inspiration from the Arab Maghreb, particularly regarding the idea of regional cooperation and its legitimacy and usefulness.

[Jibril] But the Arab Maghreb's experiment is still theoretical and has not yet materialized.

[Bisharah] We have benefited from the Arab Maghreb experiment even in its theoretical framework. I believe that it would be useful for the Arab world to know about our experiment, just as it is useful for Arab officials to know about the GCC experiment.

[Jibril] In the quest for a formula for joint Arab action there are those who believe that regional groupings hinder and frustrate joint Arab endeavors. What is your comment on this belief?

[Bisharah] Wisdom is not a monopoly. I believe that our experiment is stronger than any other experiment; it is now 5 years old. It is very important that the Arab world know about this experiment and that we subject ourselves to researchers and analysts in order to identify the shortcomings and therefore be able to overcome them and attain a unified Arab stand. We do not take lightly views that differ from ours; rather we believe that discussion of this experiment is healthy and useful. We will benefit from discussion and dialogue because we will listen with an open mind. We are aware of our Arab responsibility and are working to achieve harmony with our Arab principles.

[Jibril] During your contacts with officials in Algeria and Morocco did you discuss the idea of regional dealings between the GCC and the Arab Maghreb countries?

[Bisharah] We are operating within the Arab framework; we do not wish to appear to be a group separate from the Arabs. We are operating within the framework of the Arab League and as a part of it.

[Jibril] But there is coordination among the GCC states on fundamental Arab issues.

[Bisharah] Naturally there is coordination but we do not accept acting like a bloc within the Arab framework.

[Jibril] But this is what the others feel in this regard.

[Bisharah] I believe that we do not act as a bloc. I also believe that our role and responsibilities in the Arab world have increased and widened because in the GCC we have set as our target bringing the Arabs together and eliminating tension between the Arab countries. Since the GCC was established its member states have never hesitated to work for the achievement of a unified Arab framework for Arab relations. This is emphasized in the statements issued by our meetings and is one of our main principles. I believe that we have achieved positive and useful results in this regard.

[Jibril] The question of the Iraq-Iran war was discussed during your contacts with officials in Morocco and Algeria. In your opinion, what must the two countries do to stop the war?

[Bisharah] We have sought and are still seeking to acquaint the Arab countries in a fraternal and amicable manner with the dangers threatening the area. These dangers have escalated following the Iranian occupation of parts of Iraqi territory. Because of this occupation there have been serious developments in the area that could lead to the expansion of war. The Arab world must be made aware of the dangers threatening Arab security and peace. We therefore believe in the need for Arab solidarity in order to repel the dangers threatening any Arab area. We in the GCC are not asking for anything beyond what is possible within the Arab capabilities. We do not think that any Arab country should turn its back on the Arab security requirements when such security is clearly threatened. We are seeking in a fraternal manner to explain these dangers. As far as our area is concerned we are aware of our responsibilities and realize that we should act with prudence and moderation and should not involve the area in risks that could bring us endless problems.

[Jibril] When discussing the question of Gulf security did you propose military aid to the Gulf states from the Arab Maghreb countries?

[Bisharah] We did not discuss this subject at all.

[Jibril] I mean during your current tour.

[Bisharah] We did not discuss this subject at all. All that we explained to Moroccan and Algerian officials was the nature of the dangers the area is experiencing.

[Jibril] Therefore no military matters were discussed.

[Bisharah] Absolutely not.

[Jibril] On several occasions the Gulf states have mediated between Algeria and Morocco regarding the Sahara problem. It was always said in Morocco that so far no "comprehensive mediation" had been proposed. Did you try during your visit to Algeria and Morocco to explore the possibility of the GCC mediating as a group in order to resolve the dispute?

[Bisharah] All the discussions held during this tour focused on developments in the Gulf region and the effect of these developments on the Arab situation. We did not discuss other subjects. As I have already said, we in the Gulf have a goodwill message and seek to achieve a minimum [sic] Arab solidarity. Within this context several contacts have been held with the Arab capitals aimed at resolving problems. We in the Gulf have access to every Arab capital. Therefore we have the responsibility of making efforts with every Arab country to find Arab common ground. There is nothing further I can say in this regard.

[Jibril] During your tour of Morocco and Algeria you met with some officials in the economic sectors. Do we gather from this that you intend to establish economic relations between the GCC and the Arab Maghreb countries as a group, beyond the framework of bilateral cooperation?

[Bisharah] We did not discuss this subject. We discussed the economic situation in general. We did not discuss the establishment of joint economic projects or other specific things. We spoke about generalities and the general framework of economic cooperation between the Arab countries and the need to continue with the existing joint projects without these being affected by political differences.

Source: *Al-Majallah* (London), 9–15 April 1986, as translated in *FBIS-MEA-V–86–075*, 18 April 1986, pp. C1-C2.

Document 118

Government of Bahrain Statement on Fasht al-Dibal Dispute

29 April 1986

The Government of Bahrain expresses its regret at the action carried out by a Qatari military force against Bahraini territory and the detention of unarmed civilian workers. The Government of Bahrain considers this action a departure from the principles of good neighborliness on which the GCC is based. Bahrain also expresses its great appreciation to His Majesty King Fahd ibn Abd al-Aziz and the Government of fraternal Saudi Arabia for their good efforts to bring the parties together, contain the crisis, and restore things to normal.

Bahrain affirms its support, blessing, and total responsiveness to these efforts.

Bahrain also appreciates the positive stands of their majesties and highnesses the leaders of the GCC countries for their sympathy with Bahrain's stand, which is aimed at self-control, the preservation of the interests of the two fraternal peoples of Bahrain and Qatar, and the avoidance of violence; and their persevering quest to preserve the rights of the member countries to complete sovereignty over their territories, and the security and peace of their sons.

Source: *FBIS-MEA-V–86–083*, 30 April 1986, p. C1.

Document 119

GCC Secretariat Statement on the Resolution of the Fasht al-Dibal Dispute between Bahrain and Qatar

25 May 1986

In accordance with the agreement reached between the State of Qatar and the State of Bahrain to restore the status quo ante—an agreement that has been reached through the good and generous efforts of His Majesty King Fahd ibn Abd al-Aziz of the Kingdom of Saudi Arabia and thanks to the anxiousness of their majesties and highnesses the leaders of the GCC states to consolidate the march of cohesion and common destiny, and in response to the good intentioned guidance in this blessed month [of Ramadan]—the supervision and monitoring commission which comprises [members from] the GCC Secretariat, the Kingdom of Saudi Arabia, the State of Kuwait, the Sultanate of Oman, and the UAE, and is headed by Major General Saad al-Muwayni, has left for both Qatar and Bahrain to begin implementing the task with which it has been charged. The commission immediately began its work as of Sunday 17 Ramadan 1406 Hegira corresponding to 25 May 1986. The

GCC Secretariat hopes that the supervision and monitoring commission will complete its work at the earliest time possible and asks Almighty God to make its efforts successful.

Source: *FBIS-MEA-V–86–100*, 27 May 1986, p. C1.

Document 120

Government of Qatar Statement of Fasht al-Dibal Dispute

30 May 1986

Statement by the State of Qatar.

The State of Qatar deeply regrets the disagreement between it and the State of Bahrain concerning their maritime borders. It is a disagreement which Qatar has attempted to resolve through all fraternal and amicable means in a way that secures justice and restores rights to its owner. However, all of its attempts were fruitless as a result of Bahrain's insistence on continuing to violate the sovereignty of the State of Qatar over its maritime province.

Despite this continued violation of its sovereignty, the Government of Qatar maintained the greatest patience, tolerance, and self-control for long years to preserve fraternal relations. Bahrain, however, continued to violate the sanctity of good neighborliness which the State of Qatar takes the utmost care to preserve. It has carried out actions, which include transforming Fasht al-Dibal into an industrial island, an action which violates one of the principles of the mediation carried out by the fraternal Kingdom of Saudi Arabia—which has our gratitude and appreciation—and which provides for a pledge by each party not to carry out any action which could strengthen its legal position, undermine the legal position of the other party, or benefit the current situation concerning the issue disagreed upon.

Any such action is considered not to have happened and has no legal effect. This principle was asserted by a resolution adopted by the GCC Ministerial Council during its meeting in Riyadh in 1982.

Concerning this violation, the Government of Qatar has been compelled to stop the land filling and construction which Bahrain has carried out at Fasht al-Dibal designed to restore the situation to what it was previously, which is what the principles of mediation and the rulings of the GCC Ministerial Council's resolution were directed at, and to which Qatar had totally committed itself.

On this occasion, the State of Qatar wishes to assert its continued commitment to these principles and rulings and to express its full gratitude and profound appreciation to His Majesty King Fahd ibn Abd al-Aziz Al Saud, king of fraternal Saudi Arabia, for his good efforts in seeking to end the dispute between the two fraternal countries. It also expresses its full gratitude and great appreciation for their majesties and highnesses the leaders of the GCC countries for

the sincere care and great attention they have shown toward resolving the issue in a fair and just manner and for the good of the two fraternal peoples.

Source: *FBIS-MEA-V–86–084*, 1 May 1986, p. C3.

Document 121

GCC Secretariat Statement on Qatar-Bahrain Agreement

16 June 1986

The General Secretariat followed up the good mediation efforts of His Majesty King Fahd ibn Abd al-Aziz and his brothers their majesties and highnesses the GCC leaders which, thank God, were crowned with an auspicious agreement between the brothers in the states of Bahrain and Qatar, and which restores matters to their previous state. The General Secretariat had the honor to form the committee which attended the execution of the terms of this agreement and supervised it until its final stages. The efforts exerted by the GCC leaders and the agreement reached are a good indication of the solid relations and ties which are above anything else. They are also a confirmation of the firm GCC policy to support anything that preserves the security and stability of its states and the interests of its children. The agreement affirms the concept of profound neighborliness and intimacy between the two neighbors, Qatar and Bahrain, and enables the internal Gulf front to remain strong and cohesive and keeps the Gulf family as one family in which love and agreement prevail and which rises above incidents. It is also a confirmation of the eagerness of the wise leadership in the GCC states to keep the council a channel of Arab solidarity and a prop for joint Arab work, because the strength and unity of the council is a strength and prop for Arab solidarity.

Source: *FBIS-MEA-V–86–116*, 17 June 1986, p. C1.

Document 122

Omani Communiqué Issued following the Foreign Minister's Visit to the PDRY

17 June 1986

In response to an invitation from Dr. Abd al-Aziz al-Dali, PDRY foreign minister, Yusuf al-Alawi Abdallah, minister of state for foreign affairs, headed a delegation on an official visit to the PDRY from 15 to 17 June.

Ali Salim al-Bayd, secretary general of the YSP Central

Committee, and engineer Haydar Abu Bakr al-Attas, chairman of the Supreme People's Council Presidium, received the visiting minister and his accompanying delegation. Yusuf al-Alawi Abdallah delivered a written message from His Majesty Qabus ibn Said of Oman to his brother His Excellency Haydar Abu Bakr al-Attas, chairman of the Supreme People's Council Presidium, and conveyed the greetings of his majesty.

Official talks were held between the PDRY side led by Dr. Abd al-Aziz al-Dali, PDRY foreign minister, and on the Omani side by Yusuf al-Alawi Abdallah, minister of state for foreign affairs. The talks were held in a cordial and friendly atmosphere which reflected the intention of the leadership of the two countries in developing and consolidating bilateral relations. The PDRY and Omani sides affirmed their adherence to the agreement signed in Kuwait in 1982 between the governments of the two countries. They expressed satisfaction at the level of Omani-PDRY relations. They affirmed their keenness to achieve more positive steps to develop fraternal bilateral relations to serve the mutual interests of both fraternal peoples.

Both sides reviewed the situation in the Gulf region and the Arabian Peninsula. Stemming from the bonds of relations and neighborliness among the peoples of the region, both the Omani and PDRY sides affirmed their adherence to the good neighbor policy and noninterference in each other's internal affairs, and their keenness to achieve a larger and intimate cooperation among the countries of the Arabian Peninsula in order to achieve prosperity and progress and to preserve security and stability for the peoples and countries of the region. Both sides also reviewed the situation in the Arab arena. They affirmed the need to take more serious action to achieve Arab solidarity in order to confront all the dangers facing the Arab countries. Yusuf al-Alawi Abdallah, minister of state for foreign affairs, and the delegation accompanying him expressed their deep thanks for the good reception and hospitality accorded to them during their visit to the PDRY. He also extended an invitation to his Brother Dr. Abd al-Aziz al-Dali to visit the Sultanate of Oman. Dr. Abd al-Aziz al-Dali accepted the invitation.

Source: *FBIS-MEA-V–86–117*, 18 June 1986, p. C4.

6

From Cooperation to Confederation?

We should now return to the central question raised at the beginning: What is the nature of the GCC? In the light of this study one thing should be absolutely clear by now. Charges against the GCC of its being a tool of the United States or characterizations of it as an anti-Israeli alliance are empirically indefensible. It is true that the collapse of the shah's regime prompted the Carter administration to consider a variety of alternatives to the fallen policeman of the Persian Gulf and that these included a "security framework" which would rely on such unlikely partners as Saudi Arabia and Israel. But just before the establishment of the GCC the credibility and influence of the United States was at its lowest ebb among the Gulf Arab monarchies, especially Saudi Arabia, which in part blamed the United States for the fall of the shah's regime. And the debacle of the American rescue mission in Iran cast still further doubt on American power. Above all, the Gulf Arab states were concerned that the United States might intervene militarily in the Gulf region under the Carter Doctrine.

The notion that the GCC was created as an anti-Israel alliance is equally erroneous. To be sure, the GCC states, like all other Arab states, were, and continue to be, opposed to the Israeli occupation of Arab lands, and they join in the demand for the establishment of a Palestinian state. The GCC governments' interest in the Palestinian cause is reinforced by the fact that about half a million Palestinians live among the GCC citizens. Their homelessness is a potential source of tension in the region. But there is nothing in the record to suggest that the GCC was created to fight Israel. In fact, the GCC governments belong to the moderate faction in the Arab-Israeli conflict. This position was affirmed by their stance at the first summit meeting of the GCC leaders in Abu Dhabi in 1981 and by their endorsement of the Fahd peace plan later. It was further affirmed by a myriad statements on the Arab-Israeli conflict and the Palestinian issue over the first five years of the GCC's existence.

The most prevalent view of the nature of the GCC is equally unwarranted factually. Contrary to conventional wisdom, the GCC was not established simply in reaction to the outbreak of the Iraq-Iran war. In the first place, when the war broke out the armed hostilities were not considered as posing a major threat to the Gulf Arab monarchies. At the time, Iraq had good relations with the Gulf Arab leaders. Saddam Hussein had successfully set to rest, at least for the time being, the concern of the conservative Arab leaders over Baathist subversive activities in the region. He had made common cause with the Gulf monarchs against Sadat's Egypt over the signing of the Camp David accords and Egypt's peace treaty with Israel. Furthermore, he had opposed the Khomeini regime's bid for exporting the "Islamic Revolution" even more than had the other Arab rulers of the Gulf region.

Second, these rulers did not feel terribly threatened when the war first broke out; Iraq had the upper hand. The Iraqi forces were the ones that escalated the longtime border skirmishes with Iran to the level of a "total war" (*harb al-shamilih*), to borrow the phrase of Iraqi general Khayrallah. The Iraqi forces were the ones that occupied some 800 square miles of Iranian territory in the oil-rich province of Khuzistan. And it was the Iraqi government that was calling on not only the Arabic-speaking Iranians of "Arabistan" but also all other ethnic minorities in Iran to overthrow the Khomeini regime. The GCC leaders first became truly alarmed by the war about six months after the establishment of their organization, in September 1981 when for the first time the Iranian forces went on the offensive.

Nor was the GCC established simply in reaction to the perceived threat of the Soviet Union, although the Soviet invasion of Afghanistan had a traumatic effect on all the Gulf states and Saudi Arabia led in denouncing it within the Organization of the Islamic Conference. The timing of the Soviet invasion in particular was perturbing to the Saudis, coming as it did after the fall of the shah's regime, the perceived pro-Western and anticommunist bulwark against Soviet expansionism in the Gulf region. Furthermore, the Saudi leaders were afraid of the possibility of a communist takeover in Iran in the course of the revolutionary chaos. Yet, although the Soviet menace loomed large in the minds of GCC leaders, it was not considered to be a present and imminent threat to the Gulf royal families.

The threat that was uppermost in the minds of the Arab leaders and was most commonly shared by them was the possibility that the Iranian Revolution would prove contagious. Not only had this revolution destroyed the most powerful monarchy in the whole Gulf region, but the Islamic revolutionary movement that it had reinforced threatened to destroy all the remaining Gulf royal families as well. This fear was deepened after the fall of the provisional government of Mehdi Bazargan, or after what the Khomeini followers called the "second revolution." Until then, every Gulf government, including that of revolutionary Iraq, had hoped to get along with the new regime in Iran, in view of the participation of the National Frontists in the Bazargan government and the prime minister's own moderate stance. But once the militants seized the United States Embassy in Tehran and forced, in effect, the fall of the Bazargan government, that hope was dashed.

More critically, in the short span of time between the eruption of the Iranian Revolution and the establishment of the GCC, the virulent antiroyalist Iranian propaganda had been coupled with Iranian-inspired Shia upheavals in Bahrain, Kuwait, and Saudi Arabia. The concern of the Saudis was the greatest of all. Two Shia uprisings took place in the wake of the dramatic seizure of the Grand Mosque. Although the Shias had nothing to do with this takeover, its traumatic effect magnified the threat of the Shia uprisings when they came immediately afterwards. Given the fact that 40 to 60 percent of the work force in the oil fields of the Eastern Province are Shia Muslims, no other threat at the time seemed so near and so formidable.

The threat of the Shia turmoil in Bahrain and Kuwait might not seem to have been so great as that in Saudi Arabia, but to the Bahrainis and Kuwaitis the danger was real. Long before the Iranian Revolution, Bahrain had had its own dissident Shia movement. Bahrain's concern over the unrest of its Shia Muslims was compounded by the concurrent claim of Iranian revolutionary militants to sovereignty over the country. The Bazargan government denounced the threat of Ayatollah Sadeq Ruhani, who had warned that Iran would annex Bahrain unless it established a government modeled after the one in power in Iran; but the Iranian antiroyalist campaign intensified after Bazargan's fall and before the establishment of the GCC. Kuwait faced a lesser threat from their Shia dissidents in late 1979, but given the country's more open society and close proximity to both Iran and Iraq, Kuwait felt equally vulnerable to potential acts of subversion and terrorism. Subsequent events proved it right.

Hence, the GCC was created primarily as a vehicle of cooperation among the six Gulf Arab states for preserving monarchical regimes in the face of the perceived threat of the contagion of the Islamic revolutionary fundamentalism. As such, the claim of the GCC leaders that their grouping was "not an alliance against Iran" is technically correct. They perceived a threat larger than the Iranian revolutionary agitation. What they feared most was the tremors of the Islamic revolution among their own people and within their own societies, particularly because of the presumed susceptibility of their own Shia inhabitants to an Islamic revolutionary movement.

If this interpretation of the nature of the GCC at its inception is valid, then did it change or remain the same during the first five years of its existence? Conventional wisdom suggests that the GCC was created at the beginning as an economic grouping, modeled after the European Economic Community or the Common Market, but that subsequently it became a political and security mechanism in response to perceived threats to internal and external security of the royal families as a result of terrorism and war. The mistake in this most prevalent proposition stems from interpreting too literally the statements of the founders of the GCC. In founding the GCC, the Arab leaders said that their states would cooperate in "all fields, especially in the economic and social domains" (D1 and D2). But they did not say exactly toward what ends. All that the GCC leaders said in their first summit meeting was that they wanted to promote cooperation among the six "in order to serve their interests and strengthen their ability to hold on to their beliefs and values," without ever defining those interests, beliefs, and values. Hence, on the basis of merely what the GCC leaders did or did not say, conventional wisdom has concluded that the founding fathers of the GCC intended to create an economic community which subsequently turned out to be a security organization.

Yet, my analysis of not only the statements of the founders of the GCC but also the momentous social and political circumstances of the critical 1979–81 period shows that the GCC was never intended as an economic enterprise. Rather, it was created primarily as a political and security vehicle for cooperation among the six for the overriding purpose of ensuring the survival of their similar monarchies in the face of the revolutionary Islamic fundamentalist movement sweeping across the Gulf region in the wake of the Iranian Revolution. The reference of the GCC leaders to the cooperation of the six member states "especially in the economic and social domains" was not a statement of the central purpose of their organization, which was left unsaid. Rather, it was a statement of the kind of means that they preferred at the inception of the GCC. They then believed that they could accomplish their overriding objective by pooling the enormous economic resources of the world's six richest oil-producing states. Had not the Iranian Revolution destroyed the most militarily powerful monarchy in the Gulf region largely because of the social and economic malaise of the shah's regime? Would not the avoidance of such social and economic ills, particularly in the wake of the oil boom, help preserve their regimes from the kind of calamities that triggered the eruption of the Iranian Revolution? These were the kinds of thoughts that inclined the founders of the GCC to prefer at the beginning social and economic means to political and military means. But subsequently the perceived threats to both internal security—starting with the Bahrain plot—and external security—starting with the first successful Iranian offensive in the war in September 1981—impelled the GCC leaders to emphasize diplomatic and military means rather than economic ones. This basic shift in means, and not the purpose, of the GCC was acknowledged unequivocally by Secretary General Bisharah when he said that cooperation in the political and security domains was the prerequisite of economic integration.

My analysis of not only the creation of the GCC but also the major strategies pursued by its members during the first five years of its existence further supports the central argument of this study about the nature of the GCC. As has been seen, these strategies included efforts of the GCC states to combat subversion and terrorism, to deter the spread of the Iraq-Iran war, to integrate their economies, and to coordinate their diplomacy. On balance, most of the time and energy of the GCC states during 1981–86 were spent on efforts to prevent the spread of the Iraq-Iran war by means of both military deterrence and diplomatic coordination.

Although it might appear otherwise, the efforts of the GCC states to contain the spread of the war by diplomatic and military means were related to their overriding desire to counter the contagion of the Islamic revolutionary fundamentalism. The GCC states obviously did not wish to see the war spread to their territories. But, in fact, what they feared most was an unconditional victory by Iran. Such a victory would end the Iraq-Iran war and the threat of its spread, but it could also result in a new war by Iran against the GCC states. The GCC leaders feared that after defeating Iraq, the Iranian forces would press on to greater victories in exporting their revolution by overrunning the tiny city-state of Kuwait and easily overwhelming the meager ground forces of Saudi Arabia and the other GCC states. Iran would rejoice over the opportunity to get revenge against the GCC states, especially Kuwait and Saudi Arabia, that had repeatedly failed to heed its warnings to stop aiding the Iraqis financially and logistically.

This concern of the GCC states with the spread of the Islamic revolution as a result of an unconditional Iranian military victory in the battlefield did not necessarily imply that the GCC leaders would welcome an Iraqi victory. The Baathist republicans might stop the Iranian forces today, but an Iraqi victory would spell deep trouble for the conservative GCC regimes tomorrow. As the most populous Arab state of the Persian Gulf, a victorious Iraq would revive its old Baathist dream of establishing Iraqi hegemony over the GCC countries in the name of the Arab nation. Saddam Hussein had unfurled his Arab Charter months before the invasion of Iran as the self-appointed great power in the Arab world and aspired to leadership of the whole Third World. Even more disconcerting, a victorious Iraq might revert to its pattern of subversive activities in the GCC states. Nevertheless, despite their ambivalent attitude toward Iraq, the GCC leaders feared the perceived threat of the Islamic revolution after an unconditional victory more than any potential Iraqi subversion after an Iraqi victory.

To suggest that the containment of the war absorbed most of the time and energy of the GCC states during the organization's first five years does not necessarily mean that they did nothing else. Diplomatically, they mediated the 27 October 1982 conflict settlement agreement between Oman and South Yemen, which seems to have survived the shock of the bloody coup in January 1986. They also contained the Bahrain-Qatar disputes over the Hawar and Fasht al-Dibal islands. But it was the protracted, bloody war between Iraq and Iran that preoccupied the GCC leaders both in public and behind the scenes, both directly and indirectly through international and regional organizations, and both as supporters of Iraq and as mediators between the two belligerents. In fact, given their fear of the contagion of the Islamic revolution through the spread of the war and their essentially ambivalent attitude toward the Baathist regime in Iraq, they often seemed to play the role of the balancer in the power struggle between the two major powers of the Gulf. For example, when the Iraqis escalated the war by striking at oil tankers and at the Kharg Island oil terminal, they pressured Iraq behind the scenes not to go too far. On the other hand, when the Iranians gained the upper hand by capturing parts of the Majnoon islands in February 1984 and by establishing a bridgehead in the Fao Peninsula in February 1986, they threw their weight behind Iraq in the Arab League and in the United Nations Security Council, denouncing Iran both by name and by implication.

Militarily, too, the efforts of the GCC states in strengthening their forces during the first five years of the GCC's life were primarily in response to the nuances of the Iraq-Iran war. Even Saudi Arabia, which had been modernizing its armed forces with the help of the United States for decades, greatly intensified its military buildup after the Iranian Revolution and the start of the Iraq-Iran war. Similarly, the defense cooperation among the six was largely in response to the developments in the war. The threat of the spread of the war helped promote the idea of an integrated air defense system for the GCC region, the creation of the GCC Rapid Deployment Force headquartered at Hafr al-Batin in Saudi Arabia under joint command, and the holding of two multilateral Peninsula Shield exercises and a number of bilateral joint military maneuvers. It also prompted the adoption of the principle of indivisibility of the security of the six, although it did not create a legal obligation similar to that created by Article 5 of the North Atlantic Treaty Organization for its members, that is, that an armed attack against one or more states would be considered an attack against them all.

Although the cooperation of the GCC states in the economic field seemed to be less in response to the developments of the Iraq-Iran war, its effects should not be minimized. The founding fathers of the GCC believed that the containment of the Islamic revolutionary contagion above all required cooperation in the social and economic domains. The fact that the GCC states were concerned with the depletion of their finite oil resources only reinforced their desire to press for economic integration. Such projects as the construction of a joint oil refinery in, and a joint oil pipeline to Oman—which absorbed much study and were finally shelved largely because of the collapse of oil revenues—were clearly influenced by the threat of the spread of the war. Those economic cooperative activities least prompted by the war, such as the creation of the Gulf Organization for Investment, the abolition of internal customs, the establishment of common external tariffs, etc., had not made enough progress by the time of the sixth summit meeting of the GCC leaders to suggest whether or not they would fare better than those economic projects more induced by the war.

The GCC states also cooperated in areas related to maintaining internal security as a means of countering the threat of revolution. Beginning with the Bahrain plot, all aborted, attempted, or completed acts of terrorism were blamed on Iran as the mastermind behind these acts planned as part of the export of its revolution. The four security agreements signed by Saudi Arabia with all its junior partners except Kuwait and the draft multilateral agreement for internal security were all intended to preserve the six monarchies against internal convulsion. So were all the exchanges of equipment for riot control, intelligence information, and training, as well as all the restrictions imposed on visas, travel, and publication. The underlying political fragility of the six was rooted in a variety of demographic, social, economic, and political problems which could be exploited in the name of Islam or any other ideology. The efforts of the GCC states to detect, detain, and punish all terrorists as criminals during the first five years of their cooperation may or may not have limited the acts of political violence. But the complex, unhappy human environment that aids such acts did not seem to be sufficiently recognized in GCC official circles.

Given the pervasive influence of the Iraq-Iran war on the cooperation of the GCC states in all fields, will they continue to cooperate after the war? The preceding examination of the GCC from its creation through its first five years makes it clear that the GCC in this embryonic phase of its life was primarily a vehicle of cooperation among the six Gulf Arab states in the face of the perceived threat of the Iranian revolutionary paradigm of Islamic fundamentalism. It should now be easy to understand that the GCC states will probably continue to cooperate even after the war. There are two plausible outcomes of the war: either Iran will win the war, or neither side will win. If Iran wins in the sense of destroying the regime of Saddam Hussein, which is its overriding war objective, the GCC states will consider the threat of the revolutionary contagion all that much greater and the need for cooperation all the more pressing. If neither sides actually wins the war, the GCC states will still fear the specter of Iranian export of the Islamic revolution, as well as the appeal of revolutionary fundamentalism among their own peoples.

The question, therefore, boils down to how the GCC states will perceive the threat of the Iranian revolutionary example after the war has ended. If they continue to perceive it as menacing as before, the chances are that they will continue to cooperate closely and such challenges to their cohesion as the Fasht dispute will be contained, if not settled, in the face of the still larger threat of revolutionary contagion to the survival of the six monarchies. If their perception of the revolutionary threat diminishes, the chances are that they will find it more difficult to cooperate. In the long run, the threat perception probably will diminish. Like all other revolutionary movements of the past, the Iranian revolutionary movement probably will mellow. In *Revolutionary Iran: Challenge and Response in the Middle East*, I have shown that subtle but increasingly significant, pragmatic tendencies are discernible in Iran's Middle East policy, despite the continuing ideological and rhetorical stridency of the Khomeini regime.

If the GCC states become less concerned about the Iranian revolutionary threat, the prospects of cooperation among them will turn on their ultimate goal and intermediate objectives. Will their co-operation give way to such other objectives as the creation of a GCC economic community with the ultimate aim of GCC political unity? Although the founders of the GCC spoke of the ideal of Arab unity within the framework of the Arab League, they did not posit political unity among the GCC states as their ultimate goal as did the EEC countries in 1958. When the six countries in Western Europe decided to create a European Economic Community, they aimed at a United States of Europe. The creation of a united Europe continues to elude the Europeans even decades later, but such an ultimate goal was clearly envisaged.

Such a goal has not been adopted by the GCC despite the fact that similar ideas have been advanced by GCC leaders and officials. After a conference at Taif in October 1979, nearly two years before the official formation of the GCC, the Kuwaiti foreign minister said: "We asked if we were, that is, peoples and governments, compatible so that we can move to a unity situation, not necessarily a full unity today, rather, a step on a long road. We said let us start by establishing the *United Arab States* so that we can have one foreign policy and unify defense and judiciary together with oil policy and economy in order to preserve our internal laws as Americans did in the United States. Let us strongly study this vital matter and try it." Yet, this clarity of purpose did not exist at the time of the founding of the GCC and was never made clear by the GCC leaders subsequently. The problem first surfaced at the first summit, held in Abu Dhabi in May 1981 when Secretary General Bisharah reportedly said that the organization "is neither a confederal nor a federal one, but a cooperation council." But at the time of the organization's second anniversary, in May 1983, he said: "although the Charter does not clearly define the political theory of the GCC, we in the Secretariat have come to the conclusion that the consensus is for a confederal structure. . . . In a nutshell, the goal is confederation. This is the objective." He added, however, that "each country wants to retain its own characteristics, legislative power and sovereign attributes." This kind of confederation seems to correspond with de Gaulle's conception of European political unification, a *union des patries*. This "union of fatherlands" in the case of Europe or "union of monarchies" in the case of the GCC member countries, of course, means that each government would largely retain its own identity and freedom of action.

It remains to be seen whether in the first five years of their cooperation, the GCC states have relinquished enough of their individual freedom of action through the creation of lasting joint institutions to enable them to withstand the challenge of incohesion in the second five years. It is likely that during this period the threat of both Islamic revolutionary fundamentalism and revolutionary Iran will increasingly diminish. If so, will the GCC members then be willing and able to move forward from cooperation among a congeries of sovereign and independent states toward the establishment of a United Arab Confederation? If they can, historians will be justified in saying that the GCC leaders skillfully turned adversity to great advantage.

Appendixes
Annotated Bibliography of Select Books and Articles
Index

Appendix A
Tables

Table 1. Youth Population in the Persian Gulf Region (in thousands)

Country	1980 Total population	1980 Age group 10–34	1980 %	1990 Total opulation	1990 Age group 10–34	1990 %	2000 Total population	2000 Age group 10–34	2000 %
Bahrain	313	160	51.11	410	196	47.80	515	200	38.83
Iran	38,126	17,558	46.05	51,033	23,998	47.02	64,916	31,772	48.94
Iraq	13,072	5,884	45.01	18,136	8,343	46.00	24,198	11,525	47.62
Kuwait	1,353	600	44.34	2,101	945	44.97	2,524	1,403	55.58
Oman	891	393	44.10	1,208	541	44.78	1,651	758	45.91
Qatar	237	116	48.94	330	136	41.21	425	163	38.35
Saudi Arabia	8,960	4,059	45.30	12,908	5,776	44.74	17,804	7,965	44.73
United Arab Emirates	726	360	49.58	1,025	402	39.21	1,286	480	37.32
Total Gulf Region	63,678	29,130	45.74	87,151	40,337	46.28	113,319	54,266	47.88
Gulf Cooperation Council	12,480	5,688	45.57	17,982	7,996	44.46	24,205	10,969	45.31
More developed regions of the world	1,131,339	453,401	40.00	1,206,190	453,104	37.56	1,268,824	441,229	34.77
United States of America	223,233	95,741	42.88	245,472	94,626	38.54	263,829	93,784	35.54

Source: United Nations, Department of International Economic and Social Affairs, *Demographic Indicators of Countries: Estimates and Projections as Assessed in 1980*, ST/ESA/SER.A/82 (New York: United Nations, 1982), pp. 60–61, 304–5, 316–17, 320–21, 324–25, 328–33, 336–37.

Table 2. Citizens and Foreigners in the GCC States

Country	Total population[a]	Citizen population	Foreign population[a]	Citizens as a percentage of total population	Foreigners as a percentage of total population
Bahrain	350,798	238,420	112,378	67.9	32.1
Kuwait	1,562,190	606,800	955,390	38.8	61.2
Oman	984,000	805,000	179,000	81.8	18.2
Qatar	243,357	65,357	178,000	26.8	73.2
Saudi Arabia	9,229,107	7,079,107	2,150,000	76.7	23.3
United Arab Emirates	1,040,275	322,800	717,475	31.0	69.0

Note: reprinted from R. K. Ramazani, *Revolutionary Iran: Challenge and Response in the Middle East* (Baltimore and London: Johns Hopkins University Press, 1986), p. 261.

[a]For Bahrain: (Kuwait) *Arab Times*, no. 5498, 24 Aug. 1982, p. 7.

For Kuwait: *Middle East Economic Digest: Kuwait and the Middle East*, May 1982, p. 35.

For Oman, Qatar, and Saudi Arabia: *Demographic and Related Socio-Economic Data Sheets for Countries of the Economic Commission for Western Asia (ECWA)*, no. 3 (Beirut: UN-ECWA, May 1982), pp. 131, 115, 147.

For the UAE: *Quarterly Economic Review for the UAE: Annual Supplement, 1981* (London: *Economist* Intelligence Unit, 1981), p. 8.

Table 3. Shia Muslims in Persian Gulf Countries

Country	Total population, 1981[a]	Citizen population, 1981[a]	Shia population, 1983[b]	Shias as a percentage of total population	Shias as a percentage of citizen population
Bahrain	350,798	238,420	171,900	49.00	71.98
Kuwait (1982)	1,562,190	606,800	141,000	9.02	23.23
Oman (1980)	984,000	805,000	56,000	5.69	6.95
Qatar[b] (1980)	243,357	65,357	52,500	21.57	80.32
Saudi Arabia	9,229,107	7,079,107	350,000	3.79	4.94
United Arab Emirates[b]	1,040,275	289,892	120,000	11.53	41.39
Total	13,409,727	9,084,576	891,400	6.64	9.81
Iran[b]	41,000,000	40,000,000	38,000,000	92.00	95.00
Iraq	14,400,000	13,500,000	8,100,000	56.00	60.00

Note: reprinted from R. K. Ramazani, *Revolutionary Iran: Challenge and Response in the Middle East* (Baltimore and London: Johns Hopkins University Press, 1986), p. 259.

[a]For Bahrain: (Kuwait) *Arab Times*, 5498, 24 Aug. 1982, p. 7.

For Kuwait: *Middle East Economic Digest: Kuwait and the Middle East*, May 1982, p. 35.

For Oman, Qatar, Saudi Arabia, and Iraq, *Demographic and Related Socio-Economic Data Sheets for Countries of the Economic Commission for Western Asia (ECWA)*, no. 3 (Beirut: UN-ECWA, May 1982), pp. 131, 115, 147.

For the UAE: *Quarterly Economic Review for the UAE: Annual Supplement, 1981* (London: Economist Intelligence Unit, 1981), p. 8.

[b]Compiled from *The Middle East Military Balance, 1983*, ed. Mark Heller (Tel Aviv: Tel Aviv University, Jafee Center for Strategic Studies, 1983). There is a great difference in the percentages of Shia populations based on Heller's figures and those given by James A. Bill in "Islam, Politics, and Shi'ism in the Gulf" (*Middle East Insight* 3, no. 3 [January/February 1984]: 6). This discrepancy is especially serious in regard to Qatar and the UAE (16 and 18 percent respectively in Bill's table).

Table 4. The Military Power of the Gulf States in the 1980s

Country	Population	Troops				Military expenditures	
		Active	Army	Air Force	Navy	1983 (millions U.S. $)	As a percentage of GNP[a]
Bahrain	400,000	2,800	2,300	200	300	253	8.1
Iran[b]	42,500,000	555,000	250,000	35,000	20,000	17,370	10.6
Iraq[b]	14,900,000	642,250	600,000	38,000	4,250	10,296	46.4
Kuwait	1,750,000	12,500	10,000	2,000[e]	500	1,360	6.0
Oman	1–1,600,000	21,500[c]	16,500	3,000	2,000	1,772	28.5
Qatar	270,000	6,000	5,000	300	700	166	9.1
Saudi Arabia	8–12,000,000	51,500[d]	35,000	14,000	2,500	21,952	15.4
United Arab Emirates	1,300,000	43,000	40,000	1,500	1,500	2,422	8.0

Note: reprinted from R. K. Ramazani, *Revolutionary Iran: Challenge and Response in the Middle East* (Baltimore and London: Johns Hopkins University Press, 1986), p. 263.

Sources: Adapted from *The Military Balance, 1984–1985* (London: International Institute for Strategic Studies, 1984); *World Military Expenditures and Arms Transfers, 1972–1982* (Washington, D.C.: United States Arms Control and Disarmament Agency, April 1984).

[a]Figures are for 1982, except the figures for Iran and Qatar, which are, respectively, for 1981 and 1980.

[b]Figures for Iran and Iraq are estimates.

[c]Including some 3,700 foreign personnel.

[d]In addition, there are 10,000 foreign contract military personnel.

[e]Excluding expatriate personnel.

Table 5. GCC States Oil and Gas Reserves, 1983

Country	Daily oil exports (thousands of barrels)	Revenues from oil (thousands U.S. $)	Daily crude oil production (thousands of barrels)	Estimated proven reserves[a] (1,000 bbl)[b]	Gas reserves (billions of cubic meters)
Bahrain	160.0	2,080,000	176.00	170,000	121.4
Iran	1,718.7	19,014,000	2,441.70	48,500,000	14,000.0
Iraq	725.4	9,650,000	1,098.80	44,500,000	821.2
Kuwait	544.4	8,720,000	1,054.10	92,710,000	995.4
Oman	128.6	1,653,720	389.00	3,500,000	75.3
Qatar	268.3	3,112,000	269.00	3,350,000	1,755.1
Saudia Arabia	3,701.7	47,815,000	4,539.40	171,710,000	3,544.0
United Arab Emirates	1,077.3	12,577,000	1,149.00	32,490,000	3,150.0

Note: adapted from R. K. Ramazani, *Revolutionary Iran: Challenge and Response in the Middle East* (Baltimore and London: Johns Hopkins University Press, 1986), p. 256.

Sources: OPEC *Annual Statistical Bulletin*, 1983 (Vienna: OPEC, 1985); OAPEC *Annual Statistical Bulletin*, 1983 (Kuwait: OAPEC, 1985).

[a]From *Oil and Gas Journal* 85, no. 52 (31 Dec. 1984): 71, 114 (figures as of 1 Jan. 1985).

[b]bbl = billions of barrels.

Table 6. GCC States' Oil Refineries, 1980

Country	Location	Capacity b/d	Type
1. Kuwait	Mina Abdallah	120,000	D
	Mina Saoud	50,000	D/R/B
	Shuaiba	180,000	D/H/R/C
	Mina Abdallah	120,000	D/H
	Mina Ahmadi	250,000	D/R/B
	Mina Ahmadi (under construction)	250,000	H/L
2. Saudi Arabia	Ras Tanura	500,000	D/R/B
	Jeddah	70,000	D/R/B/H/VIS
	Riyadh	20,000	D/H/VIS/R
	Ras Tanura (under construction)	25,000	R
	Jeddah (expansion)	170,000	D/VIS/R
	Al-Jubail (under construction)	120,000	D
	Yanbu (under construction)	250,000	D
	Al-Jubail (under construction)	250,000	D
	Riyadh (expansion)	120,000	D/R/H
	Rabgh (under construction)	350,000	D
3. Bahrain	Awali	250,000	D/C/R/VIS/B
4. Qatar	Umm Said	6,321	D/R
	Umm Said (planned)	50,000	D/R
5. UAE	Umm Al-Naar	15,000	D/R/H
	Ruwais	120,000	D/R/H
	Jebel Ali	200,000	D/R/H
6. Oman	(under construction)	50,000	—

Note: reprinted from Regional and Country Study Branch, Division for Industrial Studies, *The Resource Base for Industrialization in the Gulf Cooperation Council Countries: A Framework for Cooperation* (New York: United Nations Industrial Development Organization, IS.423, 21 Dec. 1983), p. 269.
Source: GOIC, *Petrochemical Industries in the Arabian Gulf,* Nov. 1980, p. 42.
Key: B = Bitumen, C = Cracking, D = Distillation, H = Hydrocracking, L = Lubricating oil, R = Reforming, VIS = Visbreaking.

Table 7. Existing and Planned GCC Petrochemical Facilities, 1980

Country	Location	Products	Capacity thousand tons per year	Status
1. Kuwait				
KPIC	Shuaiba	Ethylene	350	Planned
		HDPE	130	Planned
		Ethylene glycol	135	Planned
		Styrene	340	Planned
		Benzene	280	Planned
		Ortho-xylene	60	Planned
		Para-xylene	86	Planned
				Planned
2. Saudi Arabia				
a) Saudi Petrochemical Co. (Shell Oil Co.)	Al-Jubail	Ethylene	656	
		Ethylene dichloride	456	
		Styrene	295	Operational in 1985
		Ethanol	281	
		Caustic soda	377	
b) Saudi Yanbu Petrochemical Co. (Mobil Chemical Co.)	Yanbu	Ethylene	450	
		LDPE	200	
		HDPE	90	Operational in 1985
		Ethylene glycol	220	
c) Al Jubail Petrochemical Co. (Exxon Chemical Co.)	Al-Jubail	LDPE	260	Operational in 1985
d) Saudi Methanol Co. (Japanese Consortium)	Al-Jubail	Methanol	600	Operational in 1983
e) National Methanol Co. (Celanese-TEXAS Eastern)	Al-Jubail	Methanol	650	Operational in 1985
f) Arabian Petrochemical Co. (Dow Chemical Co.)	Al-Jubail	Ethylene	500	
		LDPE	70	Operational in 1985
		HDPE	110	
g) Eastern Petrochemical Co. (Japanese Consortium)	Al-Jubail	LDPE	130	Operational in 1985
		Ethylene glycol	300	
3. Bahrain				
Gulf Petrochemical Industries jointly with Kuwait and Saudi Arabia	Satrat	Methanol	330	Operational 1984
4. Qatar				
QAPCO & CDF	Umm Said	Ethylene	280	Operational
		LDPE	140	
		Propylene	5	
		HDPE	70	
5. UAE				
(ADNOC)	Al-Ruwais	Ethylene	450	Under consideration

Table 7. *Continued*

Country	Location	Products	Capacity thousand tons per year	Status
6. GCC Region		Ethylene	2686	
		Ethylene dichloride	456	
		Ethylene glycol	655	
		HDPE	400	
		LDPE	800	Total operational, operational in 1985, planned, or under study
		Styrene	635	
		Benzene	280	
		Propylene	5	
		Ortho-xylene	60	
		Para-xylene	86	
		Methanol	1580	

Note: reprinted from Regional and Country Study Branch, Division for Industrial Studies, *The Resource Base for Industrialization in the Gulf Cooperation Council Countries: A Framework for Cooperation* (New York: United Nations Industrial Development Organization, IS.423, 21 Dec. 1983), pp. 273–74.

Source: Al-Wattari, *Oil Downstream* (Kuwait: OAPEC, 1980), pp. 98, 99, and SABIC, *The Fourth Annual Report for 1400 A.H. (1980 A.D.)*, p. 22.

Table 8. Gulf Cooperation Council States Customs Duties (figures in percentages)

Types of products	Bahrain	Kuwait	Oman	Qatar	Saudi Arabia	United Arab Emirates			
						Abu Dhabi	Dubay	Ras Al-Khaimah	Ajman
Food and necessities	5	—	—	—	—	—	—	—	—
Nonessential goods	10	—	—	—	—	—	—	—	—
Tobacco	30	—	—	—	—	—	—	—	—
Alcohol	70	—	75	70	—	25	—	—	—
Paints	—	—	20	—	—	—	—	—	—
Bananas	—	—	25	—	—	—	—	—	—
Records/Musical equipment	—	—	—	15	—	—	—	—	—
Selected types of steel bars	—	—	—	20	—	—	—	—	—
Standard rates	—	4*	2	2½	3†	1	3‡	2	3

Note: reprinted from *Middle East Economic Digest* 27, no. 36 (9 Sept. 1983), p. 2.

  * Selective 15–25% duty to protect local producers.

  † Selective 20% duty to protect local producers.

  ‡ 2% for products imported by air and 3% for products imported by sea.

Appendix B

GCC Chronology, 1981–86

1981

4	February	The foreign ministers of six conservative Arab Gulf monarchies (Bahrain, Kuwait, Oman, Qatar, Saudi Arabia, and the United Arab Emirates [UAE]) meet in Riyadh, Saudi Arabia, and decide to set up a cooperation council among themselves with a General Secretariat.
14	February	Formation of the GCC is announced.
24	February	A GCC committee in charge of formulating the organization's fundamental system meets in Riyadh.
7–8	March	GCC constitutional experts meet in Muscat, Oman.
9–10	March	GCC information ministers meet in Muscat.
25–26	May	The GCC's first summit meeting opens in Abu Dhabi, UAE. Abdallah Yaqub Bisharah (Kuwait) is named secretary general. The GCC's charter and bylaws are approved by the six heads of state. A working paper on joint Gulf action is issued along with a summit communiqué.
7	June	Israeli air force jets destroy the Iraqi experimental nuclear facility at Osiraq (Tamuz) near Baghdad.
9	June	GCC secretary general Bisharah condemns the Israeli attack.
22	August	GCC secretary general Bisharah condemns the United States for downing two Libyan aircrafts on 18 August over the Gulf of Sidra.
31 August–2 September		GCC foreign ministers hold their first regular meeting in At-Taif, Saudi Arabia. Their agenda covers the Fahd Peace Plan along with the GCC's proposed joint economic agreement and the Omani working paper on Gulf security (Iraq-Iran war and Soviet occupation of Afghanistan).
14	September	GCC secretary-general Bisharah arrives in Aden, the People's Democratic Republic of Yemen (PDRY), on an official visit.
21	October	GCC industry ministers convene their first meeting in Riyadh. They decide to examine common tariffs, promote joint industrial projects, and form a technical committee specializing in industrial questions.
21	October	Secretary General Bisharah arrives in Manama, Bahrain, on the first leg of a Gulf tour.
26	October	The Sixth Gulf Labor Conference opens in Riyadh (GCC plus Iraq).
27	October	Secretary General Bisharah visits Abu Dhabi to discuss joint issues.

28 October	Secretary General Bisharah visits Sultan Qabus in Muscat.
8–9 November	GCC foreign ministers meet in Riyadh; prepare second summit's agenda; identify security issues as priority.
11–12 November	Second summit meeting held in Riyadh; GCC chiefs of staff participate in deliberations; endorse the Fahd Peace Plan and review military affairs in the region; decide to convene a meeting of the defense ministers; call for end of Iraq-Iran war. Final communiqué stresses the noninterventionist policies of the GCC and its wish to deny any power of interfering in the region; it also announces the adoption of an economic agreement and states that starting with the next summit meeting to be held in Bahrain, the six heads of state will meet on a yearly basis.
12 November	GCC states agree to create a joint air defense system based on the Saudi Airborne Warning and Air Control System (AWACS).
19 November	Gulf finance ministers meet in Kuwait.
13 December	Bahrain announces that it discovered a coup plot. Coup attempt is condemned by GCC officials with the Bahraini interior minister speculating that Iran may have trained the saboteurs.
14 December	Israel annexes Syria's occupied Golan Heights.
17 December	Secretary General Bisharah condemns Golan Heights annexation in Abu Dhabi.
20 December	Saudi Arabia signs a bilateral security agreement with Bahrain.
22 December	GCC interior ministers decide to review security issues.
23 December	GCC officials to discuss sabotage plot in Bahrain.

1982

5 January	GCC military mission leaves Oman after a two-day visit (31 Dec. 1981–1 Jan. 1982).
9 January	Gulf Labor Ministers' Conference opens in Riyadh (GCC plus Iraq).
13 January	Secretary General Bisharah calls for the establishment of a GCC security network during Bahrain visit.
21 January	The United States vetoes a United Nations resolution condemning Israeli annexation of the Golan Heights (Syria). Gulf press editorials call for a boycott of the United States.
25 January	GCC defense ministers convene their first meeting in Riyadh.
26 January	GCC defense ministers conclude their meeting having discussed military cooperation among member states. Secretary General Bisharah states that concern is regional and that the ministers discussed the creation of an air defense umbrella covering all GCC states.
27 January	GCC finance and national economy ministers agree to establish a Gulf Investment Fund (GIF).
26–27 January	Iran criticizes GCC defense ministers' meeting. GCC states respond that their security quest is legitimate self-defense.

31	January	GCC oil ministers convene their first meeting in Riyadh to discuss unified oil policy.
1	February	GCC oil ministers conclude their first meeting; they agree to diversify sources of income and not rely on petroleum sources indefinitely; call for joint ventures in the oil industry (with priority going to Omani and Bahraini projects); adopt contingency plans to stockpile oil in each state. The ministers may also have discussed the construction of an oil pipeline bypassing the Strait of Hormuz.
3	February	Secretary General Bisharah arrives in Abu Dhabi for an official visit.
6–7	February	GCC foreign ministers convene their first emergency meeting in Bahrain; support Manama and accuse Iran of instigating plot to overthrow the Khalifah regime; call on Tehran to accept a peaceful settlement of the Iraq–Iran war following in the Iraqi footsteps; support Syria against the Israeli annexation of the Golan Heights; support the Palestinians in their ongoing quest for self-determination.
7	February	U.S. president Reagan states that Israel is "the only ally and only strategic asset that must be supported in the region." Editorials in GCC states' newspapers react strongly against the statement.
12	February	League of Arab States (LAS) foreign ministers convene an emergency meeting in Tunis, Tunisia, to discuss Golan Heights annexation; GCC foreign ministers are present.
21	February	Saudi Arabia signs bilateral security agreements with the UAE and Qatar.
22	February	Saudi Arabia signs a bilateral security agreement with Morocco.
23	February	Saudi Arabia signs a bilateral security agreement with Oman. Saudi interior minister Prince Nayif backs the formation of a Gulf Rapid Deployment Force.
23	February	Gulf information ministers end conference in Kuwait.
23–24	February	GCC interior ministers hold meeting in Riyadh; back joint security accord for all GCC states.
27	February	GCC military mission leaves Bahrain following consultations with Bahraini Defense Forces officials.
1	March	Gulf agricultural ministers hold their seventh meeting in Manama (GCC plus Iraq).
4	March	Qatar protests Bahrain's naming a new naval vessel after the disputed Hawar Islands and objects to naval exercises in Fasht al-Dibal.
7–8	March	GCC Ministerial Council holds third regular meeting in Riyadh; discusses Bahrain-Qatar dispute over Hawar Islands.
14	March	GCC chiefs of staff begin second conference in Riyadh.
16	March	GCC chiefs of staff discuss military cooperation among the six armed forces.
21	March	Secretary General Bisharah declares on Kuwaiti television that GCC is considering the establishment of a joint military force.
6	April	GCC planning ministers open their first conference in Bahrain.
7	April	Secretary General Bisharah announces that the planning ministers recommended the formation of a permanent "Social and Economic Planning Committee."

5–7 April	UAE president Zayid arrives in Kuwait for an official visit.
12 April	GCC states protest the 11 April Al-Aqsa Mosque shootout in Jerusalem; call for strike on 14 April throughout the Muslim world.
20 April	GCC foreign ministers hold their second emergency meeting in Riyadh to review regional and Arab developments; emphasis is on strengthening the ranks of the Arab nation against Zionist threat; express appreciation to King Khalid of Saudi Arabia for his solidarity call throughout the Muslim world with the Palestinian people; call for support for all efforts to end the Iraq-Iran war.
20 April	Qatar ratifies security agreement with Saudi Arabia which was signed in Riyadh on November 21, 1981, as well as agreement with Tunisia to employ Tunisian military personnel in the Qatari army.
24 April	GCC oil ministers hold an emergency meeting in Riyadh; may have agreed to unify policies in pricing, distribution, and orientation of production; GCC grouping emerging within both OPEC and OAPEC.
26–27 April	GCC immigration, passports, and labor committee of directors ends a two-day conference in Muscat; agree to standardize immigration and labor laws in all GCC states and to cooperate with interior ministers to safeguard the security of member states.
26 April	Saudi defense minister Prince Sultan declares that the kingdom's AWACS surveillance planes will be used on behalf of the GCC; also reiterated that the defecting Iranian plane (March 8) was returned to Iran and that the two pilots were permitted to go to Europe in accordance with their request; Sultan said that the new naval college being set up in the Eastern Province will admit GCC nationals who must attend U.S. and Pakistani colleges at the present time.
3 May	Saudi Arabia and Kuwait abolish Omani entry visas, implementing GCC interior ministers' resolutions.
4 May	GCC National Oil Company directors meet in Riyadh to discuss joint marketing and pricing policies; adopt recommendations concerning cooperation in building and operating refineries and a number of technical areas (training, information, etc.).
10 May	Secretary General Bisharah visits Sana in the Arab Republic of Yemen (ARY) where he meets Ali Abdallah Salih.
10 May	A GCC military delegation led by Saudi brigadier Yusuf al-Madani arrives in Oman for an official visit.
12 May	Bahraini amir returns from Kuwait after a two-day official visit; the two sides discuss common GCC objectives, accomplishments, and goals.
15 May	GCC foreign ministers hold their third emergency meeting in Kuwait to discuss the latest developments in the Iraq-Iran war and the return of Sinai Peninsula to Egypt; agree to reconvene on 30 May without reaching final decisions.
18 May	Saudi Arabia warns Iran not to threaten GCC states.
24 May	Bahrain's ruler arrives in Oman on an official visit; meets with Sultan Qabus to discuss GCC accomplishments and future plans.
30–31 May	GCC foreign ministers meet in Riyadh in the second part of their third emergency meeting [first part was held in Kuwait on 15 May]; review contacts between GCC states

and Iraq, Syria, and Algeria; also review Iraq's readiness to withdraw to international border; call on Iran to stop the conflict and stress the importance of maintaining a unified Arab stand; express thanks and hopes to work closely with Islamic Conference Organization (OCI) to help end Iraq-Iran war.

30	May	GCC states agree to set up the Gulf Investment Fund with a proposed capital of $3 billion (scaled down to $2.1 billion on 11 November).
6	June	GCC officials hold high-level talks with PLO leaders to discuss developments in Lebanon.
6	June	Israel invades Lebanon.
11	June	GCC statement urges Iran to observe cease-fire.
13	June	King Khalid of Saudi Arabia dies; Prince Fahd is chosen to succeed him; Prince Abdallah is new crown prince.
20	June	GCC finance ministers hold meeting in Riyadh; agree to abolish customs duties on national products of GCC states as of 1 December 1982; also agree to permit GCC nationals to invest and work in agriculture, industry, business, and vocational crafts in the six states; finally, approve new transit regulations permitting nationals to travel freely throughout the GCC states.
29	June	PLO calls for GCC states to hold an urgent meeting on developments in Lebanon following the siege of Beirut by Israeli forces.
3–7	July	PDRY and Omani diplomatic delegations meet and reach an agreement to establish diplomatic relations.
7	July	Customs duties on GCC members to be lifted.
11	July	GCC foreign ministers hold their fourth regular meeting in At-Taif to discuss developments in Lebanon.
12	July	GCC foreign ministers conclude their fourth meeting; support the Lebanese and Palestinian peoples under Israeli occupation; support Lebanon's independence and territorial integrity; stress the need to defend Lebanon and the PLO; call on the U.N. Security Council permanent members to impose sanctions on Israel for its refusal to implement Resolutions 508 and 509; denounce the United States for its veto at the Security Council; express appreciation for Iraq's offer to withdraw from all Iranian territory and hope that Iran will respond to peace overtures; express satisfaction with GCC economic accomplishments; approve the financial and administrative programs of the Secretariat.
3	August	Saudi Arabia and Kuwait endorse a new Neutral Zone accord.
1	September	The UAE implements GCC trade regulations.
13	September	Secretary General Bisharah arrives in Abu Dhabi on an official visit.
16	September	GCC information secretaries urge joint policy at their Abu Dhabi meeting for the audiovisual and news agencies and the formation of a collective plan for the welfare of Gulf artists.
19	September	GCC states hold "urgent consultations" on Beirut Palestinian camps massacres.
10–11	October	GCC defense ministers hold second conference in Riyadh; discuss "greater efforts and call for the mobilization of national potentials to ensure further coordination and military coordination between the council member states."

13–14 October	GCC petroleum ministers hold their third meeting in Muscat; discuss Gulf pollution; approve construction of an oil industrial area in Oman as well as the establishment of an oil refinery in Oman; agree to share natural gas resources among themselves and to adopt joint training methods and cooperation in technical areas; discuss the means of transporting water on returning empty tankers to GCC states; support previous decision to maintain current price of oil on international markets; warn other oil-producing states that the "GCC will not protect these countries from the consequences of their erroneous acts should they continue" to undermine the official price by exceeding their production quotas.
16 October	GCC petroleum ministers may have discussed the strategic pipeline that would bypass the Strait of Hormuz during their latest meeting in Muscat, according to local newspapers.
16 October	Oman abolishes visa requirements for GCC nationals effective 1 October 1982.
17 October	GCC interior ministers meet in Riyadh to discuss their proposed internal security pact but fail to agree on a decision.
17–18 October	GCC information ministers establish a "Permanent Committee for Information Control" at the conclusion of their two-day meeting in Abu Dhabi whose aim is to counter foreign "hostile" media; stress Islamic religion; support rulers and regimes of GCC states; and ban "indecent" articles according to the recommendations adopted by the Gulf news directors.
18 October	GCC interior ministers conclude their Riyadh meeting; approve new immigration, passports, and labor regulations; discuss internal security agreement without reaching a final decision; discuss the possibility of establishing a "Center for Security Information" which will be used in the preparation of qualified national cadres in accordance with the prerequisite of collective action.
20 October	GCC port officials hold their second meeting in Riyadh.
24 October	GCC industry ministers hold a meeting in At-Taif and agree to cooperate and coordinate industrial projects and to standardize available resources and capabilities.
27 October	Oman and the PDRY sign an agreement to normalize relations between the two countries following negotiations held in Kuwait.
28 October	GCC welcomes Oman-PDRY agreement on normalization of relations.
30–31 October	GCC trade ministers hold their first meeting in Riyadh.
1 November	GCC Ministerial Council holds its third pre-summit meeting in Manama; agrees on summit agenda; also agrees to a formula "for setting up the unified GCC military council" and to recommend to the heads of state the establishment of a permanent council of defense and interior ministers.
9 November	Third GCC summit meeting opens in Bahrain; agenda includes economic, political, military, and security topics.
11 November	GCC summit ends; heads of state agree to support Iraq in Gulf war and call on Iran to stop its belligerent actions; express gratitude to Kuwait and the UAE for having successfully resolved the Oman-PDRY border dispute; agree to establish the Gulf Investment Fund with a capital of $2.1 billion; express satisfaction on GCC-EEC cooperation; fail to reach accord on the unified internal security agreement.

| 12 | November | *Al-Watan* reports that GCC states agreed to form a Gulf military command with permanent headquarters in Bahrain which would be responsible for all military coordination, exchange of information, and coordination of arms purchases. |

| 15–21 | November | Paris-based *An-Nahar Al-Arabi wa-al-Duwali* reports in its 15–21 November issue that the GCC heads of state agreed to establish a joint air defense system at their Bahrain summit. |

| 17 | November | Kuwait's *Al-Anba* publishes draft text of GCC internal security agreement. |

| 18 | November | Kuwait submits proposals on Gulf internal security agreement to GCC Secretariat. |

| 12 | December | GCC justice ministers hold their first meeting in Riyadh to discuss unification of judicial systems and principles of jurisdiction; also discuss standardization of legislation based on Sharia, unification of criminal law, personal statutes, and court procedures. Discussions also covered a treaty on judiciary activities, implementation of courts, and judges' sentences as well as a treaty on extradition of criminals. |

| 14 | December | GCC justice ministers agree to base GCC states' judicial systems and legislation on Islamic law; agreement was also reached to publish a monthly bulletin on legislation, laws, and other topics of interest in member states. |

| 14 | December | GCC petroleum under secretaries open meeting in Kuwait to coordinate joint efforts and avoid duplicating projects. |

| 26 | December | GCC finance ministers meet in Manama to discuss GCC customs directors' report on member states' investment policy. |

1983

| 4 | January | Omani government agrees to receive and resettle its citizens in the PDRY until 30 April 1983. |

| 8 | January | Gulf News Agency directors hold their second meeting in Bahrain; discuss need to create an international telecommunications link via satellite. |

| 13 | January | Secretary General Bisharah speaks on Gulf unity to *Al-Anba*. |

| 14 | January | GCC petroleum ministers are to meet to discuss a reduction in oil production; hold "emergency" meeting on 15 January in Manama; agree to coordinate the supply of gas to GCC member states; to study the future use of heavy oil in the Gulf, and to provide oil to GCC industries; the concluding statement does not mention oil prices or reduction of production. |

| 19–20 | February | GCC foreign ministers hold their sixth regular meeting in Riyadh; review the recommendations of the finance ministers regarding the Gulf Investment Corporation and the justice ministers' unified legislation proposals; set up a Trade Cooperation Committee to discuss industrial ventures and approve the minutes of a number of committees including water and agriculture; reiterate their call for an end to the Iraq-Iran war and oppose the Tripartite (Syria-Libya-Iran) communiqué on Gulf affairs. |

| 23 | February | Gulf petroleum ministers (Saudi Arabia, Kuwait, UAE, Qatar, and Iraq) meet in Riyadh to discuss the volatile market conditions; they are joined by the Libyan oil minister to discuss a potential cut in the official price. |

| 23 | February | The Kuwaiti daily *Al-Qabas* reports that GCC states will hold joint military exercises in the framework of military coordination and cooperation. |

4 March   *Al-Qabas* reports that GCC citizens will receive unified passports with enhanced security features to eliminate forgeries.

9 March   Secretary General Bisharah reveals to the UAE *Al-Bayan* that the GCC is working on a five-year development plan toward economic integration.

14 March   At a London meeting OPEC ministers agree to reduce the benchmark oil price for Arabian Light crude from $34 a barrel to $29. They also agree on a production ceiling of 17.5 million barrels per day with Saudi Arabia acting as a swing producer.

15 March   Saudi Arabia and Qatar sign an education agreement in Riyadh to organize educational, cultural, and scientific cooperation.

27 March   GCC labor and social affairs under secretaries meet in Riyadh to discuss the unification of social organizations extending social aid to Gulf citizens and setting up joint housing projects in member states.

4 April   Gulf environmental experts meet in Bahrain (including delegates from Iran and Iraq) to discuss the Gulf oil slick that is threatening the littoral states.

6 April   The Regional Organization for the Protection of Marine Environment (ROPME) [GCC states plus Iran and Iraq] continues its meetings in Bahrain on the oil slick in the Nowruz area; health danger feared.

15 April   ROPME meeting fails to reach an agreement on protecting the Persian Gulf's environment.

20 April   GCC information ministers conclude their eighth meeting in Abu Dhabi; their communiqué calls for an end to the Iraq-Iran war and urges the Arab nation to confront the expanding Zionist threat.

22 April   According to Saudi information minister Muhammad Abduh Yamani, Arab journalists working in GCC states will see their freedom of movement and reporting increased.

22 April   Prince Sultan ibn Abd Al-Aziz of Saudi Arabia meets with Bahrain's ruler Shaykh Isa to discuss bilateral relations and defense cooperation in Manama.

23 April   GCC labor and social affairs ministers meet in Riyadh; discuss unified economic accord and the rising concern with expatriate workers. According to Saudi labor and social affairs minister Ibrahim Al-Anqari, "Cooperation between private and governmental humanitarian societies and citizens should be given priority," especially in the fields of education and recreation; the ministers also examine legislation that would protect GCC youth "from harmful habits."

26 April   ROPME member states ministers meet in Kuwait to discuss the continuing threat of the oil slick in the Gulf; no agreement is reached.

27 April   Kuwait and Bahrain sign a communication agreement; both countries will be connected by a marine cable; at present communications are conducted through satellites over the Indian Ocean; the agreement falls within the recommendations of the GCC Ministerial Council's decisions.

2 May   Shaykh Khalifah ibn Zayid, deputy supreme commander of the UAE armed forces and Abu Dhabi heir apparent, calls for joint maneuvers to be held in GCC states.

5 May   Omani foreign minister under secretary Sayf ibn Hamad al-Batashi reveals to the Cairo daily *Al-Jumhuriyah* that GCC states are studying the formation of a joint military unit.

6 May	UAE president Zayid pays an official visit to Bahrain.
9 May	GCC foreign ministers convene an emergency meeting of the Ministerial Council in Manama to discuss the Gulf oil spill and the pending Israeli-Lebanese peace treaty negotiated by Secretary Shultz in the area.
10 May	GCC foreign ministers agree to intensify efforts to end the Iraq-Iran war; *Al-Watan* reports that Kuwait will contact the permanent members of the U.N. Security Council to seek support in its mediation efforts between Baghdad and Tehran.
11 May	GCC finance ministers meet in Riyadh; discuss customs duties and seek to reduce tariffs among member states.
12 May	*Ash-Sharq Al-Awsat* announces that the GCC plans to form a committee which will shuttle between Baghdad and Tehran to mediate in the ongoing war.
14 May	The WAKH News Agency reports that a GCC delegation composed of Kuwaiti and UAE officials will visit Iran and Iraq on 16 May with a first stop in Tehran.
17 May	Bahrain's Shaykh Isa pays an official visit to Saudi Arabia.
18–19 May	GCC Ministerial Council convenes its seventh regular meeting in Riyadh to discuss Lebanon and Iraq-Iran wars.
23 May	Qatari crown prince and defense minister Shaykh Hamad ibn Khalifah Al-Thani pays an official visit to Kuwait; discusses military cooperation at all levels.
24 May	An official GCC delegation travels to Sana, ARY.
25 May	Secretary General Bisharah, at a Riyadh press conference, states that the security of the Yemens is linked with that of the GCC states.
27 May	Ibrahim as-Subhi states to *Al-Qabas* that GCC states are studying the means of establishing a unified military force to defend the region and are looking into the possibility of creating a GCC military industrialization organization.
30 May	GCC telecommunications ministers meet in Riyadh; discuss the potential for a unified network of telecommunication and a unified postal system. Other items include the unification of frequencies and the elimination of distortion and co-channel interference, the establishment of a kind of pattern of instruments, and the unification of telecommunications tariffs.
11 June	Kuwait confirms that it will participate in upcoming GCC joint military maneuvers.
6 July	ROPME officials formulate plan to combat oil slick.
21–22 July	Kuwait's interior minister, Shaykh Nawwaf al-Ahmad Al-Jabir, is quoted in *Arab Times* as saying that the amirate had finalized amendments to the GCC Internal Security Agreement.
6 August	Secretary General Bisharah visits Bahrain where he meets with prime minister in preparation for fourth summit.
10 August	GCC petroleum ministers open sixth meeting in At-Taif; discuss oil coordination system in member states.
22–24 August	GCC foreign ministers open their eighth meeting in At-Taif; discuss Iraq-Iran war and Lebanese crisis involving factionalism within Palestinian ranks; envisage economic co-

<table>
<tr><td></td><td>ordination to lead to a "Gulf Common Market" by 1990; agree to strengthen Oman economically and militarily; agree to suspend aid to any country that restores diplomatic relations with Israel.</td></tr>
<tr><td>5 September</td><td>Secretary General Bisharah arrives in Abu Dhabi on a pre-summit official visit.</td></tr>
<tr><td>25–27 September</td><td>Qatar's heir apparent and defense minister, Shaykh Hamad, arrives in Bahrain on an official visit accompanied by a high-ranking military delegation; discusses coordination in the two countries' military establishments.</td></tr>
<tr><td>29 September</td><td>*Al-Anba* reports that Qatari officials have discussed an Iranian plot to assassinate GCC leaders at their forthcoming summit meeting to be held in Doha.</td></tr>
<tr><td>10 October</td><td>GCC trade ministers open their second conference in Manama; discuss the unification of specifications and measurements in GCC states and unified trade fairs as well as food reserves.</td></tr>
<tr><td>11 October</td><td>GCC states start *Dara al-Jazirah* (Peninsula Shield) exercises near Abu Dhabi; close to 4,000 soldiers and officers participate in these first maneuvers.</td></tr>
<tr><td>11–12 October</td><td>GCC finance ministers open conference in Riyadh.</td></tr>
<tr><td>12 October</td><td>Bahrain Defense Forces commander arrives in Riyadh.</td></tr>
<tr><td>15 October</td><td>GCC states end the first stage of Peninsula Shield manuevers.</td></tr>
<tr><td>16 October</td><td>GCC chiefs of staff hold their third meeting in Riyadh; discuss Peninsula Shield I and appraise its accomplishments; prepare results for defense ministers.</td></tr>
<tr><td>23 October</td><td>Secretary General Bisharah arrives in Doha on an official visit.</td></tr>
<tr><td>23 October</td><td>*Arab Times* reports that GCC states have agreed to establish a joint radar network for the Arabian Peninsula.</td></tr>
<tr><td>27 October</td><td>Oman and the PDRY establish diplomatic relations at the ambassador levels following GCC mediation.</td></tr>
<tr><td>31 October</td><td>Iran rejects a U.N. Security Council resolution calling for an immediate cease-fire in the Iraq-Iran war.</td></tr>
<tr><td>2 November</td><td>GCC Ministerial Council's ninth meeting opens in Doha.</td></tr>
<tr><td>3 November</td><td>In a press interview Secretary General Bisharah reveals that GCC foreign ministers discussed measures that member states ought to take to deter Iran from carrying out its threat to close the strategic Strait of Hormuz.</td></tr>
<tr><td>7–9 November</td><td>GCC's fourth summit meeting is held in Doha, Qatar; form a mini-committee of Kuwaiti and Qatari officials to mediate among the different Palestinian factions fighting in Lebanon; call on United Nations to assist in bringing Iraq-Iran war to an end; call on Iran and Iraq to accept a cease-fire; support Lebanon's integrity; review military coordination among member states as well as the preliminary results of the economic agreement; schedule their next summit for November 1984 in Kuwait.</td></tr>
<tr><td>8 November</td><td>*Al-Ray al-Amm* reports that GCC heads of state agreed to create a high-level committee to discuss the Hawar Island dispute between Bahrain and Qatar.</td></tr>
<tr><td>15 November</td><td>The UAE deputy supreme commander of the armed forces and Abu Dhabi heir apparent arrives in Riyadh; meets with King Fahd.</td></tr>
</table>

16 November	A Kuwaiti air force unit flies to Riyadh to hold joint air exercises with the Royal Saudi Air Force.
19 November	Saudi crown prince Abdallah arrives in Kuwait.
21 November	A Kuwaiti Interior Ministry delegation visits Abu Dhabi to explore security cooperation potentials.
27 November	Riyadh reveals that its joint air exercises with the Kuwaiti air force is to continue for eleven days and that the types of planes involved include A-4 Skyhawks as well as F-15s and F-5s.
28 November	GCC interior ministers open third meeting in Riyadh.
29 November	GCC interior ministers conclude meeting; approve new transit regulations for GCC citizens as of 1 January 1984; approve standardization of passports and abolishing of residence permits for GCC nationals.
30 November	Kuwaiti and Saudi air force units complete their first joint military exercises.
5 December	Prince Faysal, Saudi Arabia's foreign minister, arrives in Muscat on an official visit.
12 December	A series of explosions rock Kuwait City; the U.S., and French embassies, airport control tower, and Ash-Shuaibah oil refinery are hit; the six explosions injure over 100 persons; Islamic Jihad claims responsibility.
13 December	Kuwait's bombings kill four persons and injure sixty-two; a number of Shia members of the underground *Al-Dawa* party are arrested; all GCC states condemn bombings; GCC states do not plan to call an emergency meeting of the foreign ministers, however; Kuwaiti authorities seize a number of weapons and ammunition which they display on December 18; Saudi Arabia offers security assistance; on December 19, a special court is formed to try all arrested suspects.
29 December	An official Kuwaiti statement reveals that the investigation led to several solid pieces of evidence, including the sources of weapons and the funds required to carry the bombings out; allegations that Iran may have instigated the bombings are left unanswered.

1984

9 January	GCC foreign ministers convene their sixth extraordinary meeting in Riyadh; discuss Kuwait bombings and Iraq-Iran war; declare that an attack on Kuwait is an attack on all Gulf states and offer the amirate all available resources; declare determination to confront conspiracy collectively.
13 January	GCC foreign ministers meet in Rabat, Morocco, during the OCI gathering; discuss GCC-Arab states relations.
21 January	Bahrain Defense Forces (BDF) helicopters conduct joint exercises with Qatari air force units in Qatar pursuant to GCC recommendations.
23 January	Several Royal Saudi Air Force (RSAF) F-15s arrive in Kuwait to take part in joint exercises within GCC framework on military cooperation. Exercises last for ten days during these third joint air maneuvers.
28–30 January	GCC justice ministers meet in Riyadh to discuss the issue of unifying legal systems in member states; decide to refer question to technical committee; discuss issue of ownership of real estate and consider the idea of establishing an arbitration center; recom-

mend that nationals join Sharia faculties in universities and urge member states to increase legal training among personnel.

31 January	Saudi Arabia announces that a new security force will be established to protect vital installations (oil, electricity, and water plants). The new internal security forces will be headed by Colonel Dr. Abdallah ad-Daham.
3 February	According to Shaykh Abdallah ibn Khalid Al-Khalifah, Bahraini minister of justice and Islamic affairs, GCC countries have agreed to enact Islamic laws within five years.
4 February	GCC foreign under secretaries meet in Riyadh; discuss how to coordinate their diplomatic activities within the 1961 Vienna convention treaty on diplomatic privileges and immunities.
4 February	Three Royal Omani Air Force (ROAF) Jaguar fighter planes from the Masirah air base arrive in the UAE for joint air exercises within the GCC military cooperation plans. They return to Oman on 11 February.
9 February	Soviet Communist party secretary general Yuri Andropov dies. Kuwait, Qatar, Oman, and the UAE cable condolences on 11 February. Bahrain and Saudi Arabia refrain from doing so.
10 February	The Kuwaiti newspaper *Al-Ray al-Amm* urges the GCC to accept the Arab Republic of Yemen as a full member.
12 February	Secretary General Bisharah arrives in Abu Dhabi to discuss terrorism against GCC citizens; reviews UAE ambassador al-Mubarak's assassination in Paris.
13–14 February	GCC chiefs of staff begin their fourth meeting in Doha; discuss the establishment of potential military industries in member states; Prince Sultan of Saudi Arabia, in a statement to *Al-Riyadh*, declares that the chiefs of staff are discussing military cooperation including joint naval maneuvers; the chiefs of staff also discuss steps taken to establish a joint Gulf Military College.
20–21 February	GCC defense ministers convene their third meeting in Doha; agree to consolidate military cooperation and deepen defense relations; ministers stress the necessity of concentrating on training, building national values, and self-reliance.
1 March	Reagan administration notifies the U.S. Congress of its intent to sell 1,613 shoulder-fired Stinger antiaircraft missiles to Jordan at an estimated cost of $133 million. An additional 1,200 Stingers are to be provided to Saudi Arabia.
5 March	Lebanon's President Amine Al-Jumayyil announces that the 17 May 1983 agreement with Israel on troop withdrawals is null and void. GCC states support move.
6 March	The amir of Bahrain, Shaykh Isa, arrives in Dhahran on an official visit to Saudi Arabia.
10–11 March	GCC foreign ministers convene their tenth regular meeting in Riyadh; discuss the Lebanon situation and note the efforts of Saudi Arabia in reconvening the different warring factions around a negotiating table (Lausanne, Switzerland); discuss Iraq-Iran war and note that despite past efforts, Iran rejects mediation moves; praise Iraq for readiness to negotiate an end to the conflict; agree to participate in LAS foreign ministers' conference on 13 March in Baghdad; confirm that GCC economic agreement has entered second stage of its implementation.

20 March	The Reagan administration, facing strong opposition from Congress, cancels the proposed sale of Stinger missiles to Jordan and Saudi Arabia. GCC states react with dismay.
26 March	An international team of military and medical experts conclude in a U.N. report that chemical weapons, including mustard gas and nerve agents, have been used in the Iraq-Iran war.
27 March	Six persons arrested in connection with the December 1983 bombings in Kuwait are sentenced to death. Other prisoners receive the following sentences: four receive 15 years' imprisonment, one 10 years' imprisonment, two 5 years' imprisonment and deportation, seven receive life imprisonment, and five are acquitted.
27 March	Speaking to the teaching staff and students of King Faysal University in the Eastern Province, King Fahd declared that the kingdom is studying the introduction of military conscription.
30 March	The U.N. Security Council condemns the use of chemical weapons in the Iraq-Iran war and renews appeal for a cease-fire.
1 April	Secretary General Bisharah arrives in Abu Dhabi on a two-day visit.
12 April	Saudi Arabia, Qatar, Kuwait, and Bahrain conclude air exercises in Manama within the framework of GCC military cooperation.
19 April	Bahraini crown prince Hamad departs for two-day official visit to the UAE.
22 April	UAE chief of staff Brigadier General Muhammad Said al-Badi visits Bahrain; meets with counterpart, Brigadier General Khalifah ibn Hamad Al-Khalifah.
25 April	The 362,869 deadweight ton Saudi-owned oil tanker *Safina al-Arab* is hit by an Iraqi-launched Exocet missile outside Iran's Kharg Island and subsequently declared a total loss.
1 May	Shaykh Isa lays the foundation stone of the "Arabian Gulf University" in As-Sakhir, Bahrain.
6 May	According to *Al-Qabas*, GCC states informed Washington that they rejected a U.S. proposal to develop an early joint planning strategy in response to developments in the Gulf war.
6 May	*As-Siyassah* quotes a senior Gulf source as saying that the GCC states are striving to establish an intrinsic strike force during the next five years.
6 May	Shaykh Isa of Bahrain receives a cable of thanks from Soviet president Chernenko in reply to his congratulatory message.
6 May	*As-Siyassah* reports GCC secretary general Bisharah's announcement that King Fahd of Saudi Arabia contributed 100 million Saudi riyals (about $35 million) to build permanent GCC Headquarters.
9 May	Saudi defense minister Prince Sultan declares that GCC states will conduct aerial military maneuvers in Saudi Arabia in October 1984.
9 May	The Saudi oil tanker *Al-Ahud*, attacked by Iraqi planes on 7 May near Iran's Kharg Island, is considered lost.

12 May	The Qatari interior minister, Shaykh Khalid ibn Hamad Al-Thani, starts a three-day official visit to Kuwait.
13 May	The Kuwaiti tanker *Umm Casbah* is hit by an unidentified plane in the Gulf.
14 May	A second Kuwaiti tanker, the *Bahrah*, is attacked by an unidentified plane in the Gulf.
14 May	Gulf News Agency directors meet in Riyadh; agree to coordinate and exchange news among the Arab news agencies and the GCC Information Department.
14 May	The Qatari interior minister arrives in Riyadh to attend the graduating ceremonies of the fortieth class of King Faysal Security College, which includes cadets from Qatar.
15 May	Saudi defense minister arrives in Kuwait on a four-day official visit; security issues dominate talks.
15 May	Secretary General Bisharah arrives in Doha to brief Amir Al-Thani on recent developments.
16 May	The Saudi tanker *Yanbu* is attacked by an unidentified plane at the port of Ras Tanurah inside Saudi territorial waters.
17 May	GCC foreign ministers convene an emergency meeting in Riyadh to discuss the tanker war; issue statement denouncing the attacks and agree to submit matter to an emergency meeting of the LAS (thus seeking a unified Arab stand), as well as the United Nations, in view of the threats these attacks pose to international peace and security.
17 May	Omani foreign minister al-Alawi arrives in Riyadh for an official visit.
22 May	President Reagan declares "neither we, nor the Western world as such, would stand by and see the Straits of the Persian Gulf closed to international traffic."
23 May	An official announcement from Washington says that a project to equip and train a mobile regional intervention force of Jordanian army units is being scrapped because of congressional opposition.
29 May	The Reagan administration announces that it has sent 400 Stinger antiaircraft missiles and 200 launchers to Saudi Arabia. An additional KC-10 tanker is also dispatched to support the U.S. AWACS deployed in the kingdom. The president uses his emergency powers to sell the missiles in response to increased attacks against shipping in the Persian Gulf.
1 June	The U.N. Security Council, in a GCC-sponsored resolution, calls on all states to respect freedom of navigation in the Gulf.
5 June	RSAF F-15s intercept Iranian F-4 Phantom aircraft approaching the kingdom's airspace and shoot one of the Iranian jets. The action is regretted by Riyadh but hailed by GCC states as an act of self-defense.
10 June	GCC petroleum ministers convene a meeting in At-Taif to discuss tanker war and its impact on oil sales; agree to replace for free all losses incurred in the attacks.
12–14 June	GCC foreign ministers convene a meeting in At-Taif; discuss Iraq-Iran war and the resulting tanker war as well as U.N. Security Council Resolution 552 which is perceived as supportive of the GCC. The ministers close their eleventh meeting by agreeing to coordinate peace efforts through the United Nations.

14 June	Secretary General Bisharah arrives in Kuwait for an official visit; meets with ruler whom he briefs on latest ministerial council deliberations.
23 June	GCC chiefs of staff convene an emergency meeting in Riyadh; recommendations are kept secret but probably dealt with internal security matters; recommend a $2-billion financial package for Oman to develop its air defense system and coordinate intelligence gathered by the AWACS stationed in Saudi Arabia.
27 June	Bahrain's *Akhbar al-Khalij* reports that the GCC chiefs of staff adopted an overall air defense plan for the Gulf at their extraordinary meeting held in Riyadh.
4 July	Thirty-five Iranians attempting to enter the UAE illegally are arrested in front of the Hyatt Regency Hotel in Dubai. They are tried and found guilty of breaking UAE immigration laws. After a two-week jail sentence, all are deported.
8 July	Secretary General Bisharah declares to KUNA that future shipping attacks in the Gulf will be considered as "acts of war."
10 July	Kuwaiti authorities arrest two Iranians and two Arab nationals trading in ammunition behind a grocery store. Large quantities of ammunition are confiscated.
21 July	Saudi defense minister Prince Sultan arrives in Muscat on an official visit to Oman.
28 July	GCC assistant secretary general for economic affairs, Dr. Abdallah al-Quwayz, expresses the dissatisfaction of the GCC with the EEC decision to impose tariffs on the import of Saudi methanol.
4 August	A squadron of RSAF fighters arrives at Thamarit Air Base in Oman for a two-day joint maneuvers within the GCC military cooperation framework.
11 August	GCC states announce that they are stockpiling oil for emergency use.
16 August	Within the GCC military cooperation framework, the ROAF and the RSAF conduct joint air exercises using live ammunition.
29 August	Bahrain and Qatar hold a joint naval exercise within the framework of GCC military activities.
18–19 September	GCC foreign and defense ministers convene a two-day meeting to discuss collective security. The meeting is held at the King Faysal Air Base outside Abha, Saudi Arabia; the committee approves the Defense Policy Paper and prepares it for submission to the heads of state summit in November; according to *Al-Qabas*, the committee approves the allocation of $60 million per year to bolster air defense systems and communications in member states; in addition, the daily reports that GCC foreign and defense ministers agreed to recommend the establishment of a GCC Rapid Deployment Force.
23 September	Secretary General Bisharah ends a one-day visit to Bahrain. Returns to Riyadh after meeting with Yusuf Ahmad al-Shirawi, Bahrain's minister of development and industry.
24 September	Foreign ministry under secretaries of the GCC states hold their second meeting in Riyadh; discuss various issues; no statement is issued at the conclusion of the meeting.
29 September	Kuwaiti interior minister Shaykh Nawwaf al-Ahmad al-Jabir Al-Sabah visits Qatar to discuss security cooperation measures.
2 October	GCC foreign ministers confer with U.S. secretary of state Shultz in New York during the U.N. session.

6 October	*Al-Watan* quotes Kuwait's defense minister as suggesting that the GCC would establish a joint rapid deployment force composed of two brigades to be based at Shuayb al-Batin base, 200 miles north of Jidda, Saudi Arabia.
10 October	GCC states' *Dara al-Jazirah II* (Peninsula Shield II) exercises begin in Hafar al-Batin, Saudi Arabia.
23 October	Peninsula Shield II exercises conclude.
26 October	Saudi and Omani ships hold joint naval exercises in the Gulf of Oman, which end on 1 November.
29 October	Secretary General Bisharah visits Muscat. Meets with Deputy Prime Minister for Legal Affairs Fahd ibn Mahmud Al-Bu Said.
30 October	UAE chief of staff Brigadier Muhammad Said al-Badi announces that GCC states have agreed to centralize their military colleges and institutes.
30 October	Secretary General Bisharah visits Bahrain. Dicusses preparations for fifth summit.
31 October	An OPEC ministerial conference in Geneva decides to reduce members' total output quotas from 17.5 to 16 million barrels per day following cuts in the prices of Norwegian, British, and Nigerian crude.
6 November	GCC Finance and Economic Cooperation Committee begins its eighth meeting in Riyadh.
15 November	"The Radio of the Voice of the GCC from Kuwait" begins transmission throughout the region.
19 November	GCC states agree to hold future summit meetings in Riyadh following the planned 1986 summit in Muscat.
20 November	GCC foreign ministers hold a pre-summit meeting in Kuwait; set up a Legal Committee to study legislative aspects of the Ministerial Council's agenda; agree to undertake a vigorous bid to reconcile Iran and Iraq.
20 November	Omani interior minister Badr Ibn Saud ibn Haib visits the UAE carrying a letter from Sultan Qabus to President Zayid.
21 November	GCC foreign ministers conclude their meeting; draft summit agenda, including a recommendation to accept the GCC defense strategy endorsed at the Saudi Arabian Abha resort meeting in September.
26 November	Washington and Baghdad resume full diplomatic relations originally broken following the 1967 Arab-Israeli war.
27–29 November	GCC heads of state convene their fifth summit meeting in Kuwait; discussion includes the Iraq-Iran war, collective Arab action, and defense issues. An official spokesman announces that the heads of state agreed to extend Abdallah Yaqub Bisharah's appointment as secretary general until November 1988; the council reiterates its call to work for a peaceful resolution of the Iraq-Iran war and to support the efforts carried out by the United Nations and the Good Offices Committee, which was set up by the OCI and the Nonaligned Movement; it also reiterates its readiness to carry out direct endeavors to solve the disputes between Baghdad and Tehran; it praises Iraq's attitude toward the U.N. and OCI resolutions and calls on Iran to participate in the efforts that aim at finding a solution based on attaining the rights of both parties. The council also

emphasizes the importance of U.N. Security Council Resolution 552 (1 June 1984), which proclaimed safe navigation in the Gulf and called on all parties to respect it. On the Arab front, the council calls for agreements based on cooperation and understanding; it reiterates its support for the legality of the PLO as the sole representative of the Palestinian people; it also underlines its support for the stability, independence, and national sovereignty of Lebanon within secure boundaries. Finally, the council takes note of advances in the economic field, including the GCC's joint strategy of economic development and integration.

29 November		GCC states decide to set up a joint military force to meet any foreign aggression.
30 November		A RSAF contingent arrives in Abu Dhabi to participate in joint air maneuvers with UAE forces.
16 December		Kuwait's *Al-Siyassah* reveals that GCC states plan to work together on antihijacking plans.
26 December		Saudi defense minister Prince Sultan visits Qatar; meets with Heir Apparent and Commander in Chief of the Qatari Armed Forces Shaykh Hamad ibn Khalifah Al-Thani.

1985

7–8 January		GCC labor and social affairs ministers open their seventh meeting in Bahrain; discuss the financial and administrative regulations of the follow-up bureau; and agree to appoint as secretary-general, Kamal al-Salih, to head the follow-up bureau.
13 January		Kuwaiti and Qatari naval units begin joint exercises near Doha within the GCC military cooperation framework.
20 January		A joint technical committee to mark the borders between Oman and the PDRY begins its third annual meeting in Muscat (the first time that a meeting takes place in a capital).
20 January		Saudi chief public security officer at the Interior Ministry First Lt. General Abdallah Abd al-Rahman al-Shaykh arrives in Kuwait on a five-day official visit; discusses interior security within the GCC framework.
23 January		GCC finance ministers meet with Gulf Investment Organization's board of directors in Kuwait. GIO board approves a plan for investing in the member states who hold equal shares in the $2.1-billion-dollar joint petrochemical, industrial, and livestock projects. The board also approves the organization's 1985 budget of $14 million ($4.8 billion in operations since foundation).
31 January		GCC information under secretaries meet in Kuwait; agree to coordinate Gulf media coverage stressing cultural relations, including youth activities; further agree to refrain from making false judgments following official pronouncements to limit and eliminate hatred among member states' populations.
2 February		Secretary General Bisharah visits Qatar; meets with the ruler, Amir Al-Thani, in Doha.
5 February		Kuwait's deputy prime minister discusses with his Saudi counterpart in Riyadh moves to end the Gulf war.
6 February		Bahrain's foreign minister, Shaykh Mubarak Muhammad ibn Mubarak Al-Khalifah, returns from Saudi Arabia; discusses Gulf issues with counterpart.

20 February	Secretary General Bisharah visits Manama. Meets with Foreign Minister Shaykh Muhammad ibn Mubarak Al-Khalifah; discusses upcoming GCC foreign ministers' agenda.
1 March	The second GCC-EEC Tariff Negotiation talks open in Manama to review customs fees imposed on GCC states' petrochemical exports to community members.
2 March	GCC-EEC Tariff Negotiations end without an agreement; "the two parties," however, "agree . . . to deal in the fields of trade, technology, investment activity and industrial cooperation," according to Secretary General Bisharah.
4 March	Kuwaiti and Omani air force aircraft hold joint maneuvers near the strategic Strait of Hormuz with the Kuwaiti planes operating out of Thamarit air base.
17–19 March	GCC foreign ministers convene their fourteenth meeting in Riyadh; discuss the recent escalation in the Iraq-Iran war and declare that they view these latest developments "with anxiety." The ministers further "affirm their full solidarity with Iraq in preserving the sovereignty, safety and integrity of its territory" and call on Iran to "respond to international efforts to find a peaceful solution to this war and demand [that Iran] should not cross Iraqi territory and should respect the international borders between the two countries."
27 March	UAE and Kuwaiti air force units end joint air maneuvers near and at the Al-Dafrah air base in Abu Dhabi.
6 April	Saudi foreign minister Prince Saud al-Faysal arrives in Aden on a two-day visit to the PDRY; meets with the secretary general of the Yemeni Socialist party, Ali Nasir Muhammad, and discusses bilateral and regional affairs.
9 April	GCC information ministers convene their ninth meeting in Riyadh; discuss developments in the Iraq-Iran war, Lebanon, and the Soviet occupation of Afghanistan.
11 April	Saudi finance minister Muhammad Abu al-Khayl arrives in Manama to attend the ceremony of laying the last girder of the Bahrain–Saudi Arabia causeway.
16 April	Sultan Qabus of Oman arrives in Manama on a three-day official visit to Bahrain.
18 April	Sultan visits Bahraini Defense Forces Headquarters; talks center around the coordination of arms purchase and familiarization with assorted technical systems.
18 April	Bahrain heir apparent arrives in Abu Dhabi on a visit to the UAE; meets with President Zayid.
21 April	GCC air force maneuvers start in Qatar; they last for one week and involve only helicopters.
22 April	GCC ministers of electricity and water resources hold their second meeting in Kuwait; discuss joint grids and the management of desalination plants.
23 April	Saudi petroleum minister Zaki Yamani arrives in Manama on a two-day visit; meets with Development and Industry Minister Yusuf Ahmad al-Shirawi; is received by the prime minister.
29 April	Saudi chief of staff, General Mohammad Salih al-Hamad, accompanied by a high-ranking delegation, arrives in Kuwait to discuss bilateral and GCC military affairs with Kuwaiti military officials.

6 May	GCC labor and social affairs ministers open their third meeting in Riyadh; they discuss manpower situation in Gulf states and stress the need to develop national human resources in order to replace their expatriate workers.
8 May	Iranian energy minister Ghafuri-Fard visits Saudi Arabia where he meets Foreign Minister Saud al-Faysal and Defense Minister Sultan.
9 May	Bahraini and UAE air force helicopters arrive in Muscat to participate in joint air maneuvers with ROAF crafts within the GCC military cooperation framework.
12 May	UAE president Zayid arrives in Jidda on a visit to the kingdom where he meets with King Fahd.
12 May	Saudi, Qatari, Omani, and UAE military delegations arrive in Sana (ARY) to attend the *Al-Fajr* (The Dawn) military maneuvers conducted by North Yemeni forces.
14 May	GCC finance and economy ministers open their ninth meeting in Riyadh; emphasize private sector initiatives in GCC economies and discuss customs questions among member states.
18 May	Two explosions, for which "Islamic Jihad" claims responsibility, take place in Riyadh, coinciding with a visit to Iran by Saudi foreign minister Prince Saud al-Faysal. The visit is the first by a high-ranking Saudi official to Tehran since the 1979 Iranian Revolution.
20 May	Al-Shariqah's (UAE) *Al-Khalij* attributes reports to Kuwaiti sources to the effect that GCC countries have presented comprehensive mediation proposals to end the Gulf war between Iraq and Iran. The paper states that Prince Saud al-Faysal's visit to Tehran was meant to present them to Iranian officials.
25 May	An attempt on the life of Amir Jabir of Kuwait narrowly fails when a car bomb is driven into a motorcade carrying him to the Sief Palace (two Amiri guards and a passerby are killed, however). The attack takes place ten days after "Islamic Jihad's" demand that the Kuwaiti authorities release seventeen convicted prisoners in exchange for six U.S. and French hostages held in Lebanon.
26 May	In a statement issued at the headquarters, GCC states denounce the attack on the amir of Kuwait and reemphasize member states' determination to achieve stability in the Gulf region through all available means.
27 May	*Al-Anba* reports that Kuwaiti security officials have identified the driver of the car which attempted to kill the amir. He is an Iraqi holding a Pakistani passport with a valid residency permit and a legitimate business sponsor.
28 May	A high-ranking Iranian delegation including Ali Shams Ardakani, adviser to the foreign minister, and Dr. Alaoddin Borujerdi, director of the Arab Affairs Administration at the Foreign Ministry, arrive in Abu Dhabi on the first leg of an Arab Gulf tour.
29 May	Ali Shams Ardakani and his delegation arrive in Manama from Doha on the third leg of their Gulf tour carrying a message from Iranian foreign minister Velayati.
30 May	Ali Shams Ardakani and his delegation arrive in Kuwait from Manama on the fourth leg of their Gulf tour.
2 June	Ali Shams Ardakani and his delegation arrive in At-Taif, Saudi Arabia, on the fifth leg of their Gulf tour; meet with Foreign Minister Prince Saud al-Faysal.

5 June	Yusuf al-Shirawi, Bahraini minister of development and industry, arrives in At-Taif for consultations with Saudi officials.

5 June — Yusuf al-Shirawi, Bahraini minister of development and industry, arrives in At-Taif for consultations with Saudi officials.

23 June — The United Arab Shipping Company confirms that its Kuwaiti-registered cargo ship the *Al-Muharraq* was detained near the Strait of Hormuz by Iranian naval forces on 20 June.

25 June — The amir of Bahrain, Shaykh Isa, arrives in Kuwait on a one-day visit to congratulate Skaykh Jabir on his escape from the attack on the ruler's life.

26 June — Kuwaiti authorities arrest an Iranian national carrying twenty-six photographs of Kuwaiti governmental and industrial installations.

28 June — In an interview with the London-based *Al-Sayyad* weekly, Bahraini prime minister Shaykh Khalifah ibn Salman Al-Khalifah states that GCC countries should reconsider their relations with the Soviet Union given Moscow's importance in world affairs.

29 June — GCC trades ministers open their fourth meeting in Riyadh; discuss food reserves and coordination of the purchase of foodstuffs; agree to establish a trade arbitration center for GCC countries as part of the Chambers of Commerce in member states.

8 July — The ruler of the UAE Amirate of Ras al-Khaimah, Shaykh Sakr ibn Muhammad al-Qasimi, is received by Sultan Qabus in Oman.

8–9 July — GCC foreign ministers hold their fifteenth regular session in Abha, Saudi Arabia; they condemn the attack on the amir of Kuwait, call on Iran to release the Kuwaiti vessel *Al-Muharraq* "immediately," and approve a number of items dealing with economic and labor issues.

11 July — Close to 100 persons are injured following two explosions in Al-Sharq and Al-Salimiyah districts in Kuwait. The bombs, planted in front of cafés, kill nine and are claimed by the "Arab Revolutionary Brigades Organization."

12 July — Iran releases the Kuwaiti ship *Al-Muharraq* along with all its crew and original cargo except for 2,856 tons of freight in transit through Kuwait (to Iraq?) which were unloaded at Bandar Abbas.

13 July — Saudi foreign minister Prince Saud al-Faysal arrives in Kuwait to deliver a message from King Fahd to Shaykh Jabir condemning the recent wave of bombings in the shaykhdom.

13 July — The GCC Secretariat issues a statement in Riyadh condemning the Kuwaiti explosions and affirming its support to the amirate.

29 July — President Zayid of the UAE arrives in Salalah on an official visit to Oman.

30 July — Kuwait deports nearly 4,000 persons following the Al-Sharq and Al-Salimiyah explosions on 11 July, most of whom are presumed to be Iranians and Lebanese.

4 August — *Al-Ittihad* (UAE) reports that a Dubai civil court has ordered the arrest and deportation of thirteen Iranian infiltrators who arrived in the UAE illegally.

8 August — *Gulf Daily News* (Bahrain) reports that GCC states are considering to impose a tariff of 20 percent on European goods in retaliation for tariffs imposed by the EEC on Arab petrochemical products.

11 August — Border guards in the Amirate of Sharjah arrest fifteen Iranians who were attempting to enter the UAE illegally.

12	August	Staff Major General Yusuf al-Madani, chairman of the GCC Military Committee, arrives in Manama to discuss military cooperation efforts with Bahraini officials.
2–3	September	GCC foreign ministers open their sixteenth regular meeting in Riyadh; discuss Iraq-Iran war and other issues; "regret Iran's continued refusal to respond to the efforts made to end this war through negotiations and reconciliation."
5	September	A Kuwaiti container ship the *Al-Watiyah* is stopped by an Iranian coast guard vessel. Kuwait lodges a protest with Tehran on 9 September.
7	September	Bahraini prime minister Khalifah ibn Salman Al-Khalifah arrives in Muscat on a three-day official visit to Oman.
8	September	EEC commissioner Claude Cheysson arrives in Jidda on a three-day visit to the kingdom; meets with Prince Saud al-Faysal and GCC officials; discusses GCC-EEC economic relations in the wake of an EEC decision to levy high import tariffs on GCC petrochemical products.
10	September	Omani interior minister Badr ibn Saud ibn Harib arrives in Manama as part of a tour of GCC states; leaves for Kuwait and Saudi Arabia on 11 September.
17	September	GCC interior ministers convene their fourth meeting in Riyadh; discuss security cooperation and coordination among the six states as well as issuance of a standard Gulf passport.
23	September	A number of naval units of the Royal Saudi Navy and Qatari Naval Forces arrive in Oman to hold joint maneuvers with Royal Omani Naval Forces. The exercises consist of naval mobilization operations, training in electronic warfare, aerial target practice, and artillery shelling of assumed hostile targets. In addition, participating ships practice transmitting messages among themselves and refueling as well as servicing ships.
25	September	GCC industry ministers hold their fourth meeting in Al-Khubar, Saudi Arabia; discuss GCC-EEC economic relations and agree to identify up to five industries per member state that require protection.
26	September	Oman and the Soviet Union establish diplomatic relations at the ambassadorial level.
28	September	GCC finance and economy ministers convene their tenth meeting in Riyadh; discuss export-import regulations; agree to apply the coordinated custom tariff system as of 1 January 1986.
30	September	GCC assistant secretary general for economic affairs Dr. Abdallah al-Quwayz states to *Oman* (Muscat) that a meeting between the GCC and EEC will be held in Luxembourg on 14 October to discuss GCC petrochemical exports to EEC states.
1	October	According to the Bahraini news agency WAKH, GCC countries agreed in 1982 (during the petroleum ministers' Oman meeting) to draft a formula to use a unified contract to sell their crude oil, liquid gas, and refined products. "The resolution was approved in a meeting of marketing directors of GCC national oil companies, recently held in Riyadh."
1	October	*Al-Ray al-Amm* asserts that Bahrain is considering establishing diplomatic relations with the U.S.S.R. and that contacts and consultations took place between officials of both countries. The paper concludes that "all Gulf countries ultimately will follow the steps of Muscat and Bahrain with regard to the establishment of relations with Moscow within one year at the most."

2	October	The GCC Secretariat issues a statement in Riyadh condemning the Israeli raid on the PLO Headquarters in Tunis. GCC rulers and editorials throughout the Gulf point to U.S.-Israeli cooperation efforts identifying anti-Palestinian and anti-Arab patterns. All reconfirm their full support to Arafat and the PLO.
7–8	October	GCC chiefs of staff convene their fifth meeting in Riyadh; discuss GCC military industries and their cooperative efforts in producing locally made weapons.
20–21	October	GCC defense ministers gather in Kuwait for their fourth meeting to discuss joint rapid deployment efforts. All six officials leave for the Saudi military base of Hafr al-Batin on 21 October to visit the nucleus force stationed there.
21–22	October	GCC petroleum ministers hold their eighth meeting in Riyadh; discuss threats to production and flow of oil to consumer countries; and continue to assess the need to construct a pipeline from the UAE to Oman bypassing the Strait of Hormuz.
26–29	October	GCC foreign ministers convene their seventeenth session in Muscat to prepare the sixth summit's agenda; discuss relations with Moscow; and strive to formulate a new policy toward the Iraq-Iran war.
30	October	Iraqi foreign minister Tariq Aziz arrives in Kuwait on an official visit; meets ruler; travels to Madina, Saudi Arabia, where he meets with Price Saud al-Faysal.
3–6	November	GCC rulers hold their sixth summit in Muscat; discuss Iraq-Iran war, defense and security issues, and economic relations. In their final communiqué, GCC states reaffirm their adherence to U.N. Security Council Resolutions 540 (1983) and 552 (1984), which called for free navigation in international waters and freedom of passage of merchant ships from and to the ports of the GCC states. The council calls on Iran to respect the principles mentioned in these two resolutions. With respect to the Iraq-Iran war, the GCC calls for an end to the conflict "in a manner that safeguards the legitimate rights and interests of the two sides in order to bring about the establishment of normal relations among the Gulf states." The statement, however, does not condemn Iran outright as did previous statements.
7	November	Kuwait, Oman, Qatar, and Saudi Arabia send congratulation cables to Andrei Gromyko on the occasion of the anniversary of the October Revolution.
13	November	The UAE and the Soviet Union establish diplomatic relations at the ambassadorial level.
17	November	Bahrain's heir apparent, Shaykh Hamad ibn Isa Al-Khalifah, arrives in Muscat for a three-day visit; on the same day the prime minister of Kuwait arrives in Muscat, along with Gulf and world leaders who gather in Oman to celebrate the Sultanate's fifteenth National Day.
25	November	Saudi Arabia and the EEC reach a confidential interim agreement on Gulf petrochemical exports.
8	December	Soviet ambassador to Kuwait Pogos Akopov visits the UAE where he meets Yaqub al-Kindi, director of the Foreign Affairs Department at the UAE Foreign Ministry.
9	December	Iranian foreign minister Ali Akbar Velayati arrives in Abu Dhabi from Riyadh on a one-day visit to the UAE.
11	December	Kuwaiti and Saudi air force units start a ten-day joint air exercise schedule in the GCC military cooperation framework.

11 December	Omani foreign minister Yusuf al-Alawi visits Qatar and Kuwait to deliver messages from Sultan Qabus.
12 December	Dubai grants landing rights to the Soviet airline Aeroflot for regular commercial flights, which are expected to start shortly.
15 December	Omani foreign minister Yusuf al-Alawi arrives in Abu Dhabi carrying a message from Sultan Qabus to President Zayid.
21 December	Shaykh Khalifah ibn Hamad Al-Thani, the amir of Qatar, receives Saudi defense minister Prince Sultan for consultations on bilateral defense matters.
23 December	GCC commerce and industry ministers end the fifth session of the GCC Commercial Cooperation Committee and the fourth session of the GCC Administrative Council for Standards and Measures meeting in Muscat.
28 December	Rashid Abdallah, UAE minister of state for foreign affairs, leaves for Tehran at the head of a delegation on a two-day visit to Iran at the invitation of Ali Akbar Velayati.

1986

13 January	A coup attempt in Aden is reported amid heavy fighting between rebel and loyalist forces in the capital of the PDRY, setting off serious clashes to last for several days.
9 February	GCC foreign ministers hold their fifth extraordinary meeting in Manama; discuss developments in the PDRY and the GCC's potential reactions as well as the Israeli interception of a Libyan executive jet flying from Tripoli to Damascus.
11 February	Iranian forces capture the Iraqi port city of Fao after crossing the waterway separating the city from Iranian territory. Place over 30,000 soldiers on the peninsula within twenty-four hours.
11 February	The Kuwaiti National Assembly issues a statement on the Iraq-Iran war expressing its grave concern over Iranian occupation of Iraqi territory.
11 February	GCC states call for an end to the latest Iranian offensive against Iraq, terming it a "major setback."
12 February	Saudi foreign minister Prince Saud al-Faysal leaves Riyadh to attend the League of Arab States' seven-member emergency meeting in Baghdad.
1–3 March	GCC foreign ministers open their eighteenth regular session in the wake of the rapid escalation of the Iraq-Iran war. In a concluding statement, the ministers condemn Iran's occupation of Fao and call on it to "immediately withdraw its forces to the international borders"; in addition, the ministers call on Iran to abide by U.N., OCI, and Nonaligned Movement resolutions to negotiate a peaceful settlement of the war.
5 March	GCC chiefs of staff hold a meeting at the Secretariat in Riyadh to discuss the military situation in the region.
8 March	GCC petroleum ministers hold a meeting in Riyadh in the wake of the Geneva OPEC conferences.
9 March	Kuwaiti defense minister Shaykh Salim al-Sabah Al-Salim denies an *Al-Ray al-Amm* report that the GCC rapid deployment force is presently in Kuwait.

16 March	Saudi crown prince Abdallah declares that the kingdom will defend Kuwait should the shaykhdom come under attack, presumably from Iran.
20 March	The amir of Kuwait arrives in Saudi Arabia for a one-day visit.
6 April	GCC and OAPEC Secretariat officials hold a joint meeting in Riyadh to discuss international energy developments and to increase cooperation between the two organizations.
7 April	U.S. vice president Bush meets with Secretary General Bisharah before leaving for Bahrain, the second stop of his Gulf tour, where he declares that Washington will not hesitate to take any measure if there is a threat to navigation in the Persian Gulf.
10 April	U.S. vice president Bush arrives in Sana, ARY, on the fourth leg of his Gulf tour. GCC newspapers, evaluating Bush's tour, call for U.S. action instead of laudatory words.
26 April	Qatar "seizes" the small man-made island of Fasht al-Dibal from Bahrain. Qatari forces land on the island and capture thirty men working on constructing a coast guard station (which some Gulf newspapers will later allege belonged to the GCC). GCC states appeal for a quick and peaceful resolution of the dispute.
28 April	Saudi Arabia intervenes in the Fasht al-Dibal dispute.
1 May	Qatar issues an official statement regretting its dispute with Bahrain over Fasht al-Dibal and thanks King Fahd of Saudi Arabia for his mediation efforts.
3 May	Secretary General Bisharah shuttles between Doha and Manama to end the Fasht al-Dibal dispute.
12 May	Qatar releases thirty employees of a Dutch company who were abducted on 26 April from Fasht al-Dibal.
25 May	A GCC-sponsored agreement is reached over the Fasht al-Dibal dispute. The island is to be "returned to its former state," under the monitoring of a GCC delegation.

Annotated Bibliography of Select Books and Articles

Abduljabbar, Mohammad. "The Cement Industry in the Arab Gulf States," *Arab Gulf Journal* 4, no. 1 (1984): 65–69.

Based on Gulf Organization for Industrial Consulting data, the article calls for the protection of GCC cement industries.

Abi al-Khail, Muhammad. "Al-Takamul Al-Iqtisadi Al-Khaliji: Niwat lil-takamul al-shamil" [The economic unification of the Gulf is the nucleus of comprehensive Arab unification], *Al-Arabi*, no. 303 (Feb. 1984): 36–43.

The Saudi minister of economy argues that GCC economic integration strengthens Arab economic cooperation.

Al-Akad, Sakah. *Al-Tayarat al-siyasiyat fil-khalij al-arabi* [Political currents in the Arabian Gulf] (Cairo, Egypt: Maktabat al-anglo al-masriyat, 1983).

Articulates the problems facing GCC states in their post-independence era and emphasizes the importance of petroleum as the catalyst that pulled the Gulf into the modern world.

Ali, Salamat, and Derek Davies. "The Gulf '83: A Survey," *Far Eastern Economic Review*, March 3, 1983, pp. 39–58.

With chapters on the economy, oil, investment, finance, Arab aid, the UAE, and the GCC, the survey presents a positive outlook for GCC states. Emphasis is on lack of security in region, however.

Allen, Robert C. "Regional Security in the Persian Gulf," *Military Review* 63, no. 2 (Dec. 1983): 2–11.

Argues that the GCC was established in an effort to counter perceived threats from Iran, Israel, U.S.S.R., and Iraq and that its aim is to promote a common unified position among member states.

Al-Ameri, Abdul Kader B. "Interview on the GCC," *American-Arab Affairs*, no. 15 (Winter 1985–86): 71–74.

Interview with the ambassador to the United States from the State of Qatar on GCC states' cooperation efforts.

Anckonie, Alex, III. "The Banking Sector as an Agent of Economic Diversification in Arab Gulf Countries," *American-Arab Affairs*, no. 11 (Winter 1984–85): 92–100.

Identifies the commercial banking sector as an effective mechanism for economic diversification for GCC states.

Anthony, John Duke. "The Gulf Cooperation Council," *Journal of South East Asian and Middle Eastern Studies* 5, no. 4 (Summer 1982): 3–18.

An outline of the organization of the GCC, sources of threats to and capabilities of its members, overemphasizing, however, the threat of Israel as a cause of the formation of the GCC.

al-Awadi, Badria. *Dual Majlis al-Taawun al-Khaliji wa Mustawayat al-amal al-dawliyat* [Gulf Cooperation Council States and the International Labor Organization] (Kuwait: Majlis al-Watani lil-Thakafat wal-funun wal-adab, 1985).

Analyzes GCC states' labor relations and compares them with ILO guidelines and regulations. Includes the texts of the four pertinent ILO documents to GCC states as well as the Philadelphia Declaration of 1944 in Arabic.

———. "Al-nusus al-muqayidat li-huquq al-insan al-asasiyat fil-ahd al-dual wa fi dasatir dual majlis al-Taawun al-khaliji" [Limitation provisions in the International Covenant on Civil and Political Rights and in the constitutions of the States of the Gulf Cooperation Council], *Journal of the Gulf and Arabian Peninsula Studies*, no. 40 (Oct. 1984): 43–127.

The limitation clauses embodied in the International Covenant on Civil and Political Rights are applied and compared to the constitutions of GCC states. Discusses public emergencies, public order, public morals, and the state of emergency and prescribes that national legislation or decrees should periodically be reviewed to ensure that the principle of proportionality is respected.

El-Azhary, M. S. *The Gulf Cooperation Council and Regional Defence in the 1980s*, Paper no. 1 (Exeter, U.K.: Centre for Arab Gulf Studies, University of Exeter, 1982).

After identifying the role of each GCC state in the defense of the Gulf, the author concludes that regional developments (Iranian Revolution, Iraq-Iran war, Soviet occupation of Afghanistan) crystallized the GCC's security goals. Stresses that Saudi security perceptions will, however, dominate the organization's future course of action.

———, ed. *The Impacts of Oil Revenues on Arab Gulf Development* (London and Boulder, Colo.: Croom Helm and Westview Press, 1984).

Evaluates the impact of oil revenues on GCC states' development. Several authors argue that GCC cooperation is a step in the wider Arab cooperation effort and that a combined GCC investment approach might prove to be very successful.

Beblawi, Hazem. "Gulf Foreign Investment Co-Ordination: Needs and Modalities," *Arab Gulf Journal* 3, no. 1 (April 1983): 41–59.
Argues that the effect of placing petro-funds in industrialized countries was to increase inflation rather than increase macroinvestment. Calls for direct investment in developing countries that would stimulate demand for goods produced in developed countries. Such a policy is in the interests of all parties, but it can only be made effective through coordinated action. The creation of a Gulf dinar linked to the price of oil would protect GCC states' investments.

Beseisu, Fouad Hamdi. "Sub-regional Economic Co-Operation in the Arab Gulf," *Arab Gulf Journal* 1, no. 1 (Oct. 1981): 45–54.
The establishment of the GCC is the culmination of increasing economic collaboration in the region. Reviews various sectors, ranging from fisheries to trade and the numerous joint institutions in place.

Bill, James A. "Islam, Politics, and Shiism in the Gulf," *Middle East Insight* 3, no. 3 (Jan./Feb. 1984): 3–12.
Assesses the importance of the Shia communities in the GCC states and cautions that certain Gulf officials' preoccupation with the Shia communities "deflects them from addressing the much broader and more serious challenge posed by the growing reassertion of Popular Islam in general."

Bishara, Abdallah Yacoub. "The Gulf Cooperation Council: Achievements and Challenges," *American-Arab Affairs*, no. 7 (Winter 1983–84): 40–44.
The secretary general of the GCC presents an overview of the organization's accomplishments during its first three years and identifies "Gulf public opinion" as a source of support. The GCC, according to the secretary general, needs the awareness of Gulf citizens to accomplish its goals.

de Bouteiller, Georges. "Une communauté Arabe à six qui s'organise: Le Conseil de Coopération du Golfe" [A six-member Arab community that is organizing: the Gulf Cooperation Council], *Défense Nationale* 40, no. 6 (June 1984): 83–104.
Argues that the six GCC states have 15 million people, produced 736 million-tonnes of petroleum in 1979, and have a per-capita income varying between $7,000 and $27,000. These wealthy, yet underpopulated, states must integrate their economies, harmonize development plans, and coordinate security measures to guarantee their survival. Recent efforts indicate that the GCC is destined to succeed.

Braun, Ursula. *Der Golf-Kooperationsrat: Profil, Potential, Verflechtungen* [The Gulf Cooperation Council: profile, potential, versatility] (Ebenhausen: Hans Eggenberg, Federal Republic of Germany, October 1985).
A detailed four-part study discussing the GCC's formation, interests and dilemmas, internal stability, and future prospects. Includes statistical data and selected bibliography.

Bulloch, John. *The Persian Gulf Unveiled* (New York: Congdon and Weed, 1984).
Analyzes the social, economic, and political features of the Gulf states of Kuwait, Qatar, Bahrain, and the UAE. It also highlights GCC states' accomplishments in a turbulent region of the world, foreseeing the area to be "the starting place for the final world war."

Chaoul, Melhem. "Koweit et Bahrein ou l'ambiguité de l'expérience démocratique dans les sociétés arabes contemporaines" [Kuwait and Bahrain or the ambiguity of the democratic experience in the present Arab societies], *L'Afrique et l'Asie Modernes*, no. 128 (1981): 20–42.
The idea of democracy and the exercise of pluralistic power were provisional steps for Kuwait and Bahrain to satisfy subtle domestic and regional political ends. Democratic forces remain in the region, however, and may yet spread to other Gulf states.

Christie, John. "The GCC: A Preliminary Report," *Aramco World Magazine* 35, no. 1 (Jan./Feb. 1984): 22–23.
A pictorial on the GCC with a discussion on its goals and first accomplishments.

Cordesman, Anthony H. *The Gulf and the Search for Strategic Stability: Saudi Arabia, the Military Balance, and Trends in the Arab-Israeli Military Balance* (Boulder, Colo.: Westview Press, 1984).
Discusses military and strategic developments in Saudi Arabia and other GCC states, including sources of threat to GCC states, and evaluates U.S. military assistance programs over several decades.

———. "The Gulf Crisis and Strategic Interests: A Military Analysis," *American-Arab Affairs*, no. 9 (Summer 1984): 8–15.
Calls for Iraqi, GCC, and U.S. military cooperation in the Iraq-Iran war.

Darius, Robert G., John W. Amos II, and Ralph H. Magnus, ed. *Gulf Security into the 1980s: Perceptual and Strategic Dimensions* (Stanford, Calif.: Hoover Institution Press, 1984).
The chapter on the GCC is an overview. The editors' concluding chapter on Gulf security into the 1980s calls for close U.S. military cooperation with GCC states.

Dhaher, Ahmad J. "Culture and Politics in the Arab Gulf

States," *Journal of South East Asian and Middle Eastern Studies* 4, no. 4 (Summer 1981): 21–36.
Reports that the GCC states have come to "expect modernity in their materialistic needs while maintaining a traditional mental outlook, apparently unaware of the contrast."

Djalili, Mohammad-Reza. "Le Conseil de Coopération du Golfe: quelques problèmes d'ordre structurel" [The Gulf Cooperation Council: some structural problems], *Studia Diplomatica* 36, no. 6 (1983): 625–36.
Identifies regional problems leading to the GCC's formation, including the Iraq-Iran war, the Iranian Revolution, and internal dissent. Analyzes the GCC's structural problems such as differences in size, economy, and military strengths and speculates on various regional political perceptions.

Dirasat fil-tarikh wal siyasat wal-qanun wal-iqtisad: Majmuat muhadarat al-nadwa al-diblumasiyat alati nadamatha wazarat kharijiyat dawlat al-imarat al-arabiyat al-mutahidat fi Abu Dabi li am 1401 H–1980 A.D. [Studies in history, politics, law, and economics: diplomatic activities organized by the UAE Foreign Ministry in Abu Dhabi for 1401 H–1980 A.D.] (Abu Dhabi, UAE: Ministry of Foreign Affairs, 1980).
Primarily organized for UAE diplomats, the annual colloquium held in Abu Dhabi brings together Arab researchers focusing on international affairs. These collections of studies concentrate on Gulf states' relations and include selected documents pertaining to UAE diplomatic affairs.

Duncan, Emma. "Growing Pains—The Gulf Cooperation Council: A Survey," *The Economist*, 8 Feb. 1986.
Annual survey of Arabian Peninsula states stressing the difficulties GCC states face in building a future while holding on to the past.

Dunn, Michael Collins. "Soviet Interests in the Arabian Peninsula: The Aden Pact and Other Paper Tigers" *American-Arab Affairs*, no. 8 (Spring 1984): 92–98.
Argues that the Aden Pact does not seem to be working well and that the GCC states do not fear Moscow and its surrogates but Tehran and revolutionary zeal; recommends that the United States take into account GCC states' concerns about Iran, Israel, Iraq-Iran war, rather than worry about military bases.

Al-Ebraheem, Hassan Ali. *Kuwait and the Gulf: Small States and the International System* (Washington, D.C., and London: Georgetown University Center for Contemporary Arab Studies and Croom Helm, 1984).
Examines the foreign policy and economic factors governing the activities of Kuwait and the other GCC states. Kuwait is studied as an example of a small state that has succeeded in surviving amid the troubles of realpolitik in the international arena.

Epstein, Joshua M. *Strategy and Force Planning: The Case of the Persian Gulf* (Washington, D.C.: Brookings Institution, 1987).
The most credible deterrent to large-scale Soviet aggression in the Persian Gulf, according to the author, is through conventional defense. Through numerous models, he shows how a U.S. rapid deployment force considerably smaller than that planned by the Reagan administration could defend successfully and deter credibly by exploiting key Soviet vulnerabilities in Iran.

Farley, Jonathan. "The Gulf War and the Littoral States," *World Today*, 40, no. 7 (July 1984): 269–76.
Analyzes GCC states' relations with Iran and Iraq in light of the Gulf war and identifies several significant points that may adversely affect GCC states' interests, including the Sunni-Shia cleft within Islam and regional military capabilities.

Al-Fayez, Khaled. "The Gulf Investment Corporation," *American-Arab Affairs*, no. 11 (Winter 1984–85): 34–37.
The chief executive officer of the GIC, the banking and investment arm of the GCC, discusses its goals and objectives, which include the development of the industrial, agricultural, and services sectors.

Fesharaki, Fereidun, and David T. Isaak. *OPEC, the Gulf, and the World Petroleum Market: A Study in Government Policy and Downstream Operations* (Boulder, Colo.: Westview Press, 1983).
Discusses petroleum developments in the Gulf region, asserting that GCC states grouped in response to the Iraq-Iran war and the Iranian threat. The authors state that "internal disagreements [among GCC states] could make the council's pact ineffective."

Guecioueur, Adda. "Problems and Prospects of Economic Integration among the Members of the Arab Gulf Co-Operation Council," *Arab Gulf Journal* 2, no. 2 (Oct. 1982): 43–54.
Deals with the problems and prospects of economic integration among GCC states by considering their human, natural, and financial resources with a view to assessing the existence of comparative advantages among them. It considers the integrative role of the private sector and the risks of economic and political polarization, both at sectoral and country levels, with their subsequent disintegrative effects.

The Gulf Cooperation Council, 9th ed. (Kuwait: Kuwait News Agency Documentation Department, May 1981).
Includes the GCC's charter along with short descriptions of the military situation in the Gulf, defense forces estimates for each member-state, the strategic importance of the Gulf, oil exports, pre-GCC coordination in the region, and Kuwait's attitude toward the GCC. There is also a useful chronology between 5 February

and 2 May 1981, as well as "facts and figures" on the six GCC states.

"Gulf States: Working for Integration in Industry and Agriculture," *Arab Economist* 12, no. 133 (Oct. 1980): 23–27.
Calls for the adoption of regional technical assistance, the establishment of industrial zones, financial facilities, customs exemption and protection, tax exemptions, and granting priority to local products over similar foreign ones in contracts for the supply of government provisions.

Harb, Isamat al-Ghazali. "Gulf Security and Arab National Security," *Shuun Arabiyat*, no. 35 (Jan./April 1984): 57–76.
After a brief introduction on "security" issues in the Arab world, the author, a researcher at the *Al-Ahram* Center for Strategic Studies, identifies internal and external sources of threat to the security of the Gulf. The author ties the security of the Gulf to that of the rest of the Arab world, singling out Israel as a common source of threat.

Hawla tawsiyat al-dawrat al-Sadisat lil-marakiz wal-Hayat al-ilmiyat al-muntamat bidirasat al-khalij wal-jazirat al-arabiyat" [On the Commission of the Sixth Conference of Scholarly Centers and Organizations specializing in the Arab Gulf and the Arab Peninsula] *Al-Dara*, 8, no. 1 (June 1982): 12–20.
Report on the sixth conference of Gulf scholarly centers held in Doha, Qatar, 24–28 April 1982, identifying centers and current research interests and undertakings.

"The High Cost of Gulf Leadership," *Arab Economist* 12, no. 134 (Nov. 1980): 35–37.
Assesses the 1979 oil crisis and price increases due primarily to disruptions of exports from Iran and predicts further crises throughout the region for lack of leadership in oil affairs.

Hitiris, Theodore, and Michael H. Hoyle. "Monetary Integration in the GCC: An Evaluation," *Arab Gulf Journal* 6, no. 1 (April 1986): 33–42.
Argues that monetary integration in GCC states neither can be implemented nor is necessary and cautions about premature moves toward monetary integration that would accentuate the divergence between member-states and the rest of the world.

Al-Ishal, Abdallah. "Al-ilaqat al-dawliyah fi itar majlis al-Taawun li-dual al-khalij al-arabiyah" [International relations in the framework of the Gulf Cooperation Council] *Journal of the Gulf and Arabian Peninsula Studies*, no. 37 (Jan. 1984): 61–89.
Argues that the GCC attempts to steer the political behavior of its members toward a degree of coordination and harmony and to assign specific tasks to each country during a particular crisis. Concludes that despite dif-

ferences in foreign policy attitudes, GCC states continue to display a significant degree of unity.

———. *Al-Itar al-Qanuni wal-siyasi li-majlis al-Taawun al-Khaliji* [The legal and political framework of the Gulf Cooperation Council] (Riyadh, Saudi Arabia: n.p., 1983).
This early study of the GCC identifies the reasons behind the establishment of the organization and discusses the significance of cooperation in the Gulf region. Emphasizes security issues as well as economic efforts before examining member-states' foreign policies.

Ispahani, Mahnaz Zehra. "Alone Together: Regional Security Arrangements in Southern Africa and the Arabian Gulf," *International Security* 8, no. 4 (Spring 1984): 152–75.
Regional conflicts posing direct internal threats to small powers lead them to joint efforts as is the case with the GCC and the Organization of Front Line States in Southern Africa. In turn, the author argues, regional units help contain low-level threats in suppressing interstate differences, mediating local disputes, and, allaying small-scale threats to their internal security.

Kechichian, Joseph A. "The Gulf Cooperation Council: Search for Security," *Third World Quarterly* 7, no. 4 (Oct. 1985): 853–81.
Emphasizing political and military accomplishments, the author highlights activities leading member states to sastisfy their security needs. This search is contrasted with integration prospects for GCC states.

Al-Khalij: Amal wa Mustaqbal—Majmuat min al-muhadarat wal nadawat hawla Majlis al-Taawun: Nishatuha wa Ahdafuha . . . [The Gulf: hope and future—a collection of colloquium and seminar presentations on the GCC: its inception and goals . . .] (Riyadh: Majlis al-Taawun li-dual al-Khalij al-Arabiyah, Al-Imanat al-Amat, 1983).
Divided into three parts. The first includes transcripts of presentations on Gulf unity at seminars organized by Gulf media sources and universities. In the second part, the GCC's views on economic integration are presented by the GCC assistant secretary general for economic affairs and the Saudi minister of finance. The last section includes two speeches by the GCC secretary general on Gulf security.

Khayata, Abdul Wahab. "The Future of Investments in the Gulf," *American-Arab Affairs*, no. 11 (Winter 1984–85): 6–18.
Discusses GCC states' revenues and trade policies using data for 1972–83 and identifies the problems of internal and external investments. Capital-rich countries do not feel safe in investing in "people-endowed" or "resource-rich" countries, concludes the author, who calls for "meaningful integration."

Kodmani, Bassma, ed. *Quelle Sécurité pour le Golfe?* [What security for the Gulf?] (Paris: Institut Français des Relations Internationales, 1984).

The essay on the GCC in this volume examines the organization's defensive capabilities, concluding that these are quite limited and that during an emergency GCC states may have little choice but to call on their Western allies for assistance.

Koury, Enver M. "The Impact of the Geopolitical Situation of Iraq upon the Gulf Cooperation Council," *Middle East Insight* 2, no. 5 (Jan.–Feb. 1983): 28–35.

Argues that the Iraq-Iran war has assisted better Arab cooperation in the Gulf area to counterbalance Iranian hegemony and calls on the GCC to welcome Iraq as a full member. The financial aid provided by GCC states to Iraq is seen as the price to exclude the Baathist regime from membership in the Riyadh-based regional organization.

Kubursi, Atif. *The Economies of the Arabian Gulf: A Statistical Sourcebook* (London and Dover, Croom Helm, 1984).

Organized in ten chapters, this book of "data" presents, under one cover, a myriad of statistical information on GCC states from 1970 to 1981. A few tables include data for 1982. A statistical reference work.

"Kuwait Finance Minister Foresees Big Economic Role for New Gulf Cooperation Council," *Middle East Economic Survey* 24, no. 32 (25 May 1981): 1–7.

Minister Abd al-Latif al-Hamad predicts that the GCC is "like Monet's EEC," except that Gulf states have even more in common than the European countries. His optimism is restrained, however, by acknowledged potential difficulties facing the GCC because of regional developments.

El-Kuwaize, Abdulla. "The Gulf Cooperation Council and the Concept of Economic Integration," *American-Arab Affairs*, no. 7 (Winter 1983–94): 45–49.

The assistant secretary-general for economic affairs presents his views on the potential for economic integration by stating that existing similarities at the political, philosophical, social, historical, and cultural levels bode well for GCC states. He also cautions on difficulties in the implementation phases.

Lawrence, Robert G. "Arab Perceptions of U.S. Security Policy in Southwest Asia," *American-Arab Affairs*, no. 5 (Summer 1983): 27–38.

Argues that U.S. security cooperation with GCC states must remain on a low-key basis and calls for a silent but effective partnership rather than an overt and ineffective alliance.

Lawson, Fred H. "Using Positive Sanctions to End International Conflicts: Iran and the Arab Gulf Countries,"

Journal of Peace Research 20, no. 4 (1983): 311–28.

Argues that GCC efforts to persuade Iran to end its war with Iraq in exchange for access to a large amount of capital during the late spring of 1982 were not only ignored but also met with greatly increased demands for reparations by Iran. Supports the argument that conflicts in a multipolar region will be both more likely to occur and more difficult to solve.

Lombardi, Patrizia. "Consiglio di cooperazione del Golfo. Una nuova coalizione all'ombra di Riyadh" [The Gulf Cooperation Council. A new coalition in Riyadh's shadow], *Politica Internazionale*, nos. 7–8 (July/Aug. 1982): 74–82.

The decision to establish the GCC was reached in 1979 when Saudi Arabia aimed to coordinate the economic, political, and military affairs of conservative monarchies. Also argues that the Soviet occupation of Afghanistan was a major factor leading to the GCC's formation and predicts that "joint perceptions" will strengthen member states.

Maarek, Gilles. "Du Marché Commun Arabe au Conseil de Coopération du Golfe" [From the Arab Common Market to the Gulf Cooperation Council], *Revue Tiers Monde*, no. 87 (July/Sept. 1981): 573–84.

Argues that following the unsuccessful experience of the Arab Common Market (1964), European countries look with interest to the GCC, which aims to set up regional unity on the model of the EEC. Asserts that although the GCC's goals are economic and diplomatic integration, they also include an attempt to balance relations between Iran and Iraq.

Malik, Hafeez, ed. *International Security in Southwest Asia* (New York: Praeger, 1984).

Discusses the GCC in terms of its relations with Iran, India, Egypt, and the United States.

Malone, Joseph J. "Security: A Priority for Gulf Council," *Journal of Defense and Diplomacy* 1, no. 6 (Sept. 1983): 15–17.

Argues that pre-GCC cooperation among the six Arab Gulf states was so extensive that the future must be bright. Emphasis is placed on security aspects including the ever-important acquisition of weapons and standardized training.

Martin, Lenore G. *The Unstable Gulf: Threats from Within* (Lexington, Mass.: Lexington Books, 1984).

Examines international politics of the Gulf from 1900 to 1983, evaluates Gulf territorial disputes among GCC states, and calls for a new U.S. Gulf strategy capable of assisting GCC states through both a military capability (USCENTCOM) and a revised energy policy.

Maurizi, Romano. "Il Consiglio di Cooperazione del Golfo" [The Gulf Cooperation Council], *Affari Esteri*, no. 58 (Spring 1983): 177–90.
Identifies several pre-GCC cooperation efforts, including ministerial-level meetings since 1973, as precursors to the organization and provides a positive first-year assessment despite numerous challenges both on the internal and external levels.

Mitchell, Colin. "The Gulf: Sources of Finance in the GCC," *Middle East Executive Reports* 8, no. 1 (Jan. 1985): 12–16 (Part I) and no. 2 (Feb. 1985): 14–17 (Part II).
Suggests that the banking institutions in the Gulf can provide a viable joint-venture project with whatever financing needs GCC states may have. After surveying the sources—government institutions, commercial banks, external organizations—the author discusses the offshore market in Bahrain and external specialist institutions that may assist the GCC.

Mohie el-Din, Badr. "An Economic Strategy for Arab Gulf Co-Operation in Industrialization," *Arab Gulf Journal* 4, no. 1 (1984): 37–49.
Discussing the implications of various approaches to economic cooperation and reviewing the experience with projects in the Gulf, the author identifies several promising opportunities (infant foods, edible oils, solar panels, water meters, detergents) for future joint enterprises. Concludes that regional cooperation will lead not to regional isolation but to closer integration with the Arab and world economies.

Naff, Thomas, ed. *Gulf Security and the Iran-Iraq War* (Washington, D.C.: National Defense University Press and the Middle East Research Institute, 1985).
The essay on the GCC's search for regional security concludes that member states are actively pursuing every effort within their capabilities against strong odds and calls on the United States neither to overburden the GCC with the American strategic agenda nor to fear it as a neutralizing force.

Al-Nafisi, Abdallah Fahd. *Majlis al-Taawun al-Khaliji: Al-Itar al-Siyasi wal-Istratiji* [The Gulf Cooperation Council: the political and strategic framework] (London: Ta-Ha Publishers, 1982).
The author discusses the challenges facing the GCC and its member states. Attention is focused on limitations existing in the area including the lack of political participation. Cautions on a reliance on the West to provide for member states' security needs.

Nakhleh, Emile A. *The Gulf Cooperation Council: Policies, Problems, and Prospects* (New York: Preager, 1986).
A broad background description of the six member states as well as a brief background description of the GCC's "Charter" and "By-Laws." Provides a useful per-ception of Bahraini officials and discusses five studies prepared by the Bahrain-based *Nadwat al-Tanmiya li-Duwal al-Jazira al-Arabiyya al-Muntija li al-Naft* [Development Panel for the Oil-Producing States of the Arabian Peninsula] on publicly owned projects, bureaucracy, industry, education, and population questions.

———. *The Persian Gulf and American Policy* (New York: Praeger 1982).
Devotes its third chapter to an overview of the GCC and its growing importance for U.S. interests in the Persian Gulf region.

Neuman, Robert G., and Shireen T. Hunter. "Crisis in the Gulf: Reasons for Concern but Not Panic," *American-Arab Affairs*, no. 9 (Summer 1984): 16–21.
Argues that an escalation of the Iran-Iraq war is fraught with dangers and dilemmas for GCC states and the West but does not foresee such an escalation given the war-weariness experienced by both Iran and Iraq.

Al-Nibari, Abdullah. "An Independent View of the Gulf Cooperation Council," *Dinar* 1, no. 4 (1983): 39–43.
A discussion of the GCC performance since its inception. The author identifies shortfalls including the lack of a customs union, a single external tariff, and guidelines for relations with other countries. Proposes the adoption of a customs union, strengthening indigenous political institutions by increasing public participation, and the enlarging of the GCC Secretariat to include GCC technocrats capable of implementing GCC decisions.

Niblock, Tim. "Oil, Political Change, and Social Dynamics of the Arab Gulf States," *Arab Gulf Journal* 5, no. 1 (April 1985): 37–45.
Contends that the United States is mistaken in its belief that the GCC regimes are fragile. Argues that the presence of large numbers of migrant workers, the expansion of the commercial sector, the growth of a large state administration, and the decline of peasant/nomadic groups have influenced social dynamics in ways that reinforce indigenous political structures and reduce the chances of radical political change.

Nimatallah, Yusuf A. "Economic Trends in the Gulf and Their Implications for Relations with the West," *American-Arab Affairs*, no. 7 (Winter 1983–84): 69–75.
Argues that industrialized countries can rely on GCC states for strong markets but must try harder to seek a peaceful political settlement to the Israeli-Palestinian conflict, transfer appropriate technology to GCC states, and encourage non-oil exports from GCC countries, because these steps will strengthen economic ties in general and trade in particular.

Nugent, Jeffrey B., and Theodore H. Thomas. *Bahrain and the Gulf: Past Perspectives and Alternative Futures* (New York: St. Martin's, 1985).

Reports the results of the "Bahrain Project" at the University of Southern California and covers developments in the historical, social, cultural, political, and economic settings. Bahrain's relations with GCC states are examined only in the economic sector.

Parsons, Anthony. "The Gulf States in the Eighties," *Arab Gulf Journal* 6, no. 1 (April 1986): 9–15.

Argues that GCC states, despite past experiences, enjoy remarkable political stability and that their economic problems are unlikely to seriously affect this stability. Asserts that GCC governments have managed to maintain good relations with nearly all Arab countries because they are seen as a moderating influence within the region. Concludes that the main threats in the current situation lie in the spread of terrorism and the continuation of the Gulf war.

Qatar News Agency. *Wathaiq Majlis al-Taawun al-Khaliji* [Gulf Cooperation Council documents] (Doha, Qatar: n.d.).

Includes documents in Arabic on the GCC covering the first year of the organization. In addition to the Charter and Unified Economic Agreement, several dozen speeches by senior ministers in all six states are reproduced.

Qureshi, Y. "Gulf Co-Operation Council," *Pakistan Horizon* 35, no. 4 (1982): 84–92.

Evaluates GCC states' capabilities and calls for the adoption of a joint independent security arrangement falling outside the East-West rivalry because "true nonalignment offers the only possible solution to survival."

Rajab, Yahya Halmi. *Majlis al-Taawun li-Dual al-Khalij al-arabiyah: Ruyat Mustaqbaliat; Dirasat Qanuniyah, Siyasiyah, Iqtisadiyah* [The Cooperation Council for the Arab states of the Gulf: future developments; a legal, political, and economic Study] (Kuwait: Maktabat al-Arubat lil-nashr wal-Tawzi, 1983).

A comprehensive study of the GCC, this volume describes legal, political, and economic goals of the organization and assesses its future against relevant historical background and geographic conditions. The emphasis, however, is legal and institutional in nature.

Ramazani, R. K. "The Gulf Cooperation Council: A Search for Security," in William L. Dowty and Russell B. Trood, ed., *The Indian Ocean: Perspectives on a Strategic Arena* (Durham, N. C.: Duke University Press, 1985).

Assesses the impact of the Iranian Revolution on the creation of the GCC and points out the problem of consensus building among the six with respect to the superpowers and Iraq and Iran.

———. "Iran's Islamic Revolution and the Persian Gulf," *Current History* 84, no. 498 (Jan. 1985): 5–8, 40–41.

An analysis of the perceived threat of Iran's export of Islamic revolutionary fundamentalism to the GCC states and their efforts to cope with the threat, especially in the face of ferment among Shia dissidents in the GCC area.

———. *Revolutionary Iran: Challenge and Response in the Middle East* (Baltimore and London: Johns Hopkins University Press, 1986).

Analyzes the genesis of the GCC and its diplomatic and security policies vis-à-vis the Iranian Revolution and the Iraq-Iran War.

———. "Shiism in the Persian Gulf," in Juan R. I. Cole and Nikki R. Keddie, eds., *Shiism and Social Protest* (New Haven and London: Yale University Press, 1986).

An analysis of the challenge of the Khomeini concept of security in the Persian Gulf and its influence on the social and political attitudes of the Shias in the GCC states as seen in the cases of Saudi Arabia and Bahrain as well as non-GCC Iraq.

The Resource Base for Industrialisation in the Gulf Co-Operation Council Countries: A Framework for Co-Operation (Vienna: United Nations Industrial Development Organization, 1983).

General survey followed by a study of the regional economy and its characteristics, e.g., oil revenues and labor migration. Studies of the resource base and its utilization by sectors as follows: water, agriculture, fisheries, oil and gas, minerals, recoverable wastes. Lists possibilities for coordinated industrialization and includes many statistical tables.

Rikhye, Indar Jit, Major General (Retd.). *Gulf Security: Quest for Regional Cooperation: A Report of the International Peace Academy* (New York: International Peace Academy, 1985).

This small volume highlights the GCC states' perceptions of security (internal as well as external) and stresses that (1) the superpowers, (2) the Iraq-Iran war, and (3) the Arab-Israeli dispute are the major factors affecting them. The author concludes that a joint regional defense arrangement, based on cultural and economic ties, augurs well for GCC states. Unfortunately, there are numerous factual errors in this otherwise useful study.

Rizvi, Hasan-Askari. "Gulf Co-Operation Council," *Pakistan Horizon* 35, no. 2 (1982): 29–38.

Although established to provide for member states' mutual development needs, the GCC has emphasized, according to the author, the defense and security fields. The major objective is the harmonization and improvement of joint security arrangements by modernizing and integrating available military capabilities.

Robert, Rudiger. "Der Golfkooperationsrat: Die Arabischen Golfstaaten auf der Suche nach Sicheheit und Stabilitat" [The Gulf Cooperation Council: the search for security and stability by the Arab Gulf states], *Orient* 24, no. 2 (June 1983): 235–59.

Identifies the East-West conflict, North-South division, and Iraq-Iran war as destabilizing factors leading to the establishment of the GCC in 1981. The long-term goal of the GCC, according to the author, is unification of the six states. In the short term, however, efforts are focused on "cooperation." Yet, success has only been measured in the economic sector.

al-Rumayhi, Muhammad. *Al-Khalij Laisa Nafdan: Dirasat fi Ishkaliyat al-tanmiyat wal-wahdat* [The Gulf is not petroleum: a study in development and unity] (Kuwait: Sharikat Kadhimat lil-nashr wal-tarjimat wal-tawzi, 1983).

Argues that GCC states' unification goals predate the discovery of petroleum. After a detailed discussion of trade patterns in the Gulf, the author highlights the key aspects of his research, namely demographic issues and economic commonalities. In the second part, the author discusses the GCC's economic accomplishments and offers these as evidence for future integration.

Al-Salem, Faisal. "The Issue of Identity in Selected Arab Gulf States," *Journal of South East Asian and Middle Eastern States* 4, no. 4 (Summer 1981): 3–20.

Assesses the crisis of identity among GCC states' students and identifies "citizenship" as the "only formulated identity the students of the Arab Gulf have developed within the past ten years." He states that "pan-Arabism is a myth as far as the students are concerned."

Sandwick, John A., ed. *The Gulf Cooperation Council: Moderation and Stability in an Interdependent World* (Boulder, Colo.: Westview Press and Washington, D.C.: American-Arab Affairs Council, 1987).

A collection of nine essays on the GCC emphasizing member states' economic and political relations among

themselves and with the superpowers. A novel chapter on the "Developing Legal Systems of the Gulf Countries" is also included.

Shikara, Ahmad Abdul Razzaq. *Al-Dawr al-Istratiji lilwilayat al-mutahidat al-Amiriqiyat fi mantaqat al-Khalij al-Arabi hata muntasaf al-thamaniyat* [The United States Strategic Role in the Arabian Gulf till the Mid-1980s] (Dubayy, United Arab Emirates: Al-Kazimah, 1985).

A survey of the strategic role of the U.S. throughout the nineteenth and twentieth centuries in the Gulf region. The author stresses the correlation between U.S. economic and military interests, drawing clear distinctions between them and Gulf states' own interests.

Wingerter, Rex B. "The Gulf Cooperation Council and American Interests in the Gulf," *American-Arab Affairs*, no. 16 (Spring 1986): 15–26.

Argues that the effects of the GCC in the economic and security fields bode well for U.S. interests in the Gulf, opening new opportunities for American investment and commerce. But cautions about GCC states' political fragility and calls for strengthening indigenous Gulf political participation.

Al-Yousuf, Alaa. "Industrialisation and Economic Integration in the Arab Gulf," *Arab Gulf Journal* 6, no. 1 (April 1986): 25–31.

Stresses the need for cooperation among GCC countries by identifying joint-project approaches to integration. Asserts, however, that although this was recognized even before the formation of the GCC there is little evidence of cooperation among member states in the manufacturing sector.

Zorgbibe, Charles. *Nuages de Guerre sur les Emirats du Golfe* [War clouds over the gulf emirates] (Paris: La Sorbonne, 1984).

Evaluates the impact of the Iraq-Iran war on the GCC states, arguing that the region's security is truly precarious for the stability of the area and the rest of the world.

Index